Crip Theory

CULTURAL FRONT
General Editor: Michael Bérubé

Crip Theory

Cultural Signs of Queerness and Disability

Robert McRuer

Foreword by Michael Bérubé

NEW YORK UNIVERSITY PRESS
New York and London

NEW YORK UNIVERSITY PRESS
New York and London
www.nyupress.org

Library of Congress Cataloging-in-Publication Data
McRuer, Robert, 1966–
Crip theory : cultural signs of queerness and disability / Robert
McRuer.
p. cm. — (Cultural front)
Includes bibliographical references and index.
ISBN–13: 978–0–8147–5712–3 (cloth : alk. paper)
ISBN–10: 0–8147–5712–X (cloth : alk. paper)
ISBN–13: 978–0–8147–5713–0 (pbk. : alk. paper)
ISBN–10: 0–8147–5713–8 (pbk. : alk. paper)
1. Sociology of disability. 2. Homosexuality—Social aspects. 3.
Heterosexuality—Social aspects. 4. Marginality, Social. 5. Cul-
ture. I. Title. II. Cultural front (Series)
HV1568.M37 2006
306.76'601—dc22 2005035209

New York University Press books are printed on acid-free paper,
and their binding materials are chosen for strength and durability.

Manufactured in the United States of America

c 10 9 8 7 6 5 4 3 2 1
p 10 9 8 7 6 5 4 3 2 1

Contents

Foreword

Another Word Is Possible

Michael Bérubé

I've admired Robert McRuer's work for some time now, and *Crip Theory* gives me all the more reason for admiration. Although over the past couple of years the overdue conversation between queer theory and disability studies has begun to produce new work that expands the parameters of both fields, most people—myself included—still find it exceptionally difficult to theorize multiple forms of identity, and multiple strategies of disidentification, in conjunction with each other.

At times, it has been tempting for left cultural theorists to approach this difficulty by way of the "excluded-here-is-any-account-of" gambit: in response to, say, one critic's groundbreaking account of race and class in Southern labor movements, another critic can reply, "X's account of race and class in Southern labor movements may be groundbreaking, but excluded here is any account of gender and sexuality that might complicate the analysis further." Very rarely is disability invoked in such circumstances. But at its best, the gambit is salutary, urging liberal, progressive, and left social critics to take account of intersecting cultural formations in all their vivid and contradictory complexity. Occasionally, however, it invites an "additive" approach, in which identity categories are checked off one by one as they are "accounted" for theoretically. I remember vividly a colleague rereading, after twenty-odd years, the Combahee River Collective's famous statement on the liberation of black women, one passage of which reads, "if Black women were free, it would mean that everyone else would have to be free since our freedom would necessitate the destruction of all the systems of oppression" (278), and saying to me, only half in jest: "You know, they forgot about sexuality and disability—they only got to *two* systems of oppression, maybe three."

The remark was only half in jest, though, precisely because lines of inquiry that fail to attend to one thing or another—gender, race, class, sexuality, disability, age, historical context, nation, and ethnicity (and I hope I have unwittingly left out something, so as to prove the point by example)—inevitably *do* wind up producing an incomplete or partly skewed analysis of the world. The freedom of black women would not necessarily entail the freedom of women living under shari'a law; what is true of black men is not necessarily true of black gay men, and not necessarily true of white lesbians anywhere; what is true of Chicano/a communities and class relations may not hold for Chicanos/as with disabilities and class relations. Indeed, for many reasons, disability (in its mutability, its potential invisibility, its potential relation to temporality, and its sheer variety) is a particularly elusive element to introduce into any conjunctural analysis, not because it is so distinct from sexuality, class, race, gender, and age but because it is always already so complexly intertwined with everything else. Matters become still more complicated when disability is mobilized—so to speak—as a trope within what Robert McRuer (following Michael Warner, following Erving Goffman) calls "stigmaphobic" sectors of identity communities. When that happens, you find people scrambling desperately to be included under the umbrella of the "normal"—and scrambling desperately to cast somebody else as abnormal, crazy, abject, or disabled. Thus, in his remarkable chapter on Karen Thompson and Sharon Kowalski, whose story involves disability, long-term care, and the divide between advocates of gay marriage and advocates of queerer arrangements, McRuer writes: "The stigmaphobic distancing from more stigmatized members of the community that advocates for gay marriage engage in is inescapably a distancing from disability. This is indeed literally true in one sense: commentators (such as [Gabriel] Rotello) on domesticity and marriage offer marriage (for gay men, at least) as an antidote to AIDS." As an antidote to stigmaphobia, then, McRuer offers a rigorous conjunctural analysis that leaves no form of identity behind:

> Queer communities could acknowledge that the political unconscious of debates about normalization (including debates about marriage) is shaped, in large part, by ideas about disability [and] . . . disability communities, primed to enter (or entering already) some of the territory re-

cently charted by queers, could draw on radical queer thought to continue forging the critical disability consciousness that has emerged over
the past few decades.

As *Crip Theory* shows time and again, there aren't too many people
who are as inventive and as rigorous as McRuer when it comes to reading these kinds of conjunctures. In his noncompliant chapter on "noncompliance" in the work of Gary Fisher and in Susana Aikin and Carlos
Aparicio's documentary film *The Transformation*, McRuer takes disability activists' critiques of regimes of rehabilitation and uses them to find a
"problematic rehabilitative logic" that "governs contemporary understandings of and responses to what we should still call the AIDS crisis."
He does so, moreover, by attending to scenes of "degradation" that range
from Gary Fisher's S/M fantasies to Harry Braverman's *Labor and Monopoly Capital: The Degradation of Work in the Twentieth Century*. In
the course of articulating Henri-Jacques Stiker's *A History of Disability*
to Marlon Riggs's *Tongues Untied*, McRuer does not fail to note that conjunctural analysis can produce severe identity trouble: "The proud and
sustaining *consolidation* readable in 'black' at the end of the twentieth
century could be understood as inimical to the *disintegration* put into motion by Fisher's self-proclaimed 'queer' and 'sociopathic' identities." The
subject in question here is a subject who, like Fisher, cannot quite be ac-
commodated or rehabilitated, and whose moments of consolidation and
disintegration render it impossible to read assertions of identity "pride"
as simple repudiations of identity abjection. Following Robert Reid-
Pharr, who in *Black Gay Man* argues that "even as we express the most
positive articulations of black and gay identity, we are nonetheless referencing the ugly historical and ideological realities out of which those
identities have been formed," McRuer writes, there is "no way of saying
'disabled without hearing 'cripple' (or freak, or retard) as its echo." And
yet, he adds, "that there is no way of speaking the rehabilitated self without hearing the degraded other, however, is not a univocal fact. It is, instead, a fact in multiple ways"—some of which can be recuperated, if not
quite rehabilitated, by the projects of a postidentity politics. Here, then,
is an analysis of black pride and disability activism that has been invigo-
rated and complicated by the politics of gay shame, and that retains
through it all a lively awareness of the multiaccentuality of the sign.
When McRuer turns his attention to popular cultural phenomena—
and *Queer Eye for the Straight Guy* and the James L. Brooks film *As*

Good As It Gets are nothing if not phenomena: the former for its comedic metrosexualization of masculinity, and the latter for its creepy (and therefore Academy Award–worthy) rendering of disability—the result, I think, is cultural criticism that really is just about as good as it gets. Indeed, if there's anything better than McRuer's reading of *As Good As It Gets*, teasing out the symbiotic relation between the narrative in which a gay man becomes disabled and the narrative in which he facilitates the consolidation of a heterosexual family (and, in so doing, helps to ameliorate disabilities in that family), it would be McRuer's cripping of *Queer Eye for the Straight Guy*, in which he elaborates Rosemarie Garland-Thomson's foundational work on disability images while scoring the Fab Five for their casual denigration of "mental institution chic" and "retarded" straight guys and proceeds to offer us some seriously subversive suggestions:

> A crip eye for the normate guy, I propose, would not just be a disability version of the Bravo hit, no matter how much pleasure imagining such a show has given me: "Sweetie, your university is an accessibility *nightmare*! Don't worry, honey, it is your lucky day that disabled folks are here to tell you just what's *wrong* with this place!" Rather, a crip eye for the normate guy (and because we're talking about not a real person but a subject position, somehow "normate guy" seems appropriate, regardless of whether he rears his able-bodied head in men or women) would mark a critically disabled capacity for recognizing and withstanding the vicissitudes of compulsory able-bodiedness.

The biting humor of this passage is distinctively McRuerian, a term I expect will win wider currency once the full measure of this book is taken. But just as important, I think, is its dense and savvy allusiveness: listen again, and you can hear echoes and evocations not only of the Fab Five (tonally *perfect*, I might add) but also of Judith Butler, Eve Sedgwick, and Adrienne Rich, all of whom are being mobilized—so to speak—for wholly new ends, in the service of an analysis that each of them helped to enable but none of them imagined being deployed in the context of disability.

McRuer closes this book with an optimism of the intellect and an optimism of the will: troping off the truism that each of us will become disabled if we live long enough, McRuer points us to a disability yet to come that is also a democracy yet to come. Along the way, as he moves from

Hollywood films to the Mumbai World Social Forum, from college composition programs to the debate over gay marriage, and from FOX's neo-freak show *The Littlest Groom* to Bob Flanagan's neo-freak super-masochism, Robert McRuer shows us that another world is possible, that another world is accessible, and that there's yet another way of getting there. Unlike much utopian thought in the contemporary humanities, McRuer's is grounded in materiality of the world as we know it—even as it points to a spectral world we do not yet know. Just when you thought you'd heard the last word on forms of identity and theories of cultural justice, *Crip Theory* comes along to show that another word is possible.

Acknowledgments

I am especially grateful to Joseph Choueike and Tom Murray; and to Kim Q. Hall, Angela Hewett, Dan Moshenberg, Craig Polacek, and Abby L. Wilkerson. Their generosity and love are at work in this book, and this simple acknowledgment cannot begin to do justice to the ways in which they have sustained me and kept me focused on the simple fact that another world is possible. When Joseph (and so many others) can finally move freely, they all know I hope to thank them more properly in Rio de Janeiro.

Rosemarie Garland-Thomson may not remember saying "you know, this is disability studies," as we rode the elevator up to a conference room in the Smithsonian National Museum of American History in late 1998, where we were going to discuss AIDS cultural theory with a Washington, D.C., reading group focused on theories of the body. The writing of *Crip Theory*, however, in some ways commenced with that moment. Obviously, disability theory and disability liberation would not be where it is without Garland-Thomson's foundational work. My own project, likewise, would not exist were it not for her scholarship and friendship. I am particularly grateful, as well, to the other members of that body theory reading group, including Debra Bergoffen, Carolyn Betensky, Bill Cohen, Jeffrey Cohen, Ellen Feder, Katherine Ott, and Gail Weiss. Jeffrey Cohen, in particular, has read significant portions of this book at every stage, and I have benefited immensely from his input.

The friendship and support of my other colleagues in the department of English at George Washington University have been invaluable; thanks especially to Patty Chu, Kavita Daiya, Gil Harris, Jennifer James, Meta DuEwa Jones, Jim Miller, Framji Minwalla, Faye Moskowitz, Ann Romines, Lee Salamon, Chris Sten, and Gayle Wald. I could single out each of them for large and small things: Jennifer James, for instance, knows equally well when to engage me in rigorous conversations about disability studies and intersectionality and when to send yellow tulips to my apartment. Jennifer DeVere Brody and Stacy Wolf left GWU long ago, but I continue to miss them; their ideas helped shape my thinking for this book as well. My students at GWU continually challenge me, and I acknowledge, in particular, Michael Bennett, Mara Berman, Jacob Blair, Yael Boloker, Evan Brustein, Andrea Cerbin, Joel Englestein, Keith Feldman, Robert Felt, Paige Franklin, Miriam Greenberg, Emily Henehan, Joe Fisher, Tim Nixon, Almila Ozdek, Myra Remigio, Niles Tomlinson, Aliya Weise, and Nathan Weiner. Finally, Connie Kibler gets thanked so often, it seems, in queer studies books, but I do want to acknowledge her influence. She seems to have some new idea for (or about) me with each turn of the calendar.

The more openly Marxist Expository Writing Program at GWU has been replaced with, or disciplined by, an efficient and more corporate University Writing Program, but the full and parttime members of that program know that they have my solidarity as they struggle both to sustain a critical cultural studies pedagogy and to access more just working conditions for academic laborers (including full and guaranteed health care). I am particularly grateful, again, to Abby L. Wilkerson, but also to Eric Drown, Gustavo Guerra, Randi Kristensen, Mark Mullen, Pam Presser, Rachel Riedner, and Phyllis Mentzell Ryder. Many of these colleagues have read and commented on various drafts or chapters of this book. Beyond this, Gustavo Guerra and Heidi Guerra have pulled me away from this book and toward celebratory affirmations of non-work-related aspects of life as often as anyone else, and they know how vital those times have been, for me and for Joseph.

Several colleagues listed above have also been involved in a Washington-area reading group on disability studies since the late 1990s; I thank as well my other friends in that group: Megan Davis, Lisbeth Fuisz, Susan Goldberg, Joyce Huff, Julia McCrossin, Julie Passanante, Todd R. Ramlow, Claudia Rector, and Nolana Yip.

Kim Q. Hall and Rosemarie Garland-Thomson were among those involved in the National Endowment for the Humanities Summer Institute on Disability Studies, held in 2000 at San Francisco State University. All those connected to that transformative event have had an influence on this book; I especially thank Sumi Colligan, Jim Ferris, Ann Fox, Diane Price Herndl, Martha Stoddard Holmes, Cathy Kudlick, Paul Longmore, Cindy LaCom, Carrie Sandahl, Sue Schweik, and Linda Ware.

Many others in queer and disability movements (broadly understood, and in and out of the academy) have at various points given me encouragement, feedback, and community: Stacy Alaimo, Tammy Berberi, Michael Bérubé, Brenda Jo Brueggemann, Saralyn Chesnut, Sarah E. Chinn, Sally Chivers, Eli Clare, Michael Davidson, Lennard J. Davis, John D'Emilio, Shifra Diamond, Carolyn Dinshaw, Lisa Duggan, Jill Ehnenn, Nirmala Erevelles, Beth Ferri, Anne Finger, S. Naomi Finkelstein, Chris Freeman, Terry Galloway, Noreen Giffney, David M. Halperin, Kristen Harmon, Jason Hendrickson, Mark Jordan, Alison Kafer, Ann Keefer, Joe Kisha, Georgina Kleege, Christopher Krentz, Petra Kuppers, Riva Lehrer, Kristin Lindgren, Simi Linton, Nicole Markotic, Vivian May, Ken McRuer, Madhavi Menon, David Mitchell, Anna Mollow, Sammie Moshenberg, Tom Olin, Michael O'Rourke, Ken Quandt, José Quiroga, Ellen Samuels, Dylan Scholinski, Barb Sebek, David Serlin, Tobin Siebers, Sharon Snyder, Marc Stein, Gayle Bozeman Van Pelt, Tamise Van Pelt, Priscilla Wald, Greg Walloch, and Cynthia Wu.

Finally, Michael Bérubé's editorial acumen and friendship have helped nurture this project to completion. I am grateful to NYU Press more generally, but especially to Eric Zinner and Emily Park, both for their enthusiasm and support for this project and for the critical and ongoing work they have done to support queer and disability studies.

There is a tradition on this continent that perhaps reaches back to Anne Bradstreet's *Tenth Muse Lately Sprung up in America* (1650) and that is highly developed in the acknowledgments sections of academic books in the late twentieth and early twenty-first centuries. This tradition consistently suggests that others, while they might have contributed to the successful aspects of the project, are not to be held accountable for a book's "main defects" (to adapt Bradstreet). From where I sit, writing at the turn of the millennium and 350 years after Bradstreet, this strikes me as a tradition worth inverting. If there is anything disabled, queer, or crip about this book, it has come from my collaborative work with those named above, and many others. I take responsibility, however, for the moments when crip energies and ideas are contained or diluted in what follows, and I know that others will continue to push the work of this book, and the movements that made it possible, beyond those moments of containment.

Portions of the introduction appeared previously as "Compulsory Able-Bodiedness and Queer/Disabled Existence," in *Disability Studies: En-*

abling the Humanities, edited by Sharon L. Snyder, Brenda Jo Brueggemann, and Rosemarie Garland-Thomson, MLA Publications (2002); and as "As Good As It Gets: Queer Theory and Critical Disability," in *GLQ: A Journal of Lesbian and Gay Studies* 9.1–2 (2003):79–105. Reprinted here with permission from MLA Publications and Duke University Press.

An earlier version of chapter 4 appeared as "Composing Bodies; or, De-Composition: Queer Theory, Disability Studies, and Alternative Corporealities," in *JAC: A Quarterly Journal for the Interdisciplinary Study of Rhetoric, Culture, Literacy, and Politics* 24.1 (2004):47–78. Reprinted here with permission.

A much shorter version of chapter 5 appeared as "Crip Eye for the Normate Guy: Queer Theory and the Disciplining of Disability Studies," in *PMLA: Publications of the Modern Language Association of America* 120.2 (2005), 586–592. Reprinted here with permission.

Introduction

Compulsory Able-Bodiedness and Queer/Disabled Existence

In queer studies it is a well-established critical practice to re-mark on heterosexuality's supposed invisibility.[1] As the heterosexual norm congealed during the twentieth century, it was the "homosexual menace" that was specified and embodied; the subsequent policing and containment of that menace allowed the new heterosexual normalcy to remain unspecified and disembodied.[2] As early as 1915, Sigmund Freud, in his revised "Three Contributions to the Theory of Sex," declared that "the exclusive sexual interest of the man for the woman is also a problem requiring an explanation, and is not something that is self-evident and ex-plainable on the basis of chemical attraction" (560), but such observa-tions remained—indeed, as Freud's comments literally were—mere foot-notes in the project of excavating deviance. Heterosexuality, never speak-ing—as Michel Foucault famously said of homosexuality—"in its own behalf, to demand that its legitimacy or 'naturality' be acknowledged" (*History of Sexuality* 101), thereby passed as universal love and intimacy, coextensive not with a specific and historical form of opposite-sex eros but with humanity itself. Heterosexuality's partners in this masquerade have been largely identified; an important body of feminist and antiracist work considers how compulsory heterosexuality reinforces or naturalizes dominant ideologies of gender and race.[3] However, despite the fact that homosexuality and disability clearly share a pathologized past, and de-spite a growing awareness of the intersection between queer theory and disability studies, little notice has been taken of the connection between heterosexuality and able-bodied identity. Able-bodiedness, even more than heterosexuality, still largely masquerades as a nonidentity, as the natural order of things.[4]

1

Crip Theory: Cultural Signs of Queerness and Disability emerges from cultural studies traditions that question the order of things, considering how and why it is constructed and naturalized; how it is embedded in complex economic, social, and cultural relations; and how it might be changed.[5] In this book, and in this introduction in particular, I thus theorize the construction of able-bodiedness and heterosexuality, as well as the connections between them. I also locate both, along with disability and homosexuality, in a contemporary history and political economy of visibility. Visibility and invisibility are not, after all, fixed attributes that somehow permanently attach to any identity, and it is one of the central contentions of this book that, because of changing economic, political, and cultural conditions at the turn of the millennium, the relations of visibility in circulation around heterosexuality, able-bodiedness, homosexuality, and disability have shifted significantly.

I put forward here a theory of what I call "compulsory able-bodiedness" and argue that the system of compulsory able-bodiedness, which in a sense produces disability, is thoroughly interwoven with the system of compulsory heterosexuality that produces queerness: that, in fact, compulsory heterosexuality is contingent on compulsory able-bodiedness, and vice versa. The relatively extended period, however, during which heterosexuality and able-bodiedness were wedded but invisible (and in need of embodied, visible, pathologized, and policed homosexualities and disabilities) eventually gave way to our own period, in which both dominant identities and nonpathological marginal identities are more visible and even at times spectacular.[6] Neoliberalism and the condition of postmodernity, in fact, increasingly need able-bodied, heterosexual subjects who are visible and spectacularly tolerant of queer/disabled existences.

Throughout *Crip Theory*, I take neoliberal capitalism to be the dominant economic and cultural system in which, and also against which, embodied and sexual identities have been imagined and composed over the past quarter century. Emerging from both the new social movements (including feminism, gay liberation, and the disability rights movement) and the economic crises of the 1970s, neoliberalism does not simplistically stigmatize difference and can in fact celebrate it. Above all, through the appropriation and containment of the unrestricted flow of ideas, freedoms, and energies unleashed by the new social movements, neoliberalism favors and implements the unrestricted flow of corporate capital. International financial institutions (IFIs) and neoliberal states thus work toward the privatization of public services, the deregulation of trade barriers and other restrictions on investment and development, and the downsizing or elimination (or, more insidiously, the transformation into target markets) of vibrant public and democratic cultures that might constrain or limit the interests of global capital. These cultural shifts have inaugurated an era that, paradoxically, is characterized by more global inequality and raw exploitation and less rigidity in terms of how oppression is reproduced (and extended).

Considering how these shifts have directly influenced the contemporary social construction and subordination of homosexuality and disability, my introduction thus examines the emergence of a more "flexible" heterosexual and able-bodied subject than either queer theory or disability studies has fully acknowledged. After a basic overview of the ways in which compulsory heterosexuality and compulsory able-bodiedness are intertwined, I consider how this subject is represented in James L. Brooks's 1997 film *As Good As It Gets*, which in many ways crystallizes current ideas about, and uses of, disability and queerness. Setting the stage for the chapters to come, the introduction concludes by turning to the critically disabled and queer perspectives and practices that have been deployed to resist the contemporary spectacle of able-bodied heteronormativity.[7]

In chapter 1, attesting to the ways in which crip culture is coming out all over, I name these perspectives and practices "crip theory." Examining a series of global and local examples or snapshots of coming out crip, I put forward in chapter 1 a series of contingent principles that situate the project of crip theory in relation to disability and lesbian, gay, bisexual, and transgendered (LGBT) identity politics, to queer histories of coming out, and to a focused and expansive notion of access. Such a notion of access should be at work in the counterglobalization movements that have in part inspired this project, but—I argue—often is not, given that disability is so useful, for many who would oppose corporate capitalism and corporate globalization, as the object against which an imagined future world is shaped. Cripping that future world, in chapter 1 I both interrogate and attempt to move beyond literal and theoretical efforts to locate disability (and queerness) elsewhere.

In the remainder of the book, through a series of case studies, I survey the primary institutional sites where compulsory able-bodiedness and heterosexuality are produced and secured and where queerness and disability are (partially and inadequately) contained. I understand "institution" here both in the very specific sense, as institutions such as the World Bank and my own university will be interrogated in the pages that follow, and in the more abstract sense, whereby "institution" marks the dominant understanding of a significant and structuring cultural concept: domesticity, for instance, or rehabilitation (and, of course, the specific and more abstract senses of the term are mutually constitutive). The institutions in question are domestic and legal in chapter 2; religious and rehabilitative in chapter 3. Chapter 4 is centered on educational institutions and chapter 5 on media and financial institutions.

Through readings of John D'Emilio's "Capitalism and Gay Identity," the Sharon Kowalski incident (in which custody was granted, for more than a decade, to the parents and not the lover of a Minnesota woman who experienced a disabling accident), and two AIDS narratives concerning African American and Latino men, chapters 2 and 3 focus on efforts to queer or crip domesticity and argue that LGBT subjectivities are currently forged in the contradictory space between a cult of ability (centered on discipline and domesticity) and cultures of disability (centered on networks of interdependency). In chapter 2, I begin by considering queer critiques of marriage and domesticity in order to raise questions about compulsory, able-bodied family forms. Through an examination of Karen Thompson and Julie Andrzejewski's memoir *Why Can't Sharon Kowalski Come Home?*, I contend that Thompson (Kowalski's partner) successfully challenged able-bodied ideologies of domesticity because of her engagement with queer/disabled feminist identities in alternative (and public) spaces. In chapter 3, I survey disability critiques of rehabilitation to highlight the processes through which certain locations or identifications are made safe while others are cast as dangerous and intolerable, beyond rehabilitation. The chapter juxtaposes the will to racial and sexual degradation in the journals of Gary Fisher, an African American queer writer who died in 1993, and the rehabilitative agenda represented in *The Transformation*, a documentary about Sara/Ricardo, who—before her/his death in 1996—moves from a transgendered Latina/o street community in New York to a Dallas Christian ministry and heterosexual married life. Chapter 3, without question, is working at the margins of disability studies, but it is the center of *Crip Theory* in more ways than one: the crip theory of noncompliance particularly at work in Fisher's writing (and in his collaboration with Eve Kosofsky Sedgwick, who edited his journals) could be traced in any of the other cases this book examines.

Overviewing some of the ways in which crip theory has been generated within and around the corporate university, chapter 4 focuses on a range of issues, including the politics of contingent academic labor, the pedagogies that have emerged as queer and disability studies have taken hold in the academy, and critically queer/disabled responses to the Human Rights Campaign's Millennium March on Washington. Cripping composition theory, I identify the ways in which the cultural demand to produce students who have measurable skills and who write orderly, efficient prose (a demand that is evidenced by the rhetoric of crisis that perpetually circulates around writing classrooms and programs) is connected to the demands of compulsory heterosexuality/able-bodiedness that we inhabit orderly, coherent (or managed) identities. "De-composition" emerges in chapter 4 not as the failure to achieve that coherence or managed difference but as a critical practice through which cultural workers resist such corporate demands and position queerness and disability as desirable.

The financial and media institutions (including the World Bank) that globally disseminate marketable images of queerness and disability are the focus of chapter 5. The chapter engages Rosemarie Garland-Thomson's "Seeing the Disabled: Visual Rhetorics of Disability in Popular Photography" in order to critique contemporary (tele)visual rhetorics of queerness, especially as those are captured in Bravo Television's series *Queer Eye for the Straight Guy*. I argue that the normalizing LGBT historical moment that makes possible *Queer Eye for the Straight Guy* depends on identifying and disciplining disability; I then consider some of the dangers that likewise attend the normalization of disability. The normalization of disability works through both visual rhetorics and (facilitated by those rhetorics) incorporation into the global economic disciplines of neoliberalism. Because he offered alternatives to these processes, I consider in chapter 5 the crip artistic practices of Bob Flanagan, Supermasochist. Flanagan, who had cystic fibrosis and who died in 1996, made use of the accoutrements of both disability and sadomasochism in his performance art and installations. The chapter analyzes the ways in which Flanagan's crip notions of futurity exploded a range of disability mythologies, including the spectacular mythologies that would target us all for a compromised and predictable development. Flanagan's work, I contend, set in motion signs of queerness and disability that others have taken up and extended in the interest of resisting normalization.

Finally, in an epilogue conjuring up what I call, invoking Jacques Derrida, "specters of disability" and "the disability to come," I briefly extend the reflections on futurity from chapter 5 and return, once more, to the critique of neoliberal globalization that subtends this book.

Able-Bodied Heterosexuality

In his introduction to *Keywords: A Vocabulary of Culture and Society*, Raymond Williams describes his project as

> the record of an inquiry into a *vocabulary*: a shared body of words and meanings in our most general discussions, in English, of the practices and institutions which we group as *culture* and *society*. Every word which I have included has at some time, in the course of some argument, virtually forced itself on my attention because the problems of its meaning seemed to me inextricably bound up with the problems it was being used to discuss. (15)

Although Williams is not particularly concerned in *Keywords* with feminism or gay and lesbian liberation, the processes he describes should be recognizable to feminists and queer theorists, as well as to scholars and activists in other contemporary movements, such as African American studies or critical race theory. As these movements have developed, increasing numbers of words have indeed forced themselves on our attention, so that—as Adrienne Rich's famous essay "Compulsory Heterosexuality and Lesbian Existence" exemplifies—an inquiry into both the marginalized identity and the dominant identity has become necessary. The problem of the meaning of masculinity (or even maleness), of whiteness, and of heterosexuality has increasingly been understood as inextricably bound up with the problems the term is being used to discuss.

One need go no further than the *Oxford English Dictionary* to locate problems with the meaning of heterosexuality—problems, as it were, from heterosexuality's very origins. In 1971 the *OED Supplement* defined *heterosexual* as "pertaining to or characterized by the normal relations of the sexes; opp. to *homosexual*." At this point, of course, a few decades of critical work by feminists and queer theorists have made it possible to acknowledge quite readily that heterosexual and homosexual are in fact not equal and opposite identities. Rather, the ongoing subordination of homosexuality to heterosexuality allows for heterosexuality to be institutionalized as "the normal relations of the sexes," while the institutionalization of heterosexuality as the "normal relations of the sexes" allows for homosexuality to be subordinated. And, as queer theory continues to demonstrate, it is precisely the introduction of normalcy into the system that introduces compulsion: "Nearly everyone," Michael Warner writes in *The Trouble with Normal: Sex, Politics, and the Ethics of Queer Life*, "wants to be normal. And who can blame them, if the alternative is being abnormal, or deviant, or not being one of the rest of us? Put in those terms, there doesn't seem to be a choice at all. Especially in America where [being] normal probably outranks all other social aspirations" (53). Compulsion is here produced and covered over, with the appearance of choice (sexual preference) mystifying a system in which there actually is no choice.

A critique of normalcy has similarly been central to the disability rights movement and to disability studies, with—for example—Lennard J. Davis's overview and critique of the historical emergence of normalcy or Rosemarie Garland-Thomson's introduction of the concept of the "normate" (Davis, *Enforcing Normalcy* 23–49; Garland-Thomson, *Extraordinary Bodies* 8–9).[8] Such scholarly and activist work positions us to locate the problems of able-bodied identity, to see the problem of the meaning of able-bodiedness as bound up with the problems it is being used to discuss. Nearly everyone, it would seem, wants to be normal in the able-bodied sense as well. Consequently, the critical interrogation of able-bodiedness has not always been well received. An extreme example that nonetheless encapsulates a certain way of thinking about ability and disability is a notorious *Salon* article attacking disability studies that appeared online in the summer of 1999. In "Enabling Disabled Scholarship," Norah Vincent writes: "It's hard to deny that something called normalcy exists. The human body is a machine, after all—one that has evolved functional parts: lungs for breathing, legs for walking, eyes for seeing, ears for hearing, a tongue for speaking and most crucially for all the academics concerned, a brain for thinking. This is science, not culture." In a nutshell, either you have an able body, or you don't.[9]

Yet the desire for definitional clarity might unleash more problems than it contains; if it's hard to deny that something called normalcy exists, it's even harder to pinpoint what that something is. The *OED* defines *able-bodied* redundantly and negatively as "having an able body, i.e. one free from physical disability, and capable of the physical exertions required of it; in bodily health; robust." Able-bodiedness, in turn, is defined vaguely as "soundness of health; ability to work; robustness." The parallel structure of the definitions of ability and sexuality is quite striking: first, to be able-bodied is to be "free from physical disability," just as to be heterosexual is to be "the opposite of homosexual." Second, even though the language of "the normal relations" expected of human beings is not present in the definition of able-bodied, the sense of "normal relations" is, especially with the emphasis on work: being able-bodied means being capable of the normal physical exertions required in a particular system of labor. It is here, in fact, that both able-bodied identity and the *Oxford English Dictionary* betray their origins in the nineteenth century and the rise of industrial capitalism. It is here as well that we can begin to understand the compulsory nature of able-bodiedness: in the emergent industrial capitalist system, free to sell one's labor but not free to do anything else effectively meant free to have an able body but not particularly free to have anything else.[10]

Like compulsory heterosexuality, then, compulsory able-bodiedness functions by covering over, with the appearance of choice, a system in which there actually is no choice. And even if these compulsions are in part tied to the rise of industrial capitalism, their historical emergence and development have been effaced. Just as the origins of heterosexual/homosexual identity are now obscured for most people so that compulsory heterosexuality functions as a disciplinary formation seemingly emanating from everywhere and nowhere, so, too, are the origins of able-bodied/disabled identity obscured, allowing what Susan Wendell calls "the disciplines of normality" (87) to cohere in a system of compulsory able-bodiedness that similarly emanates from everywhere and nowhere.

Michael Bérubé's memoir about his son Jamie, who has Down syndrome (*Life As We Know It: A Father, a Family, and an Exceptional Child*), helps exemplify some of the ideological demands that have sustained compulsory able-bodiedness. Bérubé writes of how he "sometimes feel[s] cornered by talking about Jamie's intelligence, as if the burden of proof is on me, official spokesman on his behalf." The subtext of these encounters always seems to be the same: "*In the end, aren't you disappointed to have a retarded child? . . . Do we really have to give this person our full attention?*" (180). Bérubé's excavation of this subtext pinpoints an important common experience that links all people with disabilities under a system of compulsory able-bodiedness—the experience of the able-bodied need for an agreed-on common ground. I can imagine that answers might be incredibly varied to similar questions: "In the end, wouldn't you rather be hearing?" and "In the end, wouldn't you rather not be HIV positive?" would seem, after all, to be very different questions, the first (with its thinly veiled desire for Deafness not to exist) more obviously genocidal than the second. But they are not really different questions, in that their constant repetition (or their presence as ongoing subtexts) reveals more about the able-bodied culture doing the asking than about the bodies being interrogated. The culture asking such questions assumes in advance that we all agree: able-bodied identities, able-bodied perspectives are preferable and what we all, collectively, are aiming for. A system of compulsory able-bodiedness repeatedly demands that people with disabilities embody for others an affirmative answer to the unspoken question, "Yes, but in the end, wouldn't you rather be more like me?"

It is with this repetition that we can begin to locate both the ways in which compulsory able-bodiedness and compulsory heterosexuality are interwoven and the ways in which they might be contested. In queer theory, Judith Butler is most famous for identifying the repetitions required to maintain heterosexual hegemony:

> The "reality" of heterosexual identities is performatively constituted through an imitation that sets itself up as the origin and the ground of all imitations. In other words, heterosexuality is always in the process of imitating and approximating its own phantasmatic idealization of itself—*and failing*. Precisely because it is bound to fail, and yet endeavors to succeed, the project of heterosexual identity is propelled into an endless repetition of itself. ("Imitation and Gender Insubordination" 21)

If anything, the emphasis on identities that are constituted through repetitive performances is even more central to compulsory able-bodiedness—think, after all, of how many institutions in our culture are showcases for able-bodied performance. Moreover, as with heterosexuality, this repetition is bound to fail, as the ideal able-bodied identity can never, once and for all, be achieved. Able-bodied identity and heterosexual identity are linked in their mutual impossibility and in their mutual incomprehensibility—they are incomprehensible in that each is an identity that is simultaneously the ground on which all identities supposedly rest and an impressive achievement that is always deferred and thus never really guaranteed. Hence Butler's queer theories of gender performativity could be reinscribed within disability studies, as this slightly paraphrased excerpt from *Gender Trouble* might suggest (I substitute, by bracketing, terms having to do literally with embodiment for Butler's terms of gender and sexuality):

> [Able-bodiedness] offers normative . . . positions that are intrinsically impossible to embody, and the persistent failure to identify fully and without incoherence with these positions reveals [able-bodiedness] itself not only as a compulsory law, but as an inevitable comedy. Indeed, I would offer this insight into [able-bodied identity] as both a compulsory system and an intrinsic comedy, a constant parody of itself, as an alternative [disabled] perspective. (122)

In other words, Butler's theory of gender trouble might be resignified in the context of queer/disability studies to highlight what we could call "ability trouble"—meaning not the so-called problem of disability but the inevitable impossibility, even as it is made compulsory, of an able-bodied identity.[11]

Reinventing the Heterosexual

The past few decades have seen plenty of ability trouble, both contingent on and fueling the gender trouble Butler traces. An example from an earlier decade in the twentieth century can demonstrate some of the ways in which able-bodied heterosexuality has changed or adapted. In his essay "Tearooms and Sympathy; or, The Epistemology of the Water Closet" (in *Homographesis*), Lee Edelman analyzes the popular representation of a sexual crisis involving a prominent member of Lyndon B. Johnson's administration and provides thereby a snapshot of dominant attitudes in the mid-twentieth century. On October 7, 1964, Walter Jenkins, Johnson's chief of staff, was arrested for performing "indecent gestures" with another man in a Washington, D.C., men's room. The arrest was made after Jenkins entered the same restroom where five years earlier he had been arrested and charged with "disorderly conduct (pervert)." That the earlier arrest had not been detected as Jenkins rose to prominence in the White House only compounded the scandal in 1964, given the widespread acceptance at the time of beliefs such as that expressed in a *New York Times* editorial: "There can be no place on the White House staff or in the upper echelons of government . . . for a person of markedly deviant behavior" (Edelman 148–149). Edelman's essay thoroughly considers how the events surrounding the Jenkins scandal codified contemporary anxieties about masculinity, homosexuality, American national identity, and national security during the Cold War. Jenkins resigned his position on October 14, 1964 (Edelman 148–151).

Edelman contends that the response to the midcentury arrest of Jenkins and many others for indecency, deviance, or perversion took at least three forms. First, the individual involved could be defined and contained as a "homosexual." This figure was understood as a distinct type of person, whose difference was legible on the body. Second, sometimes in contrast to and sometimes in tandem with the strategy of making visible an embodied "homosexual," the individual could be understood as disabled in some way; that disability, again, was supposedly legible on the body. Although Edelman himself does not use the term "disability" to describe this second strategy, he clearly invokes mental and physical differences from a healthy, fit, and able norm. In 1964, for example, Jenkins could be viewed "as the victim of some illness, physical or emotional, whose transgressive behavior did not symptomatize his (homosexual) identity but rather bespoke an exceptional *falling away* from his true (heterosexual) identity" (Edelman 162–163). This passage is notable for its twofold suggestion that, for Jenkins's contemporaries, "transgressive behavior" was a virtual property of physical or emotional difference and that health and ability were naturally linked to heterosexuality. Edelman's parentheses, moreover, are also significant, suggesting that the second strategy did not need, of necessity, to speak directly to either homosexuality (which could simply pass as "transgressive") or—even more—heterosexuality (which could simply pass as the "true" identity naturally attending the disappearance of "symptomatic" behavior).

Third, the crisis could foreground "a category-subverting alterity within the conceptual framework of masculinity itself" (Edelman 163). In other words, the contradictions inherent in the masculinity that undergirds a system of compulsory heterosexuality (whereby deviance is simultaneously desired and disavowed) could be exposed. In scandals like the Jenkins affair, this third response was, not surprisingly, the least acceptable. The spectacle of sexual, bodily, or mental difference was preferable to that of a visibly threatened masculinity or heterosexuality requiring deviance to define and sustain itself. In 1964 the first two responses prevailed: queerness and disability came together in, and were expunged from, the upper echelons of government, effectively facilitating the invisibility of compulsory heterosexuality and able-bodiedness.

Aspects of the Jenkins affair remain imaginable at the beginning of the twenty-first century, but the assumptions driving the scandal are arguably residual.[12] Throughout the 1960s and 1970s, increasingly vocal liberation movements made disability and homosexuality spectacular in new ways; LGBT people, people with disabilities, and their allies attempted to define sexuality and bodily and mental difference on their own terms.[13] Indeed, the dominant attitudes Edelman interrogates from the 1960s undoubtedly fueled the depathologizing movements of the 1970s and 1980s.[14] Feminists and gay liberationists named it "compulsory heterosexuality," and thus began the process of exposing heterosexuality's passing as the natural order of things.

Its exalted status newly in jeopardy, heterosexuality continued to be defined against homosexuality, but the identity-constituting disavowal, in the last third of the twentieth century, was made explicit. "The coming out of the homo," as Jonathan Ned Katz explains, "provoked the coming out of the het" ("Invention of Heterosexuality" 24). However severely critiqued lesbian and gay coming-out stories have been for simply replicating—in fact, demanding—the same old story of self-discovery, the anxious heterosexual coming-out story from the end of the century owes its existence to, and was necessitated by, that seemingly endless proliferation of lesbian and gay stories.[15] Snapshots from this period might include the picture of New York mayor Ed Koch declaring, "I'm heterosexual," and of Magic Johnson insisting on *The Arsenio Hall Show*, after revealing his HIV-positive status, that he was "far from being a homosexual." These and other heterosexual coming-out stories helped reassure and consolidate a newly visible "heterosexual community."[16]

The cultural representation of that reassurance and consolidation is my subject in the rest of this introduction. Following Emily Martin and David Harvey, I am concerned with the production and reproduction, at the end of the twentieth century, of more flexible bodies—gay bodies that no longer mark absolute deviance, heterosexual bodies that are newly on display. The out heterosexual works alongside gay men and lesbians; the more flexible heterosexual body tolerates a certain amount of queerness. The more flexible gay or lesbian body, in turn, enables what I call "heteronormative epiphanies," continually making available, to the out heterosexual, a sense of subjective wholeness, however illusory. As I flesh out and critique the contours of that epiphanic process, my central argument is that compulsory able-bodiedness is one of the key components of it. Precisely because of their successful negotiation of the contemporary crises surrounding heterosexuality, flexible heterosexual bodies are distinguished by their ability. Distinguished by their ability, these bodies are often explicitly distinguished from people with disabilities. Thus I argue that heteronormative epiphanies are repeatedly, and often necessarily, able-bodied ones. However, as my concluding discussion of queer theory and critical disability (as well as the remainder of *Crip Theory*) demonstrates, such a consolidation of power is not, to say the least, the only resolution imaginable.

Able-Bodied Sexual Subjects

The spectacle of homosexuality or disability may have obscured a potentially fracturing masculinity or heterosexuality in 1964, but the situation had changed considerably by the late 1990s. Indeed, 1998 might be seen as the Year of the Spectacular Heterosexual. The ex-gay movement, previously a marginal movement at best within the Christian Right, suddenly achieved national prominence, not only with the placement of full-page ads promoting its agenda in newspapers such as the *New York Times* and the *Washington Post* (the ads depicted men and women "cured" of their homosexuality), but with unprecedented coverage (of the ad campaign and the movement in general) in the mainstream media. *Newsweek*, while insisting that "few identities in America are more marginal then ex-gay," did its part to end that marginalization with a cover story on "married couple John and Anne Paulk" and other ex-gays (Leland and Miller). John Paulk himself published a book about his amazing conversion to heterosexuality: *Not Afraid to Change: The Remarkable Story of How One Man Overcame Homosexuality*. Despite naming only "homosexuality" in his book title, Paulk, and other ex-gays who told their stories, relentlessly focused on a newly visible heterosexuality. Indeed, Paulk described himself as "a heterosexual who has come out of homosexuality" (qtd. in Marble 28).

From the pages of the *New York Times* to the Oval Office itself, heterosexuality was on display, with at least one performance of spectacular heterosexuality leading to the impeachment of a president. John and Anne Paulk, after all, were not the only heterosexual couple to make the cover of *Newsweek* or *Time* that year. Despite the national crisis occasioned by the heterosexuality practiced in the Oval Office by Bill Clinton and Monica Lewinsky, however, it remained clear in 1998 that the spectacular heterosexual would survive. In and through Clinton's confession to the nation and apology to his wife and daughter, in and through the impeachment and its coverage, "proper" (married, monogamous) heterosexuality was restored and made visible—ironically, not unlike the way in which "natural" heterosexuality was restored in and through the ex-gay campaigns. The Clinton crisis did not, at least obviously, present itself as a panicked moment in which heterosexuality needed to be explicitly named in order to be shored up. Nonetheless, the Clinton affair can be seen as part of the larger crisis of the past few decades in which hegemonic (hetero)sexuality has been increasingly questioned and threatened. A dominant strategic response to that threat has been to make visible, in order to resolve, a crisis. Despite their extreme differences (the ex-gay movement, for instance, sustained an older demonization of homosexuality while the Clinton administration included and affirmed dozens of openly LGBT appointees), the contemporaneous Clinton and Paulk affairs were both thoroughly saturated with a rhetoric of healing that ostensibly restored heterosexuality to its rightful place.[17]

In this larger context, in the midst of the compulsion to impeach improper sexuality and to make visible a "healed" heterosexuality, it is perhaps not surprising that the Oscars for best actor and best actress that year went to an onscreen (heterosexual) couple in *As Good As It Gets*. For her performance as the long-suffering waitress Carol Connelly, Helen Hunt took home her first Oscar. For his performance as Melvin Udall, an obsessive-compulsive romance novelist who lives in the Manhattan neighborhood where Carol works, and whose behavior—often accompanied by sexist, racist, and homophobic comments—isolates him from almost everyone, Jack Nicholson took home his third. After Hunt and Nicholson had received their Oscars, their performances were validated even more as a large set of bleachers filled with Oscar winners from previous decades was spun onto the stage and Hunt and Nicholson were asked to join, together, that special group. Greg Kinnear, who played Melvin's gay neighbor, Simon Bishop, was nominated for best supporting actor but lost to *Good Will Hunting*'s Robin Williams.

As Good As It Gets itself, despite being nominated for best picture, was sunk as far as the main award of the night was concerned, since its competition was James Cameron's *Titanic*, the biggest box-office success of the century. In the Year of the Spectacular Heterosexual, however, it was perfectly appropriate for *Titanic* to win, since it overlaid an epic tale of heterosexual romance onto the shipwreck. Although the female protagonist (Rose Dewitt Bukater, played by Kate Winslet as a young woman and Gloria Stuart as an old woman) loses the love of her life (Jack Dawson, played by Leonardo DiCaprio) in the disaster, she remains forever true to him and tells the story of their passionate affair to a small group salvaging whatever it can from the wreckage. The divers fly her to the scene of the shipwreck to help piece together the details of what happened that night; they hope to recover a priceless necklace Rose once wore, but end up recovering much more. *Titanic* suggested that the problem of the century had not been—as W. E. B. DuBois predicted it would be in 1903—the color line, or even the class line, cartoonish depictions of bawdy working-class parties in *Titanic* notwithstanding. No, the problem of the twentieth century, symbolically resolved in its final years by this film, had been heterosexual separation and reunification. "What a shocker," queer theorist Madonna acerbically opined as she presented the Oscar for Best Original Song to Celine Dion, whose megahit "My Heart Will Go On" underscored heterosexuality's permanence. Across the century and despite catastrophe (including eighty-odd years of separation and, amazingly, death), heterosexuality prevails:

> Near, far, wherever you are
> I believe that the heart does go on
> Once more you open the door
> And you're here in my heart
> And my heart will go on and on.

The supposed timelessness of the sentiment represented by Dion's song and *Titanic* in general covered over how the film was implicated in other late-twentieth-century performances of heterosexuality.[18]

With such spectacular competition at the Academy Awards, *As Good As It Gets*—marketed not as a *Titanic*-like epic but as a mere romantic comedy—was lucky to take home any award. At the same time, it has some uncanny similarities to *Titanic*. On a much smaller scale, it is about heterosexual separations and reunifications. Beyond that, however, it is virtually a textbook example of how heteronormative epiphanies are necessarily able-bodied ones. Indeed, I read the prize-winning moment of the film's male and female leads as the culmination of an epiphanic process that begins onscreen, in the narrative of the film itself.

Although epiphany, as an artistic device, may seem to have had its (high modernist) heyday and to have now been superseded by a repeated (postmodernist) exposure of how epiphanies are always illusory or ineffective, the process retains wide currency, and Hollywood films in particular represent (and continue to produce) an intense desire for epiphany. The epiphanic moment (whether in high modernism or contemporary Hollywood film), despite its affinity with ecstatic religious experiences in which an individual is said to lose himself or herself briefly, tends to be a moment of unparalleled *subjectivity*. As the music swells and the light shifts, the moment marks for the character a temporary consolidation of past, present, and future, and the clarity that describes that consolidation allows the protagonist to carry, to the close of the narrative, a sense of subjective wholeness that he or she lacked previously.

The cultural representation of this epiphanic moment requires what Martin calls "flexible bodies," in two senses. First, the bodies experiencing the epiphany must be flexible enough to make it through a moment of crisis. *Flexible*, in this first sense, is virtually synonymous with both *heterosexual* and *able-bodied*: the bodies in question are often narratively placed in an inevitable heterosexual relationship and visually represented as able. Second, and more important, other bodies must function flexibly and objectively as sites on which the epiphanic moment can be staged. The bodies, in this second sense, are invariably queer and disabled—and they, too, are visually represented as such.

Martin's own interest in flexible bodies and the trope of flexibility crystallized when an immunology professor in a graduate course she was taking began to talk about the "flexibility" of the immune system: "In my mind, this language crashed into contemporary descriptions of the economy of the late twentieth century, with a focus on flexible specialization, flexible production, and flexible, rapid response to an ever-changing market with specific, tailor-made products" (93). The awareness of this discursive overlap leads Martin to trace flexibility's deployment across discourses of not only immunology and economics but also New Age philosophy, government organizations, psychology, and feminist theory (150–158). She consistently foregrounds the well-nigh universal pride of place given to flexibility in neoliberal economic discourses. She quotes, for instance, management guides and vision statements from companies like Hewlett-Packard: "*We encourage flexibility and innovation. We cre-ate a work environment which supports the diversity of our people and their ideas. We strive for overall objectives which are clearly stated and agreed upon, and allow people flexibility in working toward goals in ways which they help determine are best for the organization*" (144).[19]

The flexibility Martin describes is, in a sense, what Harvey elsewhere terms the condition of postmodernity. The economic and cultural crises of the 1970s engendered "a period of rapid change, flux, and uncertainty," and, for Harvey, "the contrasts between present political-economic practices and those of the post-war boom period are sufficiently strong to make the hypothesis of a shift from Fordism to what might be called a 'flexible' regime of accumulation a telling way to characterize recent history" (124). In other words, if the postwar period was largely characterized by mass production and some officially codified protections for Western workers under New Deal legislation and the modern welfare state, the period of flexible accumulation inaugurates the demise of this tenuous consensus: on the production side of the process, labor pools and practices are positioned as flexible, mobile, replaceable; on the consumption side, smaller and smaller groups, around the globe, are both generated and targeted, with products geared, again flexibly, to their specific desires. As numerous theorists of neoliberalism have argued, even as new social movements were calling for an expansion of economic and social justice, these dramatic changes in the processes of production and consumption essentially reined in or curtailed it, marking the beginning of the largest upward redistribution of wealth and other resources that the world has ever known. Culturally, these changes were facilitated by the well-nigh universal valuation of flexibility.[20]

Flexibility in the late capitalist context that both Harvey and Martin identify may seem, on the surface, to militate against subjective wholeness—a corporation like Hewlett Packard would seem, in contrast to the subjective wholeness associated with the epiphany, to value multiple subjectivities, even a certain (postmodern) fragmentation of subjectivity. I would argue, however, that this is not the case; the flexible subject is successful precisely because he or she can perform wholeness through each recurring crisis. Under neoliberalism, in other words, individuals who are indeed "flexible and innovative" make it through moments of subjective crisis. They *manage* the crisis, or at least show that they have management potential; ultimately, they adapt and perform as if the crisis had never happened. Attention must be drawn to the crisis in order for the resolution to be visible, but to draw too much attention to the subjective crisis, and to the fragmentation and multiplicity it effects, would be to perform—or act out—inflexibility. Past, present, and future are thus constantly reconsolidated to make it seem as if a subject or worker is exactly suited to each new role.

Martin is well aware of the double-edged nature of the trope:

> On the one hand, [flexibility] can mean something like freedom to initi-
> ate action: people set goals as they think best for the organization. . . .
> On the other hand, it can mean the organization's ability to hire or fire
> workers at will, as in [the *Los Angeles Times* article] "Schools to Send
> Layoff Notices for 'Flexibility,'" which describes how twenty-one hun-
> dred employees in Los Angeles were to be laid off. In this case, flexibility
> resides in the *schools*, and the employees have little choice but to com-
> ply. The powerful school system flexibly contracts or expands; the pow-
> erless employee flexibly complies. (145)

It is precisely the double-edged nature of flexibility that I find useful for
reading heteronormative, able-bodied epiphanies and this moment in the
history of compulsory heterosexuality and compulsory able-bodiedness.
The successful able-bodied subject, like the most successful heterosexual
subject, has observed and internalized some of the lessons of liberation
movements of the past few decades. Such movements without question
throw the successful heterosexual, able-bodied subject into crisis, but he
or she must perform as though they did not; the subject must demonstrate
instead a dutiful (and flexible) tolerance toward the minority groups constituted through these movements. If a residual model (such as the model
Edelman identifies from the 1960s) explicitly demonizes queerness and
disability, currently dominant and emergent models of heterosexual, able-
bodied subjectivity implicitly or explicitly stress—as in Hewlett-Packard's
support of "the diversity of our people and their ideas"—*working with*
people with disabilities and LGBT people. Martin's understanding of flexibility, however, allows us to read those more tolerant models of subjectivity critically. In many cultural representations, disabled, queer figures
no longer embody absolute deviance but are still visually and narratively
subordinated, and sometimes they are eliminated outright (or perhaps—
in the flexible new parlance—laid off). Flexibility again works both ways:
heterosexual, able-bodied characters in such texts work with queer and
disabled minorities, flexibly contracting and expanding, while queer, disabled minorities flexibly comply. Because all of this happens in a discursive climate of tolerance, which values and profits from "diversity" (a climate that even allows for the actor playing the gay character to be nominated for an Academy Award), the heterosexual, able-bodied subject, as
well as the posmodern culture that produced him or her, can easily dis-

avow how much the subjective contraction and expansion of able-bodied heterosexuality (and, as I underscore in the conclusion to this introduction, neoliberal political and economic logics more generally) are actually contingent on compliant queer, disabled bodies.

Able-Bodied Heterosexuality: As Good As It Gets?

For LGBT communities and for people with disabilities, such subordination, in a contemporary context that supposedly values diversity, is often as good as it gets. So it would seem, certainly, if we judge by the film itself, which I take here as representative of a whole range of contemporary texts.[21] Queering disability studies or claiming disability in and around queer theory, however, helps create critically disabled spaces overlapping with the critically queer spaces that activists and scholars have shaped during recent decades, in which we can identify and challenge the ongoing consolidation of heterosexual, able-bodied hegemony.

As Good As It Gets is a romantic comedy that tells the story of the budding and conflicted love affair between Melvin Udall and Carol Connelly. Simon Bishop and his dog, Verdell, inadvertently facilitate the affair, accompanying Melvin and Carol through a series of separations and reunifications. Simon, initially represented as able-bodied, is attacked in his home by burglars and, after being hospitalized for several weeks (during which Melvin is forced to care for Verdell), ends up using a wheelchair and cane for the remainder of the film. It is through the crises surrounding Simon and another character with a disability—Carol's son Spencer (Jesse James)—that Carol and Melvin's relationship develops. "Spence," according to Carol, has "gotta fight to breathe. His asthma can just shoot off the charts, he's allergic to dust, and this is New York, so his immune system fails on him whenever there's trouble. . . . An ear infection, whatever, sends us to the emergency room five, six times a month." As Carol and Melvin are placed in various situations in which they individually or together must care for Spence or Simon (or Verdell, during Simon's hospitalization), their affection and love for each other are ultimately and inevitably consolidated.

Melvin lives in a Manhattan apartment and, at the beginning of the film, is established as an unlikable character—in fact, the very first scene shows a neighbor emerging from her apartment with a light, cheery mood ("I'm so happy," she says to someone inside) that quickly changes to hostility ("son of a bitch") when she sees Melvin in the hallway. Her reaction, we learn, is due to Melvin's irritability and general meanness. As the scene continues, Melvin attempts to entice Simon's dog out of the building; when he fails, he simply picks the dog up and stuffs him down the trash chute. (Verdell is later rescued by a maintenance worker.) Melvin's irritability usually translates into explicit bigotry: until almost the end of the film he makes antisemitic, racist, sexist, and homophobic comments. His bigotry encompasses people with disabilities as well; at one point he vocalizes what John Nguyet Erni describes as "a fantasy structure of morbidity" (42). Erni is delineating cultural fantasies about AIDS in particular, but some of the cultural assumptions that he identifies—that AIDS is "invariably fatal" and people with AIDS are in some ways already dead or better off dead—circulate around other people with disabilities, who find that their bodies are read in ways that only confirm the ableist notion that such bodies face "imminent deterioration" (41). Similarly, after overhearing Carol talking with her coworkers in the restaurant about caring for her son, Melvin offhandedly remarks, "Well, we're all going to die soon—I will, you will, and it sure sounds like your son will." Melvin's banal observation about the inevitability of death depends on the assumption that Spence, because of his physical differences, will die much sooner than most.

That Melvin is played by Nicholson, a major star who can be read as portraying one of the outrageous characters he is famous for, makes it possible for the film to pass Melvin's behavior off as individual eccentricity. (If Melvin had been played by an unknown actor, he would not stand out so visibly as an eccentric or outrageous individual.) This construction of the "outrageous character" allows the audience—which, supposedly, does not identify with Melvin but nonetheless laughs at the scenes in which he makes bigoted wisecracks—to indulge without avowing its own racist, sexist, homophobic, and ableist fantasies. Melvin's bigotry is more complicated, however, than individual eccentricity, because Melvin himself is established from the start as someone living with a disability of sorts, explicitly identified later in the film as obsessive-compulsive disorder.

Obsessive-compulsive disorder pulls Melvin into the orbit of medical and psychiatric institutions designed to guarantee the production of "docile bodies." As Foucault explains: "A body is docile that may be subjected, used, transformed, and improved" (*Discipline and Punish* 136). Such bodies come into existence because of the modern era's "disciplinary methods," which make possible "the meticulous control of the operations of the body [and have] assured the constant subjection of its forces and imposed upon them a relation of docility-utility" (137). In other words, during the last two or three centuries bodies have been monitored (by disciplinary institutions and by increasingly compulsory self-policing) for signs of behavioral and physical difference that might impede their productivity; these signs of difference have been duly marked and, if possible, "transformed, and improved." Because Melvin's behavioral differences position him outside of relations of docility-utility, he is of necessity caught up in objectifying and taxonomic discourses that would "fix" him as obsessive-compulsive.

Of course, Melvin is very different from many people living with disabilities. He is certainly not one of those involved in the movement to develop a minority consciousness among people with disabilities (a reverse discourse of disability that speaks back to, or stares back at, dominant understandings of disability), and those marked as obsessive-compulsive have not yet been near the forefront of such a movement.[22] Indeed, the crisis Melvin experiences can be read as ultimately reinforcing—through its resolution—both compulsory able-bodiedness and compulsory heterosexuality.

Whether or not Melvin is a good representative of a person with disability, however, he is undeniably linked to other people with disabilities in at least four ways. First, from the beginning of the film, the audience is encouraged, even obliged, to see behavior that sets Melvin apart from others and from unacknowledged norms. As the opening scene ends and the opening credits begin, Melvin retires to the private space of his apartment, and the audience sees some of the behavior that later buttresses the diagnosis of obsessive-compulsive disorder: he ritualistically locks and unlocks the door five times (the odd number would confirm that the door was indeed locked), turns the lights on and off five times, and then proceeds to the bathroom. After dispensing with the gloves that he wears to protect himself outside the apartment, Melvin opens the medicine cabinet, which is filled with two kinds of soap, meticulously arranged on two different shelves. Melvin washes his hands under intensely hot water—saying to himself "Hot, hot!" as he does so—and, after throwing out the first bar of soap, repeats the ritual with a second bar.

Opening credits often provide filmmakers with a space in which to present "background information" efficiently; as the credits roll, many films, for instance, give the audience a sense of the setting by moving through different locations in the city or region where the story takes place. Melvin's behavior is thus flagged as something that the audience should note in order to understand fully the story it is about to see. Later his behavior is specifically differentiated from other people's as he leaves his apartment and heads to breakfast at the restaurant where Carol works— a journey he takes, again ritualistically, every day. Along the way, he is careful not to step on cracks in the pavement and to avoid physical contact with others ("Don't touch," he says nervously as he moves through the crowds). Melvin brings his own silverware to the restaurant and will eat only at a particular table in Carol's section. In one scene, she draws attention to his behavior (and to the usually unacknowledged norm) by saying, "I'm finally gonna ask—all right, what's with the plastic picnicware? . . . Give yourself a little pep talk: 'Must try other people's clean silverware as part of the fun of dining out.'"

Second, Melvin's behavioral differences congeal beneath a label that is both institutionally imposed and offered to the audience as a comprehensive explanation for his actions. At one point Melvin, clearly distressed, enters a building with the sign Fifth Avenue Psychiatric Group on the wall. He storms into his doctor's office and yells, "Help!" When the doctor (Lawrence Kasdan) insists that he "take responsibility for his actions" and make an appointment, Melvin responds, "Doctor Green, how can you diagnose someone as an obsessive-compulsive disorder and then act as if I had some choice about barging in?" The audience later learns that Doctor Green has prescribed drugs to alleviate Melvin's condition. Melvin is thus "fixed" (contained, stilled, defined) by an institution that then offers to "fix" him in the Foucauldian sense (transform, or improve). The scene in the psychiatrist's office is not a major scene (in terms of length), but it does not have to be: its function is to mark as natural modern culture's division of bodies into discrete categories (able-bodied, disabled) and the message works most effectively by simply repeating, not spelling out at length, that cultural common sense. At the same time, the end of the scene confirms its importance by invoking the film's title. Frustrated in his attempt to gain a session with his doctor, Melvin reemerges into the waiting room and says to the roomful of patients: "What if this is as good as it gets?"

Third, Melvin is located in what Martin F. Norden calls "the cinema of isolation." Norden's comprehensive history of physical disability in film demonstrates how "most movies have tended to isolate disabled

characters from their able-bodied peers as well as from each other" (1).²³
In *As Good As It Gets*, Melvin's apartment is the scene of his isolation.
The ritualistic locking represents that isolation as chosen, while the big-
otry represents that isolation as deserved.

This leads me to a fourth, and perhaps most important, way in which
the depiction of Melvin parallels other cultural representations of people
with disabilities: his disability (the anomalous behavior for which he has
been diagnosed and which sets him apart from other people) is conflated
with his character flaws (his bigotry). The film marks no separation between Melvin's disability and his bigotry; on the contrary, they are repeatedly linked, narratively and visually, and the link is naturalized. *As
Good As It Gets* and ableist ideologies in general cannot comprehend it,
of course, but there is nothing natural about this link: an obsession with
order and cleanliness that translates into ritualistic behavior that is uncomfortable for people around him (and for Melvin himself) need not simultaneously translate into bigotry. Indeed, for most people diagnosed
with obsessive-compulsive disorder, it does not.²⁴ The film is concerned
not with truth or falsity, however, but with truth effects: the message that
does not need to be sent, because it has already been received, is that there
is no material separation between disability and serious flaws in character.

A key scene in the film lays bare this conflation. Significantly, it was
one of the scenes used to market *As Good As It Gets* in previews. Melvin
and Carol are at a restaurant together for the first time, and after she
threatens to leave because of his constant wisecracks, he tries to fix things
by saying, "I've got this, what, ailment? My doctor—a shrink that I used
to go to all the time—he says that in 50 or 60 percent of the cases a pill
really helps. I hate pills. Very dangerous things, pills. Hate. I'm using the
word *hate* about pills. Hate." Melvin then reminds Carol of an earlier
evening when she told him that she would never sleep with him. "The
next morning," he says, "I started taking the pills." When she fails to see
his point, he explains, "You make me want to be a better man." The scene
slides seamlessly from a discussion of Melvin's disability and ways to deal
with it to a discussion of his character and ways to improve it. The assumption is that overcoming his disability would improve his character;
his sexism, ableism, homophobia, and racism can be treated with a pill.
By representing Melvin's disability or "ailment" *as* his character flaw, the
scene positions his story firmly in already pervasive cultural discourses of
disability.

All four of these links to representations of other people with disabilities dissolve, however, as Melvin experiences a heteronormative epiphany: as his love affair with Carol develops, the behavior audiences have been encouraged to look at slowly disappears, meaning that diagnosis of his condition is no longer relevant. The romance ends his isolation, of course, and he is represented at the end of the film not as a bigot but as a romantic with a heart of gold. During the film, in short, Melvin's identity flexibly contracts and expands. Able-bodied status is achieved in direct proportion to his increasing awareness of, and need for, (heterosexual) romance.

Both disability and nonheterosexual identity must be visually located elsewhere to allow for this subjective contraction and expansion, and the need for such a relocation or containment of difference to be visible helps explain the complex supporting role played by Simon, Melvin's gay neighbor. As lesbian existence is deployed, in Rich's analysis, to reflect back heterosexual and patriarchal "realities" or relations (178), queer/disabled existence can and must be deployed to buttress compulsory able-bodiedness. Since queerness and disability both have the potential to disrupt the performance of able-bodied heterosexuality, both must be safely contained—embodied—in others. Because of the recent historical emergence of queer/disabled subjects unwilling to acquiesce to their own abjection, however, these others are now tolerated. Indeed, even in a film that gives voice to two-dimensional homophobic and ableist sentiments, and that continues to conflate disability and character flaws, tolerance of queer/disabled existence nonetheless emerges as a necessary component of successful heterosexual and able-bodied subjectivities.

Simon, in fact, is so important to the film that he provides what might be seen as its thesis. Simon is a painter who is shown, in an early scene, working with a model whom one of his friends has recruited from the street. (It is this model and his own friends who later burglarize Simon's home.) Trying to find just the right pose with this model, Simon—with soft music breaking in to accompany his speech—provides viewers with his philosophy as a painter:

What I do is I watch. You ever watch somebody who doesn't know that you're watching them? An old woman sitting on a bus or kids going to school or somebody just waiting—and you see this flash come over them and you know immediately that it has nothing to do with anything external because that hasn't changed. And when you see it, they're just sort of realer and they're more alive. I mean, you look at someone long enough, you discover their humanity.

This insight changes everything (momentarily) for the model, who suddenly understands and accidentally falls into a thoughtful pose that Simon finds ideal. More important, this scene is offered as a context for Melvin's story. As the music suddenly shifts to a fast-paced, even anxious clip, the audience sees his legs moving through the streets of New York. The audience has already seen Melvin jumping around on the sidewalk to avoid the cracks, but the focus on his legs, by reducing him to his body parts, more efficiently objectifies him and highlights his condition. It also shows more dramatically the disruptive effect of his behavior on other people (it even causes one man to fall off his bicycle). In the context of Simon's speech, the implication is threefold. First, Melvin's humanity is not visible at this point; second, his disability, and not his bigotry, is the sign of his inhumanity; but third, a transformation can and will come: the audience will see even Melvin's humanity by the end of the film. The transformation comes as Melvin moves away from disability to a picture-perfect (heterosexual, able-bodied) Hollywood ending.

This transformation happens over and through disabled bodies—most visibly Simon's, but also Spence's. Spence requires so much care that Carol begins to miss work. Since the break in his routine is so distressing, Melvin arranges to pay for Spence's medical services, including a personal physician at Carol's home. Meanwhile, because Simon's own medical bills are so large following the break-in, and because it has broken his spirit so badly that he can no longer work, his friends convince Melvin to drive Simon to Baltimore to petition his parents for money. Because Carol feels obligated to Melvin, she can't refuse when he asks her to accompany them.

The literal transfer from New York to Baltimore is only one of a series of epiphanic transfer scenes between Melvin and Simon. The most important one precedes the Baltimore trip. Upset over an encounter in which Carol informs him that she will not have sex with him, Melvin—unable to sleep—brings Simon some Chinese soup, and the two of them sit on a bench in Simon's apartment. The men are positioned on either side of the screen: Simon, facially disfigured, wearing a cast, and using a cane, on the left; Melvin, whose body is not visibly marked as different, on the right. Melvin begins to talk about how distressed he is: "I haven't been sleeping. I haven't been clear in my head or felt like myself. I'm in trouble. It's not just the tiredness. Boy, it's. . . ." Simon chimes in and completes the thought, "—sick . . . nauseous." "Sleepy," Melvin adds, but Simon has taken over the conversation. With a pained expression, he continues: "Where everything looks distorted and everything inside just kind of aches and you can barely find the will to complain." His insight completes a transfer; whatever Melvin was experiencing when he entered the apartment, it is clearly Simon who is experiencing it now. Simon's insight somehow enables Melvin to get up from the bench, refreshed, and say (oblivious to the pain Simon continues to feel): "Yeah, I'm glad we did this. Good talking to you." As the scene opens, the two men are clearly in sync; they work together to make sense of their anomalous feelings, which are grounded, for both men, in their bodies. However, Melvin progressively sheds his sense of physical difference, so that by the end of the scene difference is wholly located in, and embodied by, Simon.

The audience "discovers Melvin's humanity" as he works with Simon through such epiphanic scenes, and as Simon flexibly complies. The extreme homophobia that Melvin exhibits early in the film subsides; he learns to be tolerant of the difference Simon embodies—or rather, of the differences Simon embodies as he comes to be the main representative not only of homosexuality but of disability. No one in the film, however, comments on the shift Melvin experiences. As I have suggested, the successful heterosexual subject performs as though there were no crisis and no shift, as though he or she were exactly suited to the new role of working with rather than against queerness and disability.

Ironically, Simon experiences a temporary heteronormative, able-bodied epiphany of his own and, through that heterosocial, if not heterosexual, experience, teaches Melvin about the flexibility that he needs to succeed with Carol. Tired of Melvin's jabs and gaffes at the restaurant in Baltimore, Carol leaves and storms into Simon's hotel room, informing him that Melvin will not come looking for her if she stays there. As he watches Carol draw her bath, Simon suddenly is inspired to draw again. She at first resists, but soon the two are laughing together, surrounded by his new drawings. Simon is so exhilarated that he rips off the cast (although he uses a cane for the rest of the film).

Simon's epiphany angers Melvin but also demonstrates to him what he needs to do. As Carol tells him in the morning, when he demands to know whether she and Simon had sex: "To hell with sex—it was better than sex.

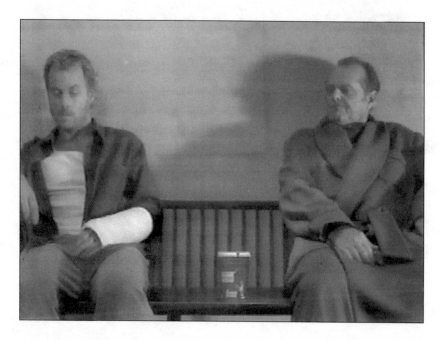

Relocating disability: Simon Bishop (Greg Kinnear) and Melvin Udall (Jack Nicholson) in *As Good As It Gets*.

We held each other. What I need, he gave me, great." Ultimately, Melvin learns the lesson, and he too works with Simon as the film moves rapidly toward its conclusion. Simon's apartment has been sublet, so after the threesome returns to New York, Melvin sets up a room for him in his own apartment. The stage is thus set for a final scene between the two men, and what Melvin needs, Simon gives him, great. After Carol calls to tell Melvin that she is sorry for getting angry with him but also is not sure if she should see him again, Melvin demands that Simon help him. "You people are supposed to be sensitive and smart," he sarcastically comments. As Simon, hobbling with his cane, follows Melvin around the apartment, he convinces him that going over to Carol's is the best thing to do. Simon, in his very last lines, facilitates the affair between Carol and Melvin, telling Melvin to "go over there, do this, catch her off-guard." Having served their purpose, Simon, disability, and queerness are then all hustled off-stage together. As Melvin turns to leave the apartment, he realizes that he has changed: he has forgotten the ritualistic locking of the door.

The film concludes with a fairly traditional reconciliation between the male and female leads. In the last frame, as Melvin and Carol enter a bakery together, he realizes that he has stepped on a crack in the pavement. Thus the heteronormative epiphany that ends the film is once more visually linked in this frame to Melvin's own able-bodied epiphany.

Critically Queer, Severely Disabled

Cultural representations of ability and heterosexuality like those in *As Good As It Gets* are unique to the past few decades. The homophobia and ableism represented in films and other cultural texts throughout the twentieth century and carefully documented by Vito Russo in *The Celluloid Closet* and Norden in *The Cinema of Isolation*—have been superseded (but not entirely replaced) by new, improved, and flexible homophobia and ableism. The more efficient management of queerness and disability suggests that a heterosexual, able-bodied culture has learned some, but most certainly not all, of the lessons of contemporary movements for liberation that queers and people with disabilities have shaped.

What if this *is* as good as it gets? It is not only award-winning Hollywood films that provoke such resignation. As George W. Bush took office in 2001, the appointment of an openly gay Republican to the position of AIDS czar covered over the antigay alliances that had propelled the new administration to power, just as the almost immediate signing of the "New Freedom Initiative" masked the fundamentally antidisabled positions that sustain both the Republicans and their New Democratic predecessors and allies. The New Freedom Initiative allows people with disabilities to take out low-interest loans to buy equipment from businesses and rehabilitation centers, but it does nothing to address the systemic economic inequality that many people with disabilities face. Most important, it is the businesses and rehab centers that receive grants for the initiative, not the people with disabilities themselves. Beyond that, the general emphasis on "smaller government" by both New Democrats and Republicans inevitably requires cutting programs on which disabled people often rely for survival. Despite the supposed emphasis on diversity, and despite the temporary visibility of disability and homosexuality even in the Bush administration, the flexible corporate strategies that currently undergird contemporary economics, politics, and culture invariably produce a world in which disability and queerness are subordinated or eliminated outright.[25]

In fact, the 2004 presidential campaign exemplifies the ways in which both U.S. political parties operate according to the flexible logic I have been delineating. In the 1990s, the Clinton administration may have included numerous openly LGBT appointees, but that did not keep the former president from suggesting, following Senator John Kerry's failed presidential bid, that Kerry should have been more supportive of antigay initiatives. Bush, in contrast, may have appealed to his conservative and Christian base through support for a constitutional amendment forever defining marriage in the United States as the union of one man and one woman, but that did not keep him, in an appeal to "moderates," from implying late in the campaign that civil union protections for same-sex couples might be sometimes appropriate. The fact that one party's homophobia is more virulent, in these examples, should not discount the extent to which both depend on flexible bodies. Neoliberalism will undoubtedly continue to exhibit or require such a dependency, even as there is likely to be vacillation between more and less apparently phobic poles.

According to the flexible logic of neoliberalism, all varieties of queerness—and, for that matter, all disabilities—are essentially temporary, appearing only when, and as long as, they are necessary. Although the disabilities resulting from the attack on Simon in *As Good As It Gets* would seem to differ from disabilities (such as Melvin's) that can be "transformed, and improved" and disabilities or conditions (such as Spence's) that are more chronic, all ultimately serve the expansion of able-bodied identity and—most important—can be moved from center stage as that expansion takes place. Similarly, the model who beats Simon and is initially represented as a street hustler, and Simon's black gay friend and colleague, Frank Sachs (Cuba Gooding Jr.), who is portrayed as a much more flamboyant character than Simon, might have very different lives from Simon himself; all have sexualities, in turn, that are different from the "sexualities" of Spence and Carol's mother, Beverly (Shirley Knight) (indeed, Spence and Beverly are represented as having no sexuality). Ultimately, however, the range of real or potential sexual identities only facilitates the heteronormative coupling represented by Melvin and Carol at the end of the film; it is no longer needed once that coupling is secure.

In the end, then, neither gender trouble nor ability trouble is sufficient in and of itself to unravel compulsory heterosexuality or compulsory able-bodiedness. Butler acknowledges this problem: "This failure to approximate the norm . . . is not the same as the subversion of the norm. There is no promise that subversion will follow from the reiteration of constitutive norms; there is no guarantee that exposing the naturalized status of heterosexuality will lead to its subversion" ("Critically Queer" 22; qtd. in Warner, "Normal and Normaller" 168–169 n.87). For Warner, this acknowledgment in Butler locates a potential gap in her theory, "let us say, between virtually queer and critically queer" ("Normal and Normaller" 168–169 n.87). In contrast to a virtually queer identity, which would be experienced by anyone who failed to perform heterosexuality without contradiction and incoherence (i.e., everyone), a critically queer perspective could presumably mobilize the inevitable failure to approximate the norm, collectively "working the weakness in the norm," to use Butler's phrase ("Critically Queer" 26).

A similar gap could be located in relation to disability. Everyone is virtually disabled, both in the sense that able-bodied norms are "intrinsically impossible to embody" fully and in the sense that able-bodied status is always temporary, disability being the one identity category that all people will embody if they live long enough. What we might call a critically disabled position, however, would differ from such a virtually disabled position; it would call attention to the ways in which the disability rights movement and disability studies have resisted the demands of compulsory able-bodiedness and have demanded access to a newly imagined and newly configured public sphere where full participation is not contingent on an able body.

We might, in fact, extend the concept and see such a perspective not as critically disabled but as severely disabled, with *severe* performing work similar to the critically queer work of *fabulous*. Tony Kushner writes:

> *Fabulous* became a popular word in the queer community—well, it was never *un*popular, but for a while it became a battle cry of a new queer politics, carnival and camp, aggressively fruity, celebratory and tough like a streetwise drag queen: "FAAAAABULOUS!" . . . *Fabulous* is one of those words that provide a measure of the degree to which a person or event manifests a particular, usually oppressed, subculture's most distinctive, invigorating features. (vii)

Severe, though less common than *fabulous*, has a similar queer history: a severe critique is a fierce critique, a defiant critique, one that thoroughly and carefully reads a situation—and I mean reading in the street sense of loudly calling out the inadequacies of a given situation, person, text, or ideology. "Severely disabled," according to such a queer conception, would reverse the able-bodied understanding of severely disabled bodies as the most marginalized, the most excluded from a privileged and always elusive normalcy, and would instead suggest that it is precisely those bodies that are best positioned to refuse "mere toleration" and to call out the inadequacies of compulsory able-bodiedness. Whether it is the "army of one-breasted women" Audre Lorde imagines descending on the Capitol; the Rolling Quads, whose resistance sparked the independent living movement in Berkeley, California; Deaf students shutting down Gallaudet University in the Deaf President Now action; or ACT UP storming the National Institutes of Health or the Food and Drug Administration— in all of these, severely disabled/critically queer bodies have already generated ability trouble that remaps the public sphere and reimagines and reshapes the limited forms of embodiment and desire proffered by the systems that would contain us.[26]

Compulsory heterosexuality is intertwined with compulsory able-bodiedness; both systems work to (re)produce the able body and heterosexuality. But precisely because these systems depend on a queer/disabled existence that can never quite be contained, able-bodied heterosexuality's hegemony is always in danger of collapse. I draw attention to critically queer, severely disabled possibilities in order to bring to the fore the crip actors who, in chapter 1 and the remainder of this book, will exacerbate, in more productive ways, the crisis of authority that currently besets heterosexual/able-bodied norms. Instead of invoking the crisis in order to resolve it (as in a film like *As Good As It Gets*), I would argue that crip theory (in productive conversations with a range of disabled/queer movements) can continuously invoke, in order to further the crisis, the inadequate resolutions that compulsory heterosexuality and compulsory able-bodiedness offer us. And in contrast to an able-bodied culture that holds out the promise of a substantive (but paradoxically always elusive) ideal, crip theory would resist delimiting the kinds of bodies and abilities that are acceptable or that will bring about change. Ideally, crip theory might function—like the term "queer" itself—"oppositionally and relationally but not necessarily substantively, not as a positivity but as a positionality, not as a thing, but as a resistance to the norm" (Halperin 66). Of course, in calling for a crip theory without a necessary substance, I hope the remainder of *Crip Theory* will make clear that I do not mean to deny the materiality of queer/disabled bodies, as it is precisely those material bodies that have populated the movements and brought about the changes I discuss throughout. Rather, I argue that critical queerness and severe disability are about collectively transforming (in ways that cannot necessarily be predicted in advance)—about cripping—the substantive, material uses to which queer/disabled existence has been put by a system of compulsory able-bodiedness, about insisting that such a system is never as good as it gets, and about imagining bodies and desires otherwise.

1

Coming Out Crip
Malibu Is Burning

A 1991 issue of *differences: A Journal of Feminist Cultural Studies* was one of the first major special issues of an academic journal on what guest editor Teresa de Lauretis called "queer theory." For de Lauretis, queer theory generally emerged from academic studies of the construction of sexuality and of sexual marginalization: How have sexualities been variously conceived and materialized in multiple cultural locations? De Lauretis explains in her introduction to the volume that the conference leading to the special issue of *differences* (which convened at the University of California, Santa Cruz in February 1990) was also intended "to articulate the terms in which lesbian and gay sexualities may be understood and imaged as forms of resistance to cultural homogenization, counteracting dominant discourses with other constructions of the subject in culture" (iii). De Lauretis cites a few other conferences that had convened around the topic, but she implies in an endnote that queer theory is not much connected to queer activism: queers in the conference hall, at least for de Lauretis in 1991, didn't have a lot to do with queers in the street.[1]

Obviously, even if the label "queer theory" itself emerged at a California conference in the early 1990s, this is only one of many origin stories, and one that might be contested in any number of ways by contemporary queer theorists.[2] For my purposes in this chapter, I cite the example simply to provide an alternative myth for the birth of crip theory. If there is, or might be soon, something that could go by the name of crip theory, and even if it similarly has something to do with studying (in this case) how bodies and disabilities have been conceived and materialized in multiple cultural locations, and how they might be understood and imaged as forms of resistance to cultural homogenization, it also has a lot to do with self-identified crips in the street—taking sledgehammers to inaccessible curbs, chaining wheelchairs together in circles around buses or subway stations, demanding community-based services and facilities for independent or interdependent living. Although I have no problem with the idea that one path to coming out crip might be going to a conference or reading about it in a book (those are, after all, paths to identification or disidentification), in general the term "crip" and the theorizing as to how that term might function have so far been put forward more by crip artists and activists, in multiple locations outside the academy.[3]

Carrie Sandahl explains that crip (which, like queer, undeniably has a long history of pejorative use) "is fluid and ever-changing, claimed by those whom it did not originally define." "The term crip," Sandahl writes, "has expanded to include not only those with physical impairments but those with sensory or mental impairments as well. Though I have never heard a nondisabled person seriously claim to *be* crip (as heterosexuals have claimed to *be* queer), I would not be surprised by this practice. The fluidity of both terms makes it likely that their boundaries will dissolve" ("Queering the Crip" 27). In what follows, I build on Sandahl's work in an attempt to imagine how crip theory might work, or what it might mean to come out crip.[4]

After a brief consideration of the term "crip" in the next section, I provide—in the remaining sections of the chapter—four meditations on coming out crip in various locations, including India, the United States, and South Africa. Situating the final meditation in southern California, however, I present it in two parts: the first (located in Malibu) is cautiously critical of a disability studies tendency to focus on the image apart from the space where the image and the (disability) identities associated with it are produced; the second (located in South Central Los Angeles) is attentive to various and local (crip) identities and practices that come into purview when the construction of identity is comprehended as a complex and contradictory process always taking place in specific locations.

Malibu in this chapter is both a literal location and—as the society of the spectacle would have it—a mythical site of arrival; those located in Malibu seemingly have it made and know who they are. South Central Los Angeles, in contrast, is a site of unmaking and dreams deferred. My consideration of South Central Los Angeles, perhaps unexpectedly, focuses on the Crips most famously associated with that location—young, African American men who are members of various Crip street gangs; I am concerned primarily with the ways in which disability functions in relation to their material reality and history. Both seemingly opposed snapshots of coming out crip in Malibu and Los Angeles, as well as the three snapshots that come before, locate human beings variously responding to neoliberalism and the condition of postmodernity. In my conclusion to this chapter, I weave these critical responses together and sketch out what might be understood as five principles of crip theory, before considering briefly a queercrip story that, in several senses, brings the urgency of crip theory home. That queercrip story is at least in part my own. Claiming disability is absolutely necessary for that story, but it is not and cannot be sufficient.

Although crip theory, as I sketch it out here and throughout this book, should be understood as having a similar contestatory relationship to disability studies and identity that queer theory has to LGBT studies and identity, crip theory does not—perhaps paradoxically—seek to dematerialize disability identity. This assertion can also be inverted: without discounting the generative role that identity has played in the disability rights movement, this chapter and book indeed attempt to crip disability studies, which entails taking seriously the critique of identity that has animated other progressive theoretical projects, most notably queer theory. The chunk of concrete dislodged by crip theorists in the street—simultaneously solid and disintegrated, fixed and displaced—might highlight these paradoxes. If from one perspective that chunk of concrete marks a material and seemingly insurmountable barrier, from another it marks the will to remake the material world. The curb cut, in turn, marks a necessary openness to the accessible public cultures we might yet inhabit.[5] Crip theory questions—or takes a sledgehammer to—that which has been concretized; it might, consequently, be comprehended as a curb cut into disability studies, and into critical theory more generally.

Crippin'

In many ways, the system of compulsory able-bodiedness I analyzed in the introduction militates against crip identifications and practices, even as it inevitably generates them. Certainly, disabled activists, artists, and others who have come out crip have done so in response to systemic able-bodied subordination and oppression. Stigmatized in and by a culture that will not or cannot accommodate their presence, crip performers (in several senses of the word and in many different performance venues, from the stage to the street to the conference hall) have proudly and col-

Toward accessible public cultures: curb cut dislodged by disability activists. Courtesy of Division of Science and Medicine, National Museum of American History, Smithsonian Institution.

lectively shaped stigmaphilic alternatives in, through, and around that abjection. At the same time, if the constraints of compulsory able-bodiedness push some politicized activists and artists with disabilities to come out crip, those constraints simultaneously keep many other disabled and nondisabled people from doing so.

Compulsory able-bodiedness makes the nondisabled claim to be crip that Sandahl tentatively imagines, in particular, unlikely for several reasons. First, a nondisabled person seriously making such a claim essentially disclaims (or refuses) the privileges that compulsory able-bodiedness grants to those closest to what Audre Lorde calls the "mythical norm" (*Sister Outsider* 116). This refusal has to be active and ongoing, functioning as more than a disavowal. In other words, nondisabled crips need to acknowledge that able-bodied privileges do not magically disappear simply because they are individually refused; the compulsions of compulsory able-bodiedness and the benefits that accrue to nondisabled people within that system are bigger than any individual's seemingly voluntary refusal of them. Second, and related, a nondisabled person claiming to be crip dissents from the binary division of the world into able-bodied and disabled—or, rather, affirms the collective crip dissent from that division. Since dissent requires comprehending the able-bodied/disabled binary as nonnatural and hierarchical (or cultural and political) rather than self-evident and universal, and since the vast majority of both nondisabled and disabled people have in effect consented to comprehending that binary as natural, it is in some ways not likely that anyone would claim to be crip, but most especially those who are nondisabled.[6] Third, even if nondisabled people engage such refusal and dissent, they risk appropriation, since the space for "tolerance" for people with disabilities that compulsory able-bodiedness and neoliberalism have generated can make nondisabled claims to be crip look like appropriation (and, indeed, nondisabled claims to be crip could quite easily function as appropriation). Attuned to some of the dangers of appropriation, liberal nondisabled allies might well be wary of identifying as crip, even if that wariness inadertently reinforces a patronizing tolerance.

As will become clear, however, in this chapter I argue in favor of unlikely identifications even as I attempt to guard against easy equations or oversimplified appropriations. Not only do I generate a critical space where certain nondisabled claims to be crip are more imaginable, I also read as crip some disabled actions and performances that may not always or explicitly deploy the term. My reasons for taking these risks can be traced, at least in part, to related risks taken in innumerable queer locations over the past few decades. In many ways, the late queer theorist Gloria Anzaldúa serves as a model for me in this risky project—in the context of this chapter she might be identified as the late crip theorist who was always adept at noting both how various progressive movements were congruent and how difficult it could be, nonetheless, to bridge the gaps between them. From one queer historical perspective, it is fortuitous that Anzaldúa writes, in *This Bridge Called My Back: Writings by Radical Women of Color*, that "we are the queer groups, the people that don't belong anywhere, not in the dominant world nor completely within our own respective cultures. Combined we cover so many oppressions. But the overwhelming oppression is the collective fact that we do not fit, and because we do not fit *we are a threat*" ("La Prieta" 209). Anzaldúa's assertion, initially published in 1981, is fortuitous because her identification with and as "queer" could be said to authorize reading *This Bridge Called My Back* as an originary text for what would later be called queer theory (although many of the other contributors to the anthology express sentiments similar to Anzaldúa's, most do so without calling those sentiments queer). Because the contributions of feminists of color are often far from central in the origin stories we construct for queer theory, Anzaldúa's 1981 assertion is an important and ongoing challengeto the field or movement.[7]

From another perspective, however, for many readers, even if such passages were not in the anthology, *This Bridge Called My Back* would still be a queer production, given its timely intervention into a monolithic white feminism and its commitment to fluidity and oppositionality, to coalition and critique of institutionalized power, and (most important) to the generation of new subjectivities. Such interventions and commitments, after all, founded a great deal of queer theory and activism of the late 1980s and 1990s. As José Esteban Muñoz insists:

> Cherríe Moraga and Gloria Anzaldúa's 1981 anthology *This Bridge Called My Back: Writings by Radical Women of Color* is too often ignored or underplayed in genealogies of queer theory. *Bridge* represented a crucial break in gender studies discourse in which any naïve positioning of gender as the primary and singular node of difference within feminist theory and politics was irrevocably challenged. Today, feminists who insist on a unified feminist subject not organized around race, class, and sexuality do so at their own risk, or, more succinctly, do so in opposition to work such as *Bridge*. (21–22)

Muñoz goes on to place his own openly queer project, *Disidentification: Queers of Color and the Performance of Politics*, in a direct line of descent from Moraga and Anzaldúa's, as part of "the critical, cultural, and political legacy of *This Bridge Called My Back*" (22).[8] For Muñoz, however, it is the range of identifications and disidentifications that *This Bridge Called My Back* makes possible, and not simply the volume's occasional use of the term "queer" that makes it such a foundational text for queer theory. Because of how the text *functions*, in other words, Muñoz risks reading the volume as queer, even if it is rarely named as such and even if some contributors might have quarreled, in various contexts, with the term (as Anzaldúa later did, even while [re]deploying it).[9]

As far as I know, Anzaldúa herself never used the term "crip," though following her death from complications due to diabetes, there have nonetheless been fledgling attempts to link her legacy to crip movements.[10] Ultimately, for me, it is less Anzaldúa's use or nonuse of crip that leads me to position her posthumously as a crip theorist and more her career-long consideration of terms and concepts that might, however contingently, function to bring together, even as they threaten to rip apart, *los atravesados*: "The squint-eyed, the perverse, the queer, the troublesome, the mongrel, the mulato, the half-breed, the half dead: in short, those who cross over, pass over, or go through the confines of the 'normal'" (*Borderlands/La Frontera* 3). Anzaldúa's famous theory of the borderlands, even as it is grounded in south Texas and centrally concerned with what she calls *mestiza* consciousness, has proven so generative for feminist, queer, and antiracist work because it simultaneously invites disparate groups to imagine themselves otherwise and to engage purposefully in the difficult work of bridge-building.

Anzaldúa may now be located on the other side of the most inexorable, overdetermined, or naturalized border—the border between the living and the dead—but that location should not preclude consideration of how she might continue to speak with crip theory, or even as a crip theorist.[11] Placing Anzaldúa's assertion that "we are the queer groups. . . . and because we do not fit *we are a threat*" next to the work of another poet, Cheryl Marie Wade, helps to illustrate my point. Wade is an award-winning poet, performance artist, and video maker; she is also the former director of the Wry Crips Disabled Women's Theatre Project. Although some of Wade's poetry is available in print form, it is also available in forms that link it to her embodied performance, so that her wheelchair, hand gestures, facial expressions, and tone of voice supplement her written text. In a performance included in *Disability Culture Rap*, an experimental video Wade codirected with Jerry Smith in 2000, Wade asserts:

> I am not one of the physically challenged—
>
> I'm a sock in the eye with a gnarled fist
> I'm a French kiss with cleft tongue
> I'm orthopedic shoes sewn on the last of your fears
>
> I am not one of the differently abled—
>
> . . . .
>
> I'm Eve I'm Kali
> I'm The Mountain That Never Moves
> I've been forever I'll be here forever
> I'm the Gimp

I'm the Cripple
I'm the Crazy Lady

I'm the Woman With Juice.[12]

Although Wade clearly rejects certain identifications (what Simi Linton and others have called "nice words" [14]), the impact of her performance depends on multiplying others: gimp, cripple, crazy lady, woman with juice. Talking back to able-bodied terms and containments, or terms of containment, Wade speaks to "the last of your fears" by implying conversely that crips cannot be contained; even the words most intended to keep disability in its place—such as, of course, the derogatory term *cripple* itself—can and will return as "a sock in the eye with a gnarled fist." And the punches keep coming: not only Wade's own performance but also the location of that performance alongside the many others represented in Wade and Jerry Smith's *Disability Culture Rap* suggest that both the number of in-your-face ways that women (and men) with juice will identify and the number of unlikely alliances they will shape is finally indeterminable.

This book is called *Crip Theory*, but imagining or staging an encounter between Anzaldúa and Wade allows me to position that nomenclature as permanently and desirably contingent: in other queer, crip, and queercrip contexts, squint-eyed, half dead, not dead yet, gimp, freak, crazy, mad, or diseased pariah have served, or might serve, similar generative functions.[13] Judith Butler, perhaps, makes a similar point calling one of her essays "Critically Queer." Positioning her own queer project, through this title, in a permanently indecipherable space (Is she critical of queer, cautioning against its use? Is she insisting that queerness is critically necessary, even indispensable?), Butler writes:

As expansive as the term "queer" is meant to be, it is used in ways that enforce a set of overlapping divisions: in some contexts, the term appeals to a younger generation who want to resist the more institutionalized and reformist politics sometimes signified by "lesbian and gay"; in some contexts, sometimes the same, it has marked a predominantly white movement that has not fully addressed the way in which "queer" plays—or fails to play—within non-white communities; and whereas in some instances it has mobilized a lesbian activism, in others the term represents a false unity of women and men. Indeed, it may be that the critique of the term will initiate a resurgence of both feminist and anti-racist mobilization within lesbian and gay politics or open up new possibilities for coalitional alliances that do not presume that these constituencies are radically distinct from one another. (20)

Cautious, in this passage, of how queer "plays—or fails to play," Butler still leaves open the possibility that it might be deployed in new ways. It is not the term itself that is crucial but whether or not, or how, it might affect or effect certain desirable futures—feminist and antiracist mobilization, coalitional alliances.[14] These desirable futures mark queer as a critical term, as crip is a critical term, that in various times and places must be displaced by other terms.

Perhaps, however, to displace Butler herself slightly, we might say, following Wade, that such simultaneous articulation and disarticulation of crip identities and identifications has been part of crip theory from the start: "I've been forever I'll be here forever/ I'm the Gimp/ I'm the Cripple/ I'm the Crazy Lady." Wade's language in these lines, regardless of whether it is spoken in performance or written, both affirms and defers her own presence. Conjuring up a range of others not in spite of but through her use of "I am," Wade perhaps mimics the words of any discounted "crazy lady" living on the streets, perhaps the "out and proud" sentiments of disability pride, perhaps neither, perhaps both. At any rate, from the beginning, and in the beginning, "cripple" or "crip" is not the last word for Wade, even as she paradoxically positions it—and gimp, and crazy lady, and herself—as the alpha and omega.

Finally, however, with its clear rejection of nice words, Wade's performance is also situated, like Butler's and Anzaldúa's, in conversation or contestation with a certain kind of liberalism—for Wade, a nondisabled liberalism that can only imagine, tolerate, and indeed materialize people with disabilities as very special people, physically challenged, differently abled, or handicapable (or, increasingly unable to effect such a patronizing materialization, it can only express frustration—not at the system of compulsory able-bodiedness nondisabled liberalism helped to build and sustains but at people with disabilities themselves, as the supposedly well-meaning lament "I just don't know what the right term these days is" might suggest). Crip theory extends that conversation/contestation, speaking back to both nondisabled and disabled liberalism and, even more important, to nondisabled and disabled neoliberalism. This book, in fact, is founded on the belief that crip experiences and epistemologies should be central to our efforts to counter neoliberalism and access alternative ways of being.

Accessing a Movement of Movements

On January 19, 2004, at the Fourth World Social Forum (WSF) in Mumbai, India, a small group of people with disabilities held a press conference. Although the WSF is often understood, and experienced by most participants, as celebrating resistance to the global reach of corporate capitalism, the mood at the press conference was decidedly not celebratory. Some critics have, in the past, charged the WSF with being almost too harmonious, but such a charge could not be leveled at the January 19 event.[15] On the contrary, discord—evident in activists' palpable anger, tension, and disappointment—dominated the press conference as disabled speakers described the ways in which they had been marginalized by the WSF's organizing committee. The committee, activists contended, had failed to provide access to the forum for people with disabilities and had refused to include a disabled speaker on the WSF's opening plenary panel. The protest garnered a WSF apology, which was in fact read at the end of the opening session, but activists remained dissatisfied with what they perceived as a merely symbolic or token gesture. Consequently, they came out once again in the evening to hold a candlelight vigil underscoring their critique.

The Mumbai protests demonstrated that disabled people would not be content playing merely a supporting role in what many have called the "Movement of Movements"—that is, the diverse global networks that oppose neoliberalism and imperialism and that collectively compose the most vibrant, fastest-growing forms of progressive activism at the turn of the millennium. In fact, I argue in this section that the protests—and this first example of coming out crip—raise both practical (and local) questions about physical space and theoretical questions about how globalization is currently conceptualized on the left. At the Fourth WSF, these questions were not addressed sufficiently. Disabled activists did make clear, however, that appended apologies would not suffice to redress the ways in which the Movement of Movements was inaccessible; in conversations about alternatives to global capitalism, crips would have to have a seat at the plenary table.

Another world is possible: disability activists in Mumbai, India. Photographs courtesy of Jean Stewart.

From 2001 to 2003, the World Social Forum took place in Porto Alegre, Brazil; the Mumbai conference was the first to be held elsewhere. Initially conceived following a range of important anticapitalist, anticorporate events in the 1990s (including, for instance, the Zapatista uprising against the North American Free Trade Agreement [NAFTA] in 1994 and protests in Seattle that led to the collapse of talks of the World Trade Organization [WTO] in 1999), the WSF was intended at first to shadow the World Economic Forum (WEF), held annually in Davos, Switzerland. At the WEF in Davos, corporate elites, economic ministers from the world's most powerful countries, and representatives from international financial institutions (IFIs) such as the World Bank and International Monetary Fund (IMF) met—in private meetings protected by a large cadre of armed guards—to discuss the future of global capitalism. In contrast, at the first anti-WEF, or WSF, in 2001, more than fifteen thousand participants met—in open meetings free from armed guards and apart from IFI or corporate regulation—to generate alternatives to global capitalism and to develop vocabularies and practices of resistance to neoliberalism.

The WSF was not formed to shape global policy but, rather, to ensure democratic spaces where open and forthright discussions of viable and humane futures could take place. The WSF's organizing committee, following the success of the 2001 meeting, found it "necessary and legitimate" to put together a Charter of Principles to further pursuit of that goal. The first principle of the WSF underscores the importance of access, broadly conceived:

> The World Social Forum is an open meeting place for reflective thinking, democratic debate of ideas, formulation of proposals, free exchange of experiences and linking up for effective action, by groups and movements of civil society that are opposed to neoliberalism and to domination of the world by capital and any form of imperialism, and are committed to building a global society of fruitful relationships among human beings and between humans and the Earth. (Fisher and Ponniah 354)

To nurture the kind of openness envisioned by these principles, however, certain exclusions were necessary. In contrast to the WEF exclusions, which were designed to protect the interests of capital and were thus symbolized quite effectively by state-subsidized armed guards, the WSF's exclusions were designed to protect the interests of voices and communities disenfranchised by the WEF and by neoliberalism more generally. Walden Bello thus explains that "some World Bank officials came and *demanded* a platform, and were told, 'No. You can speak elsewhere in the world but this is not your space'" (66). Armed organizations and representatives of political parties were also excluded, although the first three WSFs nonetheless had significant, if unofficial, ties to the Brazilian Worker's Party (Partido dos Trabalhadores, or PT), which held power at the time in Porto Alegre and the state of Rio Grande do Sul, and which had instituted a range of redistributive economic and social policies in the region. Some have criticized the PT's central role from 2001 to 2003, suggesting that Brazilian organizers, excluding representatives from political parties elsewhere, had implemented something of a double standard, given their relationship with the PT. Directly or indirectly, the move to Mumbai addressed these concerns and solidified the WSF as an event autonomous from political parties, since Mumbai was (and is) not governed by a progressive political party interested in forging ties with the WSF. The move to Mumbai suggests that, hegemonic discourses of flexibility notwithstanding, the WSF has in many ways, over the course of its history, exhibited a more democratic flexibility as it has moved to respond to various critiques from within the Movement of Movements.

The exclusion of representatives from IFIs, in particular, emphasizes the WSF's initial role as anti-Davos, whether located in Porto Alegre or Mumbai. The forum evolved away from this role over the years, however. If initially it was largely and directly opposed to the WEF, it increasingly took on an identity in its own right, concerned not just with registering opposition but with generating genuine economic and social alternatives to the policies envisioned by corporate elites in Davos and elsewhere. Hence, from 2002 on, the WSF disseminated the slogan "Another World Is Possible."

The visionary and unifying idea that another world is possible paradoxically developed at the same time that the forum was being pushed to move beyond harmony and celebration. Emerging from a perceived need to increase the representation and influence of African and Asian participants, Mumbai 2004 both reflected this push beyond celebration and addressed an important critique of the 2001, 2002, and 2003 events. If the exclusion of armed organizations, political parties, and IFIs could be justified, the exclusion of groups (from Africa, Asia, and elsewhere) marginalized by those forces clearly could not. The crip protest can therefore be said to arise directly from the critical ethos founding Mumbai 2004. Related to this, but perhaps even more important, the crip protest can be understood as congruent with the WSF's first principle (a principle of access), even as it deepens that commitment to access, founding it on an unwavering commitment to literal, local and physical, access.

A more theoretical divide had also been coming to the fore prior to Mumbai and, although the protestors did not speak directly to it, their more integral participation at Mumbai might have done much to further conversation across the divide. As Michael Hardt argues, the Movement of Movements can increasingly be read as addressing divisions between those who

> work to reinforce the sovereignty of nation-states as a defensive barrier against the control of foreign and global capital; or [those who] strive towards a non-national alternative to the present form of globalization that is equally global. The first [group] poses neoliberalism as the primary analytical category, viewing the enemy as unrestricted global capitalist activity with weak state controls; the second is more clearly posed against capital itself, whether state-regulated or not. The first might rightly be called an anti-globalization position, in so far as national sovereignties, even if linked by international solidarity, serve to limit and regulate the forces of capitalist globalization. National liberation thus remains for this position the ultimate goal, as it was for the old anti-colonial and anti-imperialist struggles. The second, in contrast, opposes any national solutions and seeks instead a democratic globalization. (232–233)

Hardt proposes that the majority of participants in the WSF may well subscribe in some way to the second position, even if, arguably, those most responsible each year for organizing the event subscribe to the first (233).

Hardt's notion that the forces of democratic globalization are in the majority or ascendancy is promising, but as with other theoretical considerations of globalization, not excluding Hardt and Antonio Negri's own voluminous *Empire* and *Multitude*, it is not always clear how disability figures into the promise. Hardt and Negri repeatedly position the immanent and creative powers of what they term the "multitude" in opposition to the homogenizing, disciplining will to transcendence put forward by "Empire." The Mumbai protests, however, might complicate this equation. In what ways, if any, can the multitude be comprehended as disabled? How does disability figure into or around the stark yet seductive opposition Hardt and Negri set up, or the stark oppositions put forward by others theorizing alternatives to Empire and corporate globalization? How has disability, in particular, figured into the modern or contemporary nation-state? To what extent, according to the terms of Hardt and Negri's argument, is the multitude always on the verge of being (necessarily) able-bodied ("what we need is to create a new social body," they write [*Empire* 204]; "we share bodies with two eyes, ten fingers, ten toes . . . we share dreams of a common future" [*Multitude* 128])? Must it always, somehow (necessarily, and negatively), guard against association with disability ("the deformed corpse of [the old] society" [*Empire* 204])? In other words, as alternative forms of globalization are conceptualized, when and where are able-bodiedness and disability *only* figures and how might coming out crip, at events like the Mumbai protests, more *positively* disfigure and rewrite such conceptualizations?

I intend for these to be open questions; a crip reading of Empire is undeniably possible.[16] Disabled activists might be well-positioned to negotiate the split Hardt identifies within the Movement of Movements, and perhaps temper the either-or implications contained in his construction of the first (antiglobalization) group's *ultimate* (that is, supposedly singular and final) goal of national liberation and the second (counterglobalization) group's opposition to *any* national solutions. To access (in all its senses) the other world that is possible, global disability activists may well have committed, at various points, to the state-based limits and regulations advocated by those who, according to Hardt's schema, directly criticize neoliberalism. Conversely and simultaneously, however, those seeking a democratic (crip) globalization may well recognize that getting many more of their comrades to that democratic space means accessing other solutions that have emerged in transnational or extranational venues.[17] If Hardt's (or Hardt and Negri's) analysis pinpoints, in short, a divide or even a potential impasse in the Movement of Movements, then crip insights or literacies might help to explode that impasse.[18]

What is clear from events in Mumbai, however, is that people with disabilities never got the opportunity to play the central part they might have in these debates, at least as they were officially constituted by the WSF in January 2004. Only three hundred of the expected two thousand disabled participants were able to attend the WSF in Mumbai. Hence, beneath banners reading "National Disability Network Solidarity Rally" and "Why Is the World Social Forum Also Marginalising Us?" disabled activists insisted on January 19 that "we do not feel we belong here. We have been struggling since the start of the conference to be recognized but no one seems to care about us and our needs." Although, for the first time since 2001, a few sessions exploring the ways in which disability and globalization are related did take place (disabled activists had demanded, "if you are coming to India and if you are having the World Social Forum in Bombay, then you can't have it without disability on the agenda"), it was not easy to secure the panels. Moreover, as Javed Abidi, one of the activists, explained, "they have given us a venue that is extremely shoddy and has a capacity of just 200 people. The venue is near a dump; there are holes in the ground; [they] have made a very shoddy ramp, where my wheelchair cannot go. It is the pits" (S. Kumar).[19] The pits, combined with the lack of other basic accommodations (such as no provision for sign language), pushed the group to hold the January 19 press conference and candlelight vigil and to protest outside the opening forum (a panel that included Arundhati Roy and other prominent speakers); "WSF shame, shame," they shouted.

Along with Abidi, the speakers for one of the official disability panels, "Disability in a Global Perspective: Nothing about Us without Us," were Anita Ghai, Anne Finger, Jean Parker, and Jean Stewart.[20] The other panelists shared the critique put forward by Abidi and the others. Stewart reported that the WSF was exhilarating but stressed that the crip protests were, for her, the highlight. Finger was struck by the organization and leadership of Indian disability activists; clearly, the protests were organized by and for an emerging Third World disability movement. Ghai also spoke at the press conference itself, calling the treatment disabled people had received "embarrassing" and claiming that WSF organizers had initially been reticent about even having official disability panels since they could not perceive how disability might be related to globalization (Mulama). Such a perception will undoubtedly be far less common in the Movement of Movements if (or as) others follow the lead of the group in Mumbai and come out crip.

Imagine This: Crip Lives and Cultures

My second example of coming out crip comes from the directors of the important 1996 film *Vital Signs: Crip Culture Talks Back*, David Mitchell and Sharon Snyder. In the preface to *Narrative Prosthesis: Disability and the Dependencies of Discourse*, Mitchell and Snyder explain that their critical negotiation of a range of

> institutions and texts brought us to inhabit an increasingly intertwined disability subjectivity. Ironically, the refusal of separate identities along the lines of "patient" and "caregiver" proved to be the monkey's wrench that brought the gears of many an institution to at least a temporary halt. We jointly plotted strategies of access, interpretation, and survival [and] the experience of disability embedded itself in both of our habits and thoughts to such an extent that we no longer differentiated between who was and who was not disabled in our family. (x–xi)

It sounds rather queer, in some ways, this pleasurable and embodied refusal of a certain kind of compulsory individualism coupled with a rigorous institutional critique, sometimes shutting institutions down and sometimes opening them up. It might be more appropriate at this point to say that queer desires and identifications that resist the commodification and normalization of the past decade (especially the commodification and normalization of gay bodies) sound rather crip.

I do not intend to put forward Mitchell and Snyder's reinvention of identity politics here for an easy equation of queer and crip experiences; indeed, as I hope my conclusion to this chapter makes clear, crip theory is necessitated at least in part by queer theory's ongoing inability to imagine such equations. It is no accident, however, that the crip intersubjectivities that Mitchell and Snyder articulate can in some ways be understood as queer. Snyder readily describes how LGBT and HIV/AIDS politics have provided one of the paths to familial and communal identification for her and Mitchell:

> I [speak and write] as a child of gay parents who sees queer culture and Castro Street life as a "parent" culture. . . . It was very early involvement in Project Inform and ACT UP (my dad's a longterm survivor) that eventually led David and me to work in disability studies as well as serious mentoring by queer theorists . . . that resulted in [the anthology we edited] *The Body and Physical Difference: Discourses of Disability*. [We] have often joked that the only film festival that would truly have "gotten" *Vital Signs: Crip Culture Talks Back* would be the SF gay/lesbian fest. Our other joke title for the video is "Disabled women, gay men, and Harlan talk back."[21]

Moreover, Jennie Livingston's *Paris Is Burning*—the acclaimed 1992 documentary about African American and Latino/a drag balls in New York City—was one of the direct antecedents for *Vital Signs*. One of the queerest aspects of *Vital Signs*, however, may be its refusal to reproduce any "parent culture," even a queer one, faithfully. If *Paris Is Burning* allowed for "narration of subcultural attitudes and practices" (Mitchell and Snyder, "Talking about *Talking Back*" 210), it also at times made use of an exoticizing anthropological gaze that *Vital Signs*, from its "talking back" subtitle on, more actively and successfully resists.[22]

Vital Signs was filmed during the opening up—to disability experiences and perspectives—of one institution in particular, the University of Michigan, Ann Arbor, which held a conference titled "This/Ability: An Interdisciplinary Conference on Disability and the Arts" in 1995. The conference was organized by Susan Crutchfield, Marcy Epstein, and Joanne Leonard, and—at the time—was only the second such conference dedicated specifically to disability studies in the humanities (the first was "Discourses of Disability in the Humanities," held at the University of Puerto Rico, Mayaguez, in 1992). The numerous speakers and performers in *Vital Signs*—including Sandahl, Finger, Robert DeFelice, Kenny Fries, and others—were all participants in "This/Ability." Crutchfield, Epstein, and Leonard agreed to the filming of some parts of the event; *Vital Signs* is the documentary resulting from the multiple interviews and performances Mitchell and Snyder collected. As individuals in *Vital Signs* "talk back" to the camera, a politicized and increasingly intertwined crip subjectivity—not unlike the subjectivity Mitchell and Snyder describe as animating their own family life—materializes. *Vital Signs*, in fact, extends to and learns from an ever-expanding range of others the crip subjectivity that Mitchell and Snyder discuss elsewhere.

Initially, Mitchell and Snyder intended *Vital Signs* to document the emergence and evolution of disability studies in the academy; their plan for observing the University of Michigan event was not unlike de Lauretis's observation of what was taking place academically, in a queer context, at the 1990 Santa Cruz conference. What resulted, however, makes de Lauretis's earlier, more straightforward academic observation, appear rather staid; Mitchell and Snyder realized that they had "the rough outline of a film about *disability culture*" ("Talking about *Talking Back*" 198). Or, as the subtitle of their documentary suggests, a film about crip culture. The evolution of Mitchell and Snyder's film underscores, as I suggested at the beginning of this chapter, that crip theory has emerged far more readily in activist and artistic venues. It also underscores not that crip theory has no place in the academy—the filming of *Vital Signs* did occur at the University of Michigan, after all, and many participants had academic affiliations—but that it—and the practices of coming out crip it makes possible—nonetheless will or should exist in productive tension with the more properly academic project of disability studies.

Mitchell and Snyder locate *Vital Signs* within a "movement of film and video in the mid-1990's that would seek to narrate the experience of disability from within the disability community itself. . . . What these visual productions all shared was a commitment to telling stories that avoided turning disability into a metaphor for social collapse, individual overcoming, or innocent suffering" ("Talking about *Talking Back*" 208–209). Toward that end, included in the video are interviews with activists such as Carol Gill and poetic and literary performances by writers such as Eli Clare (talking about cerebral palsy and "learning the muscle of [the] tongue") and Finger (reading her story of a fictionalized love affair between Helen Keller and Frida Kahlo). Solo autobiographical performance pieces in *Vital Signs* include those by Sandahl, who performed in a lab jacket with medical terminology written on it, drawing attention to the ways in which people with disabilities are treated as though diagnoses were literally written on their bodies and thus constantly available for scrutiny; and Mary Duffy, who confronted audiences as a nude Venus de Milo, thereby challenging, through her crip invocation of the highest echelons of Western art and culture, the reduction of her body to "congenital malformation."

For all of the performances and interviews documented in *Vital Signs*, Mitchell and Snyder were committed to filming disabled people speaking in their own voices. They filmed each speaker from a low angle, since they wanted their subjects "to tower over the viewer with their images punctuating their political positions and artistic caveats" ("Talking about *Talking Back*" 201). Looking back on this filmic choice, Mitchell and Snyder note Wade's performance: "When Cheryl Marie Wade . . . exclaims, 'Mine are the hands of your bad dreams—booga, booga—from behind the black curtain,' we wanted our audience to viscerally *feel* the challenge as she displays her 'claw hands' on screen" (201). The compilation that results from these images, however, ironically suggests again that coming out crip has very little to do with individuality as it is traditionally conceived. If a commitment to filming disabled people speaking in their own voices puts forward a fairly recognizable (and still important) version of identity politics, the resulting film participates in a reinvention of identity politics. Along with the individuality claimed or spoken by all of those in *Vital Signs*, Wade's "Mine" in this piece, like the "I am" I analyzed earlier, gains its meaning primarily from the larger and emergent communal (crip) context represented in the film.

Vital signs, in a strictly medicalized context, refer to that which is supposedly most undeniable about the human condition at any given moment: Are the blood pressure and temperature normal? Is the system compromised in any way by infectious agents? Is the patient's chart up-to-date? The film's supplemental understanding of "vital signs," however, like the cultural signs of disability and queerness I am tracing throughout this book, refuses the fixation on life as understood in strictly medical terms. And indeed, as the proliferation of crip identifications in the film makes clear, the system *has* been compromised by infectious agents—or, put differently, by a communicable disability agency. Even when, as in Sandahl's performance, the seemingly incontrovertible medical sign is invoked, its (singular, originary) life or presence is not guaranteed. Crip vital signs work otherwise and can never be fully or finally fixed.[23]

Even as Mitchell and Snyder later write about the making of *Vital Signs*, in an essay titled "Talking about *Talking Back*," a nonindividual crip subjectivity comes to the fore: stills from *Vital Signs* do not, in the essay, always directly gloss or exemplify what the filmmakers are arguing. Instead, these stills are included with captions excerpting part of each speaker's story, as though the speakers are providing a running (and supportive) commentary on the essay. Harlan Hahn, for instance, is depicted with the caption "Once we begin to realize that disability is in the environment then in order for us to have equal rights, we don't have to change but the environment has to change" (204). The authors do not comment directly on this observation that instead speaks—but certainly, given the repetition of such a point in many crip contexts, without Hahn as its definitive source—alongside them. If, in other contexts, coming out crip for Mitchell and Snyder made it difficult for able-bodied subjectivities, institutions, and authority to function efficiently, in the context of the film and the cultural efflorescence it represents, coming out crip—inefficiently, contagiously—allows for the emergence of new disabled subjectivities. A reinvented and collective identity politics flourishes in and around *Vital Signs*; the birth of the crip comes at the expense of the death of the (individualized, able-bodied) author.

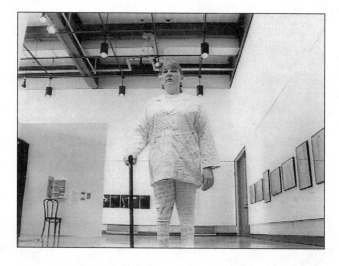

Carrie Sandahl in *Vital Signs: Crip Culture Talks Back.*

On Me, Not in Me: TAC Attack

I'm going to use myself to introduce my third example of coming out crip. In January 2004, at a meeting focused on "Interiorities" in Maastricht, Netherlands, I came out as HIV-positive. I'm not, as far as I know, HIV-positive, though like many other gay men of my generation (coming of age sexually at the very beginning of the AIDS crisis), I've had lovers who are positive and, actually, I've spent not insignificant periods of my adult life unsure of my serostatus. Nonetheless, although literal disability accommodations did get me on the plane to Amsterdam, those accommodations were not related to HIV. I came out as HIV-positive for two reasons. First, the interdisciplinary expert meeting where I was speaking was meant to explore "the experience of the inside of the body," and as the sole representative of queer theory and disability studies, I wanted to draw attention to the politics of looking into queer and disabled bodies (I wanted to raise questions, in other words, about what exactly people wanted or expected to see inside disabled and queer bodies). Second, the paper was on South Africa's Treatment Action Campaign, or TAC.

Perhaps five million people or more are living with HIV or AIDS in South Africa (approximately one in nine people). In 1998, after an AIDS activist was murdered by neighbors who were angry that she disclosed her HIV-positive identity, TAC began producing t-shirts like the one I wore at the Maastricht meeting: the front side of the t-shirt simply says "HIV POSITIVE" in block letters; the back can vary, but the version I wore declared "STAND UP FOR OUR LIVES" and "Treat the People," next to a photograph of Nelson Mandela in a TAC shirt.[24] The version I wore announced a February 2003 march for HIV/AIDS treatment, but by 2003–2004, the shirts were worn in many different contexts. The shirts are now worn, in fact, by almost everyone involved with TAC, whether in Africa, Europe, or the United States. At rallies and events, HIV POSITIVE t-shirts can be seen everywhere you look—this was the case, for instance, according to Joe Wright, who was working with TAC in South Africa at the time, at the TAC National Congress in summer 2003, which brought together delegates from around the country. Activists also often wear the shirts in more individual contexts; an HIV-negative friend of mine tells me she was approached on a South African beach by someone who came up to say "you're very brave to disclose your HIV status like that." As my friend's anecdote suggests, and as Wright reports, "the T-shirt practically shouts, 'I have HIV.' And so that's the first question many people ask whoever is wearing the shirt: 'Do you have HIV?'" Wright explains that activists generally resist or evade this question, thereby implicitly (or explicitly) insisting, "It's not your HIV status that matters most, but your HIV politics" ("Commentary").

TAC's project is not always explicitly queer, though Zackie Achmat, who founded the group, had a history of both anti-apartheid and LGBT/queer activism (his activism, in fact, helped establish the National Coalition for Gay and Lesbian Equality in 1994). Achmat, who is living with HIV, began a unique kind of "hunger strike" in 1999, refusing to take expensive antiretrovirals until they became more widely available for the many other South Africans with HIV/AIDS. In August 2003, Achmat ended his hunger strike; he now adopts what he calls a "fifty-year perspective" that will "ensure access for all and the development of a public health system." Achmat's understanding of access has consistently been both local and global, and he therefore positions himself and TAC as "part of a global movement that sees health as a human right" (Musbach).

Despite the fact that TAC's project is not always explicitly queer, Achmat's history as a gay activist certainly energized the group and there are numerous ways in which TAC's t-shirt campaign, in particular, dove-

Activists in TAC t-shirts outside Bush reelection headquarters in Arlington, Virginia. Global Day of Action on HIV/AIDS, June 24, 2004. Photograph courtesy of Sammie Moshenberg.

tails with earlier queer projects that likewise contingently universalized HIV-positive identity. In England, the Terrence Higgins Trust at one point, for instance, deployed the campaign "Safer sex—keep it up! Positive or negative, it's the same for all" (King 214). The point of the campaign was intragroup solidarity in the interests of communal and cultural survival: in contrast to heterosexuals committed to the illusory goal of "finding a safe partner," gay men at the time committed to safe practices. As Cindy Patton suggests, rather than never talking about sex in public and then endlessly interrogating one's partner in private (the U.S. heterosexual model), gay men in North America and Europe committed to an "emancipatory model" continually talked and debated safer sex in public and thus did not need to grill our partners, however multiple, in private (indeed, when the private grilling didn't happen it on some level marked one's political commitment to communal solidarity) (*Fatal Advice* 108–111; *Inventing AIDS* 46–49). These commitments (to safer practices and to textured, public conversations about sex) validated that the variety of life-affirming cultural forms and relations we had generated outside compulsory heterosexuality, and outside the couple form, would remain viable. One (and only one) of the lines of descent for TAC's t-shirt campaign might be understood as these queer projects of solidarity and contingent universalization of HIV-positive identity—projects of solidarity now largely lost as far as North American and European AIDS activism is concerned.[25]

Achmat founded TAC on International Human Rights Day, December 9, 1998. The group has three main objectives: "Ensure access to affordable and quality treatment for people with HIV/AIDS; Prevent and eliminate new HIV infections; Improve the affordability and quality of health-care access for all" (TAC: Treatment Action Campaign, "About TAC"). A major victory was scored on December 9, 2003 (the fifth anniversary of TAC's founding) when an agreement was reached allowing for generic antiretrovirals to be made available in the forty-seven countries of sub-Saharan Africa. This victory was largely attributable to the pressure TAC consistently applied, both to the South African government and to multinational pharmaceuticals such as Boehringer Ingelheim (BI) and GlaxoSmithKline (GSK). The agreement determined that (1) producers of generic antiretrovirals would be given licenses to disseminate their compounds across sub-Saharan Africa, subject to royalties, not to exceed 5 percent, to be paid to the pharmaceuticals holding name-brand patents (according to the agreement, the licenses would be "voluntary," which simply meant that BI and GSK would not be faced with governments bypassing their authority and mandating that licenses be granted to those producing generic medicine); (2) producers of generic antiretrovirals would be allowed to market and distribute their versions across sub-Saharan Africa, which would make treatment available at roughly US$140 per patient per year; and (3) producers of generic antiretrovirals would be allowed to generate new combinations from the various compounds available, which "reduces the risk of resistant virus strains appearing and is therefore an important innovation in treatment" (Rivière). Nathan Geffen of TAC insisted that this agreement was "a further sign that a new internationalism is emerging to fight the parallel globalizations of the epidemic and of intellectual propety rights," while Ellen 't Hoen of Doctors without Borders cautioned that "we need to make sure that GSK and BI do not apply delaying tactics—but the eyes of the world are once again turned on them, and they know that the legal case can be reactivated if they don't comply" (Rivière).[26]

In Maastricht, in the context of the January 2004 expert meeting on interiority, I found 't Hoen's insistence on exteriority, on keeping the eyes of the world focused on the ever-shifting machinations of multinational pharmaceuticals, multinational corporations, and neoliberalism, crucial. I called my own paper "On Me, Not in Me" both to invoke another safe sex slogan from the early days of AIDS activism and to raise questions about ways of seeing, questions about when and where looking inside the body works in tandem with the relations of looking shaped by global movements for social and economic justice and when and where looking inside the body works against those relations. Although TAC's t-shirt promises a glimpse inside, it also defers that glimpse. Ultimately, TAC t-shirts will not satisfy a desire to locate a picture (or an identity) definitively (safely?) within an individual—even as they nonetheless on some level generate that desire (and in staging a Brechtian dissonance it forces viewers of the shirt to think differently).

In my presentation, I withheld the metareflection on my own t-shirt that I am offering in the context of this chapter—a metareflection that now entails, for me personally, coming out as HIV-negative. I knew that I had been in sexual situations where HIV was unquestionably on one side of the condom, a thin layer of latex (*spatially*, that is, the tiniest barrier) and potentially a split second in time (*temporally*, again, the tiniest barrier) separating one interior space from the other. But given the ways in which my paper was functioning in that very specific rhetorical context (apparently straight and nondisabled), I declined to say which side of the latex the virus was on. In the very different context of this chapter, I find it more important to raise issues about what it means, for the purposes of solidarity, to come out as something you are—at least in some ways—not.[27] To build on the previous section, coming out crip at times involves embracing and at times disidentifying with the most familiar kinds of identity politics. In another context, away from my computer screen and apart from the imagined audience for this chapter, I will undoubtedly put on a TAC HIV POSITIVE t-shirt again. And I continue to recognize (and re-cognize) the disability insight that was not necessarily named as such when it was voiced in the 1980s: if the AIDS crisis is not over, HIV-negative status is never guaranteed. TAC's work is dedicated to emphasizing that, indeed, the AIDS crisis is not over (another slogan that formerly animated North American and European activism) and to mobilizing identifications against the global structures that sustain the epidemic by capitalizing on those most affected by it.

Crip Reality, Take One

Finally, I will put forward what might be read—at least initially—as a counterexample of coming out crip, even if it is quite recognizable as a textual disability studies analysis. In February 2004, Fox Television premiered a brief (two-episode) dating reality show called *The Littlest Groom*. Like other dating shows, *The Littlest Groom*, set in an enormous and luxurious Malibu mansion, focused on one person's consideration and elimination of a dozen or so others, so that in the end only one final date remained. Also like most (but not all) such shows, the one doing the choosing and the ones chosen were of the opposite sex; in this case, Glen Foster was put forward as the bachelor choosing from a selection of single women. Monetary prizes are usually awarded in the final episode, and although the prizes in *The Littlest Groom* were not as valuable as the prizes on other dating reality shows, the female winner, Mika Winkler, did receive a two-carat diamond ring, and Fox Television sent Foster and Winkler on a Mediterranean cruise.[28]

By 2004, viewers of dating reality shows had come to expect both these standard (even naturalized) components of the genre, as well as something supposedly unexpected—a catch or twist (or both) that seemed to set the show apart from the numerous dating reality shows that had preceded it. In this case, the catch, as the title suggests, was that *The Littlest Groom* was a short-statured man selecting his date from a group of beautiful and articulate short-statured women. Or, at least, that's what the participants assumed was taking place. Halfway through the show, Fox introduced the twist—Glen had narrowed his choices to five women when Dani Behr, the host, informed him that three new, average-statured women would be thrown into the mix. "This should be interesting," one of the average-statured women said as she kissed Glen hello and joined the group of contestants.

Disability studies and the disability rights movement make it extremely easy to critique *The Littlest Groom*: it can be read as functioning as a latter-day freak show, and Fox's marketing of it alongside another show centered on bodily (and behavioral) difference (*My Big, Fat, Obnoxious Fiancé*) only underscores such a reading—it was as though both shows were part of the extraordinary wonders audiences could discover were they to "step right up" to the circus that is Fox Television. In fact, this reading is so readily available that both mainstream discussions of the series and left-oriented critiques, almost universally, took note of *The Lit-*

tlest Groom's freak show aspects. A commercial website dedicated to the simulacrum "television news" invoked P. T. Barnum directly, accurately explaining that "P. T. Barnum made Charles S. Stratton, better known as General Tom Thumb, a celebrity in the mid-1800s and orchestrated Stratton's marriage to Lavinia Warren into a huge event breathlessly covered by the day's press." Linking Barnum's efforts to capitalize on Stratton and Warren to Fox's efforts to capitalize on *The Littlest Groom*, the article reinvoked Barnum's famous slogan, "there's a sucker born every minute" ("FOX Thinks Small"). From another location on the political spectrum, queer theorist Judith Halberstam, writing for the *Nation*, insisted that "the midget show bombed because it exposed the 'freak show' aspect of all marriage shows" ("Pimp My Bride" 45). Although neither the articles boosting or advertising the show nor, as with Halberstam's, panning or critiquing it, put forward a critically disabled reading (as Halberstam's unfortunate description of *The Littlest Groom* as "the midget show" and use of it as only a metaphor for other dating reality shows attest), the fact that it was so readily perceived as a freak show, from so many different political and cultural vantage points, lays the groundwork for a disability studies analysis.[29]

First, for the producers and for many viewers, the show was *only* about height or physical difference, and the streamlining of the program to two episodes suggested either that the network didn't believe viewers would care about getting to know these participants for more than two episodes or that the network consciously or unconsciously perceived the short-statured women as basically indistinguishable from each other (so that, again, more than two episodes would simply not be necessary). Second, a standard defense of many dating shows, including *The Littlest Groom*—that love looks beyond the exterior; that what is important is personality or what's on the inside—was belied by the fact that no other dating show had included a short-statured contestant. On *The Littlest Groom*, average-statured women may have been introduced to drive home the ideological point that what counts is not height or physical difference but the person, but for this thesis to be even partially convincing, short-statured contestants (or Deaf contestants, or contestants using wheelchairs or crutches) would have to be equal participants on *The Bachelor, The Bachelorette, Joe Millionaire, Boy Meets Boy*, and other popular dating shows. Finally, and most important, *The Littlest Groom* did almost nothing to displace dominant and gendered conceptions of beauty: all the contestants were, apparently, white and in many ways representative of hegemonic Euro-American standards of beauty. On this last point, in particular, disability studies is particularly apropos for reading not just *The Littlest Groom* but the entire corpus of reality television, from dating to "extreme make-over" shows.

And yet, if all of this positions *The Littlest Groom* as a counterexample of coming out crip, a certain disability identity politics of course also makes it possible to read the show against the grain, and I intend for my subheading— "Crip Reality"—to convey that possibility: "crip reality" need not be a substantive entity, as if anything in the genre had much to do with "reality," as it is conventionally understood, anyway. It can, rather, trace a cultural process, focusing on the myriad ways in which disabled and allied audiences in a sense "crip" culture in order to imagine and forge spaces for themselves within it. The brevity and the structure of the show might work to construct the contestants on *The Littlest Groom* as indistinguishable, but they themselves consistently foreground difference. The short-statured women in *The Littlest Groom*, including Mika, discuss age differences, education differences, and family differences (raising the issue, for instance, of growing up in a short-statured family versus growing up apart from a short-statured community). As several disability studies scholars have argued, beneath, through, or around the freak show, disability resistance is discernible. And surely—partly thanks to the short-statured women themselves—some viewers discerned such resistance; for some audience members, the pleasures of *The Littlest Groom* were undoubtedly disability pleasures, whether those pleasures emerged from the simple fact that short-statured men and women were being represented in the media as intelligent and desirable (however much that representation reinforced other problematic norms) or from subtler aspects of the show, such as the anger legible on the short-statured women's faces when the twist was introduced—anger that spoke volumes about just how aware these women were about the enfreakment process short-statured women an men are subject to on or off television.

Still, this reading can in turn be cripped, which is my main intention in this section and the next. American Sign Language represents what translates as "visual clutter" with both hands extended as though they were tiger claws—moving these up and down with a repulsed grimace on the face conveys the "noise" generated by images clashing in a visual field. And for me, the visual clutter begins with that Malibu mansion. I'm convinced enough by what Mike Davis calls "the case for letting Malibu burn" to question just how desirable disability integration into that particular corner of the society of the spectacle might be. I recognize that *The Littlest Groom* was a dating show, not (to pick another possibility from reality television) a survival show, representing its contestants withstanding the forces of nature. But locating dating shows in opulent sites of Western consumption (as though such sites were not also subject to the forces of nature) and survival shows in a non-Western "wilderness" or "wild" locations (like the Australian outback) within the West (as though such sites did not include nearby Hilton or Sheraton hotels capable of supporting television crews) is another mere convention of the genre. Viewers of *The Littlest Groom* may not have seen Malibu burn, but such a scenario is not unimaginable in this location; it is only unimaginable according to the terms of the genre.

Breaking with those terms, I want to use the scenario of Malibu burning to begin to make a different kind of sense—spatial, regional, crip sense—of the images captured by Fox Television and, in a way, by disability studies. At times, disability studies—like other fields centered on minority experiences—has put forward narrowly textual readings focused on the representation of disability and on texts consumed apart from an identifiable site of production. Crip theory resists such dislocations or, rather, insists that accessing (or making accessible) the "circuit of culture" entails attending to the sites where images and identities are produced (du Gay et al. 3–4). Locating crip identities in this way, far from displacing attention to images of disability, has the potential to generate new and perhaps unexpected images—of disability solidarity and coalition.[30]

In *Ecology of Fear*, his study of the politics of so-called natural disasters in Los Angeles, Davis examines the deadly fires that have plagued Malibu for most of the past century. Despite the fact that the Malibu area has an incredibly high propensity to wild brush fires, the location is home to some of the highest-priced real estate in the country. Wealthy homeowners and developers, rather than evacuating the area, have managed to wield their political clout to secure some of the costliest federal disaster assistance and protection available—safeguards against the destruction wrought by the fires that regularly ravage the area, destroying thousands of homes and claiming dozens of lives. Malibu residents, along with others on southern California's "fire coast" have adopted a policy of "total fire suppression" (99, 102)—that is, a policy that seeks to eliminate the possibility of ignition. This policy has had deadly effects: (1) it ignores the fact that "fuel, not ignitions" (101) feeds California's wildfires—and in

the concrete and car culture of southern California there is plenty of fuel;
(2) it disrupts the natural rhythm of relatively contained brush fires,
which are now essentially outlawed (Mexico's Baja California, in contrast, has neither the policy of total fire suppression nor the history of cat-
aclysmic fires); (3) avoiding political and economic causes for Malibu's
fires, it uniformly demonizes those individuals who ignite fires, often
homeless people attempting to keep warm; and (4) it ultimately leads to
massive cuts in services for the state's poorest residents (who are, for what
it's worth, disproportionately disabled)—because Malibu's fires are "natural" disasters rather than disasters of real estate speculation and development, residents are eligible for massive relief funds (basically, state-
subsidized insurance) designed to protect the investments capital has made
in the area. Whether we can still call *The Littlest Groom* "reality television," given that so many spatial realities are effaced by the program, is
seriously open to question.

Marta Russell's "Manifesto of an Uppity Crip" (in *Beyond Ramps*)
similarly crips the spatiality of southern California. Although she is consistently attentive in her work to the ways in which images of disability
are deployed to secure or counter able-bodied ideologies of pity, freakery,
or revulsion, Russell insists that both dominant and marginalized identities emerge in specific locations and in relation to others and that neoliberalism has made those locations and relations increasingly insecure. In
an essay ranging widely over political economy, disability identity politics, and what she and others call "the end of the social contract," Russell notes:

> Several years ago a fire erupted in a canyon in Alta Dena, California
> [near Malibu, and Malibu did burn during the Altadena fire]. Homes
> were destroyed, quite unintentionally, by a homeless man who lit a fire
> to keep warm on a cold night. The fire caught some bushes and spread
> into the hills, burning everything in its path for miles. The homeowners'
> loss was a social issue for the entire city, for if this man had had shelter
> and warmth there would have been no brush fire to burn out of control.
> The unheeded lesson of the Alta Dena fire was that we are all linked and
> until everyone is safe, no one is safe; until everyone has a home, no one's
> home is safe. (215–216)

If a certain disability identity politics allows for limited pleasure in the
short-statured integration of both Malibu and compulsory heterosexual-

ity, another kind of coalitional and postidentity, politics allows Russell to imagine southern California spaces differently, and to foreground the ways in which images of both disability and political economy should be a central concern to radical uppity crips.

Yet what might an uppity crip politics look like, and how might it function, in this space that (in Malibu and throughout the region) encompasses countless homeless people, as well as the luxuriously housed; that generates more images for global consumption than any space on earth, even if links between those images are obscured or discouraged and even if some images seem perpetually unavailable for re-presentation (in this place that purports to make *anything* available for representation); that seems to traffic equally in a hypostatization of fantasy (the dream factories of southern California generating what we all should really desire) and reality (the studios generating, and dubbing "reality," both productions like *The Littlest Groom* and action news footage of Malibu brush fires); that symbolizes and markets a peculiarly Californian version of "freedom" despite being a virtual *and* literal fortress, home to one of the largest concentrations in the world of military-industrial institutions; that allows for (and, perhaps, to return to the language of the introduction, tolerates) Los Angeles–based writer Russell identifying defiantly as an uppity crip even as thousands of others just across town, primarily African American young men, likewise identify as "Crip," with an understanding of identity that would seem to have no connection to what Russell and disability activists are getting at with their use of the term? Is it even possible for "crip reality" to figure coherently here (even temporarily or contingently), either as a substance or a process?

Crip Reality, Take Two

Although the previous section turned from disability work on the image to cultural geography (the field concerned with how meanings, histories, and political economies emerge spatially), an optimistic ambivalence in other directions is equally imaginable.[31] Permanently partial, contradictory, and oriented toward affinity (Haraway 154–155), crip reality keeps on turning.[32] Or, to adapt the words of Michael Zinzun, who was shot and blinded when he tried to stop a police beating in his L.A. community (Smith xx), crip theory puts bodies and ideas in motion:

I ain't got no big Cadillac,
I ain't got no gold . . .
I ain't got no
expensive shoes or clothes.
What we do have
is an opportunity to keep struggling
and to do research and to organize. (Qtd. in Smith 20)

The Malibu fires, for Mike Davis, are understood as necessarily connected to other events and specific communities: Davis not only challenges dominant representations of homeless people as the "incendiary Other" (*Ecology of Fear* 130); he also suggests that the construction of California wildfires as natural disasters for communities like Malibu makes it difficult to analyze (or make newsworthy) cultural disasters like tenement fires in the city of Los Angeles or political struggles like those of the largely immigrant communities who occupy such buildings. In November 1993, a month when Malibu fires were widely publicized on both a local and national scale, three occupants of a residential hotel in downtown Los Angeles died and twelve others were severely burned. The death toll in Malibu was also three, but as Davis argues, because the "property damage differed by several orders of magnitude. . . . [A] double standard of fire disaster was rubbed in the faces of the poor—in this case, Mexican and Guatemalan garment workers" (130). The immigrant workers in the building had long attempted, in struggles with the building's owners, to draw attention to landlords' (or slumlords') "notorious record of fire, health, and safety code violations" (130). Apparently neither resources nor dominant media representations could be mobilized to draw attention to these disasters. Davis, however, deconstructs the opposition between the natural fires in Malibu and the cultural fires downtown and thereby spotlights the struggles of immigrant communities in Los Angeles. Or, put differently, Davis calls back the disappeared—that is, communities whose struggles must be dematerialized in order for other Los Angeles experiences to be represented and broadcast as "reality."

The specific struggles of disabled communities, though, are another story altogether. Just as spatial analysis has largely been absent from the work done in disability studies on images (like the images of short-statured women and men in *The Littlest Groom*), disability has been largely incidental to the work of cultural geographers. In a consideration of the 1992 Los Angeles riots, for instance, Davis draws attention to the crackdown on undocumented immigrants and notes, tellingly, that "even a 14-year-old mentally retarded girl . . . was deported to Mexico" ("Uprising and Repression" 145). If Davis's work makes available for analysis the specific struggles of minority or immigrant groups, the same cannot be said about his rhetorical use of people with disabilities. In this passing example, the disabled girl herself basically only functions as what Mitchell and Snyder would call a "narrative prosthesis" for the larger story or political economy that Davis wants to put forward.[33] For cultural geography more generally, such uses of disability are not uncommon— disability amplifies theses about the excesses of capitalism or nativism or imperialism, but (and consequently) cannot function on another register, more actively or desirably engaged in the struggles geographers recount.[34]

I open this section with Zinzun, however, both to transition toward the crip reality that has more often concerned Davis and other Los Angeles writers and to suggest that disability is not, in fact, incidental to that reality. To focus in this section on the Los Angeles–based Crip street gang (actually dozens of different gangs now in existence in many locations across the country) might initially appear to dwell on a mere linguistic accident, the coincidence of the name "Crip." According to LaMar Murphy, however, gang life leads to one of three outcomes: "You're gonna be dead, locked up for the rest of your life, or paralyzed in a wheelchair." Murphy is one of four African American, disabled men interviewed in Patrick Devlieger and Miriam Hertz's *The Disabling Bullet*, a Chicago documentary film about life after gang-related gunshot injuries. Gang studies, in general, has focused more often on death and prison; this section thus calls back the (disabled) disappeared. Although I move toward a consideration of literal disability here, toward life after the bullet, I want to stress that disability has nonetheless haunted Crip reality from the beginning, in generative ways that exceed how disability has been imagined and metaphorized by cultural geography.

The origin of the Crips is at this point the stuff of mythology. One origin story has it that the name of the gang was initially an acronym, standing for "Continuing Revolution in Progress" (Hayden 167) or—alternatively—"Continuous Revolution in Progress" (Davis, *City of Quartz* 299). Whether the acronym was in circulation in the early 1970s or whether it was a later invention that retrospectively gave meaning to the gang name, it in some ways contradicts other stories about the group's origin, which would position late-1960s and early 1970s gang activity not as a function either of a thriving or continuous civil rights movement or Black Panther revolution but rather as a function of revolution's demise: "the failure of radicalism," in Tom Hayden's assessment, "bred nihilism" (167).

There are other origin myths. Perhaps the most common, and one endorsed by Stanley "Tookie" Williams (who was involved with the Crips, even as a founder, at the beginning and who was executed by the state of California in late 2005), suggests that the group was originally the "Cribs," given that members were largely young teenage, or even pre-teenage, boys, and that the name became "Crips" around 1972 when the mainstream media got it wrong (Alonso 91; Hayden 172). "Crippin'" then developed as a style throughout the 1970s, and referred at times to the Black Panther leather jackets worn by the Crips and at times to other features of dress (such as blue bandannas or earrings on the left), to robbing or stealing, or—tellingly—to the particular "crippled" style of walking advanced by the "original" 107 Hoover Crip Gang (Alonso 91; Hayden 167; Davis, *City of Quartz* 298–299).

Canes were also used as fashion accessories by the Crips, or—conversely or in tandem—as accessories useful or necessary for increased mobility. Some writers contend that the canes were not the source of the gang's name, but another story unsettles that contention: an elderly Asian American woman who was robbed by gang members reportedly told police, perhaps not coincidentally around the same time that the mainstream media purportedly got the name wrong, that she was attacked by a "crip with a stick" (Hayden 167). A version of this latter myth has a group of specifically Japanese American women attacked by a group of "young cripples that carried canes" (Alonso 91).[35]

If crippin' as a way of life undeniably marked robbery and—increasingly—violence (against rival gangs or others) or murder, it is also always (partly because its origin cannot be fixed) inscribed with other possibilities. Following the 1992 riots, for instance, numerous Crip gangs came together with members of rival Blood gangs to craft a peace treaty. They demanded improvements from the city of Los Angeles for African American communities: in educational and economic opportunities, in health care, and in living conditions (Browning 107). If the city met their demands, the Crips and the Bloods would go further: "Additionally, we will match funds for an aids [sic] research and awareness center in South Central and Long Beach that will only hire minority researchers and physicians to assist in the aids [sic] epidemic" (qtd. in Browning 108).

Davis's assessment of Crip development, prior to the 1992 riots, is stark: "If they began as a teenage substitute for the fallen Panthers, they evolved through the 1970s into a hybrid teen cult and proto-Mafia. At a time when economic opportunity was draining away from Southcentral Los Angeles, the Crips were becoming the power resource of last resort for thousands of abandoned youth" (*City of Quartz* 300). I would not want to temper Davis's sober assessment, given the reach of gang-related violence over the past three decades. With the peace treaty in mind, however, I would simultaneously want to keep at least some attention on Davis's "if," because *if* Crips (and Bloods) have been, predominantly, a hybrid teen cult and proto-Mafia, the peace treaty suggests they will have also been an interdependent network committed to building community and, significantly, disability institutions (and although the proper tense here is elusive, the present perfect progressive—attentive to what will have also been—does attempt to keep in play the promise of "if," conveying that what has happened in the past may take place in the future). Indeed, the 1992 demands actually call back, or conjure up, gang demands made in the early 1970s. At a Human Relations Conference in December 1972, when according to Davis "Cripmania was first sweeping Southside schools in an epidemic of gang shootings and street fights," those whom officials had dubbed "mad dogs" "outlined an eloquent and coherent set of demands: jobs, housing, better schools, recreation facilities and community control of local institutions" (*City of Quartz* 300).

The Los Angeles Police Department (LAPD), unsurprisingly, resisted the 1972 conference, and in the decades that followed, "has vehemently (and usually successfully) opposed attempts by social workers and community organizers to allow gang members to tell 'their side of the story'" (Davis, *City of Quartz* 300). That story, rare as it has been, generally puts forward a relatively consistent analysis: African American youth in the region come out Crip, or come out Blood, because of poverty and despair—because of their surplus role in an exploitative economy that forestalls community development and community control of capital and other vital (health care, education, recreation, employment) resources. As Davis succinctly puts it, "gang leaders have always affirmed . . . decent jobs are the price for negotiating a humane end to drug dealing and gang violence" (*City of Quartz* 300, 302). The LAPD not only has made it difficult, over three decades, for that story to speak but also, for the most part, has secured other explanations for gang activity in Los Angeles:

youth come out Crip because they are inadequately controlled or par-
ented; because they violate curfews or cross over into neighborhoods
where they don't belong; or because they are essentially criminal, incapable of any other existence. At its most extreme, the LAPD has even
posited that Crips and Bloods (metonymic of African American men
more generally) have a discrete anatomy or physiology that sets them
apart from others. In an attempt to explain why several young African
American men had died while in LAPD chokeholds, former LAPD Police
Chief Daryl Gates insisted that "we may be finding that in some Blacks
when [the carotid chokehold] is applied the veins or arteries do not open
up as fast as they do on normal [*sic*] people" (qtd. in Davis, *City of
Quartz* 272). Unable to counter such racist and biologistic sentiments—
or, rather, only capable of countering them with systemic analyses that
"normal people" could, apparently, quickly discount—gang members
have repeatedly seen the hopes generated at key moments, or in key documents such as the 1992 peace treaty, dissipated. Gates's statement was,
of course, scandalous, but from another perspective, it was simply an extreme example of more widely accepted notions that the "problem" was
located in the individual (suspected of being a) gang member and could
even be read on his body, in the ways he looked or carried himself.

Despite all of this, the 1992 truce was at least partially successful, reducing dramatically the number of gang-related killings and drive-by
shootings in the following years (Hayden 192). However, *if* gangs were
partially successful in upholding their end of the deal, the city of Los Angeles was not: fifty-five thousand jobs in the South Central Los Angeles
area were lost between 1992 and 1999. At the end of that period, the
city's overall police budget amounted to $1.2 billion, a fraction of what
was being spent on programs for inner-city youth; Hayden reports that
"just $1 million was budgeted for 'L.A.'s best,' an after-school program
for at-risk youth, and less than $2 million for gang intervention work. [In
2001] the city was accused of environmental racism for having the low-
est ration of parks to people in America, with the worst ratios in communities with the highest numbers of at-risk youth" (191–192). Crip reality, in short, continued to be defined by poverty and despair.[36]

Disability, moreover, as I suggested, is hardly incidental to that reality.
Crip origin myths ensure that disability will always be a part of the Crip
past, and the will to community institutions such as AIDS service organizations attempts to locate disability in an alternative and more democratic Crip future. Moreover, disability is without question a central compo-

nent of life in and around urban communities like present-day South Central Los Angeles, as a performance such as Lynn Manning's in *Weights* (about Manning's "personal journey from being a black man to being a blind man" following a South Central shooting), a film such as *The Disabling Bullet*, or social programs such as the Bullet Project (a peer mentoring program for young men who have experienced spinal cord injuries from gunshot wounds) demonstrate. For every death from a gunshot wound in the United States generally, in fact, there are three injuries; gunshot wounds are the fourth leading cause of spinal cord injuries (Balfanz-Vertiz et al.). As far as Los Angeles in particular is concerned, a study done by members of the Department of Surgery at the Harbor-UCLA Medical Center in Torrance, California, puts forward staggering statistics: over the twenty-nine months of their study: 272 of the 856 gunshot wounds treated were gang-related (Song et al. 810). These wounds included shots to the head and neck, chest, and abdomen and resulted in a range of temporary or permanent disabilities (810, 812). If coming out Crip does not always, or even often, mean coming out disabled, many young men in Los Angeles do, in fact, come out of their gang experiences disabled.

Although focused on Chicago, *The Disabling Bullet* and the Bullet Project are worth bringing forward here and linking to Manning's more properly Los Angeles performance because all three pieces are similarly grounded in both disability culture and urban, minority cultures. Moreover, all three demonstrate that, just as disability images might be supplemented by political economy and cultural geography, so, too, might cultural geography benefit from a sustained engagement with disability images and the "other spaces" they invoke. In other words, while I am in favor of a much more extensive engagement between disability studies and materialist analyses, and would, in fact, position crip theory as part of a material turn within the field (akin to the material turn within queer theory), I am arguing in this section for a more sustained, two-way dialogue between disability studies and cultural geography. While disability may function prosthetically to mark the futility or cost of gang violence, the ways in which economic opportunity is being drained from South Central Los Angeles, or the injustices of the Immigration and Naturalization Service (INS; since 2003 known as the U.S. Citizenship and Immigration Services [USCIS]), only spatial analyses that begin to make use of the perspectives offered by disability culture will be capable, additionally, of locating people with disabilities as part of larger, progressive struggles in a given location. But only crip analyses that locate disabled bodies in larger spatial networks will be able to forge the coalitions—particularly around race—that have thus far been elusive for disability studies.[37]

Anna Deveare Smith's interview with Zinzun for her performance piece *Twilight: Los Angeles, 1992* remains focused on alternative possibilities, past and future. Set in Zinzun's L.A. office at the Coalition against Police Abuse, the interview is conducted in front of "a large white banner with a black circle and a panther . . . the image from the Black Panther Party. Above the circle is 'All Power to the People.' At the bottom is 'Support Our Youth, Support the Truce'" (16). The invocation of the 1992 truce puts forward a vision of gang life for the future, while the invocation of the Black Panther Party founds that vision on the still-unrealized liberationist politics of the past. Zinzun's discussion with Smith of activist struggles recounts the moment of police violence that

> exploded the optic nerve to the brain,
> ya see,
> and boom *(He snaps his fingers)*
> that was it. (Smith 19)

His unsentimental discussion of that moment, however, is only the beginning for Zinzun; his central concerns— "I'm just gonna keep strugglin'" (Smith 20)—are ultimately mobilization, coalition, and the construction of new and more just Los Angeles spaces.

At Home with Crip Theory

Although it perhaps resists closure, this chapter has in some ways come full circle: beginning in Mumbai, considering global issues or movements that nonetheless always provoke very specific (local) questions of access, I ended with local or apparently isolated examples (*The Littlest Groom*, the L.A. Crips) that can nonetheless be read as both intertwined and related to larger, translocal or even global, economic, political, and cultural processes. In between, I put forward another set of inversions: crip theory can entail, as in *Vital Signs*, coming out as what you supposedly already are (but not repeating the dominant culture's understanding of that faithfully), and crip theory can entail paradoxically, as with the Treatment Action Campaign, coming out as what you are, at least apparently, not. With these questions of the local and global, of what you are and what you are not, folding into each other, we can—perhaps—at this point put forward a few tentative principles of crip theory. We might say that crip theory, coming out crip, or crippin' could—now or in the future—entail:

1. Claiming disability *and* a disability identity politics while nonetheless nurturing a necessary contestatory relationship to that identity politics. I mean not only for TAC activists coming out as HIV-positive and the deindividuated disability identities that come out in *Vital Signs* to be understood through this rubric, but also, as a counterexample, *The Littlest Groom*, since it seems clear that an isolated or dislocated disability identity politics, in that instance, potentially interferes with the more textured analysis that coalitional and spatial analyses make possible.
2. Claiming the queer history of coming out—"out of the closets, into the streets"—while simultaneously talking back to the parent culture (or, for that matter, any parent culture, including disability studies or the disability rights movement). Talking back to the queer parent culture would entail rejecting the various ways that LGBT understandings of coming out have devolved (and the ways disability coming out might devolve)—into, for instance, discovery, announcement, and celebration of individual or individualized difference.
3. Demanding that, as the World Social Forum would have it, another world is possible, or that—put differently—an accessible world is possible. "Access," however, needs to be understood, according to this principle, both very specifically and very broadly, locally and globally. An accessible world on both levels would of necessity be constructed in opposition to neoliberalism and to what Lisa Duggan calls the "cultures of upward redistribution" that have held sway for the past three decades (*Twilight of Equality* xvii).
4. Insisting that, even more, a disabled world is possible and pointing out that counterglobalization and other left movements that cannot begin to conceptualize that idea—that a disabled world is possible and desirable—as anything other than counterintuitive need to be cripped. In fact, most left movements, including most queer movements, cannot conceptualize such an idea because in general

they are tied to liberationist models that need disability as the raw material against which the imagined future world is formed. That need is arguably legible everywhere—in simple theses such as "neoliberalism disables dissent" or, more seriously, in the WSF's resistance to giving people with disabilities a voice in Porto Alegre and Mumbai. Mitchell and Snyder's work on what they call "the Eugenic Atlantic" provides further evidence of the extent to which the need to use disability as raw material against which a desired world is shaped is foundational to modernity ("Eugenic Atlantic").

5. Moving "beyond ramps," as Marta Russell put it, to questions of how private or privatized versus public cultures of ability or disability are conceived, materialized, spatialized, and populated, or how—to borrow a phrase from Sharon Snyder, who pulls it from cultural geography—"geographies of uneven development" are mapped onto bodies marked by differences of race, class, gender, and ability (533). "Malibu is burning," in this sense, might convey the crip commitment that until the other world that is possible is accessed, the sites or locations where disability identities emerge will always be interrogated and transformable, sustaining our understanding that who we are or might be can only have meaning in relation to who we are not (yet).

I said that I would conclude with a brief queercrip story that in many ways brings all of this home. Perhaps *Crip Theory* is a theoretical intervention, perhaps it is (unexpectedly) a love letter, and perhaps it is (or will become) many things besides. I don't usually write directly with someone else, as Snyder and Mitchell do, but in many ways my collective existence with my own boyfriend, with whom I have lived for more than five years, informs this analysis and this book. The home—my home or any home—is not a refuge from the convergence of the local and the global, and questions of who we are and who we are not are as pronounced there as any other location.

Though the crip theory I'm sketching out makes it impossible to do so, it's tempting to see Joseph's story as three stories. There's the story of the immigrant worker, someone who packed his bags and left Brazil in 2001, crossing the Eugenic Atlantic on a tourist visa and working a variety of jobs, including a one-day temporary catering job for one of the many events held on the day of the first Bush II inauguration—a fact I provide not to imply that he has anything but disdain for George W. Bush, but to underscore just how high up the U.S. economy's disavowed dependency on immigrant labor goes. The focus on high-profile U.S. cabinet nominees who are exposed for exploiting immigrant workers obscures the ways in which exploitation—or rather superexploitation, which is not simply the extraction of surplus value but "the production of profit under especially degraded conditions and at especially low wages"—functions (Foley 30). In such high-profile cases, the degradation of the workers themselves is only compounded by the media's focus not on immigrant work conditions but on the "embarrassment" the incident caused the official in question. When Bernard B. Kerik withdrew his nomination to direct the Department of Homeland Security in December 2004, because he had hired an undocumented immigrant for domestic labor and failed to pay taxes or social security on her behalf, ours was surely not the only Washington, D.C.–area household with experiential evidence of how hypocritical White House officials were being in their public blaming and shaming of Kerik nor were we, undoubtedly, the only ones with a certain authority to say "well, according to that logic, Bush should step down, too." Washington or any other U.S. city would cease functioning if the—often literally disabling—superexploitation on which it is founded were exposed (put differently, Washington is burning).[38] Although thi has not been a major topic in disability studies per se, it is certainly not news to cultural studies scholars more generally that the ideological consolidation of the "homeland" permanently externalizes and demonizes millions of workers already internal to the nation, even if the voices of those workers, for many reasons, are rarely recorded in cultural studies scholarship. A transfer of power was broadcast around the world on January 20, 2001, but even if (or when) the media focused on just how contested that particular transfer was, the waiters dishing up the food at inaugural events were not part of the conversation. My (admittedly unscientific) survey of those whom Joseph and I know suggests that they had plenty of critical thoughts on what was taking place.

Joseph occupied a handful of other jobs in California and Maryland, sometimes leaving after they asked for documentation (at this point he has an actual tax identification number, though to the best of our knowledge the only tax-based services he has accessed are the roads that he uses to drive to work every day). He currently takes home about $1400 a month, which is not a living wage in Washington or most other places in the U.S., and works on average 10 hours a day, five (or six) days a week. His application for immigration was legally submitted in May 2002; as of this writing, the INS is processing applications from early 2001. He is not, of course, able to secure a green card through me.

Then, there's the queer story, of phone sex and computer sex, of a wide range of erotic play, of chat rooms filled with men (or, filled with blips on the screen generated by people with many different gender identifications). Coming of age in Rio de Janeiro, specifically the area of the city known as Zona Sul and the neighborhoods of Botafogo and Copacana, Joseph's interpretation of his same-sex desire and activity led to a specifically gay identification not unlike my own in the United States. Still, in Brazil and the United States, we have both been significantly influenced by what Richard Parker calls, in his study of Brazilian homosexualities, "diverse cultures of desire, organized around varying forms of same-sex practice and . . . cultures of resistance, which provide at least partial protection from the violence, stigma, and oppression encountered in the outside world" (42). Language barriers when we first met, in fact, ensured that some of the things we were proposing to each other—since, as queers, we were dutifully starting with sex and working backward—weren't exactly translating, but those barriers quickly dissolved. And since he moved in with me in September 2001, we have maintained sustaining connections to queer cultures of desire, in Washington, Rio de Janeiro, and other locations (including cyberspace); if homeland security depends on locating Brazil and other places elsewhere, the vitality of our own home depends on the opposite. When I hear an exuberant "*Bicha!*" and laughter, for instance, I know that Joseph is on the phone or computer with his friend Fabio in Rio; we are wired to Brazilian cultures of desire even if concerns about his visa make it impossible (perhaps permanently) for us to be there physically. And although marriage would seem to provide a limited answer to these concerns (currently not available to bi-national same-sex couples, anyway), we are not particularly interested in it (for committed political reasons) and in some ways much more concerned about how it would work, potentially, to jeopardize our connection and commitment to others, to the cultures of desire and resistance that have allowed our relationship to flourish.

And finally, there's the disability story, as Joseph lost sight in one of his eyes in May 2004 and is now diagnosed with multiple sclerosis, which he has probably had for quite some time, including when he packed his bags and moved and including when he logged on to the Internet to see what queer connections he might make in this new space. This diagnosis added to our lives, almost overnight, countless visits to ophthalmologists and neurologists, worry about copayments and insurance, and drug companies sending us pamphlets titled things like *Multiple Sclerosis: A Guide for Families* (Kalb) (incidentally, our family—which includes, among many others, former lovers in Chicago and Maryland and lesbian friends in North Carolina—wasn't represented in the guide).

Even if Joseph is essentially excluded from the (ruins of the) U.S. welfare state, disability identities that had been formed in that context fortified the unexpected transition we were making. I've often wondered whether John Hockenberry's theory of the "quantum view of disability," which "allows you to dare to think that you can have lived two lives, two bodies occupying two places at once" was a retrospective theory rather than one that emerged, as it seems to in his autobiography, at the time of the car accident that led to his disability (25). Hockenberry puts the theory forward to counter "the old Newtonian view of the universe [that] states that disability is like a brake on the wheel of life that runs you down with friction" (24). While my question about the timing of the emergence of Hockenberry's theory may be unanswerable, at this point I can indeed say that the innumerable disability counteridentifications and counterstories that emerged from the disability rights movement and disability studies, and that were solidly in place at the time of Joseph's diagnosis, made a quantum view comprehensible. Even if he was eligible for virtually no "disability benefits" from the state, by 2004, he (or we) could nonetheless say "I'm disabled" and have that be the beginning of a resistant, not tragic, story. As we worried about insurance, about getting Portuguese translation for some of the more confusing points about MS, about status questions (either about who I was or who he was) from Caremark or Shared Solutions or any other new agency we were encountering, we also found ourselves laughing about just how sexy Washington's newest disabled diva was.

We're just one home, but the view from here is local and global and daily engages questions of who we are, who we are not, and who we might become. I've learned a lot from queer theory and disability studies, in isolation and in their still-tentative points of convergence, but at this point, if we didn't have crip theory, we would have to invent it. And by that we, I suppose I mean those of us who identify as or with Brazilian, gay, immigrant workers with multiple sclerosis, as well as the rest of us. Though perhaps if another world is really accessible—a world beyond ramps and gay marriage, beyond identity politics and analyses that would isolate the cultural from the economic and vice versa—that opposition is

At home with disability. Photograph by author.

or should be untenable. Crip theory might function as a body of thought, or as thought about bodies, that allows for assertions like the following: if it's not even *conceivable* for you to identify as or with Brazilian, gay, immigrant workers with multiple sclerosis, then you're not yet attending to how bodies and spaces are being materialized in the cultures of upward redistribution we currently inhabit. Call me crip, but I do believe that such unlikely identifications, as well as yet-to-be-imagined (queer and disabled) cultures of downward redistribution, remain possible.

2

Capitalism and Disabled Identity

Sharon Kowalski, Interdependency,
and Queer Domesticity

On November 18, 2003, the Supreme Court of Massachusetts ruled that the state was discriminating against lesbians and gay men by denying them the right to marry. The court gave Massachusetts lawmakers six months to rectify the situation, meaning that marriage licenses for same-sex couples would be issued as early as May 2004. In February 2004, the Massachusetts legislature debated the issue from a few different directions, voting down both a compromise "civil unions" bill that would mirror a bill passed in Vermont in 2000 granting same-sex couples the benefits of marriage without the name and a constitutional amendment that would officially ban marriage between two men and two women in the state. If it had passed, the amendment faced a potential two-year lag before it could be implemented, as it would have gone before Massachusetts voters for approval only in 2006. Legal marriages for same-sex couples thus commenced in Massachusetts in May 2004, although Governor Mitt Romney insisted—making public again a racist 1913 law intended to restrict interracial unions—that couples from elsewhere could not be married in the state if their marriage would not be legally recognized back at home.

Meanwhile, as the debates raged in the Massachusetts legislature in February 2004, Mayor Gavin Newsome of San Francisco began issuing marriage licenses to same-sex couples in the city. Lesbian and gay marriage had been banned in California since 2000, following passage of a statute known as the Knight Initiative, but hundreds of couples nonetheless lined up outside San Francisco City Hall, joining Newsome in what was essentially an act of civil disobedience. Longtime activists Del Martin and Phyllis Lyon, who had founded the lesbian organization Daughters of Bilitis (DOB) in 1955 and coauthored *Lesbian/Woman* in 1972, were the first to be married in the San Francisco action. Although both the DOB and *Lesbian/Woman* could be interpreted in many ways as assimilationist (the organization and the book, for instance, each sharply critiqued the queer distinctiveness of butch/femme roles and identities—or, rather, were unable to comprehend the ways in which butch/femme identities had been shaped as often-defiant alternatives to heterosexual respectability), the expressions on many of the faces outside City Hall suggested that participants desired something else.[1] Images of the long lines were broadcast from coast to coast and for some, perhaps, the civil disobedience suddenly called into being a San Francisco that had not existed since the late 1980s/early 1990s heyday of radical AIDS activism.

Newsome was not the only public figure to defy state policies. In what at times appeared to be a tidal wave of civil disobedience, officials in New Mexico, Oregon, and New York also issued marriage licenses. Sympathetic clergy members defiantly performed wedding ceremonies. In New York City, the display window in a Manhattan Kenneth Cole store positioned two male mannequins and two female mannequins side by side with signs and arrows marking the distance to San Francisco and to New Paltz, New York, where Mayor Jason West, a member of the Green Party, was issuing marriage certificates. Domestic partners were coming out all over, having civil ceremonies, and returning home as married couples.

The end of the year, however, brought another kind of spectacle altogether. Missouri voters, months before the November election, passed a constitutional amendment banning same-sex marriage in the state, and Virginia Governor Mark Warner signed into law a bill that reached even further, banning other legal forms that might recognize same-sex couples, such as civil unions or domestic partnerships. Despite President George W. Bush's support for the measure and Republican control of both the House of Representatives and the Senate, a vote in the U.S. Congress that would have begun the process of amending the Constitution to ban same-sex marriage failed. Nonetheless, statutes or bills like the ones in Missouri and Virginia passed in fourteen other states in the election year of 2004, and many people believed that conservative opposition to same-sex marriage was decisive in carrying Bush to a second term. Whether or not that was the case, some socially conservative groups in early 2005 made clear that they expected a payoff: they would support Bush's broader economic and political agenda (including privatization of social security) as long as he followed through on his efforts to secure the Constitutional amendment.

For conservatives and liberals observing these spectacles, there always seems to be two, and only two, very clear choices. Indeed, many people considering LGBT rights at the turn of the century (including many LGBT people themselves) are still surprised to learn that queer communities have actually been deeply divided over the issue of gay marriage. Conservatives may believe generally that the issue is part of a broader and unified "gay agenda," but the liberal consensus in many locations also invokes relative unity; liberals tend to believe that gay marriage is simply a matter of fairness. According to the liberal consensus, the process of change that began with victory in Vermont in 2000—with the approval of legally sanctioned civil unions—is not only "progressive" but unequivocally a Good Thing, akin to other signs that gay men and lesbians are more securely "out in public" than we were even a decade ago. After the civil unions bill passed through Vermont's House and Senate in 2000, in fact, Governor Howard Dean linked it to basic liberal ideals that "have been incredibly important to the success of this country," declaring: "This is a vote that is about principle, and that principle is respect for everyone—and that is regardless of gender, ethnicity, sexual orientation, race, or any one of a number of factors that makes us different" (qtd. in Dahir 61). A later cover story for the national gay and lesbian newsmagazine the *Advocate* participated in the ongoing construction of Dean—who had gone on to declare his candidacy for president and who was for a time the Democratic Party's front-runner in 2003–2004—as the figure of liberal common sense. A smiling Dean appeared beneath the headline "A Civil Union President" and was offered, apparently, as the antidote—or at least as a refreshing and clearly liberal contrast—to the smirking, self-satisfied Bush. At the end of 2004, after antigay victories in the November elections, Dean had been surpassed as the representative figure of common sense: the *Advocate* named San Francisco's Newsome "Person of the Year," not—of course—because he had gained notoriety for a range of punitive, pro-development positions targeting homeless populations (such as curfew initiatives designed to keep homeless people out of view), but again because of his self-evidently refreshing liberal views in a historical moment of hostility: because of his courage to take a stand on the single issue of same-sex marriage.[2]

The liberal consensus represented variously by figures like Dean and Newsome—who are framed by the parlance of the gay marriage movement as "straight allies"—positions support for civil unions or gay marriage at the turn of the century as part and parcel of support for diversity and respect for cultural distinction or difference. Thus, the consensus would also generally affirm as positive television shows like *Ellen, Will and Grace*, and *Queer As Folk* (which provided more popular representations of lesbians and gay men during the 1990s than ever before), or groups like the Human Rights Campaign (which was the most visible and well-funded organization working to secure LGBT rights during the decade). The Human Rights Campaign (HRC), which always happily affirms diversity but which—in contrast to the National Gay and Lesbian Task Force (NGLTF)—declared early in 2003 that it would not take a position on the war in Iraq because it was not perceived as "a gay issue," focuses on more targeted issues like hate crimes legislation, domestic partner benefits, gay marriage, and repealing the ban on gays in the military. At their "Action Center and Store" in Washington, D.C., one can learn about these projects while purchasing rainbow earrings and other queer fashion accessories. About all of these cultural developments, from *Will and Grace* to gay shopping, queer theorists and activists are likewise ambivalent, which would, undoubtedly, also surprise many who support LGBT rights.[3]

Yet queer studies and activism, along with—to widen the cloud of witnesses observing these developments—disability studies and disability activism, have not taken account of the arguments I put forth in this chapter, which suggest that intracommunity debates over gay marriage and other "normalizing" issues are centrally about disability and disability oppression (and not just because the HRC Action Center and Store, like so many other buildings in Washington, D.C., is down a steep flight of stairs). Two suggestions thus undergird my analysis in this chapter: first, that queer communities could acknowledge that the political unconscious of debates about normalization (including debates about marriage) is shaped, in large part, by ideas about disability; second, that disability communities, primed to enter (or entering already) some of the territory recently charted by queers, could draw on radical queer thought to continue forging the critical disability consciousness that has emerged over the past few decades—what I am calling in this book crip theory or crip culture. If the appeal to two communities inevitably replicates the very division I want to question, however, I also want to reemphasize that I am not presuming in this chapter a stark or absolute separation between queer and disability communities, especially since the text that is at its center, Karen Thompson and Julie Andrzejewski's *Why Can't Sharon Kowal-ski Come Home?*, is equally about lesbian sexuality and disability identity.

In what follows, I provide an overview of contemporary queer critiques of marriage and domesticity and begin to ask how disability figures into those conversations. I then consider the history of queer opposition to domesticity, drawing on and expanding John D'Emilio's foundational 1980 article "Capitalism and Gay Identity." I conclude with a close reading of *Why Can't Sharon Kowalski Come Home?* that supplements that queer history; I argue through that reading that the expanded public sphere that lesbian and gay historians and queer theorists have called for intersects with what we might call the "accessible public sphere" that crip theorists and activists have begun to imagine and materialize. The bourgeois public sphere, as it has been most famously theorized by Jürgen Habermas, is founded on principles of independence and ability, and is thus inimical both to the broader conception of access that disability theorists and activists have produced and to the alternative (and interdependent) public cultures that queer theorists, and radical social theorists more generally, have advocated.[4]

Cripping Domesticity I

In 1991, Nan Hunter, noting that lawsuits in Hawaii and the District of Columbia had been filed by same-sex couples seeking the right to marry, wrote prophetically: "The effort to legalize gay marriage will almost certainly emerge as a major issue in the next decade" (106). Hunter's prediction was completely borne out by the 1990s. Given the backlash I have just recounted, however, especially the antigay spectacle of the 2004 U.S. elections, most LGBT commentators, including advocates for legalized marriage, would have to acknowledge that the focus on marriage rights has brought mixed, if not largely negative, results. Long before 2004, failure in Hawaii led to a referendum rewriting that state's constitution so that marriage would be defined as the union of one man and one woman and the Defense of Marriage Act (DOMA), which codified the same definition of marriage on a national level, was signed into law by President Bill Clinton.

The political climate of backlash could seem to mandate a united front. As Michael Warner writes: "What purpose could be served by a skeptical discussion of marriage now, given the nature of the opposition?" (*Trou-*

ble with Normal 83). Drawing on queer critiques of the marriage rights movement, however, such a skeptical discussion is precisely what Warner provides: "The image of the Good Gay," he writes, "is never invoked without its shadow in mind—the Bad Queer, the kind who has sex, who talks about it, and who builds with other queers a way of life that ordinary folk do not understand or control" (114). Consistently, the marriage rights movement has been about manufacturing images of the Good Gay, sometimes explicitly so, as when the April 21, 1997, cover of the *Nation* presented readers with an image of two gay men and their cat safely ensconced in their living room ("Creating a New Gay Culture: Balancing Fidelity and Freedom," the headline read), or when Gabriel Rotello, the author of the article, along with other highly paid, neoconservative writers, invoked the image of the well-behaved, domesticated lesbian couple as the model for the poorly behaved, undomesticated gay man. Many lesbians, at the height of these debates, did not appreciate being cast as poster children for the new gay culture, but the usefulness of the image was what was at stake, not the complex reality of lesbian lives.

Of course, given that disability studies is one of the main conditions of possibility for my analysis of these developments, I use the metaphor of the poster child advisedly.[5] Nevertheless, I do think that the deployment of images in the lesbian and gay marriage rights debate makes use of the logic of the poster child: the images presented reassure the viewer that the figure in question is not as abject as one might have assumed, or at least that he or she is trying valiantly not to be so abject. There is even something "cute" about these images, even when they don't include a kitty: viewers could or even should extend pity to couples trying so hard, and they could even, perhaps, redirect resources to help them (and the marriage rights debate has, in fact, often invoked the resources that straight couples have that "even the most committed" gay or lesbian couple is denied). As with the poster child in disability contexts, one dominant effect of the image is to shut down other possibilities for thinking about identity, community, democracy, and justice. Warner highlights this, drawing on Erving Goffman's stigma theory to stress that the lesbian and gay emphasis on normalizing issues such as marriage deploys a fundamentally "stigmaphobic" strategy, "where conformity is ensured through fear of stigma" (*Trouble with Normal* 43). The stigmaphobic strategy is most troubling, for Warner and other queers, because it proscribes larger discussions of social justice and queer cultural generativity. To cite just one crucial example: most of the complaints about lesbian and gay partners

Cover of *The Nation*, April 21, 1997.

not being able to get health insurance through their spouse have not included an acknowledgement of how many people in general don't have
adequate health insurance, let alone a broader critique of the corporate
health insurance industry (a critique that was fairly basic to earlier gay
liberationist and feminist writing).[6]

Hunter and others, however, approach the issue from a different direction: "family," "marriage," and even "parenting" could be redefined
through these conversations, they argue. Indeed, the very unevenness of
family law, the variability of regulations from state to state and from locale to locale, "may help to denaturalize concepts like 'marriage' or 'parent,' and to expose the utter contingency of the sexual conventions that
. . . construct the family" (106). Although my theoretical sympathies are
more with those holding an uncompromised position against the institution of marriage (and I'm influenced here as much by longstanding tradi-

tions within feminism as within gay liberation and queer theory), I understand and appreciate Hunter's work, which I concede has the potential to be exactly right. Even though, from a Foucauldian perspective, I see analogies to the ongoing "reform" of the prison that ultimately serves to keep a system of docility and delinquency running smoothly, I do concede that lesbians and gay men inhabiting the categories of "marriage" and "family" will change those institutions.[7] My main problem with the emphasis on how lesbians and gay men will change (at some unspecified point in the future) the meaning of marriage is how that emphasis obscures the fact that we have already proliferated multiple queer alternatives to straight ways of relating. In the end, many more people have found satisfaction leaving marriages in search of those queer alternatives than will ever find satisfaction in the lesbian and gay rush toward marriage (and I do mean to invoke an able-bodied metaphor when I speak critically of the *rush* toward marriage).

I'm most interested, though, in the fact that Hunter's critique is not made in the abstract. The argument for redefining the family is made in an article on Sharon Kowalski—indeed, in an article that begins with an epigraph from the Minnesota State District Court, which in 1991 finally granted guardianship of Kowalski (a woman who had become disabled in 1983 following a car accident) to her lover Karen Thompson: "Sharon Kowalski is the child of a divorce between her consanguineous family and her family of affinity, the petitioner Karen Thompson. . . . That Sharon's family of affinity has not enjoyed societal recognition in the past is unfortunate" (Hunter 101). Kowalski and Thompson were living together as a closeted couple in St. Cloud, Minnesota (and both working at St. Cloud State University), when a drunk driver crashed into the car Kowalski was driving, killing Kowalski's niece, mildly injuring Kowalski's nephew, and seriously injuring Kowalski herself. Kowalski's parents Donald and Della refused to recognize the relationship between Kowalski and Thompson and, over the course of seven years, Minnesota courts consistently granted custody to Donald Kowalski, despite Sharon's repeated requests to go "home" with Thompson. Donald Kowalski not only refused to acknowledge that his daughter and Thompson were lovers and that his daughter's stated preference (through various bodily signs and communication-assistance devices) was to live with Thompson, but even that his daughter could have any preferences at all. "It doesn't really mean much to Sharon what she was," Donald Kowalski testified in court; as far as he was concerned, Sharon Kowalski was "totally helpless," by which he meant not that Sharon needed assistance with mobility, eating, and other functions but that Sharon could not conceivably care what happened to her or where she was (Thompson and Andrzejewski 136). Thompson writes of this particular court scene: "Both Donald Kowalski and [his lawyer] seemed to believe that disabled people no longer have any identity, let alone sexuality." Throughout Thompson and Andrzejewski's book, Della Kowalski is also implicated in this belief, which virtually guaranteed that Sharon Kowalski would spend the bulk of the 1980s in a nursing home. Thompson herself counters the Kowalskis' sentiments, writing, "I had learned that being in diapers and having to be turned every two hours does not make a person less human, less able to feel, to care, to love, to think, to dream of a future" (136).

This is indeed a more compelling context for thinking about marriage rights, though it would seem to introduce a paradox. To summarize the two conclusions I would draw from this overview: from one perspective, marriage is normalizing, and unquestionably, disability activists and theorists have critiqued innumerable normalizing issues, since the emphasis on "normalcy" has invariably been oppressive to people with disabilities. I would in fact claim that the stigmaphobic distancing from more stigmatized members of the community that advocates for gay marriage engage in is inescapably a distancing from disability. This is indeed literally true in one sense: commentators (such as Rotello) on domesticity and marriage offer marriage (for gay men, at least) as an antidote to AIDS, and their commentary thus distances presumably HIV-negative couples from AIDS communities and the cultures that people with AIDS and their allies have shaped. As early as 1983, people living with AIDS themselves argued that the irrational fear of AIDS is always as much or more a fear of *people* with AIDS—and Rotello's proposal of marriage as prophylactic is nothing if not irrational. It is, in fact, what Cindy Patton would call "fatal advice."[8]

From another perspective, however, the drive toward marriage potentially works *for* disability. *Why Can't Sharon Kowalski Come Home?* is peppered with references like "if I were [Sharon's] legal spouse, they wouldn't be questioning my involvement or the time I spent with her" (17) and "I was outraged by the injustice of the situation. If we had been legally married, we wouldn't have had to go through this additional strain" (33). I will ultimately argue that, partly because of Thompson's outrage at these injustices, the politicized stance Thompson and Andrzejewski construct in *Why Can't Sharon Kowalski Come Home?* represents or puts forward a much more sophisticated queercrip consciousness, but at this point I simply want to highlight the paradox: gay marriage works against disability, gay marriage works for disability.

Cripping Domesticity II

Most queer critiques of the marriage rights movement stress the normalizing effects of gay marriage. I've tried to complicate those critiques by figuring disability into the conversation: the debates about marriage and domesticity suggest that gay and lesbian subjectivity is currently forged in the contradictory space between what we might call a *cult of ability* (that includes the Good Gays who are capable of sustaining a marriage, who are not stigmatized by AIDS, and who went to Washington in 2000 for the Millennium March) and *cultures of disability* (that include AIDS activism and the lesbian feminist traditions of health care activism that preceded it, alternative ways of relating collectively and sexually, acknowledged interdependency, and communal care).[9] The long lines outside San Francisco City Hall in 2004—if, indeed, both the normative pull of marriage and the affective pull of earlier forms of activism helped form them—represent well how subjectivities emerge in that contradictory space.

Our history, however, provides an even more elaborate critique of marriage, or at least of the supposedly "traditional" family structure that places marriage at the center. In "Capitalism and Gay Identity," John D'Emilio has famously argued that nineteenth-century economic shifts away from a system of household production (and in the southern United States, slavery) and to a "free labor" system allowed for the emergence of gay identity. As men and some women were sent out into a newly defined "public sphere," some people began, more obviously, to shape an identity around their same-sex desire, and gay and lesbian communities became visible in many urban areas. At the same time, to offset the instability of the shifting economic system, the domestic realm in the cultural imagination was consolidated in opposition to the public realm of labor and production: no longer a place of interdependency for survival, home became a site where one could supposedly find emotional satisfaction and happiness. As Karl Marx himself argued, inadvertently confirming such a domestic consolidation: "The worker . . . only feels himself outside his work, and in his work feels outside himself. He is at home when he is not working, and when he is working he is not at home" ("Economic and

Philosophic Manuscripts" 74). Heterosexual relations, in this context, were released from the imperative to procreate and reimagined as connected to love and intimacy. D'Emilio makes clear, however, beyond Marx, that some workers, while perhaps still "outside themselves" at work, resisted the ideological demand to find themselves at home and generated new selves and communities elsewhere. As the home was reinvented as both private and heterosexual, then, a "gay identity" became available in public.

Although capitalism allows for the emergence of gay identities and communities, D'Emilio argues that the relationship between gay men and lesbians and capitalism is contradictory, precisely because of the new ideological role played by the family and domesticity:

> On the one hand, capitalism continually weakens the material foundation of family life, making it possible for individuals to live outside the family, and for a lesbian and gay male identity to develop. On the other, it needs to push men and women into families, at least long enough to reproduce the next generation of workers. The elevation of the family to ideological preeminence guarantees that capitalist society will reproduce not just children, but heterosexism and homophobia. In the most profound sense, capitalism is the problem. (110)

Addressing this paradox in his conclusion, D'Emilio calls for an expanded, more radically democratic public sphere. If one response to the contradictions of capitalism would be to reform the private sphere so that gays and lesbians were incorporated into straight ideologies of domesticity, consumption, and even reproduction (which was undoubtedly happening by the end of the twentieth century, in ways D'Emilio and most LGBT activists could not have anticipated in 1980), another would be to proliferate alternative public cultures where all of us (gay and nongay) have "autonomy and security" (111), and where we cannot wholly predict in advance the creative shape our identities and communities might take (we might call this the will to the least restrictive environment). D'Emilio writes: "[We need] structures and programs that will help to dissolve the boundaries that isolate the family, particularly those that privatize childrearing. We need community- or worker-controlled daycare, housing where privacy and community coexist, neighborhood institutions—from medical clinics to performance centers—that enlarge the social unit where each of us has a secure place" (111).

Building on D'Emilio's analysis, a great deal of work remains to be done on what I will call in this chapter the able-bodied family. Although many have noted that people with disabilities are often socialized in isolation from other people with disabilities (not unlike most gay men, lesbians, transgendered people, and bisexuals—this is, in fact, the most frequently cited connection between disability and LGBT movements), and although the rhetoric of coming out that now permeates disability studies suggests at its best not simply declaring oneself to be disabled (a truth one has "discovered" deep inside) but, as I implied in chapter 1, coming out to a political and cultural *movement* where disability or crip identities and cultures are collectively shaped and reshaped, a lot remains to be said about whether (or how) able-bodied ideologies, domesticity, and the family intersect.

Perhaps this particular conversation is underdeveloped because it would seem to be quite different for disability. As the public realm of labor and production that D'Emilio discusses was consolidated in the late nineteenth century, it would seem to be fundamentally about the emergence not of a disability identity but of an able-bodied identity. For instance, the twenty-fifth anniversary edition of Harry Braverman's landmark *Labor and Monopoly Capital: The Degradation of Work in the Twentieth Century*—a book which traces these economic and cultural shifts (and which, in fact, was one of the inspirations for D'Emilio's "Capitalism and Gay Identity")—uses on the cover as its representative image a series of stills from early-twentieth-century scientific management studies. These range of motion studies were designed to guarantee that workers moved efficiently and productively; the work of efficiency experts like Frederick Taylor and Frank and Lillian Gilbreth thus played a large part in the emergence of the identity of the able-bodied worker. Whether or not this was the self workers expected to find away from home, able-bodied identities were nonetheless produced in the disciplinary space of the factory. That new public identity, in turn, would seem to ensure that disability was more of a concern in the private or domestic realm (and the gendering of the range of motion photographs, as well as the already-extant nineteenth-century identity of the female "invalid," would seem to substantiate that private/public split).[10]

I want to resist that understanding of the emergence of able-bodied and disabled identities in and around the public/private divide. The ideological reconsolidation of the home as a site of intimacy and heterosexuality was also the reconsolidation of the home as a site for the develop-

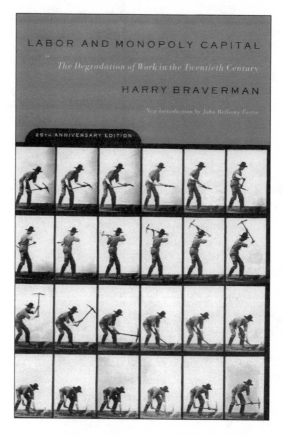

The emergence of the able-bodied worker: scientific management stills from *Labor and Monopoly Capital: The Degradation of Work in the Twentieth Century* by Harry Braverman (twenty-fifth anniversary edition).

ment of able-bodied identities, practices, and relations. The Kowalski affair is partly a legacy of this ideological conflation: Donald and Della Kowalski's inability to imagine a queer domesticity for their daughter was simultaneously an inability to imagine a disabled domesticity.

Not wholly unlike the new gay and lesbian identities that were in many ways discrete from the isolated acts of other eras, minoritized disability identities, over the course of the twentieth century, have emerged in multiple public locations: from the League of the Physically Handicapped protesting Works Progress Administration exclusions in the 1930s to the Rolling Quads demanding access to UC-Berkeley in the 1970s, from disability studies conferences in the past two decades to the Internet, where groups like WinVisible—Women with Visible and Invisible Disabilities— have articulated disability to and in other movements (such as the global women's strike and counterglobalization activism more generally), or where individuals with disabilities have simply entered chat rooms that allowed them to imagine or generate new desires or identities. Even the Deaf President Now action at Gallaudet University or late 1980s actions in New York and Washington spearheaded by the AIDS Coalition to Unleash Power (ACT UP) could be understood as part of this phenomenon. Although initially both movements were, at least in part, about refusing disability (so that the consensus seemed to be "we are not disabled, we are people living with AIDS" or "we are Deaf, not disabled"), individuals and groups have begun to reimagine them, over the past decade, as participating less in a refusal than in a public reinvention of disability (so that, for instance, both forms of activism were featured prominently in the Smithsonian National Museum of American History's groundbreaking exhibition in 2000 on the Disability Rights Movement). And of course the public and collective reinvention of disability identities continues: antiwar activism as disability activism has flourished beneath slogans like "Make Access, Not War," "Another World Is Accessible," and "Nursing Homes Are Weapons of Mass Destruction." Being at home with these and other disability identities was not simply inconceivable to Donald and Della Kowalski but disruptive of a primary site where their able-bodied consciousness was forged.

Consolidating the Able-Bodied Home

At the turn of the last century, as the home was being reinvented as heterosexual, a group of "experts" known as domestic scientists, in league with (and sometimes married to) efficiency experts, were at the forefront of the simultaneous reinvention of the home as able-bodied. Indeed, domestic scientists were the efficiency experts of the newly conceived "private" sphere. In 1902, one domestic science expert, Henrietta Goodrich, declared:

> Home economics aims to bring the home into harmony with industrial conditions and social ideals that prevail today in the larger world outside the home. This end can never be accomplished till the home in pop-

ular conception shall embody something more than the idea of personal relationships to individual homes. Men in general must admit consciously that the home is the social workshop for the making of men. No home, however, isolated can escape the social obligation that rests on it. (Qtd. in Ehrenreich and English 168)

Goodrich's insistence that no home could escape its social obligation notwithstanding, in reality the new home initially represented an almost-impossible ideal, to which many (or most) individuals and groups could never hope to aspire. The architects of this new domestic space not only maintained a strict gendered division of labor (which simultaneously nurtured the new heterosexual identities and intimacies), they also opposed the orderly, managed home to the (perceived) unruly, disorderly homes of the poor, people of color, and (especially) immigrants. Indeed, the new ideological consolidation of domesticity and management in many ways made the spaces where such groups resided unimaginable as "home." It was, in fact, the home (that is, the white, middle-class home), "brought into harmony with industrial conditions and socialideals" in the larger world, that would forestall what Theodore Roosevelt and others called "race suicide."[11] As Foucault would perhaps have it, the disciplinary space of the able-bodied home was not initially imposed on subjugated populations from on high; the bourgeoisie first constructed and occupied such a space themselves.

The emergence of domestic science was in part related to what Barbara Ehrenreich and Deirdre English have called "the domestic void." As the home became more established as a primary site for consumption rather than production, white, middle-class women (who, despite the advances of first-wave feminism, were being shut out of many educational and professional venues) were left with nothing to do. Domestic science experts filled the void and professionalized the home, just as (mostly) male doctors, scientists, and academics were professionalizing other realms. As Ehrenreich and English explain: "The domestic scientists hoped to forge a direct pipeline between the scientific laboratory and the average home. They seized any science, any discipline, any discovery, which could conceivably be used to upgrade a familiar task" (157). It was through their efforts that housecleaning and housekeeping became household management. The new "science of right living" enlisted women in a campaign against idleness, germs, and supposedly unsanitary domestic conditions (153).

Disability would be virtually inconceivable in this newly configured space, dedicated as it was to ability and "the making of men," and thus the era of domestic science was not surprisingly an era of accelerated institutionalization. In an examination of "noncriminal state institutions in Illinois," James W. Trent Jr. observes that the population in 1915 was "20,934, housed in seventeen facilities, compared with 1,061 inmates in three facilities in 1869"—an increase of 1,500 percent (98). In his overview of various institutions around the United States, Trent also notes the "pressure to admit more and different types of inmates"—a pressure that guaranteed that people with a range of cognitive and physical disabilities and as many adults as children were institutionalized during the early decades of the twentieth century (98–99). Bertha Flaten was an inmate with epilepsy at the Faribault State School and Hospital in Minnesota. Following her death, Faribault buried her, like thousands of other women and men at institutions around the country, in a grave with a simple concrete stone marked "number 7."[12] Disability rights activist John Hockenberry writes of an institutionalized uncle simply erased from the family memory (334–353). Michael Bérubé, in his memoir about his son with Down syndrome, recounts that "expert" medical and scientific advice as late as the 1970s was to "institutionalize [the] baby" and tell "family and friends the child was stillborn" (*Life As We Know It* 30).

Disability studies has often debated the connection between illness and disability.[13] The early twentieth-century consolidation and spread of the able-bodied home that I'm tracing did not produce a sharp distinction between the two. Priscilla Wald's work on "carrier narratives," and on the story of Mary Mallon (or "Typhoid Mary") in particular, examines the ways in which housewives were compelled to contain infection through better household management. Containing infection also meant being wary of others, like the Irish immigrant and domestic worker Mallon, who supposedly posed a threat to the health and safety of the home. But the concurrent institutionalization of people with disabilities and domestic science experts' repeated, even unrelenting, focus on "ability" and efficiency, suggests that disability was as much of a threat to this new and well-managed space as infection.

As "the homosexual [became] a species" discursively at the turn of the last century (Foucault, *History of Sexuality* 43), then, so, too, did the person with cognitive and physical disabilities. Put differently, people with disabilities or illnesses were objectified and pathologized in new ways as authority to name and describe disability decidedly shifted to medical and

Bertha Flaten's gravemarker. Faribault State School and Hospital, Minnesota. Courtesy of Division of Science and Medicine, National Museum of American History, Smithsonian Institution.

psychiatric institutions (and away from other venues, such as the church and the freak show). Emergent domestic ideologies—ideologies that in fact became dominant in the United States as the industrialized American century continued (and that were embraced even by groups they had initially demonized)—facilitated these processes of objectification and pathologization. If a logic of institutionalization and "expertise" was pulling people with disabilities from the home, able-bodied domestic ideologies were pushing them.

Hence, far from emerging as the "private" counterpart to the new and public able-bodied identity, disability during the period was more firmly linked to ideas of pathology, loss, lack, and isolation and was opposed to the intimacy and security associated with (heterosexual and able-bodied) domestic space. Only the collective disability identities and movements that emerged later in the century—as people with disabilities began to speak, "often in the same vocabulary, using the same categories by which [they were] medically disqualified" (Foucault, *History of Sexuality* 101)—could oppose such a consolidation of ability, domesticity, and heterosexuality. And, not surprisingly, the models for living that have been put forward by the disability rights movement, such as the Independent Living Movement that began in Berkeley, California, and elsewhere in the

1970s, have generally opposed, implicitly or explicitly, both institutionalization and dominant models of domesticity. An accessible society, according to the best, critically disabled perspectives, is not simply one with ramps and Braille signs on "public" buildings, but one in which our ways of relating to, and depending on, each other have been reconfigured.

Even though a central contention of this chapter is that the Kowalski affair is partly a legacy of these consolidations of ability, heterosexuality, and domesticity, obviously, at the turn of the twenty-first century, we inherit the space of the domestic in complex, contradictory ways. The Kowalski affair, however, is thoroughly marked by that complexity and contradiction. Shifts in capitalism and patriarchy over the past thirty years have undeniably introduced a certain amount of "flexibility" into family forms; the "brave new families" that Judith Stacey and others have described come in many varieties. In Minnesota, however, much more starkly than in many other states, new and flexible family forms are associated with particular regions, most notably the more diverse Minneapolis–St. Paul areas and academic areas such as St. Cloud, where Karen Thompson and Sharon Kowalski lived and worked at the time of Kowalski's accident. In the industrial northern part of the state where Donald and Della Kowalski lived—the location known as "the Iron Range" because of the dominance of the mining industry—"traditional" family forms are valued and indeed have become more entrenched as fluid and postmodern familial alternatives, associated largely with the Twin Cities, have become more vocal and visible.

Family forms on the Iron Range are hardly traditional, in the sense that they are less than two centuries old, and their debt to efficiency experts at work or at home suggests that the interests of capital shaped them at least as much as the interests of labor. Nonetheless, the heterosexual and able-bodied family is perceived as traditional, as surely as alternatives in other locations are perceived as threats. Particular commitments to Christianity on the Iron Range compound that threat: the Iron Range is more deeply and obviously religious than other areas of the state, and "traditional" understandings of the family clearly buttress that religious fervor.

Casey Charles explains that "the so-called Range mentality, a fierce independence combined with a distrust of urbanization and its progressive social values, grew out of a history of hard work in hard conditions under hard bosses" (21). Hard bosses and exploitative conditions helped to secure both able-bodied identities and the sense that such identities needed to be (re)produced for the future. Charles's account of the Kowalskis' life in Nashwauk, Minnesota, exemplifies this understanding of security and reproduction:

> Donald Kowalski took early retirement from Hanna Mining Company, where he had risen to a position of foreman in the taconite mines in the 1960s and 1970s. He had saved enough money to buy some land outside of Nashwauk, where he and his wife, Della, raised three children, Sharon, Debbie, and Mark. He also raised some cattle and operated a bulldozer to supplement his pension, wanting to give each of his children a piece of the property on which to raise their families. (22)

As far as Donald and Della Kowalski were concerned, the only recognizable family form was the able-bodied/heterosexual family. And the institutions Karen Thompson encountered in her attempts to challenge her enforced separation from Sharon Kowalski for seven years only confirmed the Kowalskis' (mis)recognition.

Dependency and Interdependency, Out in Public

In the early chapters of *Why Can't Sharon Kowalski Come Home?*, Karen Thompson herself explicitly holds to values of independence, self-reliance, and (by extension) isolation. She too associates these values both with the particular variant of Protestantism (Presbyterianism) she practices and—like those living on the Iron Range—with what she perceives as longstanding regional attributes. Indeed, Karen, discounting the alternatives already internal to the region, usually associates values of independence, self-reliance, and privacy with Minnesota as a whole or with the Midwest generally (her own family of origin lives in Ohio).[14] She works as an assistant professor of physical education and recreation at St. Cloud State University, where she enjoys her job but does not particularly connect her situation to others—especially other women—around her. Indeed, Julie Andrzejewski, the colleague with whom Karen eventually forms a friendship after Sharon's accident, is—for a long time—unable to convince Karen to participate in a class action lawsuit alleging systemic discrimination at the university on the basis of gender. When Karen receives her settlement from the case, she feels like a fraud, because of her ongoing reluctance to interpret her experience as connected to the experience of other women.

The early chapters of *Why Can't Sharon Kowalski Come Home?* relate the story of Karen and Sharon's affair before Sharon's accident. Like Karen's experience of herself as a professor, the affair is characterized by an insistence on independence—an insistence that disallows identification of the women's relationship as "lesbian" and that, indeed, even forestalls use of the word. Inverting Teresa de Lauretis's assertion that "it takes two women, not one, to make a lesbian" ("Film and the Visible" 232), in the story of Sharon and Karen's romance, it takes two women to maintain the façade that their relationship is *not* "lesbian"—that it is, instead, simply about two unique individuals who love each other. Thompson writes: "At this time we weren't ready to think or talk about any of the ramifications of two women loving each other. I felt that it was Sharon, the *individual*, I had fallen in love with, regardless of whether she was a woman or a man" (Thompson and Andrzejewski 14).

In the months before the accident, Sharon becomes increasingly uncomfortable with the refusal of connection and identification. When the couple attends a concert featuring lesbian performers Meg Christian and Cris Williamson, Sharon is "ecstatic . . . feeling support that had been missing for so long. She felt like she belonged for the first time, like she was part of a family. She wanted to talk about it, to admit who we were, to go out afterwards to socialize with other gay people" (Thompson and Andrzejewski 22). Karen, in contrast, experiences the concert as "traumatic": "I felt on display, or labeled in some way. . . . For the first time in our lives, we could have touched each other in public, held hands, hugged each other or exchanged glances without worrying about how someone else would interpret them. But I sat as far away from Sharon as possible" (22–23). The model of privacy on which the women's lives are founded comes with a limited (and isolating) understanding of "family" that they are trying to replicate: security and intimacy are associated with the "home," but that home is not supposed to open up onto spaces like the space collectively produced by the women at the concert. Ironically, before the accident, Karen and Sharon are a closeted female couple, but their insistently private affair is actually not very different from Della and Donald Kowalski's marriage. In alternative public spaces, Sharon begins to detect an alternative model of "family" that would position the couple as connected to—as, in many ways, dependent on for survival—other lesbians.

After the accident, Sharon and Karen discover quickly that, regardless of the similarities between their relationship and a private, heterosexual "marriage," and regardless of how hard they have been working to support the dominant model of family, the institutions they encounter are structured to deny the validity of their efforts and to produce truths that will naturalize the family as heterosexual and able-bodied. The first institutions that participate in this naturalization are the hospitals and nursing homes that initially care for Sharon. Immediately after the accident, in fact, Sharon and Karen's family is deemed invalid:

> I stuttered into the intercom [at St. Cloud Hospital], "I would like information concerning Sharon Kowalski. Is she here? . . . Can I see her? What's her condition?"
>
> A voice responded, "What is your relationship?" After some hesitation, I said, "We live together and I'm a close friend."
>
> "I'm sorry. We can't give out information to anyone except immediate family members," the intercom spit out. (Thompson and Andrzejewski 4)

Over time, an initial custody agreement allows for equal visitation for Karen and the Kowalskis at the various medical facilities that care for Sharon. Two intersecting trajectories, however, characterize Karen's engagement with these establishments. The first trajectory brings Karen into contact with an increasing number of individual professionals who observe that Sharon's rehabilitation moves much more rapidly and is much more consistent with Karen's central participation. The second, ominous, trajectory absolutely contradicts the first: proliferating medical "truths" about Sharon's condition suggest that she is not improving and even that Karen's participation in Sharon's life is impeding improvement (because, as these medical truths begin to imply, only her "real" family, in consultation with medical experts, can know what is best for Sharon). These medical truths are at times individual, in that the Kowalskis do enlist (and pay) various individual professionals to testify that Karen's visitation rights should be curtailed and that Sharon should remain in a nursing home indefinitely. As often, however, these medical truths seem to be a function of the structure of the medical institution that cannot comprehend a lesbian and disabled life for Sharon outside of their purview.

During the initial days of the crisis, Karen turns to her church for sustenance and finds some support from the associate pastor of the First Presbyterian Church where she attends. When a woman attacks her verbally, saying, "You must have allowed Satan to twist the love you had for Sharon into something else to try to get you away from Christ" (Thompson and Andrzejewski 107), Karen mentions the support of the associate pastor. After he learns of the incident, however, the pastor retracts his support: "While I want to support and help you any way I can, I would appreciate it if you wouldn't use my name to others in the church. There are certain factions within the church that simply wouldn't accept this" (108). Karen thus learns quickly that the religious institution, like the hospital and the nursing homes, provides only certain kinds of "care" and ultimately protects only certain kinds of families: "I felt like I had been kicked in the solar plexus. . . . I had hoped that he would help others accept me as a member of the 'family of the church.' I felt betrayed once again. Knowing I didn't have the strength to handle another emotional crisis, I felt I had no choice but to leave the church. No one reached out to me" (108).

The justice system is the institution that most contributes to the protection of the heterosexual and able-bodied family. Over the course of *Why Can't Sharon Kowalski Come Home?*, numerous court cases attempt to adjudicate various questions: Who will be Sharon's primary guardian? Will Sharon be allowed to go home after her initial rehabilitation, or will she be transferred to a nursing home? Will Karen be allowed to participate in Sharon's recovery at all? Karen's faith in individuals is especially evident as she participates in the early proceedings, often thoroughly convinced that her own case is airtight and that anyone seeing the "evidence" will undoubtedly recognize that Sharon does better in rehabilitation with Karen than anyone else and that Sharon's interests will be best served by avoiding a protracted stay in a nursing home. Indeed, Sharon's own *stated* desires are introduced as evidence into some of the proceedings, and these stated desires consistently support Karen's interpretation of the situation.

The courts, however, repeatedly side with the Kowalskis and their lawyer, Jack Fena. The testimony of the medical personnel the Kowalskis bring to the court (supporting their contentions that Karen is detrimental to Sharon's recovery and that Sharon could not possibly live outside a nursing home) is consistently given more credence than the evidence introduced by Karen and her lawyers, even though the personnel in question have often never worked with Sharon directly, have only observed her quickly one or two times, or are reporting on an area outside of their own particular expertise. Moreover, the construction of judicial and medical truths is mutually constitutive: spurious medical evidence is introduced in court, and even noted in court as spurious, but is later taken as both legal and medical truth precisely because it has been introduced in court. Ultimately, Donald Kowalski is granted full guardianship, which comes with the legal right to decide who will interact with his daughter: Karen Thompson, her lawyers, civil liberties groups, and—significantly—disability rights groups are all denied access to Sharon Kowalski (Thompson and Andrzejewski 156). Just as medical and legal "truths" are mutually constitutive, so, too, are Donald Kowalski's actions and beliefs about lesbian and disability identities: unable to imagine a queer and disabled domesticity, Donald Kowalski confines Sharon to a nursing home and keeps her from coming in contact with all those (public) movements and identities that would make queer and disabled publicity (and domesticity) imaginable.

The last major institution working against Karen is the mainstream media. The first headline in the case, in the *St. Cloud Daily Times* on October 18, 1984, reads, "Gay Issue Clouds Fight for Custody" (Thompson and Andrzejewski 80). The article begins by depicting Sharon as a "quadriplegic," despite her demonstrated capacity to use her arms and fingers to operate communication-assistance devices and other tools. Additionally, the article pathologizes Karen; Donald Kowalski insists Karen is "about as sick as they come. . . . They don't come much sicker" (80, 81). Unable to represent lesbian domesticity as anything other than alleged, the *St. Cloud Daily Times* introduces Karen as "an assistant professor at St. Cloud State University (SCSU) who claims to have carried on a secret lesbian relationship with Kowalski for the past four years" (80–81).

Thompson describes the article as "more objective than most" (Thompson and Andrzejewski 80); later articles prove to be even more harmful. Her own university's paper, for instance, quotes Jack Fena: "I think the gay community has been brainwashed in this case by Ms. Thompson and I believe that if they were to view the medical records thoroughly, they wouldn't give Ms. Thompson five cents to continue these attacks on Sharon Kowalski and her family" (Thompson and Andrzejewski 184). Karen, of course, is conspicuously outside of Sharon's "family" in Fena's statement. And although Fena's appeal to "the medical records" is anything but "thorough," it nonetheless contributes to the construction of legal and medical "knowledge": "Even some lesbians in Minnesota became convinced by the articles that there was no evidence that Sharon and I indeed had a relationship" (184).

Although her faith in individual good will and her inability (at least at first) to perceive systemic injustice lead her to expect that representation will be fairly straightforward (that is, that media institutions will simply perceive how things "really are" and will then represent them "accurately" to a reading or viewing public), Karen eventually learns that mainstream media—like the medical, religious, and judicial institutions she has encountered—is similarly structured to protect (by keeping private) the heterosexual and able-bodied family. Indeed, most mainstream media sources, with their commitment to "two sides of a story" (a commitment that Karen undoubtedly would not have questioned prior to the accident), simply refuse to report the case, since the Kowalskis refuse to participate.

This cumulative situation pushes Karen away from the simple private life that she had desired (and that she and Sharon had implicitly, and sometimes explicitly, agreed to support) to a public (and even activist) life associated with lesbian sexuality and disability. She begins to travel around the country, to speak to communities that have formed because of a commitment to lesbian and gay, feminist, and disability issues (and even to communities that have specifically formed "Free Sharon Kowalski" groups). She quickly perceives that the feminist networks she discovers, in particular, have been in many cases explicitly shaped to contest the medical, religious, legal, and media institutions she has encountered. And the capacity to contest these institutions has been shaped not from a model of the private and independent home but from an alternative model of home and community, where individuals, couples, and "families" are dependent on each other and where "home" is always contiguous to other sustaining locations. A shift that occurs for Karen while on a speaking tour in Boston helps to illustrate what she learns out in public:

> [The] lesbian and gay community had organized with disabled activists to bring me [to speak in Boston]. Once again, people took me into their community and welcomed me into their homes. I was amazed to find that many of the women had almost no possessions. They spent all their extra time and money organizing for causes. They had a real sense of community and purpose. Though I didn't necessarily want to live like them, I began to think that I was missing something valuable, that my life was too shallow.
>
> I realized that I had never spent this much time with women. One afternoon the Boston organizers "kidnapped" me to drive me to a lesbian clambake. The old me would have felt extremely uncomfortable being with a group of women I didn't know, especially if they were lesbians. But it shocked me to realize that I felt at home. For the first time I un-

derstood Sharon's feelings of being with "family" at the Meg and Chris [*sic*] concert. . . . Instead of being totally drained after a presentation, I was learning to become revitalized from being with women. (Thompson and Andrzejewski 186–187)

Karen opens herself up, in the final chapters of *Why Can't Sharon Kowalski Come Home?* to a specifically feminist notion of interdependency. This notion of interdependency is not without its dangers; as Eva Feder Kittay notes, an emphasis on interdependency is often a cover for "the mutual (often voluntary) cooperation between essentially independent persons" (xii). Because the education of Karen Thompson has so thoroughly entailed a critique of independence (and the institutions that sustain it), however, I would argue that the idea of interdependency she comes to value aligns with Kittay's insistence that "interdependence begins with dependence" (xii). Indeed, it is ultimately Sharon's dependence on Karen, and vice versa, that queers and crips the family. The feminist, queer, and disabled relations of interdependency Karen encounters in alternative public spheres expose the inadequacies of the able-bodied/heterosexual family. Those relations also make clear for Karen the structural connections between the supposedly "private" family (offering heterosexual and able-bodied intimacy and security) and the general "public" sphere (sustaining relations of exploitation, but obscuring such relations by privileging ideologies of "independence" and protecting heterosexual and able-bodied identities and homes).

Conclusion: At Home with Sharon Kowalski

Worrying that the lesbian and gay community might be "selling out" with its emphasis on marriage and other normalizing issues (particularly those tied to privatization and consumption), Alexandra Chasin writes: "I consider a value on access to be the defining difference between progressive and liberal agendas" (22). Chasin does not acknowledge it, but discussions about what access might mean are most developed within disability contexts. *Why Can't Sharon Kowalski Come Home?* and innumerable other critiques emerging from the disability movement work to value and materialize access. Which is certainly not to deny that Thompson herself cannot speak to or around the contemporary same-sex marriage movement; she has, in fact, allowed her name and struggle to be used in HRC materials (Charles 180, 188). It is, rather, to suggest that the crip story she and Julie Andrzejewski put forward in *Why Can't Sharon Kowalski Come Home?* cannot be fully contained by a normalizing movement or a liberal agenda. In the end, that story is not so much a tale of arrival (indeed, the memoir literally cannot be about arrival as it was written in the midst of Thompson's legal battle) as it is a tale of becoming: becoming queer and disabled in the generative, adaptive, world-making sense—becoming crip.[15]

Sharon Kowalski is now home in Clearwater, Minnesota, with Karen Thompson and Patty Bresser, another woman who joined the family in 1992. Thompson began a relationship with Bresser in the early 1990s but insisted that "Sharon and I would always be a package deal. If anyone could learn to love me, they would have to love us both" (Schneider 13). It's a fairly queer domestic arrangement, suggesting that queerness, in its most critical sense, might generate disability, while disability might breed queerness.[16]

Perhaps if Kowalski and Thompson had been married a great deal of conflict could have been avoided. Yet ultimately this would only shape an accessible private space for Thompson and Kowalski while keeping inaccessible more expansive and democratic spaces where crips and queers might yet remake the system that produced the Kowalski affair in the first place. As *Why Can't Sharon Kowalski Come Home?* concludes, as she encounters lesbian, gay, feminist, and disability activists, Karen thinks and writes about gender oppression, AIDS, homelessness, and even the injustices and exploitation endemic to transnational capitalism. She links her struggle to the struggles of others. Thompson and Kowalski's story can thus be read as much more than the simple incorporation of a privatized couple into a system that guarantees and requires the primacy of the ablebodied and heterosexual family. Somewhere outside of that privatized space, disability activists like Thompson, Kowalski, and Bresser continue to shape fluid and critical identities and creative, radically democratic ways of relating that are neither predictable in advance nor containable within straight ideologies of domesticity.

3

Noncompliance
The Transformation, Gary Fisher, and the Limits of Rehabilitation

The story of Sharon Kowalski and Karen Thompson, from the previous chapter, could be understood at least in part as a story of competing understandings of rehabilitation. Donald and Della Kowalski believed that there was little possibility of rehabilitation for Sharon, given the extent of her disabilities. For the Kowalskis, who or what their daughter had been in the past or could be in the future didn't "really mean much to Sharon" anymore (Thompson and Andrzejewski 136). Thompson, in contrast, arguably came to perceive rehabilitation in more holistic terms: physical and language therapy for Kowalski was possible, and it could include Thompson herself and the queer/disabled community. Moreover, the therapy need not be conducted solely in institutions such as hospitals and nursing homes; instead, physical and language therapy—with the right kind of public, communal support—could be an integral part of the queer/disabled domesticity envisioned by both women following Kowalski's accident. The very title of Thompson and Julie Andrzejewski's memoir, *Why Can't Sharon Kowalski Come Home?*, marks this conflict over rehabilitation—or, more precisely, over the "return" that rehabilitation (which at its root suggests the return to a former role or capacity) might or might not facilitate. A variety of legal, medical, media, and religious institutions colluded to make the queer/disabled rehabilitation or return that Kowalski and Thompson hoped for unthinkable.

From another perspective, however, Kowalski and Thompson in some ways *refused* rehabilitation. The queercrip consciousness that emerged for both women over the course of the memoir made a return to their former existence—able-bodied, closeted, private, privatized—less imaginable and undesirable. Kowalski's parents, in contrast, arguably only embraced dominant understandings of rehabilitation: for them, able-bodied/heterosexual normalcy began at home, and if Sharon could not return to such a state of normalcy, then she would have to remain incarcerated in nursing homes.

Around 1996

In this chapter, I address disability studies critiques of ideologies of rehabilitation more directly, through consideration of a few texts produced in the normalizing decade after Sharon Kowalski did, in fact, return home to live with Thompson and Patty Bresser. In 1996, PBS premiered Susana Aikin and Carlos Aparicio's documentary *The Transformation*. *The Transformation* was a sequel to Aikin and Aparicio's 1990 documentary *The Salt Mines*, which focused on African American and Latina transgender communities living on the streets of New York City—specifically, in the area known as "the Salt Mines" because salt (for use on the city's streets in winter) is stored there. Members of a Dallas-based Fundamentalist Christian ministry saw a news report about the Salt Mines on network television and targeted the communities represented in it for transformation; Aikin and Aparicio's later documentary, consequently, tells the story of Sara, who—before her death from complications due to HIV/AIDS—joins the Christian ministry and returns to her former life as Ricardo. *The Transformation* details Ricardo's journey from the transgender streets of New York to a housed, married, and Fundamentalist Christian life in Dallas.

Also in 1996, Eve Kosofsky Sedgwick edited and published the journals and short fiction of her former student Gary Fisher. *Gary in Your Pocket: Stories and Notebooks of Gary Fisher* appeared three years after Fisher's death from HIV/AIDS. It is a return of sorts; in the words of Don Belton, who wrote the introduction to *Gary in Your Pocket*, the collection "is a resurrection of the power and seduction of Gary's conversation. It is a good vessel of Gary's voice" (xi). According to Belton, Fisher himself described that voice as the voice of a "black, queer sociopath" (qtd. in Belton ix). This self-description, presumably, in part alludes to the sexual fantasies and activities detailed throughout Fisher's writing. In the journal excerpts published in *Gary in Your Pocket*, most of the multiple sexual activities described, especially in the last few years of Fisher's life, are wrapped up in sadomasochistic fantasies; they are also often anonymous (with Fisher going nameless, using an assumed name, or taking on a label or identity such as "slave") and consummated in public or semi-public spaces. Fisher particularly returns quite often to Buena Vista Park near his apartment in San Francisco, but he also seeks encounters on the phone and—at least in a few of his final fantasies—in a reconstructed "kinky hospital" (251). Fisher's exploration of sexual domination and submission and a world of masters and slaves, moreover, often explicitly includes, in the excerpts published in *Gary in Your Pocket*, fantasies of racial degradation.

It was when Belton and Fisher discussed the possibility of publication that Fisher insisted, "Where can a black, queer sociopath get a fair hearing anyway?" (qtd. in Belton ix). In Belton's interpretation, Fisher "did not write for publication" and was in fact quite "ambivalent about the machinery of publication" (xi, ix). As Fisher apparently perceived it, the available forms for publication could not comprehend his identifications; in particular, the proud and sustaining *consolidation* readable in "black" at the end of the twentieth century could be understood as inimical to the *disintegration* put into motion by Fisher's self-proclaimed "queer" and "sociopathic" identities. Put differently, as Fisher himself well knew, almost thirty years of collective action had made available (through various machineries of publication) understandings of black identity that specifically resisted white conflations of "blackness" with anything "sociopathic" or "queer" (broadly and negatively understood). Such activism had done its work in other contexts as well; the proud consolidation likewise readable in "black gay" and even some versions of "black queer" identification by the mid-1990s would similarly be undone by, because defined in opposition to, sociopathic behavior (or—even more—identification).[1]

This chapter, then, centers on two men of color in the normalizing gay 1990s, considering two returns, and (perhaps) one rehabilitation. Neither man survived the 1990s, though there were certainly efforts made by others in the decade to chart paths for individual and communal survival. I mention two such efforts at the outset of my analysis, because for me they haunt *The Transformation*, *Gary in Your Pocket*, the world of 1996, and this chapter. The first effort is invoked, in a few ways, by Belton's introduction, and even by his opening paragraph. Bearing witness to the loss around him, Belton writes: "Gary Fisher's death came in a season of deaths of young black men I called Brother. During that bitter and long harvest, he fell along with the novelist Melvin Dixon, documentary film-maker Marlon Riggs and my birth brother Morris who shot himself to death one Monday morning having abandoned his routine preparations to go into this downtown Philadelphia office" (vii). It is not only the inclusion of Marlon Riggs on Belton's list that calls to mind the documentary *Tongues Untied*, or even that the film itself, produced and directed by Riggs in 1989, is named by Belton on the next page, by Sedgwick in her "other contexts for reading *Gary in Your Pocket*" in the afterword to the volume (284), and by Duke University Press in their blurb for the book on the back cover. More important than the insistent naming of *Tongues Untied* is the fact that the two primary rhetorical strategies of the film—indeed, the rhetorical strategies that frame it—are rumbling behind almost everything Belton writes.

Tongues Untied opens with images of black men playing basketball, while a chorus of black male voices chants, "Brother to Brother to Brother to Brother." It closes with images of a black gay pride parade interwoven with historical civil rights footage (Martin Luther King Jr. and others marching to Selma, Alabama) and the thesis—put forward in block letters—that "Black Men Loving Black Men Is *The* Revolutionary Act." Even as he commemorates death, Belton conjures up these strategies for survival: the explicit repetition of "Brother" and the literal naming of four men (Brother to Brother to Brother to Brother) implicitly calls back the film's ultimate "revolutionary" thesis about the world-making potential of black men loving black men. Indeed, conjuring up the world he believed he contingently formed with another friend (who had also recently died from HIV/AIDS), Belton writes much more explicitly: "We laughed, agreed, argued, mind to mind, eye to eye, brother to brother. In those moments he was what Gary was for me, and what my birth brother, nine years my senior, would never scale the stony wall of black masculine silence to become: a chosen brother" (viii).

The strategies for overcoming silence and the theses about black brotherhood encapsulated in Belton's introduction and in *Tongues Untied* were undeniably vital throughout the 1990s. However, Belton's own connection to Fisher (and by extension his connection of Fisher to these theses) notwithstanding, they were not necessarily the rhetorical strategies or theses put forward by Fisher himself—or, for that matter, by Ricardo, although some members of the street community of the Salt Mines are black and *The Transformation* also puts forward a sibling discourse, albeit one more oriented around sisterhood than brotherhood. In some ways, in fact, Belton's introduction confirms what Fisher himself asserted, since "queer" and "sociopath" cannot easily get a hearing in it, cannot easily coexist with the particular kind of black identification Belton prioritizes. Again, that proud and consolidated black identification helped lay down important paths for individual and communal survival, but they were not paths Fisher (or Ricardo) followed in any obvious sense.

The second path for survival was forged too late for both men and may not have been available to them or effective for them, even if they had lived a few more years. At the end of the year that saw the publication of *Gary in Your Pocket* and the premier of *The Transformation*, *Time* magazine named Dr. David Ho "Man of the Year." Ho's individualization was more a function of *Time*'s conventions; although the cover did not make it clear, the magazine was actually highlighting less Ho's singular achievements and more his participation on research teams that led to the development of protease inhibitors, which achieved worldwide attention in 1996. Protease is an enzyme HIV utilizes to replicate itself; protease inhibitors block that replication and, from the mid-1990s on, when taken in therapeutic combination with other HIV drugs, proved highly successful for some patients. These combinations became known popularly as "drug cocktails." Drug cocktails (which were generally patient-specific, developed in consultation with one's doctor) initially required compliance with an extremely difficult regimen: they had to be taken every day, throughout the day, at certain times of the day, in certain combinations, with or without food, and so forth. The worldwide attention on protease inhibitors and drug cocktails in 1996 was most pronounced in July at the 11th International AIDS Conference, in Vancouver, British Columbia.

It would be difficult to overstate the ways in which Vancouver marked a perceptual shift in relation to HIV/AIDS. Undeniably, doctors, scientists, and researchers attending the conference felt relief that, for once, a positive and major advance in AIDS research and therapy could be discussed. The perceptual shift toward optimism was fueled even more, however, by problematic media representations, from Andrew Sullivan's egregious article "When AIDS Ends" in the *New York Times Magazine* to *Time*'s own cover of Ho, which pictures him, in profile, gazing at a constellation of bright colors.[2] The vibrant oranges, reds, and yellows are reflected in Ho's glasses, obscuring his eyes, though his mood is readable through the faint trace of a smile on his face. The picture may call to mind a doctor reading an X-ray or an MRI on a lightboard, but it is an abstraction and a mystification; we are not—in other words—given Ho or his colleagues involved in the actual labor that led to the development of protease inhibitors, perhaps analyzing Petri dishes or gazing into microscopes. In the end, the metonymic invocation of a range of twentieth-century scientific ideologies is more urgent for *Time*: Ho's picture suggests that science sees into the future, that advances in medicine will ultimately conquer disease, or that the heroic individual researcher will discover the cures that rid the world of sickness or impairment. Beyond that, the funky, psychedelic colors simultaneously position Ho within another set of (emergent) ideologies: here is one of those technological innovators from the fast-paced, cybernetic, and neoliberal 1990s; the picture could almost function, as effectively, on the cover of *Wired* magazine, along with the caption "Is This a Great Time or What?" (Frank, *One Market under God* 51).[3]

1996 may have ended, at least for *Time*, on this upbeat note, but clearly it was not such a great time for everyone. Wearing buttons with ironic slogans such as "Don't Worry, Be Happy" and asserting more directly "Greed Equals Death" and "Demand Access for All," activists worked in Vancouver to challenge the easy optimism that both the media and the pharmaceutical companies poised to profit from the new protease inhibitors were fueling. Both Fisher and Ricardo, of course, died before protease inhibitors became available. It is nonetheless appropriate to keep the demand of access for all in mind when considering their stories, given that securing access to any and all AIDS therapies, both before and after Vancouver, has consistently been more difficult for queer men of color.[4]

The next section of this chapter introduces disability studies critiques of rehabilitation; throughout, my contention is that such critiques provide a useful context for reading *The Transformation* and *Gary in Your Pocket* (and, less directly, *Tongues Untied*). In some ways, HIV/AIDS is not susceptible to "rehabilitation" in the classic twentieth-century sense I sketch out here, but I argue that—perhaps all the more because of its difference from other conditions or impairments—a problematic rehabilitative logic nonetheless governs contemporary understandings of and responses to what we should still call the AIDS crisis.[5]

Throughout, I bring my theses about the rehabilitative logic at work in the AIDS crisis to bear on questions about degradation: what it might mean, how it might work, where and why it appears, and why (or whether) it generates such shock or revulsion. Clearly, in this chapter, questions about degradation are raised most explicitly by Fisher's journal ("should I go back," he asks at one point, "'defile' myself . . . for the thrill

Cover of *Time* magazine, December 30, 1996.

of it? Have I thought about why I do this?" [195]). I contend, however, that such questions are inevitably in circulation in any cultural context or movement that depends on identity or, perhaps more directly, in any cultural context that depends on rehabilitation (two dependencies that are not always as far removed from each other as they might appear). The twentieth-century dream of rehabilitative return might appear to be completely and exactly opposed to degradation, but Fisher's prescient linkage of degradation to complex questions of return—"should I go back"—suggests that the cultural poison that human degradation is conventionally assumed to be might be internal, not external, to the conventionally medicinal machinery we think we know as rehabilitation. My primary (queer and crip) goal in this chapter is one that is both dangerous and nearly impossible at the present moment: because of my faith in what Belton calls his "resurrection," I want to keep the questions raised by Fisher alive. With those questions alive and on top (another near impossibility that arguably both rehabilitates and degrades Fisher), I want to resist (or perhaps put forward) the rehabilitation of degradation and put forward (or perhaps resist) the degradation of rehab.[6]

Rehabilitation and Its Discontents

According to Henri-Jacques Stiker, rehabilitation came to prominence as practice and ideology following World War I. The sheer quantity of soldiers returning home with disabilities produced a situation Stiker labels "startling." I quote at length the scene he sets for the emergence of modern notions of rehabilitation:

> At the close of what the European nations called the Great War without knowing to what extent this qualifier was relative, a startling number of men were discharged injured for life. They were called *mutilés de guerre* "maimed war veterans" on the model of those disabled by accidents at work. The "mutilated" were not only amputees. Mutilation applied to all alteration of integrity, of integralness. It amounted to a degradation, but one by removal—or deterioration—which has the effect of suppression. The maimed person is someone missing something precise, an organ or function. Thus, the first image presented by this change in terminology is that of damage. The war has taken away, we must replace. (123)

It would be difficult to call the therapeutic impulses and rehabilitative energies that emerged from this context malevolent. Indeed, Webster's definition of *degrade*—since it seems to signify, at every turn, processes to be avoided—affirms how solidly the history of rehabilitation is founded on good intentions:

> **degrade** *vb* [ME *degraden*, fr. MF *degrader*, fr. LL *degradare*, fr. L *de* + *gradus* step, grade—more at GRADE] *vt* (14c) **1 a :** to lower in grade, rank, or status : DEMOTE **b :** to strip of rank or honors **c :** to deprive of standing or true function : PERVERT **d :** to scale down in desirability or salability **2 a :** to bring to low esteem or into disrepute **b :** to drag down in moral or intellectual character : CORRUPT **3 :** to impair in respect to some physical property **4 :** to wear down by erosion **5 :** to reduce the complexity of (a chemical compound) : DE-COMPOSE ~ *vi* **1 :** to pass

from a higher grade or class to a lower 2 *of a chemical compound* : to become reduced in complexity

Considering the apparent meanings of degradation, it is quite striking how thoroughly the will to rehabilitate, at its inception, negates the will to degrade: if the proud "grade, rank, or status" of returning soldiers was somehow endangered by war injuries, rehabilitation promised a restoration of rank, honors, and "true function." If (at times quite literal) standing was deprived, rehabilitation restored it, eliminating the perversion attending other (nonstanding) positions. Rehabilitation increased esteem and repute; rehabilitation ensured desirability and—without question—salability. The corruption in character that impairment, in respect to some physical property, appeared to mark need not matter; quite literally, rehabilitation ensured that physical, intellectual, and "moral" differences need not materialize. Finally, rehabilitation restored complexity; if the degradation, in Stiker's words, "of integrity, of integralness" seemed to simplify the *mutilés de guerre*, reducing them to "injured for life," the complex machinations of rehabilitation resisted such a reduction and (re)produced complex modern men.

For Stiker, "the rehabilitation initiative," despite its connection to returning soldiers, "applied to congenital cases as well as to the adventitious" (122). If "a new will is born: to reintegrate" (124), theoretically no disabled body would be excluded. This theoretical conception—essentially, "make it new"—is not, I should make clear, of necessity in contradiction with the practices of institutionalization I discussed in chapter 2, or with the desire for the able-bodied worker or the emergence of the able-bodied home. On the contrary, throughout the twentieth century, both the ideologies and practices of institutionalization and domesticity I discussed in the last chapter and the ideologies and practices of rehabilitation depended on and helped to produce the "assumed prior, normal state" Stiker analyzes (122). And that now quite entrenched "assumed prior, normal state," in turn, depends on and helps to produce barriers to disability consciousness, identity, and culture. That the state "assumed prior" actually follows the production of bodies, pleasures, and barriers that could be comprehended as coming first has not kept the rehabilitation initiative from functioning efficiently for almost a century.[7]

Stiker insists that "a society cannot live with a consciousness of its deepest motivations, any more than you can speak a language while being conscious of all the grammatical rules to which you are subject" (169).

Tracing the cultural grammar of rehabilitation, Stiker repeatedly identifies identity and integration as two of its most constitutive components and outcomes; moreover, both would be understood, within this diagram, as fundamentally different components, outcomes, or—to stick with the cultural grammar metaphor—parts of speech, from degradation. The notion of identity Stiker has in mind is not concerned with the distinct or distinguishing features of an individual or group but with generic sameness. Thus, his notion of identity is not necessarily the notion put forward by identity movements of the late twentieth century, including disability movements, although—as will become clearer later, in my readings of *The Transformation* and *Gary in Your Pocket*—I think that it is impossible to shed entirely the problems with identity in Stiker's sense and that these problems continue to haunt later, identity-movement conceptions of identity. To separate the two notions (however contingently): two objects on a table could, in one sense, be said to "have an identity" if each has something absolutely unique about it; conversely, those objects could be said to "have identity" if and only if they are essentially the same. It is the latter meaning of identity that is most clearly operative in the cultural grammar of rehabilitation; the former, apparently, in the cultural grammar of identity movements. Hence, Stiker writes, "rehabilitation marks the appearance of a culture that attempts to complete the act of identification, of making identical. This act will cause the disabled to disappear and with them all that is lacking, in order to assimilate them, drown them, dissolve them in the greater and single social whole" (128) The practice of rehabilitation "succeeded in making alterity disappear" and founded a world where "identicalness reigns, at least a rough identity, a socially constructed identity, an identity of which citizens can be convinced" (131–132).

Integration attends such a conception of identity quite logically; indeed, once identity has been fixed, integration must follow: "[The disabled] are designated in order to be made to disappear, they are spoken in order to be silenced" (134). Stiker makes quite clear that what he means by integration is a place at the table, integration into society as it is. As with "identity," the ideology of rehabilitation can only comprehend "integration" according to its own terms: "Everyone agrees on this point: even when everything is set to brake the process, readjustment must be to society as society is presently constituted" (135). What we might call the rehabilitative contract ("everyone agrees"), then, essentially stipulates that, in return for integration, no complaints will be made, no suggestions for how the world, and not the disabled body or mind, might be molded differently. No complaints will be made even if the contract in effect relegates disabled people to the margins: "Society's wish is to make identical *without making equal*. In fact, measures and actions on behalf of impaired citizens tend to efface their difference but not establish them on the same level economically and socially" (150–151).

Most important, in order for the rehabilitative system to function efficiently, "disability cannot be a confrontational position" (137). Confrontation equals disintegration, in all its senses, as—in the previous chapter—*Why Can't Sharon Kowalski Come Home?* demonstrated. Because those initially making decisions about Kowalski's future perceived emergent queercrip subjectivities as absolutely confrontational, disintegration ensued: Kowalski could not go home with Karen Thompson; the physical and mental improvement Thompson (and many of her allies) clearly measured could not be admitted as truth by members of the nursing home administration or staff, or as evidence in court, so that these institutions essentially ceased functioning with any efficiency on Kowalski's behalf; and the signs of improvement Thompson and others measured would in fact be reread (or rewritten) as signs of deterioration. Rehab demands compliance or—more properly—makes noncompliance unthinkable. It is at this point that the two different senses of identity appear to be most opposed: sign here, the final stipulation of the rehabilitative contract seems to say, you will have identity (generic sameness without equality) not identity (disabled or LGBT distinctiveness or distinction).

Stiker describes his own account, because of "the need to understand what has underpinned rehabilitation" (185), as more theoretical than historical. David Serlin, in *Replaceable You: Engineering the Body in Postwar America*, provides a more properly historical account of rehabilitation. Focusing specifically on the United States, Serlin examines a selection of ways in which the body was literally reinvented or reengineered in the 1950s. For instance, Serlin considers, in one of his case studies, Henry Dreyfuss's work with the Veterans Administration to construct model prosthetic limbs (50–56). The Dreyfuss arm or hand was made of stainless steel and ended in a functional split hook. Serlin links this sleek, "undeniably *moderne*" prosthesis, "a product of the design-conscious mid-1950s," to contemporaneous crises surrounding masculinity and labor: the streamlined Dreyfuss hand "offered corporate bureaucrats a vision of a white-collar hand for the newly emerging white-collar world that would come to dominate the workscape of American cities" (54–55). Serlin calls this race for a prosthesis appropriate to new masculinities and seemingly ameliorative of the crises effected in labor (by declining numbers of secure jobs in industry and manufacturing and rising numbers of insecure service positions) "the other arms race" of the 1950s (54). The training associated with rehabilitation earlier in the century, according to Serlin (training that largely attempted to integrate workers into an industrial labor force), was in some ways (and anxiously) supplemented or supplanted by the mid-century physical and social engineering associated with the Dreyfuss hand.

If rehabilitation prepared (or repaired) workers for productivity, Serlin suggests that additional imperatives (tied not only to production but also to consumption) were at least in part driving the engineers of mid-century: "The white-collar sophistication that Dreyfuss's design team attempted to impart through both product and marketing reflected not the contents of contemporary rehabilitation manuals but those of period magazines like *Playboy* and *Esquire*, whose advertisements regularly featured high-tech appliances or multifunctional Herman Miller furniture" (55). Neither Stiker and Serlin, however, nor the interwar emergence of rehabilitation and the post–World War II emphasis on design are as opposed as they might at first appear. Whether the social, cultural, and bodily processes at work go by the name of rehabilitation or engineering, degradation is what they are defined against. Serlin writes: "The Dreyfuss hand may have promised to restore anatomical function and neutralize emasculation," just as post–World War I rehabilitation movements promised, "but perhaps it could also confer self-esteem and cultural capital" (55). Social engineering, in other words, promised not the low esteem or disrepute of degradation but a rehabilitated self-confidence, not the undesirability or devaluation of degradation but a restored marketability.

Stiker's more theoretical account is concerned with excavating a rehabilitative logic that was entrenched or sedimented throughout the twentieth century. Despite (or rather because of) Serlin's careful attentiveness to the historical specificity of the Dreyfuss hand and other mid-century attempts to rebuild the body, the sedimentation of that logic is apparent in *Replaceable You* (and, in fact, Serlin notes that his case studies are "saturated by the discourse of physical rehabilitation" [12]). Even on the issues of visibility or invisibility, where their accounts might be said to differ most obviously, Stiker and Serlin are largely in accord with each other. Stiker claims that rehabilitation made disability disappear, completing the act of identification, of making identical. Serlin's 1950s engineering arguably and conversely makes disability appear, in that the Dreyfuss hand and other technologies were not out of sight but on display, spectacularly resolving crises that both able-bodied and disabled people were experiencing. Identity as generic sameness, however, grounds both accounts, whether the specific issue is the integration of disabled workers into (able-bodied) productivity or the integration of able-bodied/disabled consumers into a new and uncertain economy. Serlin's conclusion, in particular, strikes me as of a piece with Stiker's critique of rehabilitation, even down to the ways in which a world war sets the scene for the next chapter in the history of generic sameness: "At the end of the war, an amputated arm or leg may have provoked associations between anatomical dysfunction and a lack of reliability, sturdiness, fortitude, or commitment. But by the 1950s, the utterly functionalist, aesthetically integrated, and mass-produced Dreyfuss hand offered a new kind of social prestige as well as a new model of masculine labor" (55–56).

People of color, from one perspective, were not the ideal subjects for hegemonic processes of either twentieth-century rehabilitation or social engineering. Black soldiers returning from World War I, for instance, found themselves facing ongoing segregation rather than the integration anxiously imposed on other *mutilés de guerre*, and the Dreyfuss hand's mid-century resolution of the crises facing a shifting work force would seem to be, first and foremost, a resolution of crises facing a white male workforce that needed to be integrated quickly into a corporate service economy.[8] This does not mean, however (by any means), that people of color were not subject to discourses of rehabilitation—the ideological saturation that Serlin conjures up, like any saturation, permeated everywhere. In fact, the perceived failures of the black family or of black communities more generally proved very useful to rehabilitation initiatives and helped to entrench those discourses. From another perspective, in other words, people of color were precisely the ideal subjects for hegemonic processes of rehabilitation. During the era when ideologies of rehabilitation coalesced, segregation and economic injustice for African Americans, according to Roderick A. Ferguson, were unlikely to be understood, by sociologists or the culture at large, as systemic inequities and more likely to be understood as signs that nonnormativity and pathology were somehow endemic to African American family life. Integration into the peculiar disciplines of twentieth-century liberal capitalism entailed diagnosing that pathology and, if possible, rehabilitating the subject. Indeed, the title of Ferguson's study, *Aberrations in Black*, attests to the pride of place held by African Americans, in particular, in rehabilitative logics; after all (and again), the assumed prior, normal state absolutely requires the aberration.[9]

Into the Closet and off the Streets: The Transformation

Near the end of his account of rehabilitation (originally published in 1982 but revised, updated, and republished in 1997), Stiker tentatively considers whether the model he puts forward "is now perhaps in retreat, confronted with the questions posed by multiple disability, diseases of the genome, AIDS" (189). In contrast to the inclusion or making identical of rehabilitation, the AIDS crisis in particular seemed to depend on exclusion and difference; especially during the 1980s, people with HIV/AIDS were regularly marked as absolutely different, or seen as marked by absolute difference, and were excluded from schools, religious institutions, hospitals, public transportation, the "general population," and even—almost—from the Americans with Disabilities Act (ADA).[10] At the same time, as new social movements took identity into their own hands, fractures could be traced in the consensus that making identical was always and everywhere desirable. Identity and integration, in the classical rehabilitative sense, were perhaps in retreat. Yet Serlin, in particular, insists on the ongoing power of the world that rehabilitation and engineering wrought: "Perhaps we underestimate the capacity of ideology to unravel and, under conditions of its own choosing, to reconstitute itself in complex ways that often exceed our abilities of explanation" (20). Stiker, too, even as he ponders whether his analysis has contemporary relevance, concludes that "for all that, the force of what came into play as a consequence of work accidents, war injuries, the generalization of social security . . .—none of all this can be whisked away, as if we were starting again at zero" (189). In this section, even as I turn to a very different context where the past supposedly *can* be washed away (by the blood of Jesus Christ), I concur with Serlin's and Stiker's implication that a rehabilitative logic continues to govern, in complex ways, who we can be.

The Transformation opens with Terry, the director of the Dallas-based ministry intent on converting Ricardo and others, introducing Ricardo to viewers. "Let's talk about Ricardo," Terry says twice before pulling out a photo album that includes classic before and after shots. Directing Aikin and Aparicio's camera to zoom in on the two shots, Terry points from one photograph to the other and lays out the terms of Ricardo's transformation:

> First of all—uh, you can probably focus on this—let's find Ricardo in here, so that *everybody's* on the same page; how's that sound? This is Ricardo. When I met Ricardo, he was Sara. He was the gang leader, the mentor, of *all* the drag queens out there. He got most of 'em into drag, into crack, showed 'em how to work the streets and everything else. This was him shortly after he came off the streets. The thing that makes him unusual is that he is *enormously* charismatic. He attracts people, he has power, he has presence, he has a personality—uh, as they say he could sell tennis shoes to paraplegics, that kind of personality—but there was something missing. And what was missing is that he never knew what it was to be a man.

With these words (Terry's assertion of what Ricardo supposedly never knew following the insistent and repetitive articulation of the masculine pronoun), the screen fades to black and the film's title—*The Transformation*—appears onscreen.

Terry's voice continues as the scene opens once again on a different kind of before and after sequence; the before and after shots that precede the film's title, in other words, are matched by a before and after sequence that follows it. In the "before" half of the sequence, it is a cold day in New York, and after panoramic perspective shots and a caption locate viewers in the Salt Mines of 1989 (the camera first focuses on the smoke-stacks next to the Salt Mines and then on the debris-filled area itself), a single figure emerges from one of several large bins. She is soon joined by several others, warming themselves around a fire, laughing, and putting on make-up.

Terry's voiceover, as this scene commences, ensures that several visual and narrative associations are in place at the outset. There are, of course, two narratives at work here—the Christian ministry's story of transgression and salvation and the filmmakers' story of Sara/Ricardo's transformation. The latter story, it seems to me, is at least in part intended to be a critical commentary on the former, but that critical commentary is not didactic, and throughout *The Transformation*, the evangelicals' perspectives and practices are thoroughly (and I think fairly) represented. What is most striking about the opening of the film, however, is how much both stories—regardless of whether one is a critical commentary on the other—share the set of associations established at the outset. In the first half of the before and after sequence, the streets of New York are represented by the Salt Mines, and viewers learn to associate with those streets homelessness, poverty, debris, decay, and lack of warmth. Also out in the open here are racial, linguistic, and national diversity, as well as bodies and genders that can be read, in several senses, as "out of place." In Talmadge Wright's study of inner-city homelessness, to be out of place entails "risking inspection by others, having one's identity defined by others as suspect, as 'deviant,' or 'criminal,' or as just 'sick.' Homeless bodies, poor bodies, visible to passersby, visible to the streets, are open to the public's gaze, to the gaze of authority" (1). Certainly, the two competing stories in *The Transformation* in the end differ as to whether the gender transgression made visible in the film is to be tolerated or targeted for transformation, but both nonetheless rely on an authoritative gaze and, interestingly enough, at least according to the logic of this opening scene, each concurs, on some level, that gender transgression an displacement go hand in hand.

The film establishes a few other associations with the streets of New York. Although it is not yet clear in the opening scene, the film (and both stories) will also ultimately associate HIV/AIDS, drug addiction, and other disabilities with the streets. Community is clearly represented at the outset, but it is community that—in what is legible as its degradation—troubles both stories. Finally, Sara (as Sara) is present in the opening, which ends with members of the Christian ministry—who, as Terry's voiceover explains, had a photography studio a few blocks away from the Salt Mines—descending on this community in hopes of rescuing its members. Terry explains that *48 Hours* had done a piece on "the salt mine kids" (forging yet another association with the streets, this time with adolescence or juvenility), and he and his partners decided to take them food and see if they needed help. The group in the Salt Mines was initially "hostile," but of the group of thirty or forty, Terry explains that fourteen have "made the change" and come off the streets. Before the "after" half of the sequence begins, Sara herself is interviewed, and explains (in Spanish with English subtitles) that she came to the United States from Cuba and couldn't wait to get here. After arriving in this country, however, she regretted her decision because, as she explains, in America, "if you have no money, you are nothing."

The after half of the sequence opens on a domestic interior in Dallas and represents Ricardo (as Ricardo) praying with a circle of other Christians. Although he is dressed in a flowery shirt and although earrings are visible, his hair is short and black (a decided contrast to Sara's long, blonde hair), and his appearance is supposed to signify conventional masculinity. The group holds hands as it prays, and Ricardo is positioned between Betty (later identified as his wife) and Jim (identified in the next scene as one who, along with his wife Robby, took Ricardo into his home and "discipled" him when Ricardo began his transformation). The group's prayer, however, even more than the setting, underscores the change that has taken place and the contrasts with what has come before. Ricardo is heard first, now speaking in English, thanking Jesus Christ for everything he has done. "Thank you for everything, Lord," Ricardo says. "Thank you for Betty; thank you for a lot of people who have been around me—all these people that love me, Lord. Thank you for your help financially; everything, Lord." A woman's voice is heard over Ricardo's at this point, interjecting "thank you Lord, hallelujah, amen." As similar interjections continue in the background, Jim begins his own prayer on Ricardo's behalf:

> Father, we just thank you for the *change* in Ricardo and in his life. Father, we thank you that you have brought him from such a, from such a deep and a dark hole, Lord, but that you have lifted him out of that place. Father, you have set him up, Lord. You have *stuck* him in the devil's face and you have said, "Look, at what I can do. . . ." We see the transformation taking place even now, Lord, and we thank you for that transformation in Ricardo's life and in his heart.

The group's prayer attests not only to their sincere belief in a heavenly father but also to their conviction that he has (over)seen Ricardo's transformation and declared that it is good.

If Sara was out of place, or lost, Ricardo—through the Lord's amazing grace—has been found, or located. His new location is associated with domesticity, heterosexual marriage, and religious, linguistic, and (most important) gender conformity. Despite the fact that viewers have only seen Sara in an open, and rather well-lit, environment, her world is described as "a deep and a dark hole," and despite the fact that viewers at this point have only seen Ricardo in a rather dim interior, his world calls forth a language of openness and expansion. Turning the outside in and the inside out, the Lord apparently associates Sara's life on the streets with a dangerous and feminized interiority and Ricardo's domesticity (which brings him out, sets him up, and sticks him in the devil's face) with emergence, penetration, and freedom. Ricardo, for his part, associates his new life with community and financial security. Sara's thesis is in some ways borne out in this scene: if in America, without money, on the streets, you are nothing, then with money, off the streets, you are something. Or, at least, you *have* something: although community seems to exist in the Salt Mines, judging by his prayer, it is only in Dallas that Ricardo feels he has people around him who love him. He also has a home, a wife, and health care.

It is tempting to read the final possession as the only one that really matters. As José Esteban Muñoz points out: "It is not difficult to understand why Ricardo has made this transformation. The chief reason is his health status. Ricardo was living with AIDS. His already tragically shortened life span would have been even more painful if he had continued to live on the street in poverty and malnourished" (163). Many of the things that Ricardo and others say in the film, moreover, discount his investment in most other aspects of his transformation. Betty makes clear in an interview that sex is not a major component of the couple's marriage, and Ricardo himself notes (in an interview again conducted in Spanish) that he enjoyed, in his past life, both the sex that he had with men and his own life as a woman. Even the final scene of *The Transformation*, when Ricardo is near death, emphasizes that he preferred his former existence as Sara: in Spanish, he explains that "I'm on my way out. That's the way AIDS works," but as the interview continues, after he affirms that he "repented" for his past life, he switches to English and says, "Even now that I have my wife and everything—if I had the choice I would choose to be a woman." Ricardo chooses to translate these final sentiments, as though to underscore their importance: his English assertion suggests that, even in the face of the compulsory translation he has been subjected to on multiple levels in Dallas, his desire to live as a woman remains. This final interview, then, along with several others throughout *The Transformation*, only confirms Muñoz's conclusion that the need for health care and a home—not *necessarily* a commitment to Fundamentalism, heterosexual marriage, and linguistic and gender conformity—motivated Ricardo's actions.

Ricardo's individual moments of noncompliance, however, do nothing to dislodge the terms of the contract he has essentially signed, a contract

Ricardo (right), Betty, and others at a Dallas
church service in *The Transformation*.

that in the end completely depends on a rehabilitative logic of identity, a
logic that, in turn, discounts difference and noncompliance, essentially
making them disappear. Certainly, in *The Transformation*, that contract
is inflected with the particular valences of late-twentieth-century Fundamentalist Christianity, but this conflation of rehabilitation and salvation
arguably only consummates a long-standing engagement. Especially in
the United States, twentieth-century Fundamentalism and dominant ideologies of rehabilitation have lived parallel lives. The Reverend Charles
Sheldon's 1897 novel *In His Steps, or What Would Jesus Do?* is only one
example, securing not only the secular but the spiritual link between productivity and generic sameness or lockstep conformity: blessings, financial success, and ultimately salvation come from walking like Jesus would
walk, talking like Jesus would talk.[11]

HIV/AIDS is not susceptible to rehabilitation in the strict sense of return or restoration of a former state or capacity. Perhaps the only classic
twentieth-century rehabilitation apparent in *The Transformation*, in fact,
is drug rehabilitation, since the drug use that Terry claims "most of 'em"
are "into" in the Salt Mines has ceased in Dallas, both for Ricardo and
Hugo, another member of the ministry (who had formerly lived on the
streets as Gina). Yet Stiker argues that, throughout the twentieth century,

"the great majority of people affected by the consequences of illness or accident adhere without hesitation to the idea of rehabilitation and, as a result, to that of the empirical normality of the social state of things (salaried industrial employment, living conditions, type of family, sexual norms, etc.)" (144). It may be impossible for the members of Terry's ministry to restore HIV-negative status, but they nonetheless secure—both in the sense of "making safe against adverse contingencies" (including the contingency of Ricardo's resistance) and "putting beyond hazard of losing or of not receiving"—a rehabilitative compliance that places Ricardo precisely on the path Stiker maps. Affected by the consequences of illness (and perhaps addiction), and in return for the treatment of his illness, Ricardo must consent to the "empirical normality" that others demand. Everyone involved in his transformation perceives that empirical normality both as something that preexisted Ricardo's transgression and as the natural outcome of his rehabilitation.

The compliance secured in the film is most obvious in Ricardo's living conditions, type of family, sexual behavior, and gender identity/presentation, but labor is in fact part of the bargain as well—even if it is not precisely Stiker's "industrial employment." At one point in the film, Terry sits down with Ricardo and Betty in another domestic interior and explains, in a patronizingly slow English, "You're going to be traveling with me, all over the United States, to tell people where you came from, to help us raise money for the [ministry's] buildings." Terry then produces the before and after shots of Sara and Ricardo—although the album now includes a final shot of Betty and Ricardo together—and explains that a brochure will be produced using the photographs as evidence (Terry pauses to ask Betty what "brochure" is in Spanish, but Ricardo assures him that he understands). "Now what's really important," Terry continues, "is that you have to really practice your English, okay? Because, see, I can tell 'em what you went through, but you went through it, you lived it." Ricardo's job, defined by Terry and the ministry, is to tell his unique story or testimony. Within a few months, Terry explains, the two will be on the road with this testimony almost every weekend.

The scene is a relatively minor one, and viewers of *The Transformation* never actually see Ricardo telling congregations his story. It is nonetheless an important scene for exposing, in a perhaps unexpected way, the degradation that attends Ricardo's rehabilitation. For Harry Braverman, in *Labor and Monopoly Capital: The Degradation of Work in the Twentieth Century*, the primary feature of capitalist degradation is a separation of conception and execution. Labor, in other words, has in Braverman's interpretation increasingly been segmented for more and more people over the last century so that what is conceived at one level and by one (ever-shrinking) group is executed—without input or challenge—at another level by others. For Braverman, this marks degradation in several senses: for the vast majority of workers, labor has been reduced in complexity, the actions they must carry out are generally repetitive and uninteresting, and they are permanently barred access to the locations where decisions are made and to the prestige that attends those locations. Despite Braverman's focus on factory and office labor, it is still true that—according to Braverman's terms—Ricardo's rehabilitation requires his degradation, regardless of the fact that narration of his (or anyone's) own story would seem to depend on autonomy and subjectivity.[12]

Sara's autonomy and subjectivity, in fact, helps to illuminate the degraded aspects of Ricardo's work and living conditions. Despite the undeniable harshness of the living conditions in the Salt Mines, dignity largely attends Sara's living situation, according to a broad reading of Braverman's terms: on the level of gender, sexual desire, community, behavior, and even (with some definite qualifications that I return to below) work, Sara conceived and put into motion who she would be. Which is not to deny that Sara experienced who she was as something that was in some ways nonindividual, bigger than herself, and innate or inherent— as something that preceded her life on the streets of New York. It is simply to say that conditions of community and freedom existed for Sara at least to the extent that dignity attended her status as a human being and was not an achievement or outcome of empirical normalcy, domesticity, marriage, or rehabilitation. Most important, she was not inhabiting and executing an identity conceived for her elsewhere by her patrons (or by the Lord). If traces of dignity are at all apparent in Sara's life and in the street communities represented in *The Transformation*, they are not what Michael Warner would identify as the traces of "that kind of dignity we might as well call bourgeois propriety." That kind of dignity, according to Warner, "is closely related to honor, and fundamentally an ethic of rank. It requires soap. (Real estate doesn't hurt, either.)" The other kind of dignity, significantly possible—it would seem—without real estate (or without a job like Ricardo's that will guarantee real estate for others), "is inherent in the human. You can't, in a way, not have it. At worst, others can simply fail to recognize your dignity" (*Trouble with Normal* 36).

Terry, Jim, Betty, and the others fail to recognize Sara's dignity. All those who participate in Ricardo's rehabilitation fail in this respect, including Ricardo at his most compliant (that is, Ricardo most of the time). Ricardo himself may actively and at times vocally desire (to be) Sara, but his rehabilitation depends on her degradation: aberrant, reduced in complexity, invisible even in the hypervisibility of the Christians' ubiquitous "before" shots, Sara is, to use her own terms, essentially "nothing."

The fact that, while attempting to document fairly the ideas and actions of the evangelicals, Aikin and Aparicio also attempt to capture something of Sara's dignity—and literally, through footage from *The Salt Mines*, allow her to speak in *The Transformation*—attests to the competing agenda of their film. As documentary filmmakers, however, Aikin and Aparicio commit to a particular filmmaking ethos and, through that ethos, set themselves the nearly impossible task of valuing *both* Sara and Ricardo (this is a nearly impossible task, of course, given the ways in which the rehabilitation and identity of one depends on the degradation and silencing of the other). Their film must attempt to comprehend both Ricardo and Sara, however, if—as Aikin herself suggested in an interview when *The Transformation* aired as part of PBS's *P.O.V.* series—the film is to succeed at opening up "some kind of discussion or thought about what it means to be tolerant, what it means to accept others as they are, what it means to be compassionate with other people, without imposing our views on them." According to Aikin, such tolerance "is one of the most beautiful values of our culture, [even though] it is buried in the sand in so many instances." It is of course possible to read Aikin's points as specifically critical of the imposing Christian ministry, but—in an attempt to realize the tolerance the film professes—she studiously avoids directly chastising them (or Ricardo).

Ironically, Aikin's comments were initially broadcast, quite literally, at the limits of tolerance; immediately following the *P.O.V.* interview, PBS dutifully informed viewers that some might find the material to follow "offensive." Still, even if and as PBS effectively calls into being a population unable to tolerate what they are about to see, Aikin and Aparicio, through *The Transformation* itself, are partially successful in achieving their goal of tolerance. The main strategy they use for reaching this goal is the inclusion of other members of the community of the Salt Mines; other, competing stories speak, autonomously and without commentary, alongside the story of Sara/Ricardo. Any criticism of "others as they are" thus never comes directly but only on the level of reception or decoding, as viewers make their own sense of the different choices members of the community have made.

The very title of the film could theoretically apply to at least one figure whose story is included and represented as essentially the opposite of Ricardo's. The figure in question—Jovanna—had also appeared in *The Salt Mines* and, at one point, the filmmakers include clips of her from 1989, bundled up in front of a fire outside, smiling, and speaking directly to the camera (in English):

> I don't have no American dream. My dream is my dream. It is not an American dream. And I feel very strongly about that. My dream is my dream and it's not American. And my dream . . . what is my dream? To one day have a job and a home that I can go to, to be looked and to be treated like a regular human being. That simple. It's not too much to ask for, is it?

In *The Transformation*, Jovanna is living a very different life. Jovanna's mother and her biological sister Sandra have found the means to help Jovanna, and she is living as part of a vibrant, housed, and happy family life. Sandra explains (in Spanish) that once Jovanna realized the family needed her—particularly Jovanna's brother (who, according to Sandra, has "a drinking problem") and her nieces—she was able to transition off the streets for good. Jovanna's room, in *The Transformation*, is one she shares with her mother and, without exception, the film represents the family, and the community in which they are located, as embracing Jovanna. In fact, the after sequence that follows Jovanna's 1989 description of her dream shows her entering a crowded apartment where salsa music is playing and a Halloween party is in progress. Jovanna, as Jane Russell, wears a gorgeous purple gown and her sister, as Marilyn Monroe, wears a white dress and blonde wig. "Oh, you look beautiful, Jovanna," their hostess says as they enter. At the Halloween party, Jovanna and Sandra may be just two little girls from Little Rock, but Jovanna is also happily a woman in all other aspects of her life. Sandra has even acquiesced to Jovanna's request that she be buried as a woman.

Jovanna has apparently achieved her dream and (also apparently) without compromise: nothing about her story in *The Transformation*, in particular, requires her to relinquish the political or proto-political perspective that was nurtured in the Salt Mines and that leads her to pointedly critique the ways in which "the American Dream" requires what

Wright calls "refuse spaces": "spaces in which one is refused—refused services, refused dignity, refused human rights, refused the basics of food, clothing, and shelter, and refused medical care" (106). The fact that Jovanna feels "very strongly" that her dream is not American suggests that she recognizes the mythical American Dream's contingency: the American Dream is contigent upon refuse spaces; it produces—or, in several senses, develops—such spaces. Those, in turn, "who live in such spaces, such as the homeless, are then treated by association as equivalent to human 'refuse'" (T. Wright 107). Used to being treated like human refuse, Jovanna feels very strongly that other dreams are needed. By underscoring—even as it is realized—that Jovanna's dream is not American, *The Transformation* effectively sustains her earlier critique.

No longer out of place, Jovanna is also no longer subject to the peculiar and degrading disciplines attending those who inhabit refuse space, those who have been cast as human refuse. Two scenes exemplify the transformation she has experienced in this sense. In the first, Terry, Ricardo, and Hugo attempt to find Jovanna in New York, unaware that she is living with her mother and sister. Speaking to the camera on a busy street, Terry explains that this is "his" (that is, Jovanna's) corner. Already implicitly qualifying, however (through his patronizing and insistent use of the masculine pronoun), the question of whether Jovanna and the others living on the streets have a right to possess anything, Terry proceeds to go further and to make stunningly literal his disciplinary, rehabilitative authority. First, he confers with a police officer who, without surprise or outrage, listens patiently to Terry's story of being a minister who works with "drag queens, transvestites, and transsexuals, getting them out of the city, getting them out of the lifestyle." Second, and more explicitly, he peppers the area with "WANTED" signs. The signs seeking Jovanna's capture faithfully repeat all the elements commonly associated with a classic poster in this genre, with the criminal's picture below the word "WANTED," printed boldly across the top, and instructions for what to do once she's apprehended across the bottom. Or he, as the case may be: these signs specifically seek "'Jovanna' Hector Lopez"; the scare quotes, drawing on yet another convention of the genre, effectively render "Jovanna" little more than an alias. Signs of another reality altogether, these posters point to Hector Lopez. And the desire for Hector is backed up with a fifty-dollar reward, which—as Terry explains—is "a lot . . . on this street." The inhabitants of this space, "refused services, refused digity, refused human rights," will find it hard to refuse, in Terry's estimation, fifty dollars.

Jovanna, however, is no longer on the streets and is thus more equipped to resist Terry's rehabilitative agenda—an agenda that has completely incorporated Ricardo, who helps Terry tape the "WANTED" signs to street poles. On the street, Terry can repeatedly insist that he has "a place" for Hector in Dallas and—since everyone seems to agree that the Salt Mines are clearly no place and that "a place" is better than no place—can expect that he will encounter no authoritative resistance to his plan (indeed, he can expect the authorities to facilitate his plan). In the scene that follows, however, in Jovanna's home, Terry's authority is, as it were, checked at the door. "We have twenty-seven people who pray for you every day," Terry says in the slow and emphatic English he uses with those who have lived in the Salt Mines, but he fails to gain a hearing: Jovanna is more interested in showing her breast implants to Ricardo and Hugo and in conveying to Hugo how shocked she is that his implants have been removed ("oh, Gina!" Jovanna says with a look of disbelief on her face). Terry—attempting to regain control of the conversation—insists that the implants are "dangerous" and that Hugo could have gotten an infection from them. While infection is certainly possible if and when a breast implant ruptures (Terry is not particularly teaching Jovanna anything she doesn't already know), Terry's deployment of "danger" is more in the interests of a much more expansive ideological consolidation: danger attends gender out of place and is, in fact, endemic to transgender street communities. Danger needs to be contained; the "place in Dallas" is the antidote to such danger. *The Transformation*, however, strategically (and effectively) offers Jovanna's *own* place as an alternative to Terry's special, rehabilitative place in Dallas.

Jovanna's place also suggests that Sara could have been located as Sara; in the larger project of the film, Jovanna's story is offered as an example of "what it means to accept others as they are, what it means to be compassionate with other people, without imposing our views on them." As I suggested, however, Aikin and Aparicio's filmic ethos, stressing tolerance, is ultimately only partially successful. Success here is partial both in the sense of being incomplete and in the sense of tolerating some figures more than others. If, as Jacques Derrida reminds us, tolerance has problematic "biological, genetic, or organicist connotations," at some point a "quasi-organic and unpreventable—in short, a natural—phenomenon of rejection can be expected" (qtd. in Borradori 128). The film, in a sense, stages such a rejection, despite—or, as Derrida would have it, through—its "tolerance." Some concluding thoughts on that rejection should effectively call back questions about degradation that I will engage more thoroughly, in relation to Gary Fisher, in the next section.

The figure whom both the *The Transformation* and an ethos of tolerance ultimately fail to encompass is named Gigi.[13] The film's inability to locate Gigi is in some ways symptomatic of an inability to locate and value queer and crip community on the streets or in the Salt Mines. Jovanna's story can unquestionably serve as an alternative to Ricardo's—offering identity as distinctiveness as an answer to identity as generic sameness—but it cannot easily (without trouble) comprehend the spaces where identity perhaps disintegrates, and where human beings *nonetheless* shape generative and resistant ways of being. Essentially, the film (like most texts, including my own) cannot wholly comprehend impossible spaces. If agency is part and parcel of identity and integration (as it is for both Ricardo and Jovanna), then—within the frame or narrative structure of the film—it is difficult to access or represent traces of agency, or agency effects, tied to spaces of disintegration.

Gigi appears in two key scenes in the film, the first mediated by video. Aikin and Aparicio film Gigi and her friend (or lover) Edwin sitting on railway tracks in New York; the filmmakers then deliver Gigi's message to Ricardo in Texas. The video functions like a Derridean postcard, in several senses: it reaches someone different from its intended recipient (Gigi's message, to Sara, essentially does not reach her, but Ricardo); it is officially a private message (in Spanish) from Gigi to her long-lost "sister," but is (through the magic of *The Transformation*) out in the open, for anyone to read (translated into English, via the filmmakers' captions); and it puts into play messages that challenge the truth-telling power of the film's other stories (not only Ricardo's rehabilitation but its counterpart, Jovanna's reincorporation or reintegration into her family and community of origin).

"Who is writing?" Derrida asks. "To whom? And to send, to destine, to dispatch what? To what address?" (*Post Card* 5). Gigi, too, begins her videogram with a question, one that would seem at least to answer the question "to whom?" were it not for the fact that the question of Sara's existence both precedes and permeates the message:

> What can I say, Sara? I don't know. . . . But, anyway, I'd like to see you and hug you. I haven't forgotten you. You were my special friend. I'm glad you've changed but I've missed you a lot. Don't forget me, because I carry you always in my heart. . . . Edwin also sends his love—he does-

n't talk anymore. Look at him! He's really fat! [Edwin, who is not particularly fat, smiles and Gigi laughs.] We never forget you, our little sister—you're still my sister. To hell with that man business . . . to me you're always a woman!

The video postcard complete, the camera follows Gigi and Edwin as they walk, arm-in-arm, down the tracks.

Before Aikin and Aparicio film Gigi's message, they talk to her and show her pictures of Ricardo's wedding ("What a killer you are, Sara!" Gigi says when she sees Ricardo in his tuxedo). They also ask her, explicitly, if she is okay living on the streets. For better or worse, she nods yes, even if the weight of what follows partially complicates her affirmation: "I've lived in the street for seven years. Seven winters, seven falls, seven summers, seven springs. And I'm still alive and that's all that matters." Gigi also expresses in this interview an understanding of the choices Ricardo made; in the only reference to her friend as "he," Gigi explains that when he found out he was HIV-positive, the church and the transformation were Ricardo's only options. He had to do what he did because living and dying on the streets would have been "impossible."

It is not entirely true, however, that being alive (in a literal, biological sense) is all that matters to Gigi: her transgender dignity and her love for Edwin also matter. The only other scene that includes her underscores both these points. The scene—in which Terry, Ricardo, and Hugo encounter Gigi on a New York street at night and attempt to convince her to come to Dallas—also underscores that disability is best left to the streets. A rehabilitation that makes disability disappear (or that promises to do so) is apparently preferable to the degradation of living with disability out in the open. Significantly, whether or not he conceived of it on his own, it is Ricardo who delivers that implicit thesis. When Gigi says to him, "What am I going to do with Edwin?" Ricardo answers, without a moment's hesitation or reflection: "Leave him, Gigi. Start a new life. You're killing yourself." In the videogram, according to Gigi (since Edwin himself "doesn't talk anymore"), a smiling Edwin had sent Sara his love and was included in the "we" that could "never forget" her ("to forget"—*olvidar*—conveying here "to treat with inattention" and "to disregard intentionally"). Ricardo (rehabilitated, domesticated, housed), in direct contrast to these sentiments from the street, delivers—in regards to this disabled figure who doesn't speak but who can never forget him—the most inhospitable lines of the film: "Leave him, Gigi."

The scene is a difficult one, literally (for the participants) and cinematically. Gigi's final audible (and translated and captioned) words in *The Transformation* are "Oh God! I need a cigarette . . . do you have a cigarette?" Ricardo, who has already been represented as apparently free from addiction of any kind, ignores both the question and Gigi's explicit acknowledgment of what she needs. Worried, as he says, about what might happen to her, Ricardo redoubles his efforts to convince Gigi, essentially, that he knows better what she needs. Though Gigi continues to speak, the camera pulls back and her words are no longer intelligible. Like Edwin, she doesn't talk anymore in the film; *The Transformation* does not (and cannot, according to the logic of tolerance) resolve her story as it does the stories of Ricardo and Jovanna.

When Gigi informs Ricardo, before they (and the camera) pull away from Terry and Hugo, that he knows exactly why Gigi will not leave the street (that is, she refuses to change or to read her gendered existence in the pathologizing way the Christians require), the intimacy between the two, as well as a shared history of transgender dignity, is evident. I do not want to idealize Gigi's life, however, and will emphasize that the film represents Ricardo's concern for her safety as genuine. Indeed, to return to the question of work that I mentioned earlier in relation to Sara, Ricardo exhibits a clear sense that Gigi's work conditions are not only potentially beyond her control but potentially lethal: "You can get killed by any trick who finds out you're a man. Most of the drag queens we used to know are dead."

Like Terry telling Jovanna about the dangers of breast implants, Ricardo is not telling Gigi anything she doesn't already know, but it is easier to read Ricardo's concern for his sister as authentic. Ricardo's genuine concern for Gigi as an individual, however, cannot be divorced in this scene from the ways in which discourses of safety function ideologically, as part of what Wright calls "authoritative strategies":

> Authoritative strategies are employed to establish a place as "proper," as a place within which understandable and controllable things will happen. A "proper" place is a place where social events occur that are understandable to authoritative decision makers. Conversely, to be "out of control" or "out of place" is to not be in a "proper" place. As bodies considered "out of place" by housed society, the homeless are subject to the continual gaze of authority to ensure that their actions will not violate "proper" social boundaries. (181)

If indeed Ricardo is concerned about Gigi in this scene (as I believe he is), Ricardo's rehabilitation has guaranteed that such concern can only be articulated through authoritative strategies. Ricardo's statement—"you can get killed by any trick who finds out you're a man"—is seductive because it is reasonable; indeed, Gigi *could* get killed by any trick who finds out she is biologically male. Seduced by reason, however, we could lose sight of how thoroughly nonuniversal and bourgeois (this) rationality is, contingent on unspoken premises such as "the world is properly divided into two genders," "Gigi is a man," and "violence is an understandable or logical outcome when sex or gender are discovered out of place." Gigi concurs (by running her finger over her throat) that she could be killed but apparently manages to disregard all the unspoken premises that for Ricardo attend the possibility of danger. Ricardo, however, can no longer disregard such premises, as his subjectivity depends on them. In the face of these ideological and physical pressures, Sara might have understood Gigi's need for a cigarette (or a hit), but Ricardo cannot.

To position Gigi's resistance, her love for Edwin, and her refusal to leave the streets as having value is not to romanticize her life or to suggest that being homeless—or homeless and disabled—is preferable to having food, shelter, and health care. It is, rather, to keep alive (in ways *The Transformation* itself does not) Gigi's critique of the degradation proferred by rehabilitative and bourgeois authorities—those who would, essentially, see Gigi (and Edwin and Sara and the community of the Salt Mines) dead already. Similarly, to imply that Jovanna's story, even as it is offered as an alternative to Ricardo's, partakes of comparable strategies of identity and integration in order to put forward a message of tolerance, is not to discount the urgency of that message. It is only to suggest that probing or testing the limits of rehabilitation and compliance may at times be as vital as, or more vital than, acquiescing to them.

Submissive and Noncompliant: The Paradox of Gary Fisher

The rehabilitation of Gary Fisher has perhaps already begun, if—before I officially begin this section—I, like Sedgwick, present you with "other contexts for reading *Gary in Your Pocket*":

> The received wisdom, in straight culture, is that all of its different norms line up, that one is synonymous with the others. . . . If you deviate at any

point from this program, you do so at your own cost. And one of the things straight culture hates most is any sign that the different parts of the package might be recombined in an infinite number of ways. But experience shows that this is just what tends to happen. If heterosexuality requires the entire sequence, then it is very fragile. No wonder it needs so much terror to induce compliance. (Warner, *Trouble with Normal* 37–38)

Even in his resistance, Fisher produced nothing like the independent, manly blackness that we see displayed in figures like [Frederick] Douglass. The gesture that Fisher illustrates—the black man with three, possibly four, fingers up his ass, the black man caught in an act of self-pleasuring (or self-degradation depending on one's point of view), the black man taking direction from the obviously self-deluded white—is hardly designed to rearticulate our most precious models of black subjectivity. (Reid-Pharr 141)

Michael Warner and Robert F. Reid-Pharr are, of course, queer public intellectuals; in good faith, it is important to underscore that they consistently attempt to write noncompliance with heteronormativity, and affirmation of other ways of being, into existence. One paradox facing (and shaping) the queer public intellectual, however, is that she or he so often speaks or writes about challenges to authoritative systems like heteronormativity from authorized, and heteronormative, spaces (often, but by no means always, the small space for authoritative queer speech that has been forged, or granted, within the academy).[14] Queer in the broadest sense, Warner and Reid-Pharr ensure, or assist me in ensuring, that what Reid-Pharr calls "the shock of Gary Fisher" can still be registered (135). As authorities, they/we nonetheless inescapably mediate and (partially) rehabilitate him.

Approaching Fisher through "other contexts"—like framing him, editing him, placing him in your pocket—contains him in ways that restore him to a rationality and intelligibility that he, paradoxically, constantly questioned or probed. Conversely, however, for me to approach Fisher unmediated—perhaps beginning with his raw sentiments that "sperm is addictive for niggers, as addictive as crack for niggers who can't see beyond the white goo" and that he is "PROUD TO BE A NIGGER" (239)—would also imply that he is (this time directly) knowable or containable in some way (and this particular passage, and my re-presentation of it, is disturbing because, on some level, we—when the "n word" is used—think "we know what that means").[15] To put forward such an implication of knowability would be, to adapt Reid-Pharr, "obviously self-deluded" on my part.

To return (Fisher) to a conventional structure seems both safe and unsatisfying. Fisher's capacity as a writer to put a reader or critic in such an impossible position attests to his literary and philosophical mastery, although to attest to his mastery is not exactly to honor his own stated (and apparently deepest) desires. Despite these conundrums, and however unsatisfying it may be, the structure of this section is as follows: beginning at the end (of Fisher's life and of the journal selections Sedgwick has included in *Gary in Your Pocket*), I first consider the crip critiques that are legible in regard to rehabilitation proper in Fisher's writing (that is, in regard to the therapeutic treatment he undergoes at various stages in the progression of HIV disease). Second, building on Reid-Pharr, I briefly weave these critiques into Fisher's sadomasochistic will to degradation, paying particular attention to what that will to degradation suggests about identity trouble more generally. Third, I return to *Tongues Untied*, considering how Fisher unsettles the revolutionary (or perhaps rehabilitative) agenda of Riggs's film. I conclude with some—hopefully generative—reflections on form and obsessive-compulsive disorder (OCD), not by any means to fix Fisher with an additional diagnosis but to affirm or validate his reflections on the limits of identity and identification. The traces of OCD discernable in what is potentially one of the most open-ended, uncontainable forms (the personal journal) illustrate well Fisher's work at and on the points where identity disintegrates. "I'm really going to have to burn this," Fisher writes at one point (143). Resisting the apparent compulsion to incinerate his words, Fisher still manages, paradoxically, to generate a text that is almost too hot to touch.[16]

Fisher is, arguably, not the best candidate for articulating disability critiques of rehabilitation, at least according to the dominant terms of a late-twentieth-century disability identity politics: he was not out and proud; he was, instead, extremely closeted about his HIV status until very close to the end. "Over many years," Sedgwick explains in her afterword to *Gary in Your Pocket*, Fisher "shared the knowledge with very few of even his close friends, until less than a year before his death when an acute health breakdown necessitated a long, frightening hospitalization" (275). Despite living in San Francisco and studying at Berkeley for most of his HIV-positive years, Fisher was not apparently incorporated into the

HIV/AIDS or disability community, even though it would be difficult to find locations in the United States with more vibrant or resistant communities organized around both identities, especially—in regard to HIV/AIDS—in the late 1980s and early 1990s.[17] At times, in fact, disability identification seems to consist, for Fisher, almost solely in what one could call his crip identification with Sedgwick: "It wasn't until after I was diagnosed with breast cancer in 1991 that we began to get real. . . . I remember describing to Gary what I'd experienced as the overwhelming trauma of half a year of chemotherapy-induced baldness," she writes (279, 281); he writes (to her) in turn, "I had a small battle with KS [Kaposi's sarcoma] recently. The kimo [*sic*] made me ill even at such low dosages. I can't imagine. . . . I guess I need to talk to you" (qtd. in Sedgwick, *Gary in Your Pocket* 279).

Fisher's connection to Sedgwick is nonetheless in some ways sufficient. If it takes at least two people to make a crip, there are certainly ways in which *Gary in Your Pocket* suggests that Fisher and Sedgwick school each other in the art of crip noncompliance: "Eve reminded me of something I'd told a doctor whose question seemed too specific for any patient . . . I told him: 'Doctor, I'm sorry, I'm not all here. Maybe it's a defense mechanism, I don't know, but part of me has gone away .' . . . Eve experienced the same defensive removal" (262). Sedgwick writes elsewhere about her connection to communities of gay men living with HIV/AIDS—communities that had, over the course of the 1980s and 1990s, learned to question rigorously medical and scientific authority (*Tendencies* 12–15). The passages in *Gary in Your Pocket* that weave together her experiences and Fisher's provide intimate, touching illustrations of that connection: "I love it when she says 'lots of love to you' into my machine. I should answer immediately"; "I'll need Eve's help buying hats" (265, 266).

Of course, I'm approaching in this section of my chapter a text that was edited by Sedgwick; given that *Gary in Your Pocket* was compiled after Fisher's death, Sedgwick had a key role in constructing Fisher, herself as a figure in Fisher's story, and the relationship between the two. Clearly, however, Fisher and Sedgwick were more than aware of the ways in which their relationship could be read in straightforward and hierarchized terms: teacher/student, editor/author, (white) patron/(black) writer; they discussed these issues before Fisher's death. Sedgwick writes: "Gary and I were both very conscious of a history of white patronage and patronization of African American writers, the tonalities of which neither of us had any wish to reproduce. Sexuality was a place where Gary was interested in dramatizing the historical violences and expropriations of racism; friendship, authorship, and publication, by contrast, were not" (285–286). By foregrounding the teacher/student, patron/author relationship, Sedgwick puts it under erasure, as does Fisher in many ways, even if (or as) his desire to please his former teacher is often apparent ("She's on my case too. It's time to get busy and I'm still putzing" [265]). I argue even further, however, that—at the limits of these overdetermined and hierarchized relationships—*Gary in Your Pocket* accesses alternative (crip) possibilities. Among those possibilities is the multifaceted and multiauthored critique of rehabilitation and will to degradation that the text/Fisher/Sedgwick puts forward.

There are many examples of this critique in the final journal entries included in *Gary in Your Pocket*. An entry dated June 17, 1993, however, provides a particularly good example of Fisher and Sedgwick's collective crip critique, even though Sedgwick is not mentioned in it. A woman who appears to be a social worker (but who might be simply a philanthropist-cum-social worker) comes into Fisher's hospital room. Fisher does not detail in this entry exactly what her role in the hospital is, but she seems to have some involvement in creating pleasant surroundings for hospitalized individuals. She begins to talk with Fisher about what he describes as "the rather awful impressionist print on the wall [that] looks like bad Seurat." The woman—who apparently purchased the print herself on a trip to Europe—"thought it would be relaxing." Fisher insists, point-blank, "It's not." Fisher does not, however, give the woman *herself* this sober, dismissive assessment; it is what he writes in his journal, along with the assertion that the print "detracts from the incredible view of the city that has sustained me for 3 weeks now" (267).

The *actual* exchange between the two, very different from the sentiments Fisher records in his journal, is significant enough to quote at length:

> The old woman went on to detail the obvious—a woman [in the print] is walking what looks like a goat, taking him to be tethered she thinks. "Many patients in this room," she says, "have found this very relaxing." I'm sure she meant the picture in toto and not just walking the goat. She moved along so quickly in her remarks that I wasn't sure I was supposed to speak but I finally commented that I liked the hedge and the grass because they remind me of home. They do not. Indeed the way they ob-

scure the houses of the street beyond them has bothered me (I don't believe she ever looked at me, not even during her mundane greeting—the
whole of it was so rote as to be completely unmemorable and worth
writing about only as a trophy to the hollowness of so much effort, action, and concern, care—many, if not all, things medical! *and* so many of
the caretakers. Hollow!)—she then said: "I thank you for sharing that
with me," and then she left. I said thank you with a stinging sincerity, I
hope. Were those last words of hers dismissal or did she intend to pile
my observation on top of the others who'd said, collectively at least, the
picture relaxed them? (267–268)

Like Ralph Ellison's Invisible Man, Fisher overcomes the subject of this
entry with yeses, undermines her with grins, and agrees her to death and
destruction. In what is traceable, by the end, as a collective—if always
spectral—refusal by "many patients" to give the woman the relaxation
and sincerity that she needs and that the therapeutic, rehabilitative relationship requires (a collective refusal that, of course, appears to be ac-
quiescence), Fisher quickly learns his part here, even if it is not immediately clear what the script would have him saying or doing. Once he
learns his predictable part, Fisher dutifully plays it, but through his lie
registers a victory against "all things medical" and rehabilitative, and
against the many sincere caretakers who need him to be a compliant
patient.

The spirit presiding over this scene, however, is not so much Ralph
Ellison as Audre Lorde. In a famous scene in Lorde's *Cancer Journals*, a
well-meaning representative from the organization Reach for Recovery
comes into Lorde's hospital room following her mastectomy. She offers
Lorde "a soft sleep-bra and a wad of lambswool pressed into a pale
pink breast shaped pad." "Her message," Lorde notes, "was, you are
just as good as you were before because you can look exactly the same"
(42). Later, it becomes clear that Reach for Recovery expects this identity as generic sameness from all the women accessing their services;
Lorde is told when she goes to their offices that if she does not wear a
prosthesis it is "bad for the morale" of patients and of the organization
(59). In contrast to Fisher, Lorde does not directly lie and refuses the
padded bra with the pale pink pad, but like Fisher, she does confide
some sentiments not to the social worker but to her journal: "I looked
away, thinking, 'I wonder if there are any black lesbian feminists in
Reach for Recovery'" (42).

Whether or not Fisher himself is directly drafting what Henry Louis Gates Jr. might call (as he does in regard to the relationship, across time and space, between Alice Walker and Zora Neale Hurston) one of "the most loving revision[s] . . . we have seen in the tradition" (255), it seems to me that Sedgwick—through her inclusion of this particular episode, from "the thousands of pages of notebooks and journals that Gary kept" (287)—is. Which is not to suggest that Fisher's echo of Lorde is unintentional: his knowledge as a teacher and student of African American literature certainly makes such a connection plausible.[18] But what is even more clear is that, like many women with breast cancer, Sedgwick turns to *The Cancer Journals* for sustenance. In the year of Fisher's death (1993), in fact, she described the book as "an immensely important account of dealing with breast cancer in the context of feminist, antiracist, and lesbian activism" (*Tendencies* 13). I feel as confident, in fact, that Sedgwick intentionally writes Fisher's anecdote into a tradition that incorporates Lorde as Sedgwick herself feels confident that Henry James intentionally writes about anal pleasures. Of course, Sedgwick's defiant affirmation of intentionality in regard to James and anality is in the queer interests of what she terms "an audience desired" ("Inside Henry James" 138). The crip noncompliance that Fisher and Sedgwick author here, especially through the invocation of others who disidentified with their rehabilitation, likewise calls forth an audience desired. That audience is not desired—as with Fisher's and Lorde's social workers—for its docility or its boosterism in regard to "morale" but rather for its playfulness, trickery, and creativity. Lorde identifies the collective "love of women" ("the sweet smell of their breath and laughter and voices calling y name") as the force that sustains her through *The Cancer Journals* (39). The love of Sedgwick and a host of imagined others whose bodies, minds, and laughter are not ultimately contained or stilled by rehabilitative initiatives—the love of crips, in other words—sustains Fisher through his own hospital journals.

Even the entries that can most be interpreted through the lens of compliance contain its opposite and conjure up another audience, sometimes—to shift the meanings of audience—another kind of audience with the health care practitioner in question. In an entry dated May 19, 1993, and specifically composed as a letter to Sedgwick, Fisher—after saying that he hates his doctor for "my crazy symptoms"—suggests alternatively that he has "accumulated so much love and respect (maybe a little lust too) for this man that I will take his next prescription unquestioned—

same way I used to have sex" (257–258). If taking a prescription unquestioned marks compliance as we think we know it, the remainder of
Fisher's sentence unsettles such a conclusion, to say the least. To a figure
identified as "Master Park" (presumably the same Park he later imagines
calling up for "kinky . . . games" when he is hospitalized [251]), Fisher
had written a few years earlier, "I enjoy being your nigger, your property
and worshipping not just you, but your whiteness. . . . I really wanted
your cum and more of your piss" (230–231). The doctor whom Fisher
loves and hates is hearing little more than a "yes" when his prescription
is dispensed, but Sedgwick (in the entry addressed to her) and readers of
Gary in Your Pocket inescapably hear something quite different, given
that numerous entries like the one to Master Park have preceded this
medical scene. What looks like compliance on an ordinary day is something else altogether. Taking Fisher at his word here ("same way I used to
have sex") means recognizing that his "yes" to the doctor contains the desire for degradation and that the doctor's prescription, to be taken in
some sort of religious and sexual ecstasy, contains cum and piss.

Sometimes, however, Fisher's resistance is more straightforward,
through wry, perceptive readings of medical or bureaucratic (in)efficiency.
Saying that he "refused, sometimes wholesale" to follow a doctor's orders, that "they couldn't stick or poke or scan me in any way without my
permission," Fisher quickly learns how things work and can immediately
identify when "someone had fucked up" (261). When he informs his
nurse that the doctors have made an error interpreting his symptoms and
prescribing a solution, "she looked at me like I'd farted" (262). The nurse
insists not only that an error would be impossible, given that "errors in
this profession . . . could be costly," but also that Fisher is having
headaches even though he says he is not. "My god, what if I made a mistake?" she says. "We can't change anything without a doctor's consent."
Fisher replies simply, "You're making a mistake now" (262). Clearly
aware that the system is not working, Fisher refuses to participate and lets
this scene play out, until the nurse finally discovers that indeed an error
has been made and offers "the most profuse apologies" (262).

At least once in the selections included in *Gary in Your Pocket*, Fisher
directly and literally escapes from the Alta Bates Summit Medical Center
where he is being treated. Alta Bates may offer "comprehensive services
designed to meet the health care needs of the diverse communities of the
greater East Bay Area" (Alta Bates, "About Us"), but Fisher—invoking
the original *Psycho*—still calls it the "Bates Inn" (259). In this scene, he

is literally identified (tagged, in fact) as a patient, but he takes pleasure in disguising that identity and resisting the complicated machinery that encompasses and indeed engenders the "AIDS patient." "Snuck out of Alta Bates," he writes:

> If my sleeve rises too high (I used the 2nd button) the white and gray ID bracelet will be noticeable to this keenly observant jewish fellow sitting next to me. Snuck out of AB, took off the throw-away smock, the ones with the 40 snaps that seem to fit any other 40. . . . Took off all that stuff at Brad Lewis's urgence. He told me I'd have to sneak out, because not sneaking out would cost me my Medicaid coverage (which I don't really have anyway, yet). My last bill, by the way, was $18,000. I have to laugh whenever I look at it, all the procedures, chemicals and equipment I don't remember or understand. Just a strange concoction of symbols on 8–10 pages, two rows, the second one boasting amounts, and $5,470 for cancer drugs (in 5 days) would have to be a boast. (251)

Undoubtedly, the "needs" of the diverse communities Fisher moved through still exceed Alta Bates's capacity for "comprehensive services." The costs for HIV medication, conversely, have escalated to a point where Fisher's boast could be easily outdone by some later resident of the Bates Inn.

The laughter at economic and medical systems clearly designed with the interests of capital, not human beings, in mind is to me the crux of this passage and the feature that most locates Fisher in crip traditions of noncompliance and even desertion. "Cripping," as Carrie Sandahl puts it, exposes "the arbitrary delineation between normal and defective and the negative social ramifications of attempts to homogenize humanity . . . disarm[ing] what is painful with wicked humor" ("Queering the Crip or Cripping the Queer?" 37). Sandahl does not specifically identify the economic system in which crips are currently located as among or grounding the things that are painful, but capitalism, infamously, does homogenize humanity, creating "a world after its own image" (Marx and Engels 477). Sandahl clearly connects cripping to alternative worlds and performances, however, which—as she suggests elsewhere—allow "for a multitude of imaginary identifications across identities" ("Black Man, Blind Man" 602). Thus, it is significant that Fisher escapes to a performative space of creativity, blackness, queerness, disability, and hope: leaving Alta Bates, he laughs and heads to the Alvin Ailey American Dance Theater (a dance troupe that was still thriving four years after Ailey's own death from complications due to AIDS) (Fisher 251).[19]

Laughing at, jarring, or exiting from systems of exploitation or oppression are such longstanding black traditions that I have to question, on some level, the Reid-Pharr assertion at the beginning of this section: that is, the idea that the figure Fisher writes into existence "is hardly designed to rearticulate our most precious models of black subjectivity." A good portion of Zora Neale Hurston's career, to choose just one twentieth-century example, was dedicated to collecting and preserving (cherishing, making precious) the ways in which black subjects disarmed what was painful with wicked humor. In this tradition, and especially from a disability perspective, Fisher rearticulated, in multiple senses and with virtuosity, powerful and resistant models of black subjectivity. Reid-Pharr, however, does not exactly have the disabled and noncompliant Fisher in mind in his argument, but the (seemingly) submissive Fisher, the figure Fisher himself described as "a fit, intelligent black slave with a keen desire to please" (qtd. in Sedgwick, *Gary in Your Pocket* 281). Despite the fact that I—engaged in the impossible and perhaps self-deluded work of honoring him—have only approached this enslaved figure obliquely (as, in the last section, I in some ways could only approach Sara obliquely), he appears over and over again in *Gary in Your Pocket*: "I want to be the TOY. . . . That's what being a faggot's all about, right?" (188); "I'm on my knees again, before God. Tall, white, wary of me, trying to work him into a froth of masterliness" (208); "The simplicity of it astounds me and yet I have no words for it, just an image, at once holy and profane, of the nigger on his knees taking cock juices into his body" (238–239).

Reid-Pharr's argument about this submissive figure is that he unsettles "the philosophical and aesthetic ambitions of what has come to be known as Black American culture," which turns "precisely on the necessity of establishing a live blackness, a corporeality that does something other than announce social death" (136). The "nigger corporeality" Fisher materializes, according to Reid-Pharr, repudiates life on these terms and deliriously embraces death (135). Reid-Pharr argues that Fisher forces a recognition that "there is no black subjectivity in the absence of the white master, no articulation in the absence of degradation, no way of saying 'black' without hearing 'nigger' as its echo" (137). I find Reid-Pharr's theses largely convincing, despite my qualifications above (that is, my contingent location of Fisher in vibrant black traditions). Indeed, I find Reid-

Pharr's assertions—which, in part, could be said to locate a will to degradation operative in and through rehabilitation—largely in accord with or foundational for my own, including my assertion at the beginning of this chapter that the problems that attend rehabilitation (with its demand for identity as generic sameness and its dependency on degradation or on the aberration) inevitably also attend late-twentieth-century identity-movement conceptions of identity. "Even as we express the most positive articulations of black and gay identity," Reid-Pharr writes, "we are nonetheless referencing the ugly historical and ideological realities out of which those identities have been formed" (137). Fisher's articulation of "nigger pride" and his embrace of "what being a faggot's all about," in other words, are not original to him; they can be traced even (or especially) to the locations that seem to oppose them the most.

It is not Reid-Pharr's subject, but there is a sense in which disability could claim a certain pride of place in what he is arguing, given that there is (literally) no way of articulating the very word "disability" in the absence of "ability"—and, indeed, in the absence of the mastery that, as most would have it, naturally attends able-bodiedness. And to carry these points further, there is likewise no way of saying "disabled" without hearing "cripple" (or freak, or retard) as its echo. That there is no way of speaking the rehabilitated self without hearing the degraded other, however, is not a univocal fact. It is, instead, a fact in multiple ways. Identity depends on degradation in Reid-Pharr's sense—that is, resistant identities always reference the ugly historical and ideological realities from whence they emerged—but identity depends on degradation in another, redoubled sense: to the extent that identity-movement identities are rehabilitated identities ("gay is good [not bad]," "black is beautiful [not ugly]," "disabled and proud [not pitiful]"), they are also in some ways normative identities that inevitably incorporate generic sameness *in and through their distinctiveness* and that require and produce degraded others. This is not to deny a certain indispensability to the identity politics of the past few decades (indispensability conveying both necessity and unshakeability, regardless of our desires or intentions); as I suggested in chapter 1, crip theory would not emerge without such a politics. It is to locate and value (and in some ways, mourn) a certain rigor in projects like Fisher's that push the limits of such a politics, that appear in fact to be the most opposed to identity politics proper.

This rigor is not always legible in *Tongues Untied*, and not simply because the "revolution" invoked by the film's concluding, and nation-building, thesis—Black Men Loving Black Men Is *The* Revolutionary Act—could be seen as in tension with the reformist history called up by the film's use of historic civil rights footage. On the contrary: the film is in some ways, and ironically, most rigorous with that association; as Ferguson argues in *Aberrations in Black*, "liberal ideology captivates revolutionary nationalism" (3). In other words, revolutionary nationalism in the 1960s and 1970s inherited from reform movements a liberal failure "to conceptualize the multiple specificities and differences that constituted their various subjects" and (again, like liberal reformism) "normalized the suppression of subaltern gender, racial, and sexual identities" (126). Although it does not directly test the limits of their respective political projects, *Tongues Untied* nonetheless makes visible these associations between reform movements and revolutionary nationalism.[20]

If Ferguson's theses make it possible to apprehend these linkages in *Tongues Untied*, they also make accessible the film's (il)logic, its less rigorous moments. And what the film cannot know or acknowledge is, indeed, that aberrations in black are produced as necessary correlates of the nonaberrant (rehabilitated) black and gay revolutionary nationalists the film celebrates. Or, at least, in this case, aberrations in black leather: the SM subcultures of San Francisco—undoubtedly captured by the camera during the very years Fisher and other black, Latino, and Asian men he writes about were active members of them—are filmically constructed as necessarily both degraded and degrading. Fisher cannot be a black gay man because of his will to degradation; according to the logic of the film, which in an autobiographical sequence has Riggs fleeing Castro and Market Street cultures, a normative black gay identity comes only from exiting the spaces where Fisher, or traces of Fisher, or crips like Fisher, might be found.[21]

John Champagne writes, in the analysis of *Tongues Untied* that first broached the ways in which it demonizes SM subcultures: "This granting of a subjectivity necessarily depends . . . on the figure of the undisciplined gay and lesbian body, who continues to act as a foil for a normal that can make sense only in terms of what it is not" (84). A foil for the normal in so many ways, seeking out or desiring undisciplined bodies, Fisher took pleasure in what Jeffrey J. Cohen calls a "historically specific masochistic *assemblage*, an intersubjective sexuality that almost always involves a transposition of institutionalized dominance and submission into unexpected arenas of performance" (79). Ironically, *Tongues Untied*—at least through its concluding thesis about black men loving black men and the (singular) revolutionary act—can be read as forwarding both an inter-subjective sexuality and expected arenas of performance. Or, we might say (according to a strict reading of this thesis), an intersubjective sexuality performed in expected (rehabilitated) arenas—this particular revolution, in other words, expects compliance. Reading Fisher alongside *Tongues Untied* makes clear that he cripped rehabilitative agendas even before he was disabled.

Conclusion: "It's a big big room and it's full of everybody's hope I'm sure"

This is not a diagnosis. Nor is it intended to provoke a rehabilitation. With such disclaimers (or perhaps tributes to Magritte) in the background, however, one could argue that, sprinkled throughout Fisher's writing, there are traces of OCD: lines signifying new beginnings, outlines marking the rigid form future entries will or should take, worries he cannot shake about who might be reading him, obsessive questions about tense or punctuation. To cite just a few of the dozens of possibilities: "Neatness seems to inspire me. I'm not sure why" (123); "That's not the way it was supposed to be. . . . there won't be any more of what happened today" (139): "It's time to set some guidelines for this journal and future ones. This may be a conglomeration of materials, but its point is to show my daily progression and/or regression" (142): "Boy, tense still scares me—the most basic tool of my trade and I can't be sure" (270). I do not find these examples interesting because they fix Fisher, but because they show Fisher himself working or testing the limits. In the space of the personal journal, where he could, conceivably, enjoy a sort of limitless freedom (at least from written form or order), Fisher hems himself in, worrying about and working over the tiniest things. And yet, simultaneously, there are conversely innumerable entries (often the ones most ecstatically describing sexual activities) where such concerns about form, order, syntax, and punctuation—not to mention the cultural grammar of rehabilitation—appear to be deliberately repudiated ("I AM PROUD TO BE A NIGGER," in particular, marking an entry that concludes with no period, no punctuation).

Reid-Pharr writes that he is "not attempting to rehabilitate Fisher for those wary of perverse black subjectivity. On the contrary, Fisher's genius turns on his ability to spoil all our expectations, to deform our most cherished models of human subjectivity" (141). Reid-Pharr's work on Fisher is not in conversation with disability studies, though he does reverse here, in a potentially generative way, the usually negative metaphorical use of "deform." I do wonder, however, from a position internal to disability studies and the disability rights movement, whether the rehabilitation of Fisher (or anyone) can be so easily disclaimed, whether—in fact—the OCD-like moments in his journal position even Fisher himself both claiming and disclaiming rehab. Even if, as Reid-Pharr and numerous other queer theorists would have it, we must be able to grapple with the spaces where identity unravels, with what we might call the myriad crip forms that identity trouble takes, we still inhabit a world sedimented with rehabilitative logics speaking us.

Of course (and this is itself an OCD insight), the obsessive discipline that marks rehabilitation and the grandiose repudiation of that discipline could be seen as of a piece. Indeed, it's not difficult to see Fisher's worry over minutiae as simply the inverse of his at times Whitmanian (or perhaps Whitmanic) efforts to think and write differently, expansively: "I want to write large. Don't I want to write large?" (271). Fisher's "big big room" "full of everybody's hope" is one such expansive effort; it is the impossible space he imagined five months before he died, in an entry (the last one included in *Gary in Your Pocket*) dated September 19, 1993. "40 million people will have it by the end of the decade," Fisher writes, "I'm in good company. I'm in plenty of company. I'm less afraid. It's a big big room and it's full of everybody's hope I'm sure" (272). The forty million figure makes it clear, to call back Jovanna from *The Transformation*, that even if it's Fisher's dream, it's not an American dream, because Fisher is obviously thinking globally. Additionally, Fisher was also quite close in his projections: in the year 2000, an estimated thirty-six million people were living with HIV/AIDS, three million died, and more than five million were newly infected. Almost twenty-two million people had already died by 2000, the vast majority of them nonwhite and without access to protease inhibitors or other therapies.

What I have written about *The Transformation* and *Gary in Your Pocket*—these two texts from around 1996—does nothing to change this other, post-1996, story. Put differently, what I have written does nothing to change these staggering numbers that are now part of history, as surely as it does not literally resurrect Sara/Ricardo or Fisher. In 2005, however, I could imaginatively put myself in Fisher's place: fifty million people will have it by the end of the decade. That future story can be changed, and the questions about identity, community, rehabilitation, and political economy that *The Transformation* and *Gary in Your Pocket* raise—questions about who is encompassed when "marginalized groups . . . render themselves visible" and who is not, and why (Champagne 70); questions about how to materialize what David Harvey calls "spaces of hope" and who is currently shut out of spaces that matter, and why—invite that change.

Rehabilitated identities, however necessary or inescapable, are not sufficient for making Fisher's big big room, which invokes that post-1996 story, accessible. But *The Transformation* and *Gary in Your Pocket* do keep in play some of the most important and ongoing challenges of crip theory, or more simply of progressive queer and disability movements at the turn of the century: the challenge of always imagining subjects beyond LGBT or disability visibility, tolerance, and inclusion; the challenge of shaping movements that, regardless of how degraded they are, can value the traces of agency, resistance, and hope that are as legible where identity disintegrates as where it comes together.

4

Composing Queerness and Disability

The Corporate University and Alternative Corporealities

Most teachers and students of writing experience the cultural practice of composition as a difficult, messy, disorienting affair—the encounter between a writer and the blank page or computer screen, like any encounter between two bodies, can leave one, as Tina Turner suggests in "What's Love Got to Do with It?", dazed and confused:

> It may seem to you
> That I'm acting confused
> When you're close to me.
> If I tend to look dazed,
> I read it someplace
> I got cause to be.

Turner's claim to have "read someplace" about the disconcerting effects of the more general encounter between self and other, moreover, is amply borne out by anti-identitarian theories of the past few decades that document the impossibility—given the ways all identities are continually shaped and reshaped in and through multiple communities and discourses—of composing, or writing into existence, a coherent and individual self.

More than fifty years ago Kenneth Burke argued that composition is a cultural practice that would seem to be inescapably—even inevitably—connected to order.[1] *Webster's Dictionary* authoritatively defines "composition" as a process that reduces difference, forms many ingredients into one substance, or even calms, settles, or frees from agitation:

> compose *vb* composed; composing [MF *composer,* fr. L *componere* (perf. indic. *composui*)] *vt* (15c) **1 a :** to form by putting together : FASHION <a committee *composed* of three representatives—*Current Biog*> **b :** to form the substance of : CONSTITUTE <*composed* of many ingredients> **c :** to produce (as columns or pages of type) by composition **2 a :** to create by mental or artistic labor : PRODUCE <~a sonnet sequence> **b** (1) : to formulate and write (a piece of music) (2) : to compose music for **3 :** to deal with or act on so as to reduce to a minimum <~their differences> **4 :** to arrange in proper or orderly form @~her clothing: **5 :** to free from agitation : CALM, SETTLE <~a patient> ~*vi* : to practice composition

In his study of the uses of language and strategies of resistance in an urban Chicano/a community, Ralph Cintron describes composition or writing as a "discourse of measurement" that is, especially in the exclusionary institutional forms it usually takes within the academy, "highly routinized" and controlled by an "ordering agent" (210, 229):

> Writing is the making of an order and the blank surface is that space or servant that bears the order. Typically, writing catches the eye, but the surface that receives the writing does not. In this sense, writing contains the stronger presence, and the surface that receives the writing is defined by that presence. The surface, then, is an ordered, limited space cleared of obstacles and ready to be acted upon by an ordering agent wielding a highly routinized tool.

How, then, to acknowledge and affirm the experiences we draw from multiple academic and nonacademic communities where composing (in all senses of the word) is clearly an unruly, disorderly cultural practice? Can composition theory work against the simplistic formulation of that which is proper, orderly, and harmonious? If, as the dictionary definition suggests, composing is somehow connected to labor, is it possible to resist the impulse to focus on finished products (the highly routinized, "well-made" essay; the sonnet sequence; the supposedly secure masculine or heterosexual identity) and to keep that labor in mind as we inquire into what composition means and into what it might mean in the future? To adapt Michael Hardt and Antonio Negri, what vital role might contemporary composition have in the production of producers (*Empire* 32)? What would happen if, true to our experiences in and out of the classroom, we continually attempted to reconceive composing as that which produced agitation—to reconceive it, paradoxically, as what it is? In what ways might that agitation be generative?[2]

Although it is by no means universally acknowledged (to judge by how little or how slowly pedagogical and institutional practices have changed), there is nonetheless widespread critical recognition at this point that composition, as it is currently conceptualized and taught in most U.S. colleges and universities, serves a corporate model of efficiency and flexibility.[3] What we might call the current "corpo-reality" of composition guarantees that instruction is often streamlined across dozens of classes at a given institution, with standardized texts (handbooks, guides to the writing and research process, essay collections) required or strongly encouraged (either by campus or departmental administrators or by publishing houses). Inside and outside the university, corporate elites demand that composition courses focus on demonstrable professional-managerial skills rather than critical thought—or, more insidiously, "critical thought" is reconceptualized through a skills-based model ultimately grounded in measurement and marketability, or measurement for marketability. The most troubling feature of our current corpo-reality is that composition at most institutions is routinely taught by adjunct or graduate student employees who receive low pay and few (if any) benefits: the composition work force, at the corporate university, is highly contingent and replaceable, and instructors are thus often forced to piece together multiple appointments at various schools in a region.

I find these arguments that composition serves a corporate model of efficiency convincing, and it is vitally important for teachers and scholars of composition and composition theory to remain attentive to the ways we are positioned to serve professional-managerial interests. In many ways, however, despite the material base of these critiques, they remain strangely *in*corporeal—in other words, these critiques are not yet especially concerned with theorizing *embodiment* and/in the corporate university. Perhaps this is because corporate processes seem to privilege, imagine, and produce only one kind of body on either side of the desk: on one side, the flexible body of the contingent, replaceable instructor; on the other, the flexible body of the student dutifully mastering marketable skills and producing clear, orderly, efficient prose.

Chapters 2 and 3 focused on highly charged institutional and institutionalized sites where cultural signs of queerness and disability appear and where, in many ways, they are made to disappear to shore up dominant forms of domesticity and rehabilitation, respectively. In this chapter, I turn to another institutional site, the contemporary university, where anxieties about disability and queerness are likewise legible. In particular, I extend the critical dialogue on composition and the contemporary university by arguing for alternative, and multiple, corporealities. I contend that recentering our attention on the composing bodies in our classrooms can inaugurate and work to sustain a process of "de-composition"—that is, a process that provides an ongoing critique of both the corporate models into which we, as students and teachers of composition, are interpellated and the concomitant disciplinary compulsion to produce only disembodied, efficient writers. Most important, I make the somewhat polemical claim that bringing back in composing bodies means, inevitably, placing queer theory and disability studies at the center of composition theory.[4]

Interrogating but not resolving one of the paradoxes at the heart of composition (whereby composing is defined as the production of order and experienced as the opposite), I argue for the desirability of a loss of composure, since it is only in such a state that heteronormativity might be questioned or resisted and that new (queer/disabled) identities and communities might be imagined.[5] In the sections that follow, then, I first sketch out more thoroughly the paradox in which composing bodies find themselves, locating specifically the ways in which composition undergirds heteronormativity and heteronormativity undergirds composition. Next, in order to challenge such understandings of composition, I argue for what I call the "contingent universalization" of queerness and disability. Finally, I briefly consider two composition courses at George Washington University, along with the institutional context that both enabled and endangered them, in order to materialize the processes of decomposition that I advocate. The institutional machinery that I critique most pointedly in the coda to this chapter largely concerns itself with managing difference, with producing what Stuart Hall calls "the difference that may not make a difference" ("What Is This 'Black'?" 467). Conversely (and perversely), the cultural studies pedagogy that has been accessed, continuously and collectively, at GWU has insisted on materializing the difference that makes a difference, even if and as that difference is "by definition contradictory and . . . impure, threatened by incorporation or exclusion" (471). Writing at GWU—as well as writing in and around the corporate university more generally—remains a critical process, regardless of attempts to generate, and manage, the desire for finished products (finished products marked particularly, as I will demonstrate, by the GWU brand). Ultimately, ongoing writing processes in the corporate university make clear that composition can, as David Halperin writes about queerness, "open a social space for the construction of different identities, for the elaboration of various types of relationships, for the development of new cultural forms" (66–67). This chapter sketches some of the ways in which that queer process proceeds.

Composing Straightness/Straight Composition

As I suggest in chapter 1, feminists and queer theorists have demonstrated for more than three decades that heterosexuality, particularly for women, is not a choice but a compulsory identity that secures a dominant patriarchal system. Compulsory femininity (for women), masculinity (for men), and heterosexuality are (re)produced in and through a wide variety of cultural institutions. Eve Kosofsky Sedgwick has famously (and wryly) observed: "Advice on how to help your kids turn out gay, not to mention your students, your parishioners, your therapy clients, or your military subordinates, is less ubiquitous than you might think. On the other hand, the scope of institutions whose programmatic undertaking is to prevent the development of gay people is unimaginably large" (*Tendencies* 161). The finished product that emerges from this "unimaginably large" institutional matrix is the supposedly secure masculine or feminine heterosexual identity; the institutions that Sedgwick nods toward here are highly invested in a process we might describe as "composing straightness"—compulsory heterosexuality, with its correctly gendered and embodied participants, is continually produced from the disorderly array of possible human desires and embodiments.

But composing straightness is no easy affair. As Judith Butler's body of work makes clear, the compulsory nature of gendered positions ensures that those subjected to the system (all of us) are catapulted into endless attempts to get it right—into repetitions (of masculinity, femininity, heterosexuality) that, in their proliferation, ironically threaten to destabilize the very identifications that any given performance would purport to fix. The fact that heterosexuality is destined to fail and always in process, however, does not change the fact that most people understand it as wholly natural. Although heterosexuality is without question a product of complex cultural, economic, and historical processes, it is by no means experienced as such. The finished heterosexual product is so fetishized that the composition process cannot be acknowledged; the institutions that compose straightness thus simultaneously produce ideologies that render the process itself virtually unthinkable.

The institutions in our culture that produce and secure a heterosexual identity also work to secure an able-bodied identity. Fundamentally structured in ways that limit access for people with disabilities, such institutions perpetuate able-bodied hegemony, figuratively and literally constructing a world that always and everywhere privileges very narrow (and ever-narrowing) conceptions of ability. Advice on how to help your kids turn out disabled, not to mention your students, your parishioners, your therapy clients, or your military subordinates, is less ubiquitous than you might think. Certainly there are innumerable institutions devoted to a *medical* model of disability; indeed, the scope of institutions designed to secure a medical model of disability (i.e., designed to proffer advice on how to help your kids turn out pathologized) is unimaginably large. The disability rights movement and disability studies, however, are the only forces shaping locations where the *cultural* model of how to turn out disabled is available, and the scope of these cultural and political movements currently pales in comparison with the scope of institutions that (re)produce dominant understandings of able-bodiedness.

I will talk more about queer/disabled responses to this state of affairs in the next two sections of this chapter. The main reason I underscore the ways in which a disavowed composing process undergirds compulsory able-bodiedness and heterosexuality, however, is to consider how similar normative processes are at work in our current understandings of composition. My contention is that "straight composition"—that is, common sense or currently hegemonic understandings of composition—requires similar compulsory identifications and engages in similar disavowals. Despite the best efforts of many individual composition theorists and instructors, and despite a decades-long conversation about process and revision, composition in the corporate university remains a practice that is focused on a fetishized final product, whether it is the final paper, the final grade, or the student body with measurable skills. If this emphasis is not necessarily (or even often) pronounced in a given individual classroom, it is nonetheless pronounced at the level of administrative (or governmental, or corporate) surveillance of those classrooms. Individual instructors—and even institutions—may focus on process, in other words, but corporate elites nonetheless want to see a return on their investment. Contemporary composition is a highly monitored cultural practice, and those doing the monitoring (on some level, all of us involved) are intent on producing order and efficiency where there was none and, ultimately, on forgetting the messy composing process and the composing bodies that experience it.

The contemporary cultural and socioeconomic contexts in which writing studies is located are what most concern me in this chapter. In order to understand these contemporary circumstances better, however, it's worth pointing out briefly that the much more general linkages I am making here are not entirely new, even if the particular convergence of composition, heterosexuality, and able-bodied identity has not been detailed. The composition of a coherent and disciplined self in modernity has, in fact, often been linked to the composition of orderly written texts. In 1690, for instance, in his *Essay Concerning Human Understanding*, John Locke wrote: "Let us suppose the mind to be, as we say, white paper void of all characters." Tamar Plakins Thornton begins her study *Handwriting in America: A Cultural History* with this dictum, describing it as Locke's "now-famous notion of the human being as a tabula rasa, who acquires reason and knowledge through experience" (3). Although *Handwriting in America* is not focused on the history of composition in the United States per se, Thornton similarly links the formation of subjectivities to the ways in which writing has been conceptualized. "How could the development of the human self and the acquisition of writing skills," she asks, "have anything to do with each other?" (3). With Locke's dictum as a backdrop, Thornton proceeds to answer her own question by tracing ideas about handwriting that emerged and developed in the eighteenth century alongside opposing ideas about print. Thornton contends that the filling of the blank page—the composition of a handwritten text—simultaneously composed a self with a recognizable location in a social order hierarchically arranged according to class, gender, and occupation. The self written into existence by men of commerce, for instance, was meant to be distinguishable from that written into existence by gentlemen and ladies, who in turn composed selves that could be properly distinguished from each other.

Thornton's history could be understood as diametrically opposed to the points I am making about contemporary composition, subjectivity, and postmodernity, especially since the (printed) finished products of most composition courses have very little to do with handwriting. As Thornton demonstrates, in the eighteenth century, the perceived close link between handwriting and subjectivity contrasted to the perceived *distance* between print and subjectivity: "As men and women exploited the impersonality of print to its fullest, they came to understand handwriting in contradistinction to print and to make handwriting function in contradistinction to the press, as the medium of the self" (30). I would argue, however, that contemporary ideas about composition more properly descend from the ideas about handwriting that Thornton excavates than from the ideas about print that were dominant in the early days of a print culture.[6] Certainly in the nineteenth century when composition became compulsory in American universities, handwriting would have been the medium of choice, but this is not the only reason I would place composition in such a line of descent. As queer and disability studies have repeatedly shown, the bourgeois culture of the past few centuries has only become more obsessed with the composed, self-possessed, "normal" subject, properly located in a hierarchical social order. If some of the disciplinary practices shaping such a self can be clearly tied to handwriting in the eighteenth century, when a normalized, bourgeois culture was still emergent, they have undoubtedly become unmoored from such a specific location in the centuries since then. Even though Thornton tucks Michel Foucault away in only one endnote in her study (204–205 n.16), some of his general insights in *Discipline and Punish* could more thoroughly extend her own. *Discipline and Punish* purports to examine "the birth of the prison" but of course ends up demonstrating that docile bodies are produced in a range of cultural locations: the schoolroom, the clinic, the asylum, the workplace.[7] Similarly, the composed self that emerges in Thornton's history of handwriting has ultimately come to be produced in other locations, which are centrally concerned with the acquisition of writing skills.

Although we could thus be said to inherit in contemporary composition studies the legacy Thornton traces, that legacy is now compounded by the postmodernizing urgency that characterizes this particular moment in the history of capitalism and the history of the university. For those administering composition inside and outside the university, it often seems that there is perpetual panic about students' perceived lack of the basic (professional-managerial) communication skills they supposedly need. We may inherit an Enlightenment legacy where the production of writing and production of the self converge, but the corporate university also extends that legacy in its eagerness to intervene in, and thereby vouchsafe, the kinds of selves produced. The call to produce orderly and efficient writing/docile subjects thus takes on a heightened urgency in our particular moment.

Through my linkage of two varieties of composition in this section, however, my desire in the end is to keep in play the critical possibilities that are inherent in Butler's theory of gender trouble. That is, if composing straightness and able-bodiedness is always on some level impossible, then perhaps the same could be said about straight composition. The perpetual panic over what is supposedly *not* happening in composition classrooms and what supposedly *needs* to be happening there guarantees that our identities are indeed compulsory, even if—or precisely because—we are not getting those identities exactly right. If we are thus catapulted into cycles of repetition as students and scholars of composition, following Butler we could argue that the repetition ensures that straight composition is inevitably comedic, impossible to perform dutifully, and without incoherence. De-composition and disorder always haunt the composition classroom intent on the production of order and efficiency.

There is, however, nothing comedic about certain material cycles of repetition that are part of the scenario I describe—the cycle of repetition, for example, whereby a given instructor, year after year, pieces together numerous teaching positions in composition but receives neither a living wage nor security in return. If all of our classrooms are virtually de-composed, they are not necessarily "critically de-composed"—that is, actively involved in resisting the corporate university and disordering straight composition. And, indeed, critical de-composition is impossible on an individual level, impossible without what Butler labels "collective disidentifications" with the efficient identities we are compelled to corporealize (*Bodies That Matter* 4).

In the conclusion to his ethnography of the Chicano/a community he calls "Angelstown," Cintron reflects on the composing process, which encourages students "to shape language in school-appropriate ways . . . reinforcing what is standard and conventional and sloughing off the dialectical and disruptive" (231). Cintron finds a "saving grace" even within such rigidity, a saving grace which he describes as "the sweetness of critique that always finds the remainder, the forgotten, the hidden, and thereby, exposes as illusion that sense of control, that sense of a ruling self in control" (231). There is a certain pathos in Cintron's conclusion, however, that would be less pronounced if "the saving grace of critique" were not so seemingly individual and if it could be more clearly articulated to collective political projects specifically concerned with *embracing* the disruptive.[8] For Cintron, a certain kind of order is inevitable:

> Call it a vicious pleasure: written language seems to offer a ruling self, whether author or reader, the special opportunity of reducing language and experience to something manageable and, thus, to create an order. Even if the order sought is that of disorder, as in certain kinds of poetry, what gets created is a domesticated version of disorder, in short, the appearance of disorder, rather than the being of disorder. (229)

We might perpetually lament this conservative impulse at the center of composition, but—for Cintron—we cannot eradicate it. We can, instead, simply take solace in the sweetness of critique that finds the remainder, the forgotten, the hidden.

The sweetness of critique seems to me less infused with pathos when imagined through collective disidentifications, however. All writing, even writing committed to disorder, may reduce language and experience to something manageable, but surely there is a difference between the "school-appropriate" writing Cintron cites—writing that helps to maintain a hegemonic social and economic system—and the collective writing practices that would speak back to the particular institutional circumstances in which we find ourselves, even if, without question, the resistant writing in turn can and should still be subject to the sweetness of critique.

Butler writes: "It is important to resist that theoretical gesture of pathos in which exclusions are simply affirmed as sad necessities of signification. The task is to refigure this necessary 'outside' as a future horizon, one in which the violence of exclusion is perpetually in the process of being overcome" (*Bodies That Matter* 53). Queer and crip theory, if conceptualized as indissolubly linked to collective queer/disabled movements outside the university, are sites for continually imagining the collective disidentifications that make possible the refiguring Butler describes. Positioned to critique the finished products heteronormativity demands, queer/crip perspectives can help to keep our attention on disruptive, inappropriate, composing bodies—bodies that invoke the future horizon beyond straight composition.

Aren't We All Queer/Disabled?: Speaking Back to Straight Composition

If the fetishized finished product in the composition classroom has affinities with the composed heterosexual or able-bodied self, I would argue that the composing body, in contrast, is in some ways inevitably queer/disabled. Sedgwick, after considering the features that characterize the composed heterosexual self, particularly listing (for more than a page) "the number and *difference* of the dimensions that 'sexual identity' is supposed to organize into a seamless and univocal whole," contends that queerness refers to "the open mesh of possibilities, gaps, overlaps, dissonances and resonances, lapses and excesses of meaning when the constituent elements of anyone's gender, of anyone's sexuality aren't made (or *can't be* made) to signify monolithically" (*Tendencies* 8). Able-bodied identity, similarly, emerges from disparate features that are supposed to be organized into a seamless and univocal whole: a standard (and "working") number of limbs and digits that are used in appropriate ways (i.e., feet are not used for eating or performing other tasks besides walking; hands are not used as the primary vehicle for language); eyes that see and ears that hear (both consistently and "accurately"); proper dimensions of height and weight (generally determined according to Euro-American standards of beauty); genitalia and other bodily features that are deemed gender-appropriate (i.e., aligned with one of only two possible sexes, and in such a way that sex and gender correspond); an HIV-negative serostatus; high energy and freedom from chronic conditions that might in fact impact energy, mobility, and the potential to be awake and "functional" for a standard number of hours each day; freedom from illness or infection (ideally, freedom from the *likelihood* of either illness or infection, particularly HIV infection or sexually transmitted diseases); acceptable and meaurable mental functioning; behaviors that are not disruptive, unfocused, or "addictive"; thoughts that are not unusual or disturbing. Optimally these features are not only aligned but are consistent over time—regeneration is privileged over degeneration (read: the effects of aging, which should be resisted, particularly for women). If the alignment of all these features guarantee the composed able-bodied self, then—following Sedgwick on queerness—we might say that disability refers to the open mesh of possibilities, gaps, overlaps, dissonances and resonances, lapses and excesses of meaning when the constituent elements of bodily, mental, or behavioral functioning aren't made (or *can't be* made) to signify monolithically.

One could easily conclude from these circumstances that we are all disabled/queer, since all of us (at some point and to some degree—or to some degree at *most* points) inhabit composing bodies that exist prior to the successful alignment of all of these features. I want to both resist and advance this conclusion. Obviously, definitional issues have been central to both queer and disability rights movements—who counts as queer, who counts as disabled? As Simi Linton points out, following Carol Gill: "The problem gets stickier when the distinction between disabled and nondisabled is challenged by people who say, 'Actually, we're all disabled in some way, aren't we?'" (Linton 12–13; Gill 46). Similar complacent assertions are made about queerness—"actually, we're all queer in some way, aren't we?"—and I believe it is important to resist such assertions, recognizing them as able-bodied/heterosexual *containments*: an able-bodied/heterosexual society doesn't have to take seriously disabled/queer claims to rights and recognition if it can diffuse or universalize what activists and scholars are saying as really nothing new and as really about all of us. In other words, the question "aren't we all queer/disabled?" can be an indirect way of saying, "you don't need to be taken seriously, do you?"

In some very important ways, we are in fact *not* all queer/disabled. The fact that some of us get beaten and left for dead tied to deer fences or that others of us die virtually unnoticed in underfunded and unsanitary group homes should be enough to highlight that the heterosexual/queer and able-bodied/disabled binaries produce real and material distinctions.[9] However, recognizing that the question "aren't we all queer/disabled?" can be an attempt at containment and affirming that I resist that containment, I nonetheless argue that there are *moments* when we are all queer/disabled, and that *those disabled/queer moments are desirable*. In particular, a crip theory of composition argues for the desirability and extension of those moments when we are all queer/disabled, since it is those moments that provide us with a means of speaking back to straight composition in all its guises. Instead of a banal, humanistic universalization of queerness/disability, a crip theory of composition advocates for the temporary or contingent universalization of queerness/disability.[10]

The flip side of the fact that there are moments when all of us are queer/disabled is the fact that no one (unfortunately) is queer/disabled *all* of the time—that would be impossible to sustain in a cultural order that privileges heterosexuality/able-bodied identity and that compels all of us, no matter how distant we might be from the ideal, into repetitions that approximate those norms.[11] Critical de-composition, however, results from reorienting ourselves away from those compulsory ideals and onto the composing process and the composing bodies—the alternative, and multiple, corporealities—that continually ensure that things can turn out otherwise. Put differently, critical de-composition results from actively and collectively desiring not virtual but critical disability and queerness. Instead of solely and repeatedly asking the questions Cintron rightly cites as central to "school-appropriate" writing instruction— "'Have you chosen the right word?' 'Can this be made clearer?' 'Your argument here is inconsistent.' 'Are you being contradictory?'" (231)—we might ask questions designed to dismantle our current corpo-reality: How can we queer this? How can we crip it? What ideologies or norms that are at work in this text, discourse, program need to be cripped? How can this system be de-composed?

I recognize that the general point I am making here is one that has been central to a certain mode of composition theory for some time. Although I want to complicate the project, I in fact believe that one of the conditions of possibility for my own analysis here is precisely the collective and ongoing project, within composition theory, of arguing for the difficult but necessary work of continually resisting a pedagogy focused on finished products.[12] To take just one example, William A. Covino writes:

> In even the most enlightened composition class, a class blown by the winds of change through a "paradigm shift" into a student-centered, process-oriented environment replete with heuristics, sentence combining, workshopping, conferencing, and recursive revising, speculation and exploration remain subordinate to finishing. . . . While writing is identified exclusively with a product and purpose that contain and abbreviate it, writers let the conclusion dictate their tasks and necessarily censor whatever imagined possibilities seem irrelevant or inappropriate; they develop a trained incapacity to speculate and raise questions, to try stylistic and formal alternatives. They become unwilling and unable to fully elaborate the process of composing. (316–317)

As I asserted at the beginning of this chapter, however, such critiques remain decidedly incorporeal—composition theory has not yet recognized (or perhaps has censored the "imagined possibility") that the demand for certain kinds of finished projects in the writing classroom is congruent with the demand for certain kinds of bodies. Not recognizing this congruence, in turn, can bring us to a point where the imagined solution is the sort of *disembodied* postmodernism Covino calls for. I'm suggesting that queer theory and disability studies should figure centrally into the work that we do in composition and composition theory—that, in fact, they already do in some ways figure centrally into that work, since the critical projects that we have been imagining, projects of resisting closure or containment and accessing other possibilities, are queer/crip projects. In other words, a subtext of the decades-long project in composition theory focusing on the composing process and away from the finished product is that disability and queerness are desirable.

Composing Queerness, Composing Disability: De-Composition in Practice

Desiring queerness/disability means not assuming in advance that the finished state is the one worth striving for, especially the finished state demanded by the corporate university and the broader oppressive cultural and economic circumstances in which we are currently located. It means striving instead for "permanently partial identities" (Haraway 154). Indeed, through Donna J. Haraway, we might understand disability/queerness as "not the products of escape and transcendence of limits, i.e., the view from above, but the joining of partial views and halting voices into a collective subject position that promises a vision of the means of ongoing finite embodiment, of living within limits and contradictions, i.e., of views from somewhere" (196). Critical de-composition, in other words, entails recognizing and participating in the multiple and intersecting critical movements—what Haraway calls "an earth-wide network of connections" (187)—that would resist, or stare back at, the corporate "view from above." Haraway writes: "We need the power of modern critical theories of how meanings and bodies get made, not in order to deny meaning and bodies, but in order to live in meanings and bodies that have a chance for the future" (187).

A more limited but crucial (or, perhaps more positively, precisely such a local/located) "network of connections" characterized the Writing Program at George Washington University for most of the past decade. This program was responsible for English 10 and 11, the two-semester com-position sequence that fulfilled a literacy requirement for almost all first-year students. In contrast to more streamlined, "efficient" writing pro-grams, the courses taught at GWU did not employ standardized texts, nor did they necessarily share, across sections, a conception of the kinds of writing projects students should be working on (although we discussed our varying conceptions continually). The courses were organized as writing-intensive seminars, and many or most were semester-long explo-rations of specific cultural studies topics such as international feminisms, rhetoric and technology, or contemporary youth cultures. The rhizomatic program was nurtured by the work of an openly Marxist director, Dan Moshenberg. Over time, faculty in the program (including Moshenberg) instituted movement of the discussions in our classroom out in public: the second semester concluded with an annual "Composition and Cultural Studies Conference" involving close to one thousand students presenting their work, or attending to and debating others' work, in Deaf studies, disability studies, queer studies, postcolonial studies, rhetoric and democ-racy, and a host of other topics.[13]

In this section, I describe some of the courses I was able to shape within this critically de-composing context, where cultural studies perspectives and pedagogies were actively and collectively at work. These descrip-tions, however, should not be read merely as culminating the theories I developed in previous sections, if culmination (or even a simple example), by bringing the discussion to a particular, fixed point, generates a man-ageable order, reduces difference, and calms, settles, or frees from agita-tion. Indeed, at least some of those observing the Writing Program at GWU—described variously by the English department and others as "stakeholders"—perceived it to be unmanageable, and composed a less unruly alternative. In May 2002, at an "Academic Excellence" manage-ment forum, the English department at GWU learned that our Writing Program was being dismantled, that a new program would be instituted outside the department, that it would be staffed entirely by non-tenure-track professors, and that it would more directly focus on skills acquisi-tion and measurable achievement. This proposal had been in develop-ment for almost a year, although faculty teaching in neither the Writing Program nor the English department more broadly were consulted. Thus, after describing in this section some of the classes I taught in GWU's Writ-ing Program, I will insist in my coda that de-composition is a process that is always commencing; the fact that specters of queerness and disability are conjured away suggests, in fact, that the struggle never culminates but is and must be ongoing.

The English 10 and 11 courses I shaped were centered on disability studies and/or queer studies and had titles such as "Reading and Writing a Crisis: Rhetoric, AIDS, and the Media" and "Critical Bodies: Disability Studies and American Culture." I taught the "Critical Bodies" course, a composition course organized as an introduction to disability studies, for the first time in the fall of 1999 (I repeated the course in the fall of 2000). I followed that course, in the spring of 2000, with a composition course organized around lesbian, gay, and bisexual studies and called "Out in Public: Contemporary Lesbian, Gay, and Bisexual Movements."[14]

As the "Critical Bodies" course began, many students expected its structure to fit the structure they were coming to recognize from most college classes, with a body of material to be mastered and writing assignments that would be successful if they competently reflected that mastery back to the instructor. This general structure in fact dovetailed with many students' preconceived notions of disability, which tends to be understood in Western cultures according to a subject/object model—that is, what can "we" (a group assumed to be able-bodied) do for or about "them" (the disabled or "handicapped")? Several things quickly helped to shift this professional-managerial ethos, not the least a classroom atmosphere where students felt comfortable about "coming out" in relation to disability. Since disability studies in the humanities specifically rejects the objectifying/pathologizing model that would position people with disabilities as always talked about by others and instead produces spaces where people with disabilities speak in their own voices, the material we were reading encouraged students with disabilities to position themselves as subjects. In fact, coming-out stories (stories students were telling about themselves or their families) proliferated more in and around this particular course than in any of the numerous LGBT studies courses I have taught. Most disabilities are not readily apparent, so able-bodied students in the class could initially proceed with the efficient model intent on mastery of an already-composed body of material. The material we were actually reading, however (especially theoretical pieces early in the semester that located disability within a larger history of "normalcy"), as well as the alternative corporealities that were being claimed or cited by other students (around, for instance, diabetes, or learning disabilities, or hard-of-hearing identitis), quickly challenged this mindset.

Ironically, alternative corporealities often emerged in what would seem at first to be an entirely "disembodied" medium.[15] Students were required to participate all semester in a discussion on a listserv that linked all three of the sections I was teaching. This was certainly one of the kinds of writing which students were required to "produce" in the course, but it encouraged de-composition and directed attention to (individual and nonindividual) composing bodies in that the important feature of this writing assignment was not the product but the ongoing critical conversation that would never be completely finished or orderly (especially since students reported that it spilled over into other venues, into conversations they were having with friends or in other classes). At various points in the semester, some of the authors we were reading—Abby L. Wilkerson, Michael Bérubé, and Ralph Cintron—either joined the listserv briefly or responded to questions students had written (after distributing the questions to the authors, I later posted their answers to the listserv). Certainly the texts we were reading by these authors initially appeared to students as finished products, but the class eventually had good reasons for questioning such an appearance, as the seemingly authoritative voices that had composed those texts were called back to rethink them.[16]

In the spring, although I had taught the course on lesbian, gay, and bisexual movements before, the issues I have been discussing throughout this chapter were particularly pronounced, given that the semester was going to end right after the controversial Millennium March on Washington (MMOW) for lesbian, gay, bisexual, and transgendered rights. In fact, the MMOW, which was held on April 30, 2000, strikes me as a quintessentially "composed" event that was nonetheless haunted from the beginning by disorder and de-composition, by queerness and disability. In 1998, leaders of the Human Rights Campaign (HRC) and the Universal Fellowship of Metropolitan Community Churches (MCC) called for the march. From the beginning, the leadership of the march was top-down, with the leaders alone defining which issues were to be central to the event. Grassroots organizers around the country were critical of the fact that they were not consulted, of the consistent lack of attention to anything more than token diversity throughout the planning process and of the monolithic focus by march leaders (and HRC more generally) on "normalizing" issues such as marriage rights as opposed to more sweeping calls for social justice and for a critique of the multiple systems of power (including corporate capitalism) that sustain injustice.[17] Far from critiquing corporate capitalism, HRC was and is understood by many critics as craving corporate sponsorship (and, in fact, corporate logos were so ubiquitous at the march, alongside HRC symbols, that one was left with the sense that the march represented something like "the gay movement, brought to you by AT&T and other sponsors"). Earlier marches had been organized at a grassroots level and had in fact centrally included a larger, systemic critique, and many activists in communities around the country, as well as most queer theorists working in the academy, felt that this march had thus been organized without an adequate awareness of either queer politics or history. By the time of the march, even mainstream media such as the *Washington Post* and the *Nation* had covered the controversy.[18]

As an openly gay professor teaching both queer cultural studies and disability studies in Washington, D.C., it was important to me to take advantage of this highly charged moment. From the beginning of the class, students had been reading about historical splits within the gay movement, particularly the ongoing tension in twentieth-century lesbian and gay history between radical liberationist and liberal reformist politics. Students had read extensive selections from the work of John D'Emilio (and, as in the disability studies class, had in fact been in conversation, via our class listserv, with D'Emilio), who traces these historical tensions from the 1950s through the 1980s in his *Sexual Politics, Sexual Communities: The Making of a Homosexual Minority in the United States 1940–1970* and *Making Trouble: Essays on Gay History, Politics, and the University*. As I emphasize in chapter 5, a radical liberationist tradition places an emphasis on difference and distinction: not necessarily on essential difference but, rather, on how queers are *made* different by an oppressive society and how a minority identity emerges precisely because of the positions gay men and lesbians occupy within a larger, dominant structure (similar analyses have of course emerged within the disability rights movement over the last few decades). Since oppression according to this tradition is structural and not just a matter of individual prejudice, collective action is needed: sexual minorities need to speak in their own voices, and alongside multiple others. In contrast, a liberal reformist tradition emphasizes sameness; the catch phrase of this tradition is the perennial "gays and lesbians are just like everyone else." Individuality and individual prejudice are stressed more than structural oppression or collective action, and, over the past fifty years, liberal reformists have often appealed or even deferred to "experts" (doctors, ministers, and, more recently, celebrities).

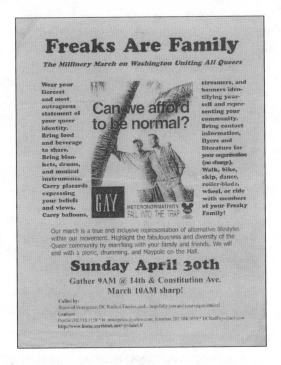

"Walk, bike, skip, dance, roller-blade, wheel, or ride with members of your Freaky Family!" Flyer calling for opposition to the Millennium March on Washington, April 30, 2000. Author's personal collection.

During the spring of 2000, this tension was being played out just beyond the walls of my composition class. We had also read Michael Warner (*The Trouble with Normal*) and Sarah Schulman (*Stagestruck*) on the contemporary commodification and normalization of the movement, and I had examined with students a series of ads directed at gay consumers. The ads that evoked the most discussion were intended to work as a set: a colorful ad for "Equality Rocks," HRC's April 29 concert to celebrate the MMOW (the ad featured corporate logos and pictures of Ellen DeGeneres, Melissa Etheridge, and other celebrities who had become overnight "leaders" of the movement simply by coming out) and a flyer from "Freaks Are Family," a local group that had been formed by members of the D.C. Radical Faeries and Bi Insurgence to protest the homogenization of the movement generally and the MMOW particularly. HRC's message that gays and lesbians are "just like everyone else" had definite appeal for many, and some students resisted, even angrily, both my own and other students' critique of HRC and the suggestion that the construction of gays and lesbians as a "niche market" might be problematic. Other students, however, found themselves completely compelled by the alternative corporealities offered by the Freaks Are Family contingent and sought the group out on April 30 in order to demonstrate their support.

My use of "alternative corporealities" to describe what Freaks Are Family offered is meant quite literally: without question, the small group of about fifty protesters was more diverse than the MMOW more generally. The Freaks Are Family contingent included a range of body types, as well as clearly identifiable members of trans, leather, bear, bi, and faerie communities. Diverse and perverse erotic proclivities (decidedly not the homogenous and domesticated married identity sought after by the MMOW), multiple genders, and various disabilities were also represented—and these could be read both on protesters' bodies and through the signs that we carried (which differed sharply from the mass-produced signs displaying HRC's ever-cryptic blue and gold equals sign). In contrast to this proliferation of corporealities, HRC and the MMOW—like the straight composition I have been critiquing throughout this chapter—offered only an orderly and singular corpo-reality.

Coda: Freakin' Composition

With the image of my students searching for the freaks, I intend to put my students' work and the (queer/disabled) composing bodies that were at the center of our composition class in conversation with at least part of the earth-wide network of (de-composing) connections outside the walls of our classroom. In the end, however, this chapter is not offered as a specific "nuts and bolts" way to conceptualize the kinds of classroom practices that will compose queerness or disability (that is, the classroom practices that will participate in critical de-composition), and not only because most composition instructors aren't likely to have the MMOW on hand when they construct their syllabus. De-composition ultimately is inimical to "nuts and bolts" approaches that somehow streamline the process of composition instruction through manuals, teaching "strategies" exchanged like recipes, and the like. Such streamlining removes composition and composition theory from the realm of critical thought and secures its place in the well-run corporate university. De-composition does result, however, from *ongoing attentiveness* to how a given composition class will intersect with local or national issues such as the MMOW.

The well-run corporate university, in turn, will invariably work to fix de-composing processes. To call back Hardt and Negri, the production of not simply products but student and faculty producers will exacerbate crises that the corporate university will always attempt to transcend. Although many in the English department objected, the May 2002 management forum that reconceptualized writing instruction at GWU eventually led to the formation of a new and autonomous program, the University Writing Program. The literacy requirement for students was also revised: students must now take University Writing 20 (UW20), a one-semester composition course, during their first year, and then must follow this with two Writing in the Disciplines (WID) courses. In contrast to what was often explicitly antidisciplinary in the old program (and to what will remain antidisciplinary in the writing program to come), the new University Writing Program, with its mandate to produce a student body that will go on to write first within very particular boundaries and second—marked by the GWU brand—within neoliberal professional-managerial contexts, is literally disciplining.

Teachers in the new program are required to order one handbook from among five or six possibilities and they must address in the classroom issues of grammar and punctuation (though faculty members continue to insist that they will make the determination as to how this requirement is met). Certain requirements are now attached to the first-year writing course, regarding both the number of pages of student writing that will be generated over the course of the semester (twenty-five to thirty pages of finished writing spread over three papers, at least one of which must involve research) and, with a little more leeway, what will count as effective "outcomes" of the course (there was no agreement but rather continual debate on these particular issues in the old program, though students in the old program generally wrote well over thirty pages each semester). Both UW20 faculty and WID instructors are explicitly charged with incorporating revision into the classes they teach. Certain structural factors, however, are working to ensure that revision in relation to writing at GWU will ultimately vouchsafe particular kinds of finished products and docile bodies.

Although initially the administration insisted that the new program would be staffed solely by (non-tenure-track) full-time assistant professors, as early as fall 2004 graduate teaching assistants and part-time faculty on several tiers (some with benefits, and some without) began teaching in the program. At that time, most part-time faculty at GWU were paid $2,700 a course and received no benefits, although a selection of "regular part-time" faculty hired in the new program received a little more than twice this amount, with some benefits. Regular part-time faculty in the University Writing Program were teaching three courses during the school year; their full-time counterparts, at well over twice the salary with full benefits, were teaching four. "Regular," of course, implies some continuity; as of this writing, there was no continuity for regular part-time faculty members from year to year. Some of those teaching on regular part-time lines, moreover, explicitly needed disability-related health care coverage.

The University Writing Program was phased in over three years, with incoming students initially tracked randomly into either the new program or the old program. By the 2005–2006 school year, all incoming students were in the new program. Especially during this period, when the program was in its infancy, faculty members were evaluated repeatedly over the course of the semester; "oversight" and "assessment" are among the keywords of the new program. Part of this assessment includes the collection of sample student essays (for every student in UW20) from the beginning and the end of the semester (though it is still not entirely clear who will read the hundreds of essays collected, nor is it yet clear what will exactly mark improvement).

After initially informing faculty, during the 2003–2004 academic year, that they could no longer hold a public conference focused on student writing, the administration relented and said that the conference could be held, with three provisions: the words "cultural studies" could not be used to describe the conference, the event could not include both students tracked into the new program and students tracked into the old program, and no funding would be made available for an autonomous event that involved students in the old program. The Composition and Cultural Studies Conference has consequently folded, and, instead, as a 2004 article advertising the new program in the *Association of American Colleges and Universities* newsletter explains, GWU will now hold, each spring, a "University Writing and Research Symposium." The *AAC&U News* article says nothing about the fact that students randomly tracked into the old Writing Program were forbidden to participate in the symposium, nor does it mention that the symposium replaced a vibrant antidisciplinary writing event with a six-year history. The article instead celebrated the fact that students, in a public forum, could demonstrate mastery of the forms of writing specific to their disciplines: "Students in the sciences might present poster sessions . . . students in business classes might use Power Point presentations." In line with the administration's requirement, the words "cultural studies" do not appear in the piece.[19]

The *AAC&U News* article is what Mike Davis might call a "booster" narrative (*City of Quartz* 24). Davis writes of the ways in which boosters and booster narratives, in the early part of the twentieth century, "set out to sell Los Angeles—as no city had ever been sold—to the restless but affluent babbitry of the Middle West" (25). The booster narratives generated for this marketing project essentially constructed Los Angeles as the land of eternal sunshine and quaint Spanish missions; Davis opens his section on boosters with an epigraph from Charles Fletcher Lummis insisting that "the missions are, next to our climate and its consequences, the best capital Southern California has" (24). Efficient productivity and profit were among the "consequences" that the intended audience of these narratives might expect, largely as a result of Los Angeles's notorious antilabor "open shop."

The ready availability of booster narratives in relation to the University Writing Program, more than anything else, demonstrates the ways in which those administering the new program only want "revision" that is safe, contained, composed; the corporate university, in other words, seeks immunity from authentic revision, from writing generated by unruly queer/crip subjectivities, from de-composition. This is evidenced by the fact that the booster narrative *must not be revised*; in repetitive language at times stunningly similar to the language Davis associates with efforts to sell Los Angeles, the University Writing Program's booster narrative—always yearning for an identifiable finished product—has been made public: "Our goal is to produce the best writing program in the country. . . . We expect to say, with no hesitation, that when you graduate from GW, you will be able to write well and that others will recognize this capability in you—that writing competency is an essential characteristic of a GW education" (Ewald 3). There are no missions on GWU's campus (though, ironically, one academic building is in fact located in a former church that is architecturally reminiscent of a Spanish-style mission), but it's always sunny—and always will be—according to the new program's (master) booster narrative. Storms are brewing, however, anywhere and everywhere that the corporate university generates contradictions like the one

I am teasing out in this paragraph: revision is mandated, revision is forbidden. The production of producers within that contradictory—literally impossible and unlivable—context is bound to generate unexpected revisions. The new program will inevitably de-compose.

Although clearly the will to a finished—and marketable—product is strong, the future of writing instruction nonetheless remains contested at GWU, which is actually located (paradoxically, as far as the sunshine of boosterism is concerned) in the neighborhood of Washington, D.C., known as "Foggy Bottom." Many of the faculty hired for the new University Writing Program formerly held positions in the old, and although they have been shut out of many key decisions (particularly around hiring and assessment), they have managed to secure some victories, most notably a small class size (fifteen students) and courses that largely remain focused on cultural studies topics, even if the language of cultural studies has been conjured away by some who are heavily invested in the new program. Specters of disability and queerness have appeared at the margins of the new program, and how those specters will affect its current corporeality remains to be seen. The faculty in the new program includes at least one nationally recognized scholar in disability studies, whose current work, notably, centers on disability movements resisting conceptions of "diagnosis." Courses in the new program have already included one focused on freak shows and another on sexuality, identity, and anxiety.[20] Such work, however, is arguably viewed with a great deal of suspicion by those invested in a particular and contained view of writing at GWU, and some candidates for positions in the new program whose work is directly in queer or disability studies have been perceived as having an "agenda" (and have, consequently, not been hired).

As I draw attention to anything positive or generative about the preservation of some queer, disability, and cultural studies content even as the program more explicitly dedicated to a cultural studies pedagogy was dismantled, it could be said that I'm fiddling as Foggy Bottom burns, or—more directly—that I'm not comprehending what Thomas Frank calls the "conquest of cool" as it operates in neoliberalism generally and in and around cultural studies in particular. Topic-based composition courses, in other words, could be read as integral to the corporate university, not as forces potentially opposing it. In my mind, however, such a conclusion (while in some ways true—the corporate university *will* incorporate topic-based courses, along with any other kind of course, into its strategic plans for excellence) gives up on writing and forgets what Hall argues about the ways that cultural hegemony works. According to Hall: "Cultural hegemony is never about pure victory or pure domination (that's not what the term means); it is never a zero-sum cultural game; it is always about shifting the balance of power in relations of culture; it is always about changing the dispositions and the configurations of cultural power, not getting out of it" ("What Is This 'Black'?" 468). Hall's formulation suggests that processes of de-composition always pose dangers in and for the corporate university. Recognizing—and indeed teaching—that means not ceding to the right a skill worth having and sharing with others: the capacity for continually linking questions of identity to questions of political economy. This chapter (and this book) are part of a much larger and collective pedagogical effort to claim queer and crip sites where those linkages can be forged and can work against the current neoliberal order of things.

Certainly in this chapter I intend to position queer theory and disability studies at the center of composition theory, and in the interests of such a project, my highlighting of the ways in which disabled/queer questions and issues, or de-composing processes, haunt the newly composed program is intended to affirm, in the face of dangerous transitions, what Paulo Freire called "a pedagogy of freedom." But I do not centralize disability studies and queer theory in order to offer them, somehow, as the "solution" for either a localized or more general crisis in composition; queer theory and disability studies in and of themselves will not magically revitalize a sometimes-tendentious and often-beleaguered field. I am nonetheless hopeful that disability studies and queer theory will remain locations from which we might speak back to straight composition, with its demand for composed and docile texts, skills, and bodies. Despite that hope, and with the transitions at my own institution in mind, I recognize that composition programs are currently heavily policed locations and that the demand for order and efficiency remains pronounced—mainly because that demand and the practices that result from it serve very specific material interests. Crip and queer theory, however, do provide us with ways of comprehending how our very bodies are caught up in, or even produced by, straight composition. More important, with their connection to embodied, de-composing movements both outside and inside the academy, they simultaneously continue to imagine or envision a future horizon *beyond* straight composition, in all its forms.

5

Crip Eye for the Normate Guy
Queer Theory, Bob Flanagan, and the Disciplining of Disability Studies

In "Seeing the Disabled: Visual Rhetorics of Disability in Popular Photography," Rosemarie Garland-Thomson argues that representations of disability in photography, over more than a century, have generally fallen into four broad categories. These categories or modes include, first, the wondrous, which places the disabled subject on high and elicits awe from viewers because of the supposedly amazing achievement represented (and even the most quotidian activities, such as eating and drinking, are at times understood through the rubric of the wondrous); second, the sentimental, which places the disabled subject in a more diminished or lowly position, evoking pity, and establishing a relationship between viewer and viewed not unlike the custodial relationship of parent and child (indeed, the sentimental mode often deploys images of children); third, the exotic, which makes disability strange and distant—a freakish, or perhaps transgressive, spectacle (in fact, Garland-Thomson at times directly calls this mode the "transgressive"); and finally, the realistic, which brings disability close, naturalizing disability and potentially minimizing the difference between viewer and viewed (and which, it is important to note, Garland-Thomson insists is just as constructed as the other three modes).

"Seeing the Disabled," which first appeared in print in the important disability studies anthology *The New Disability History: American Perspectives*, continues the field-defining work for which Garland-Thomson is well known at this point. The essay reiterates some of the central disability studies insights that have transformed scholarship in the humanities and social sciences over the past decade (and that have founded studies such as this one): it focuses on the construction and representation of disability rather than supposedly self-evident bodily truths; it critiques the medical model; it puts forward a minority thesis to displace the cultural compulsion to understand disability only in relation to loss, lack, or pity; and it makes explicit the connection between work in disability studies and work in feminism and other fields concerned with identity and identity trouble. It also takes disability studies in new directions, generously providing a critical taxonomy that scholars in the field can immediately use as a foundation for countless other projects.

I choose "generous" quite carefully to describe what Garland-Thomson accomplishes with this essay; throughout her work, Garland-Thomson reflects an astute awareness of the transformations that are occurring in the academy, and, consistently, she facilitates those transformations by generously inviting others to reconceptualize and reinvigorate their work through an encounter with disability studies. Always, the invitation is to take this new field in whatever exciting, unpredictable directions they can dare to imagine.[1] Garland-Thomson shares this generosity with many other prominent figures in disability studies; like feminism, queer studies, Latino/a studies, and other movements that have laid the groundwork for, or that have developed in tandem with, disability studies, this is a collective endeavor and those involved are eager to spread the enthusiasm. Some of the most innovative work in the humanities today has resulted from all of this generosity and enthusiasm.

The signs of the transformation are everywhere: disability studies classes (in literature, philosophy, history, rhetoric/composition, performance studies, and other disciplines), as well as disability studies programs, are cropping up in several countries; hundreds of scholars around the world are linked to DS-HUM, the Disability Studies in the Humanities listserv; and disability is one of the most popular topics right now in the academic publishing world—most prominent university presses have begun to publish in the field, and special disability issues of journals such as *Public Culture*, *Social Theory and Practice*, *GLQ: A Journal of Lesbian and Gay Studies*, and *NWSA* [National Women's Studies Association] *Journal* have appeared. In 2002, the Modern Language Association (MLA) published the landmark anthology, edited by Sharon L. Snyder, Brenda J. Brueggeman, and Garland-Thomson, *Disability Studies: Enabling the Humanities*—meaning that a volume now exists bearing the imprimatur of the largest and most important professional organization for scholars working on modern languages and literature (the volume includes a much-condensed version of Garland-Thomson's "Seeing the Dis-

abled," titled "The Politics of Staring"). The MLA has done more than
simply publish a definitive, or *the* definitive, volume, however. The organization occasionally promotes, and funds, high-profile conferences
around issues understood to be of central importance to the profession;
in March 2004, it hosted at Emory University a four-day gathering on
"Disability Studies and the University." The presentations from this
event—papers from more than thirty well-known disability studies scholars—were subsequently published in a special cluster of the MLA's journal *PMLA*.[2] "Someday soon," Michael Bérubé writes in the afterword to
Disability Studies, "disability studies will be widely understood as one of
the normal—but not normalizing—aspects of study in the humanities,
central to any adequate understanding of the human record" (343). Arguably, in many locations, today looks a lot like the day Bérubé imagines.
All things just keep getting better.

Working Like a Homosexual?: Visual Rhetorics of Queerness in Contemporary Culture

My use of the refrain "all things just keep getting better," from Bravo
Television's Summer 2003 megahit *Queer Eye for the Straight Guy*, allows me to put my consideration of Garland-Thomson's essay and my
celebration of the success of disability studies in the academy to the side
temporarily as I consider a different, even more recent, and perhaps unlikely, cultural phenomenon. *Queer Eye for the Straight Guy*, in which
five gay experts in grooming, fashion, interior design, dining, and "culture" make over a "straight guy" whose supposedly disastrous appearance and living space provide the premise for the show, premiered in June
2003 and scored Bravo TV record ratings (not coincidentally, *Boy Meets
Boy*, a dating reality show in which a gay man chooses a date but is not
told that some of the contestants are straight, aired immediately before
Queer Eye for the Straight Guy in June 2003 and held Bravo's second-
place rating for that year). During the opening of each episode, to the beat
of Simone Denny's "All Things (Just Keep Getting Better)," the stars of
Queer Eye are introduced by their area of expertise, and as they walk
through a drab, black-and-white semiurban space, it is instantly transformed into living color.

The so-called Fab Five made *Queer Eye* a gay media phenom; nothing
like it had been broadcast before, and no other gay or lesbian show has

had such a meteoric rise to prominence. NBC, Bravo's corporate partner, consequently broadcast shorter (half-hour) versions of some of the episodes in some areas, and Jay Leno signed up to have *The Tonight Show* done over by the Fab Five. Clinique reportedly wanted to send Kyan Douglas, grooming expert, "every product it has ever made or ever will make in hopes he'll use some of them on the air" (Glitz 40). By early 2004, a hardcover companion volume to the show—Ted Allen et al.'s *Queer Eye for the Straight Guy: The Fab 5's Guide to Looking Better, Cooking Better, Dressing Better, Behaving Better, and Living Better*—was available for sale in a range of mainstream and LGBT venues, from Borders Bookstores and Amazon.com to the Human Rights Campaign's Action Center and Store and the gay-targeted book club, ISO Books. Every version of *The Fab 5's Guide* was essentially the same, picturing the stars of the show on its cover in stylish black suits, but consumers purchasing the book could choose one of five different background colors. Customers who bought this particular visual rhetoric of queerness also bought titles like Scott Omelianuk and Ted Allen's *Esquire's Things a Man Should Know about Style* and Carson Kressley's *Off the Cuff: The Essential Guide for Men—and the Women Who Love Them*.[3]

Both the general marketing frenzy and the more specific dish (like Clinique groveling for some queer attention) make it clear why, in many ways, *Queer Eye* functions as such an easy target for cultural theorists. In *Subculture: The Meaning of Style*, Dick Hebdige famously argues that dissident subcultures inevitably face two kinds of incorporation: commodification—evident in *Queer Eye*, which basically functions as a queer commercial for everything from Bed, Bath, and Beyond to Urban Outfitters—and ideological dilution. Ideological dilution ensures that the potential threat to the dominant culture posed by the subculture is "trivialized, naturalized, domesticated" (Hebdige 97). This, too, is clearly evident in *Queer Eye*, not least in what it asks us to consent to before we even start watching the show or consuming its products: the nonthreatening (and even reassuring) idea that indeed there are two distinct types of "guys," queer and straight. Forget about queerness as a descriptor for what doesn't fit neatly within a heterosexual/homosexual binary; forget about queerness as a critique of compulsory heterosexuality or as a critical lens for denaturalizing all sexual identities. In many ways, *Queer Eye* naturalizes sexual identity and stages for viewers a rapprochement between gay men and straight men (and the sometimes not-so-subtle misogyny of the show facilitates that rapprochement). "Straight guys are so much fun," fashion expert Kressley says in one episode, but if part of the fun of queer theory (not to mention more than a century of queer sub-cultural practice) has been watching that compulsory identity unravel, that is no longer necessarily the case. As long as we agree that gay men and straight men are distinct, and—incidentally—as long as we're look-ing at the straight guy, supposedly, we can all get along.[4]

Most queers, of course, could easily complicate such a critique of *Queer Eye*, however, before—perhaps—redoubling it. There is limited pleasure in the transformative power these gay men wield, power that res-onates with the fantasies, or even the experiences, of many gay people. When the show came out, I joked, for instance, that my own drab gray department was suddenly filled with beautiful Benjamin Moore colors the day I walked in. This was merely a joke, but it nonetheless attempted to mark what Matthew Tinkcomm, in an important book on camp, capital, and cinema, calls "working like a homosexual." Working like a homo-sexual—which Tinkcomm defines in relation to filmmakers Vincente Minelli, Kenneth Anger, Andy Warhol, and John Waters—consists of a camp luxuriating in the potentially excessive cultural values that gay peo-ple produce when "paradoxically it would seem that no subject is ever prohibited from exerting him- or herself on capital's behalf" (5). In other words, Tinkcomm, shifting the discussion of camp from the realm of con-sumption to the realm of production, argues that even as we are com-pelled to produce ourselves as commodities, "the passionate failure to strive for a compulsory identity" is possible and desirable (15) and that, instead of simply producing ourselves as blank commodities and objects that erase entirely the history of their production, we might produce com-modities (including ourselves) that bear the mark of queer labor and that thus hint at alternative values.

Queer Eye, however, makes it difficult to work like a homosexual. If the traces of at least some of the disruptive ways camp has functioned his-torically are readable—even if recommodified—in *Queer Eye* and the many products available in its wake, the show itself emerges in a nor-malizing historical period that insistently domesticates camp and other disruptive queer forces: as I suggest in chapter 2, the dominant gay move-ment—and certainly the most prominent organization, the Human Rights Campaign—has a slick, corporate feel; marriage rather than a feminist or queer critique of marriage occupies many people's attention, gay and nongay; media invisibility has been replaced by, at this point, in-numerable figures who "just happen to be gay"; and a minority thesis that formerly emphasized positionality—that is, the idea that in a homophobic and heterosexist culture gay men and lesbians are *made* an oppressed minority—has been largely superseded by the naturalizing minority thesis that emphasizes essence: some guys are straight, some guys are queer.

Attending to this larger historical context for *Queer Eye for the Straight Guy*, I draw at least two conclusions. First, the camp pleasures of the show—pleasures that have entailed in the past disidentifying with normalcy—partially obscure how *Queer Eye* participates in the larger normalizing processes we are currently enduring. Second, and conversely, the seemingly marginal flashes of disability in the show at the same time attest to those processes. "That's so mental-institution chic" (or, more directly, "He's so retarded!"), one of the Fab Five will readily say, either when they first arrive at the straight guy's home or at the end, when they are watching—stout cocktails in hand—his final performance on closed-circuit television. If his face is twitching, "Maybe he's got Tourette's"; if he fumbles in the kitchen or elsewhere, "It's like he has a mechanical hand"; if he seems confused at all, "Guys, I think we have a real live Rain Man on our hands." Yes, queer theory and disability studies have come together in incredibly generative ways over the past several years, but that academic fact should not lead us to discount the more widespread cultural fact that our normalizing moment (like all normalizing moments) depends on identifying and containing—on *disciplining*—disability. It also depends—paradoxically, given how much a version of queerness is supposedly on display here—on containing, on disciplining, queerness.

I would certainly not suggest that humor at the expense of disability is anything but culturally ubiquitous. In other words, I recognize that the Fab Five's banter is hardly unique to them. The kind of humor Carson, Kyan, and the others deploy is actually everywhere, from the playground to the office party, regardless of whether it feels—either positively or negatively—somehow original to them. Karen Tongson, in a book review attempting, at least in part, to account for the phenomenon of *Queer Eye*, writes that "the pleasure many queers derive from *Queer Eye for the Straight Guy* comes not from the glistening example of the groomed straight man 'made better' at the end of the show but from the laughs that come when we, along with the 'Fab 5,' delight in the spectacle of his hapless state" (633). Although her assessment is slightly different from my own attempt above to account for the limited pleasure in *Queer Eye*, I agree with Tongson's thesis about the pleasure "many queers" derive from the show. I question, however, the "we" she invokes, if that "we" forgets that it is involved in a cultural practice that is ultimately so widespread as to be banal: identifying a hapless state, linking it metaphorically to disability, and laughing at it. My main critique of this humor, however, is not simply that it exists—I can imagine democratic, carnivalesque spaces (including the spaces generated by some queer/crip performers) where laughter at someone (or at ourselves) in a hapless state is desirable and life-affirming for everyone involved.[5] My critique, rather, is specifically of the fact that this banal disability humor—"he's so retarded!"— functions particularly efficiently in and for an LGBT normalizing moment that disciplines disability and queerness.

The paradox of disciplining queerness when queerness is unquestionably so spectacular brings me back to the somewhat different disciplinary issues with which I started. "More analysis than evaluation," Garland-Thomson insists in her essay on photography, as she moves from the wondrous, through the sentimental and exotic, to the realistic mode, "the discussion here does not suggest a progress narrative in which the culture marches invariably toward a state of egalitarian enlightenment" (339). Disability studies makes it possible to analyze visual rhetorics of disability in their plurality and oppose that plurality to the singularity (and supposedly nonrhetorical truth) of the medical model. However, plurality does not vouchsafe progress: "None of these rhetorical modes is in the service of actual disabled people; indeed, almost all of them appropriate the disabled body for the purposes of constructing, instructing, or assuring some aspect of than ostensibly nondisabled viewer" (340). Garland-Thomson stresses that the visual rhetorics she identifies "wax and wane, shift and combine, over time as they respond to the purposes for which they were produced" (339). In other words, some things *don't* keep getting better; visual rhetorics of disability do not *necessarily* improve over time, nor do they posit (or construct, instruct, or assure) a disabled viewer.

I concur with Garland-Thomson's wariness about progress narratives, but—given the larger essay, which ends with something of a fanfare on a realistic-mode photograph of President Bill Clinton's undersecretary of education Judith Heumann—I can't help feeling that the thesis requires me, as a reader, to engage in a fairly straightforward disavowal. That is, I know that assertions of decisive differences between our present and a problematic past, appeals to things like a seemingly unprecedented "climate of integration and diversity" (366), and triumphant conclusions are generally the necessary components of a progress narrative and, when present, sufficient for constituting said narrative, but in this case, I consent as a reader to not see it. Call it a queer eye for the progress narrative, but you will have gathered that I dissent: Secretary Heumann, in Garland-Thomson's essay, is as counterposed to the closeted Franklin Delano Roosevelt as her era is to his; the realistic mode is three times "radical" in the space of two pages; and it explicitly supplants the wondrous, sentimental, and exotic modes. Additionally, the full-page concluding photograph of Heumann flanked by flags in her Education Department office arguably participates in progress-centered, and very American, narratives of arrival.

Heumann, moreover, is not alone in her arrival; the realistic mode in general appears in "Seeing the Disabled" to mark a decisive cultural advance.[6] Another example of the realistic, immediately preceding the official Department of Education photograph, represents "the upscale disability fashion photography featured in magazines that target the disability market, such as *We Magazine*" (368). Two side-by-side photographs depict a conventionally handsome, middle-aged white man in two different sports jackets that neither cover up nor draw much attention to his prosthetic arm. Garland-Thomson's caption reads: "The Disability Rights movement has generated a rhetoric of the ordinary in contemporary advertising that appeals to the disability market and suggests an ideology of diversity and inclusion" (369). Like the Heumann photograph, which is not qualitatively different from any other photograph of a state official, the *We Magazine* selections are not unlike other images produced by the larger fashion industry. The caption, however, does underscore a difference between the realistic mode more generally and the visual rhetorics of disability that have preceded it: people with disabilities materialize in the caption, both as producers and as consumers. Garland-Thomson's claims that none of the modes work in the service of "actual disabled people" notwithstanding, the disability rights movement, in the conclusion to her essay, has helped to "generate," or produce, the realistic mode and a (new) disability target market is largely consuming it.

The incorporation of disabled people into early twenty-first-century production and consumption processes may not be as accomplished as *Queer Eye* suggests LGBT incorporation into those processes is, but the fashions of *We Magazine* and the progress they mark are of a piece with the progress, and the "looking and living better," marked by the Fab Five.

And that incorporation is marked by some of the same (sometimes quite promising) paradoxes: if all subjects must exert themselves on capital's behalf—and I would include here Heumann in her Education Department office, the disabled model in *We Magazine*'s studio, and Garland-Thomson and myself working on these images—clearly within and around locations impacted by the disability rights movement, there is now a will to generate alternative, disabled values. Garland-Thomson's re-presentation of four photographic rubrics, in particular, posits both disabled and nondisabled critical viewers of them and, in fact, works these images over and makes them mean something new. To choose just one straightforward example from her essay: a classic twentieth-century "poster child" shot may not have been intended, when the March of Dimes was founded, for viewers with a critically disabled consciousness (342).[7] It may have carried, as well, a sentimental meaning that was not to be questioned, and that able-bodied viewers eagerly consumed. In Garland-Thomson's work on the image, however, new, different, and critical meanings are generated in excess of the original producers' intent and in the interests of an imagined viewing community that approaches, or accesses, such an image from a different direction.

Disabled people and their allies, then, are in fact incorporated into contemporary economies, however tenuously, and—as far as images of disability are concerned—disabled people, again however tenuously, are at work both producing and consuming the images in circulation within those economies. And since incorporation into processes of production and consumption is most evident in and around the realistic mode, on some level a progress narrative is built into the trajectory of "Seeing the Disabled," despite Garland-Thomson's suggestion otherwise. I would argue, however, that the issues here extend far beyond Garland-Thomson's (or my own) writing; it seems to me that a cultural progress narrative toward the realistic mode for representing disability, even if it is still in many ways emergent, very much precedes (and in some ways enables) any scholarship on it.

Related to this, there is one other argumentative strand that troubles me in "Seeing the Disabled," this time because I am at least inclined to be convinced by portions of it: "Realism aims to routinize disability, making it seem ordinary. As such, it has the most political power in a democratic order, although one could argue that the transgressive most effectively achieves social change in democracies" (363). My first question about this seductive argument is: if one could argue that the transgressive most effectively achieves social change—and in a post-Stonewall, post-HEW takeover, post-ACT UP, post-ADAPT, post-Sex Panic!, post-Battle for Seattle world, such an argument would have a lot going for it—then why not argue it?[8] And my second question may partially answer my first: if we are in the realm of routinizing a particular cultural construction and making it seem ordinary, are we not potentially in the realm of ideology?

"Routinizing and making something seem ordinary" is actually a fairly good description of what Roland Barthes called myth-making. From soap powders to wrestling matches, Barthes's queer eye for the French bourgeoisie of the 1950s pinpointed the ways in which myth-makers appropriated cultural and historical objects or signs and attached new meanings to them. This new, second order of signification was then made to seem natural. In the essay on "Photography and Electoral Appeal," for instance, Barthes contends that political "photography constitutes . . . a veritable blackmail by means of moral values: country, army, family, honour, reckless heroism" (*Mythologies* 92). None of these moral values magically inhere in any given photograph of a politician, whether the photograph is of Pierre-Marie Poujade for Barthes or of John Kerry or George W. Bush for us. Myth-making, however, makes these moral values seem self-evident, makes the values *seem* to inhere magically; ventriloquizing the images, Barthes imagines them saying, naturally, "*Look at me: I am like you*" (91; italics in original).[9]

The fact that Barthes's larger project in *Mythologies* includes an attentiveness to both electoral photography and advertising, moreover, suggests an awareness, on his part, of how a variety of myth-making, visual rhetorics for the mid-century French bourgeoisie were working in concert. In particular, visual rhetorics at work in the state were functioning relatively harmoniously with visual rhetorics at work in the market. In fact, the essay on French politicians directly follows an essay on "The New Citroën," which argues that "cars today are almost the exact equivalent of the great Gothic cathedrals . . . the supreme creation of an era, conceived with passion by unknown artists, and consumed in image if not in usage by a whole population" (88). The Citroën does not, naturally, speak, but of course its status as a commodity fetish—as "a very queer thing," as Karl Marx would say (*Capital* 319)—makes it appear to speak (though not to reveal the history of its production). Barthes doesn't, this time, ventriloquize, but the Citroën's message too seems fairly clear: "Look at me; people like you want to have me."

The Return of the Transgressive: Burning Candles for Bob Flanagan

Chela Sandoval argues the following:

> Barthes's radical aim in *Mythologies* is to challenge [the] formation through which Western meaning, consciousness, and ideology are produced, and thus to rescue the irreproachably good, compliant citizen-subject of Western culture as she/he unerringly enters this sensuous experience, this living prison house of meaning. Barthes's strategy is to demonstrate how meaning is conjugal, erotic, and satisfyingly naturalized. (95)

"Seeing the Disabled," it is important to emphasize, purports to acknowledge such ideological maneuvers; to return, in good faith, to Garland-Thomson's claims: "The rhetoric of realism is just as constructed and convention-bound as the rhetorics of the wondrous, sentimental, or exotic" (344). This claim, however, is at least partially undone by the disavowed progress narrative that weaves together visual advances in the state and the market (and although the market emerges at various points in Garland-Thomson's discussion of the other three modes, it is only the realistic that thoroughly weaves together market and state) and by the subordination (through a brief dismissal) of the exotic/transgressive. The quick subordination of the transgressive, in particular, makes it seem as though there were, in fact, something inherently better (and more satisfying), because less bound by the able-bodied conventions of the past, about the realistic mode. In this section, I call back the transgressive to consider whether it might be understood otherwise.

And since we're talking about bondage, I tie Bob Flanagan, the self-proclaimed "supermasochist" "famous for pounding a nail through his penis" ("Seeing the Disabled" 358), to this discussion. As Garland-Thomson notes when she brings him forward as an example of the exotic mode, and before she subordinates the exotic mode to the realistic, Flanagan incorporated into photographs and performances "cape, chains, piercings, and the oxygen mask characteristic of cystic fibrosis to discomfort his viewers" (358). In, "Visiting Hours" an installation at the Santa Monica Museum of Art and the Museum of Modern Art (MOMA) in New York City, Flanagan and his partner/mistress Sheree Rose staged a performance that included a beating characteristic of their erotic and sexual practices together. The beating was at once therapeutically useful for Flanagan (clearing the respiratory system, keeping the lungs as free of mucus as possible) and, presumably, erotically satisfying for both participants. Flanagan's life, relationship with Rose, performances, and poetry were documented in Kirby Dick's 1997 film *Sick: The Life and Death of Bob Flanagan, Supermasochist.* "I was so excited to learn about an artist with cf," one admirer wrote on January 4, 1998, the second anniversary of Flanagan's death at age forty-one. "Wherever I am today, I will burn a candle for you, Bob" (Compton). And CF individuals and communities were not alone burning those candles; after Flanagan's death in 1996, bdsm chat groups and listservs were abuzz with what they perceived as an incalculable loss. "Bob Flanagan Is Dead," the email's subject line proclaimed, over and over again, in posting after posting.[10]

On some level, clearly, CF and bdsm communities, encountering visual representations of Flanagan, received the message "Look at me: I am like you." In these particular subcultural contexts, however, that message functions differently from the ways in which it functions in relation to the electoral photography Barthes discusses, or in relation to his most famous example from *Mythologies*—a photograph of a young, black Algerian soldier, wearing the colors of the French colonial empire and saluting, presumably the French tricolor. As with electoral photography, the image of the French colonial subject provides what Barthes calls "spectacular comfort" (91). And, significantly, that spectacular comfort sends a message that reassures in the face of, or actively against, the contingencies of the future; it "is somehow frozen, purified, eternalized. . . . *The French Empire? It's just a fact: look at this good Negro who salutes like one of our own boys*" (124; italics in original). Just as electoral photography seeks to reassure so that the (neo)liberal state seems inevitable and functions more efficiently (particularly in its role as guardian of the interests of capital), Barthes's famous example suggests that the picture of the Algerian solider reassures so that the French Empire might function more efficiently. Paradoxically, since efficiency simultaneously signifies that a dynamic system is moving forward but that it is also decidedly not being jarred or redirected, we could say that such photographs attempt to mark a progress that is essentially going nowhere.

In contrast, Flanagan's radical crip images (and his writing and interviews, as I suggest below) generally put into play the multifaceted message "fuck the future." "Look at me: I am like you," the images indeed say to some people, but they add a certain heady contingency: "Look at me: I am like you . . . maybe. But we're not like the others and we might, you and I, be able to imagine something other than, different from, or beyond all of this." It is a contingency and investment in futurity, that Richard Kim, in his essay "Fuck the Future?" identifies as "utopian and queer" (qtd. in Duggan, "Down There" 385). Attempting to account for why "we" might have such an investment, Kim writes:

> It might be because we have a queer relationship with some future person, who might or might not identify as queer. Looking back at what is preserved of our present, such a person will not find the familiar and familial trace of their own descent, and failing to find his or her own mirror image in the past, he or she will be able to take little comfort in the assumption that what holds so true for them now will remain true in the future. But such a person might, in a moment of danger, seize hold of our present as their memory. Our present, and our present relationship with the past, might be that momentary, irretrievable spark of hope in their past that, though we are dead, will reveal to them a way to survive at the margins of time and space. (Qtd. in Duggan, "Down There" 385–386)

Critically queer, and radically crip, Flanagan's images sometimes suggest little more than "Bob Flanagan's sick." In a moment of danger and noncompliance, however, "some future person" or collectivity might detect in that sick message the seemingly incomprehensible way to survive, and survive well, at the margins of time, space, and representation (they might, in fact, detect that surviving well can paradoxically mean surviving sick).[11]

Flanagan himself repeatedly affirmed that a range of meanings might be detected in his writings and performances. An interviewer asked him once, for instance, "What do you think of the juxtaposition of metaphors: being sick equals SM?" An entirely valid, and at this point well-established, line of disability studies theorizing, would have, perhaps, disciplined or sent away/exorcised the metaphorical conflation (and, arguably, this important theoretical tradition, like Garland-Thomson's "Seeing the Disabled," requires prioritizing a certain realism).[12] Flanagan, however, perversely embraced and extended the metaphor: "My last show in New York and L.A. was titled 'Bob Flanagan's Sick.' I purposely used that title, and there were three different meanings: (1) Bob Flanagan's sick in the head [mentally], (2) Bob Flanagan's sick [physically], and (3) This is Bob Flanagan's show called 'Sick'" (Juno and Vale 27; brackets in original). A few things are notable about Flanagan's crip response. First, he essentially answers the interviewer's "What do you think of the juxtaposition of metaphors: being sick equals SM?" with his own, supermasochistic, "I think I like it." Or, put differently: "More, please." Second, although he enumerates "three different meanings," his answer does not preclude a proliferation of meanings beyond three (or four, or more). Indeed, the fact that Flanagan adds a third meaning to the two the interviewer puts before him is a good indication of the pleasure he takes—in performance, in his writing, and in his life—testing and extending the limits of meaning and metaphor. Such pleasure, moreover, was clearly something Flanagan sought to offer to others. In Tinkcomm's sense, in fact, Flanagan worked like a homosexual, even though he was not gay: even as he exerted himself on capital's behalf, as a masochistic erformer, Flanagan put on display nonheteronormative, excessive sexual and bodily pleasures that audience members were encouraged (potentially, and without any coercion) to test out themselves.[13] And without question, for many in the specific *subcultural* audiences that saw Flanagan perform (that is, not so much at MOMA as at venues like the SM Beyond Baroque Club in Los Angeles), that is precisely what they came for: to discover (and invent) possibilities that they might test out and extend (on) themselves.[14]

Third, although the final meaning—"This is Bob Flanagan's show called 'Sick'"—is apparently the most literal or (seemingly) metaphor-free, Flanagan's move from meaning one to meaning three cannot really be read as a march forward. On the contrary, he clearly delights in the queer ways in which the meanings of "sick" are inextricably associated, one meaning constantly folding back into another. For Flanagan, the multiple meanings of "sick" are as erotically bound together as he and Rose. And although those meanings can be contingently separated (as, certainly, he and Rose were, in the end, two separate people), Flanagan questions whether or why that separation would be desirable, just as SM sex and performance can (sometimes) be about questioning whether or why Western individuality is always and everywhere so desirable.

Linda S. Kauffman suggests that "bad girls and sick boys" like Flanagan often ask such questions: "Why . . . are certain things—foods, bodily functions, sex acts, fetishes—taboo?" (15); they subject themselves, in other words, to answering sometimes-impossible questions about and at cultural limits. Consequently, bad girls and sick boys (or sick girls and bad boys) are also invariably subject to a diagnostic gaze that would determine what is causing their deviance.

Flanagan's most famous prose poem, "Why," illustrates well (and responds to) this subjection. To excerpt selections from "Why" is already to discipline it, in a nonconsensual way; the poem proliferates and does not prioritize answers to the invasive question "Why do you do it, Bob?" To quote only some of those answers is in some ways—like the doctor or psychiatrist looking for the key—to undermine important functions of the poem (and you can almost hear the doctor now, can't you? "I want to go back to one particular thing you said a moment ago that seems to me especially significant"). "Why" implicitly insists that the key is not to be found and performatively demonstrates that the "answers" will keep coming. Perhaps, in fact, the only ethical interpretive relation to the poem would be an erotic one that acknowledges entering it sadistically, in order to linger over the (exotic) passages that are most pleasurable or that hold the most promise for transporting a reader elsewhere. I can, however, only *presume* Flanagan's consent to such a sadistic reading; ultimately, the poem puts a reader in something of an interpretive bind.[15]

"Why" could be said to "preclude even a trace of the sentimental or the wondrous, insisting instead on the empowerment of the transgressive" (Garland-Thomson, "Seeing the Disabled" 360). Flanagan begins:

Because it feels good; because it gives me an erection; because it makes me come; because I'm sick; because there was so much sickness; because I say FUCK THE SICKNESS; because I like the attention; because I was alone a lot; because I was different; because kids beat me up at school; because I was humiliated by nuns; because of Christ and the crucifixion; because of Porky Pig in bondage, force-fed by some sinister creep in a black cape . . . because of what's inside me; because of my genes; because of my parents; because of doctors and nurses; because they tied me to the crib so I wouldn't hurt myself; because I had time to think; because I had time to hold my penis; because I had awful stomach-aches and holding my penis made it feel better; because I felt like I was going to die; because it makes me feel invincible . . . because it's in my nature; because it's against nature; because it's nasty; because it's fun; because it flies in the face of all that's normal (whatever that is); because I'm not normal. . . . (64–65).

The published version of "Why" continues for two full pages. Versions of "Why" that were performed, however, or that were part of Flanagan and Rose's installations, sometimes ran in loops that had no clear beginning or end.

There are many things I like (and find empowering) about the excerpts I have chosen here. Flanagan's answers are contradictory; if "it's in my nature" seems to put forward a recognizable minority defense of why he does it, the proud embrace of "it's against nature" undoes that defense. These excerpts also repeat, but unfaithfully, classic—even canonical—causal explanations. Flanagan's mother indeed worried that she had somehow "caused" his masochism: "Knowing how odd we all are," Flanagan once said about his siblings and himself, "I think my mother thinks that if she'd done something differently, we'd all be 'normal'" (Juno and Vale 84). Flanagan (sadistically or masochistically, depending on your perspective) takes up this compulsory narrative about parents (and mothers in particular) causing deviance, and thereby interrupts his mother's (much more faithful) repetition of it. Although the general, liberal response to the parental worry "What did I do to cause this?" is an insistent and reassuring "Nothing" (reassurance again marking a progress going nowhere, since in some sense the traditional, heterosexual family structure is protected from too much criticism through such an answer), Flanagan offers a different kind of reversal: if there's a "you" who caused abnormality (and, paradoxically, there both is and isn't a causal "you" in his "Why"—or, rather, the causal you both appears and disappears), Flanagan sees little reason for worry or alarm. Indeed, in a perverse twist on "all things just keep getting better," he sees cause for celebration in the fact that he has been made abnormal.

The poem contains several other paradoxes. Holding the penis is both urgent and entirely banal, a mere accident of the time Flanagan had on his hands. The earnest insistence that "Christ and the crucifixion" were responsible is also offset by what comes next—it's difficult to sustain the importance of being earnest when Christ cavorts with Porky Pig. Finally, and most important (at least for the points I am contingently making about these very particular excerpts), even though Flanagan's "FUCK THE SICKNESS" is, through capitalization, literally emphasized more than anything else in the poem, "Why" remains a slap in the face to any classic disability overcoming narrative. Cystic fibrosis is not "overcome" through bdsm as surely as bdsm is not a direct (singular, determined) outcome of what Flanagan experienced living with CF.

Flanagan repeatedly drew attention to how his life interrupted classic disability narratives more generally and the standard narrative of CF, in particular. As a child, both Flanagan and his sister (who died when she was twenty-one) were located—or fixed—within standard CF narratives. Indeed, Flanagan himself (or, to be precise, "Robert Flanagan, Jr., 14, Costa Mesa") had been named "first poster child for the newly organized North Orange County Chapter, National Cystic Fibrosis Research Foundation." The July 23, 1967, article is reproduced in its entirety, complete with a picture of a young Flanagan playing the drums (captioned "Cystic Fibrosis Poster Boy"), in Andrea Juno and V. Vale's collection of interviews with Flanagan, *Bob Flanagan: Supermasochist.* "Cystic fibrosis struck alternate children in the family of Mr. and Mrs. Robert Flanagan, Sr.," the journalist explains, and proceeds to put forward the true story of the Flanagan family, and through them the true story of CF, "a hereditary disease, believed carried by a recessive gene" and "variously called 'fibrocystic disease of the pancreas,' 'pancreatic cystic fibrosis' and 'mucoviscidosis.'" Since the mythology of the poster child depends on his or her asexuality, the Flanagan poster boy story cannot, of course, reveal that "Mrs. Robert Flanagan" actively worries about her children's potential sexual deviance, even though, at fourteen, Flanagan was an adolescent who had actively been fantasizing about masochism and experimenting with various bodily pleasures or sensations for quite some time. The article does recount Mrs. Flanagan's concern that Robert Jr. was "a sickly baby, who wheezed as he fought for breath, and suffered pneumonia at two weeks." When the family moved to California (from New York—the poster boy article can conceivably be read as both a progress narrative and even, in its narrative structure, a Western), "the true nature of Robert's difficulty was diagnosed." At this point in the story, medical authority intervenes, and "since diagnosis and treatment, both children [Robert and his sister] have been in improved health." Upon this recognizable foundation, the more elaborate architecture of the poster child can easily be erected: the article proceeds to inform readers about the available treatments; to revel in the amazing things that Robert Jr. can now do, thanks to that treatment (he likes "to sketch, paint portraits, play drums . . . and tinker in his workshop"); and to lament that there is still no cure—and will never be one, without the support of "citizens," who are asked to call the organization if they "wish to help in the fund drive" (29).

That Robert Jr. will die young is implied in the article, but also cannot be explicitly stated because that eventuality is precisely what the imagined citizenry—busily engaged in consolidating their own subject positions through what Paul K. Longmore calls "conspicuous contribution" (134)—is hoping to forestall. Newspaper representations of the latter part of Flanagan's life, however, had no problem discussing death. One Los Angeles performance included in *Sick*, for instance, positions Flanagan onstage in a coffin, appearing to be dead, while a video of him speaking plays on a screen at the back of the stage: "All the articles about me start that way: 'Bob Flanagan should be dead already,' that's what they say [audience laughter]. 'But he isn't;' that's what they always say. 'Instead, he nails his dick to a board.'" The adult Flanagan apparently still liked to tinker in his workshop, but citizens in these later articles are not encouraged to send their dimes so that he might continue the behavior.

Flanagan inhabits and essentially explodes both the poster child and the dead-already mythologies, in some ways literally fucking the compulsory future that both portend. His explosion of these mythologies, in turn, affects other people with CF (including would-be poster children) and makes it quite difficult for various disability mythologies and machineries to function efficiently around them. Progress going nowhere, apparently, is nowhere near as enticing to some boys and girls as ways to survive at the margins or limits of time and space. Flanagan's transgressive representation offers, to some crips, precisely such a meditation on ways to survive at those limits.

One of Flanagan's anecdotes illustrates all of these points well, and is thus worth quoting at length:

> *L.A. Style* did an article on me which . . . describes me hanging by my wrists, talks about CF, and basically talks about sex and sickness. It starts out saying, "Bob Flanagan should be dead by now of cystic fibrosis." The writer talks about the disease, about my sister, and describes some of the things I've done to myself, some of the shows, and talks about SM. A lot of people have seen that article; at summer camp [where Flanagan sometimes worked with children with CF] a CF kid came up to me and said, "Hey—saw you in that magazine, *man!*" I asked him, "Where'd you see it?" "In the Cystic Fibrosis Foundation office in Orange county." I couldn't believe it. It turned out that they have a clipping service, and the woman who runs the foundation office was so pissed that she was running around the office screaming, "This isn't good for CF! This isn't good for CF!" The foundation depends on cute little dying kids . . . those posters of kids with big eyes and sad faces say-

ing "I'm going to die—we need money for research." And I'm like the
poster child from *hell* saying, "*Don't* give us money because we'll grow
up to do things like *this!*" (Juno and Vale 28)

In *Bob Flanagan: Supermasochist*, this anecdote is positioned overleaf
from the reproduction of the 1967 poster boy story about Robert Jr. If the
line of causality leading *to* his CF/SM identity is performatively blurred
in "Why," the chaotic line of causality leading *from* that impossible identity is, in this anecdote, clearer: the poster child from hell isn't good for
the CF mythology, or any other disability mythology. Most dangerously,
this anecdote suggests that an undead Flanagan might walk the earth and
recruit others.

One scene in *Sick*, in particular, literally represents such a possibility,
as Sara, a young Canadian woman, visits Flanagan and Rose and ex-
plores their workshop (examining, among other things, the coffin Flanagan used in some performances). Sara has cystic fibrosis and uses her
"wish," from the Make-a-Wish Foundation, to meet Flanagan (or, literally, to meet "Bob Flanagan: Supermasochist," since—as she says in the
film when she talks to the camera about her wish—all she had was the
Juno and Vale volume, which functioned as a type of "Bible" for her).

The Make-a-Wish Foundation emerged in the late 1970s and now purports to "grant the wishes of children with life-threatening medical conditions to enrich the human experience with hope, strength, and joy"
(Make-a-Wish, "About Us"). My description of the seventeen-year-old
Sara as "a young Canadian woman with CF," then, is in some ways in-
accurate, since the Make-a-Wish Foundation needs or requires her to be
a "girl" or a "child." Just as Robert Jr. cannot be a nascent pervert, Sara
is not supposed to be a young adult with sexual desires. That Sara's wish
is to meet Bob Flanagan: Supermasochist, however, marks the transgressive potential for rupture in the Make-a-Wish mythology as surely as the
L.A. Style article on—of all places—the bulletin board in the Cystic Fibrosis Foundation office in Orange County marked the potential for rupture in the poster child mythology (a potential that was, of course, recognized by the screaming office manager). Although the Fuck-the-Future
Foundation is unlikely to be up and running anytime soon, it is not
unimaginable and in some ways always internal to the Make-a-Wish
mythology.

Longmore argues that "poster children are made the means by which
nondisabled people can prove to themselves that they have not been cor-

rupted by an egocentric and materialistic capitalist order. . . . The cere-
monial counterimage to conspicuous consumption is conspicuous contribution" ("Conspicuous Contribution" 136). As a late-twentieth-century
manifestation of this process, Make-a-Wish completes the circle; the
"children with life-threatening medical conditions" are themselves located, through the foundation and thanks to the conspicuous contribution of others, within situations of conspicuous consumption. "I'm going
to Disneyland!" is the catch phrase that sums up this process; it is a
phrase that has its origin in Make-a-Wish's activities, even if—by the end
of the twentieth century—it was widely recognized and deployed, sometimes comedically, in a range of locations. Alexandra Chasin discusses its
1993 use, for instance, on Ellen Degeneres's sitcom *The Ellen Show*:
"After Ellen comes out in therapy, her therapist asks, 'What are you going
to do now?' Ellen's response is automatic: 'I'm going to Disneyland!' The
irony is that Ellen is already in Disneyland. . . . [She] emerges into gay
consciousness and identity through commodity consumption in a world
in which Disney stands as the premiere symbol of commodification" (55).
Chasin is critical here of how thoroughly LGBT people, as LGBT people,
were being incorporated into contemporary consumption processes in the
1990s; her larger study, *Selling Out: The Lesbian and Gay Movement
Goes to Market*, details extensively the ways in which LGBT "consciousness and identity" was founded on conspicuous consumption. What's interesting about Chasin's Ellen Degeneres example, however, is how it depends on a prior, disabled, emergence into consciousness and identity
through commodity consumption. It is because that prior emergence is so
mythologized, so far beyond critique (how could one critique the desire
of a child with a life-threatening illness to go to Disneyland?), that the
catch phrase can so easily travel to other locations. In one of the most
spectacular (and flexible) movements of late-twentieth-century capitalism, in other words, the conspicuous consumption of people with disabilities authorized the conspicuous consumption of others.

Clearly, Sara's wish also incorporates her into contemporary consumption processes. Plane tickets were booked and hotel reservations
were made; at some point in the past, the Juno and Vale volume was purchased. But if maintenance of the Make-a-Wish mythology has required
a great deal of labor, *Sick* presents viewers with figures (Sara, Flanagan,
Rose, and even Sara's mother) who work it differently. When the camera
person asks Sara, following her visit to Flanagan and Rose, what her "involvement with their kind of sexuality" is, Sara responds: "I guess it's just

the same thing, I think, with Bob—being able to control your body for a change, being able to control *something*." Sara's mother interjects politely that "it wasn't the S and M that attracted her," but Sara counters that, indeed, "that was certainly *part* of it. . . . It does *interest* me and, I mean, like, I'll go out of the house with collars wrapped around my neck and stuff. . . . It certainly attracted me because you don't hear about people with diseases being like that; you always hear about them being sick and feeble, you know, and they don't really do anything." Essentially shifting consideration of the Make-a-Wish mythology and the standard CF narrative from the realm of consumption to the realm of production, Sara—following Flanagan—tests out alternative ways of being and, even as she talks decisively and unsentimentally in this interview about the probability of her own death, alternative ways of surviving.

To return to "Seeing the Disabled" with this more textured understanding of Flanagan's practice allows for an alternative reading of the essay. Clearly, in Garland-Thomson's "Seeing the Disabled," the full-page photograph of Flanagan, which is taken from the cover of the Juno and Vale volume and depicts Flanagan with an oxygen mask, hospital cape and gloves, and SM gear (collars, chains, and weights), is the queerest image in the piece—not, of course, according to the terms of *Queer Eye* but in Kim's (and much of queer activism's) "queer and utopian" sense. Significantly, however, in the shorter, MLA version of the essay (that is, in the version that is inescapably more authoritative, more disciplined), Flanagan's is one of the photographs that is cut. I'm not critical of the essay's condensation in and of itself, but I do find myself wondering how the excision of Flanagan functions (and even if the longer essay was written second, condensation and excision are *in effect* the right words, because the shorter essay appeared in print second). What I additionally find myself wondering, particularly after this consideration of Flanagan's work, is this: If indeed the rhetoric of realism is just as constructed as the rhetoric of the exotic, how might an alternative construction of the longer essay—one that concluded not with Secretary Heumann but with Flanagan—function?

Such a construction of "Seeing the Disabled" might make more visible a fifth photographic mode, a mode we might recognize as the hegemonic. Garland-Thomson insists that all of the photographic rhetorics manipulate the viewer, so I would contend that her essay at its best actually invites the re-cognition I'm proposing. In my estimation, however, it's important to define the hegemonic mode more directly, particularly because

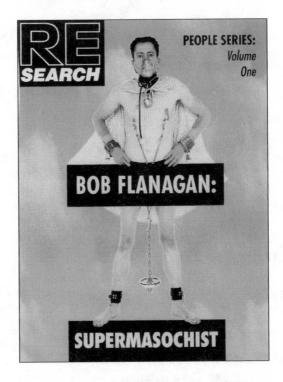

"Look at me, I am like you . . . maybe."
Bob Flanagan, Supermasochist.

neoliberalism seems to be deploying disabled realism quite efficiently—and winning consent to particular ways of being in the process. The hegemonic mode, then, to put forward a rather straightforward (Gramscian) definition, elicits consent to the dominant economic and political ideologies of a particular historical order.[16] Hence, in the era of the freak show (and the rise of industrial capitalism), while the realistic mode might be barely discernible or emergent, the exotic, or a combination of the exotic and wondrous, would be hegemonic (and functioning very differently from now). As Garland-Thomson herself writes, in her important work on the American freak show: "The immense popularity of the shows between the Jacksonian and Progressive Eras suggests that the onlookers needed to constantly reaffirm the difference between 'them' and 'us' at a time when immigration, emancipation of the slaves, and female suffrage confounded previously reliable physical indices of status and privilege such as maleness and Western European features" (*Extraordinary Bodies* 65) These historical tensions engendered images, exotic photographs that fulfilled what Garland-Thomson identifies as the cultural need for the "extravagant and indisputable otherness of the freak" (65). In our own era, in contrast, the ways of looking that constructed and reassured the Jacksonian "common man" are present but residual—in other words, no longer dominant or hegemonic.

Any of the four photographic rhetorics that Garland-Thomson delineates can be deployed as the hegemonic mode and—by extension—any of the four rhetorics can be deployed in a counterhegemonic fashion. In an era marked by, say, the hegemony of the sentimental it might be more difficult to dislodge the dominance of the sentimental mode by redeploying it in a counterhegemonic way, but it is certainly not impossible or unthinkable. What makes me wonder about the ways in which an essay not excising but concluding with Flanagan would function is precisely Flanagan's construction, in our own historical moment, of a counterhegemony: "sick," his photographs and performances scream, in an era obsessed with (and capitalizing on) a narrow and oppressive understanding of the body, health, and fitness; "pervert," they insist, in the face of either docile family values or a benign and "tolerant" multiculturalism. Most important, they say "work it" (meaning, do it differently, do it otherwise, imagine the unimaginable outside) in contexts calling for efficient production and compulsory consumption. And the fact that, both before and in the wake of Flanagan's death, we can distinctly perceive alternative communities and communal norms ("norms without producing effects of normalization," as David Halperin might say [109]) attests more than anything to the counterhegemonic role Flanagan played.

Kauffman suggests that the artists she considers in *Bad Girls and Sick Boys*, including Flanagan, "deal with fantasies that have not been coopted by consumer culture" (15). Such an assertion is importantly not quite the same thing as saying these fantasies are not, in the end, cooptable. To insist that Flanagan is not co-optable, in fact, would put forward another progress narrative going nowhere, since such an insistence would need to posit a move forward to a satisfying (and ultimately reassuring) endpoint. Arguably, Flanagan's work so often functions transgressively partly because he was aware of the perpetual (and disciplining) possibility of co-optation. *The Pain Journal*, for example, which Flanagan composed during the final year and a half of his life, repeatedly rails against the art world and is in some ways quite critical of Rose's embrace of it.

Flanagan was fabulous not because he looked at the straight guy and saw someone in a hapless state who could be spruced up so that conspicuous consumption and heteronormativity could continue apace. Rather, Flanagan's queer eye for the straight guy (very broadly conceived) recognized seduction—in other words, an insidious attempt to win or elicit consent—in the straight guy's winning smile and demeanor. Essentially invoking his safe word (refusing, that is, to go there) and continually becoming the poster child from hell, Flanagan imagined crip existence as atypical and reached for something beyond the current order.

A Place at the Table: The World Bank Sees the Disabled

My conclusion to the previous section intentionally (and playfully) echoes and reverses Garland-Thomson's conclusion to "Seeing the Disabled," which suggests that "the realistic mode is most likely to encourage the cultural work the Disability Rights movement began. Imagining disability as ordinary, as the typical rather than the atypical human experience, can promote practices of equality and inclusion that begin to fulfill the promise of a democratic order" (372). Although I very much like (and share) Garland-Thomson's emphasis on the promise, the realistic mode for representing disability—it seems to me—potentially effects promises (or, perhaps more precisely, contracts) in our own era that might be worth questioning. Moreover, the disability rights movement (like Heumann herself, as will be more evident below) can be comprehended as nonsingular and contradictory—as, decidedly, a "rights" movement firmly located within and compatible with the "order" of the liberal and neoliberal state, but also as a radical liberationist movement, which—like many of the other social movements that emerged in the 1960s and 1970s—"called the system's bluff. . . . and broke through the barriers that had constrained the reform-oriented . . . movement," to adapt John D'Emilio (*Making Trouble* 244–245).[17]

It is more difficult for the official, and realistic, Heumann photograph to perform the counterhegemonic work I have been ascribing to Flanagan, more difficult—at the current moment—for it to open up such contradictory questions and uncertain but hopeful futures. Garland-

Thomson argues that the realistic mode holds the most political power in a democratic order. While not entirely disputing that assertion, I would amend it to suggest that the realistic mode for representing disability identity has hegemonic power in a very particular moment in the history of liberal democracy, namely neoliberalism. I could make a case that participation in the hegemonic, neoliberal mode of our own time is already operative in the Clinton-era photograph (especially as that state photograph comes into focus next to an advertisement), but it's even clearer to me in another set of photos, accompanying the World Bank's press release announcing Heumann's appointment as the new adviser on "Disability and Development."

Again, the photographs in question are generally official or semiofficial shots, though representations of Heumann herself are this time included alongside a collage of people with disabilities from elsewhere, presumably from the World Bank's client countries. These client-country photos can perhaps be read as distant or exotic, at least as far as viewers in the West are concerned in that we are indeed encouraged to read these images as "elsewhere." I suggest, however, that the realistic mode is more discernible in this collage, and the text of the press release invites such a reading: "Disability is not a tragedy," Heumann points out, "but rather a normal part of life. It is a tragedy when disabled people are excluded from the economic mainstream of society. Discrimination has denied hundreds of millions of disabled people around the world their right to receive education, health care, housing, transportation, and equal employment opportunities" ("Disability in the Mainstream"). As long as people with disabilities are denied such freedoms, talking points like these remain absolutely indispensable, and they make evident Heumann's history as a disability activist and educator from the early 1970s. Inevitably framing a viewer's reading of the collage, such talking points bring the disabled subject of the photograph close, minimizing the distance that might otherwise exist between, in this case, a disabled or nondisabled (Western) viewer and (non-Western) viewed.

This realistic representation is brought to you by the World Bank, however, which holds certain truths to be self-evident (and it is because of widespread opposition to these supposed truths that the streets erupt in Washington, D.C., whenever the World Bank's annual meeting comes to town): privatization is always and everywhere a good thing; privatization of public services (to echo Heumann, education, health care, housing, transportation) can help countries cope with economic and social crises; markets around the world should be opened up to what Marx and Engels called "that single, unconscionable Freedom—Free Trade" (469); and government or public regulation of those markets should be minimized. In many countries the World Bank policies designed to ensure that countries pledge allegiance to this neoliberal consensus have been disastrous: the imposition of "user fees" and the privatization of health care, water, education, and electricity has had disproportionately negative effects on people with disabilities, people with HIV/AIDS, women, people of color, the elderly, and poor people (groups that are, of course, not mutually exclusive). I cannot discount the genuine pleasure we as readers and viewers are likely to take in the spotlighting, in the press release, of Heumann's decades-long activism. But as the World Bank makes a particular construction of disability and disability identity seem ordinary, two other maneuvers in relation to disability are obscured: first, the fact that the World Bank is basically capitalizing on disability, on these images; and second, and related, the fact that the World Bank's general neoliberal policies might be understood as antidisabled regardless of these pictures, regardless of what's happening in the Office of Disability and Development. In other words, disability, and even disability activism, made to seem ordinary, can still be deployed in the service of normalizing dominant mythologies—in this cae, neoliberalism, trickle-down economics, the Washington consensus.

The press release for the Office of Disability and Development could be understood as what Amitava Kumar and others call World Bank Literature, a multifaceted and imaginative concept that Kumar intends to be "a provocation" that does "not assume a distinct referent" (xvii). Kumar cites Michael Hardt and Antonio Negri, who examine the ways that "the creation of wealth tends ever more increasingly toward . . . biopolitical production, the production of social life itself, in which the economic, the political, and the cultural increasingly overlap and invest one another" (qtd. in Kumar xviii). A concept like "World Bank Literature" allows for the interrogation of that new world order. Rosemary Hennessy, responding to Kumar's questions—"Where is the literature of the new economic policy? Where is the literature of the World Bank?"—contingently divides the concept in two: "The literature of the World Bank can be found in the World Bank" (that is, in the myriad documents the institution itself generates), and the literature of the World Bank can be found in "the critiques of the Bank and its legitimating narratives that are now being generated by an emergent social movement" ("¡Ya Basta!" 40–41). In the epilogue that follows this chapter, thinking through what I call the disability to come, I'm more focused, if briefly, on the latter. The press release from the Office of Disability and Development is an example of the former.

The often-insidious normalizing processes, or the processes of biopolitical production, at work in the media industry that brings us *Queer Eye* and in the economic consensus that brings us the World Bank are also at work in the humanities today, of course; the realistic mode as hegemonic formation potentially links not only media, market, state, and trans-state institutions but also the contemporary academy. And especially in the era of the corporate university that I discussed in chapter 4, resisting these processes is necessary if disability studies is to become, as Bérubé imagines, a normal but not normalizing part of the humanities. Perhaps it will take a crip eye for the normate guy to facilitate such resistance. Normate is an indispensable theoretical concept coined by Garland-Thomson in her earlier work on not ordinary but *Extraordinary Bodies*: "This neologism names the veiled subject position of cultural self, the figure outlined by the array of deviant others whose marked bodies shore up the normate's boundaries. The term *normate* usefully designates the social figure through which people can represent themselves as definitive human beings" (8). A crip eye for the normate guy, I propose, would not just be a disability version of the Bravo hit, no matter how much pleasure imagining such a show has given me: "Sweetie, your university is an accessibility *nightmare*! Don't worry, honey, it is your lucky day that disabled folks are here to tell you just what's *wrong* with this place!" Rather, a crip eye for the normate guy (and because we're talking about not a real person but a subject position, somehow "normate guy" seems appropriate, regardless of whether he rears his able-bodied head in men or women) would mark a critically disabled capacity for recognizing and withstanding the vicissitudes of compulsory able-bodiedness. The capacity is needed because, regardless of who actually populates the "array of deviant others" Garland-Thomson writes about, compulsory able-bodiedness always requires such an array to function efficiently—or flexibly, since again I'm linking these processes to the current moment in the history of capitalism. It takes a crip eye for the normate guy to see this flexibility in action.

Rewriting a disability studies truism helps me bring these points home. Sooner or later, if we live long enough (so we often say), we will all become disabled. Another twist on the truism is that disability is the one identity that each of us will, at some point in our lives, inhabit. I don't want to dispute these foundational disability studies points, and as long as we endure systems of oppression like compulsory able-bodiedness (which have generally prohibited people with disabilities from becoming subjects because it was assumed they could not exert themselves on capital's behalf), they are worth emphasizing—but I do want to invert them: sooner or later, if we live long enough, we will all become normate. And if the established disability studies point is worth repeating, again and again, the queer disability studies point I'm excavating is worth resisting, especially as disability studies becomes, rightly and desirably, one of the normal aspects of study in the humanities.

The fact that, if we live long enough, all of us will become normate is arguably the dominant story of the gay movement at the turn of the twentieth century. Resistance to becoming normate, consequently, has over the last decade engendered some of the most critically queer work around, from performances by artists like Flanagan and Rose to Gay Shame counterfestivals in New York and San Francisco (festivals that protest both narrow understandings of gay embodiment and the fact that Gay Pride is now brought to you by Budweiser) to queer theory—by Michael Warner, Lisa Duggan, Phillip Brian Harper, Samuel R. Delany, and others—that relentlessly draws our attention to the ways in which our most vital public cultures are being circumscribed or privatized out of existence. It may be impossible to say, right now, that someday soon, that circumscription will cease—it's hard to deny the bleakness of the world we currently inhabit. But, keeping a crip eye on the horizon, we should nonetheless continue to demand access to other worlds—worlds that are public, democratic, expansive, and extraordinary.

Epilogue
Specters of Disability

From the protests at the Mumbai World Social Forum in chapter 1 to the World Bank's capitalization on disability images in chapter 5, we might conclude that a specter is haunting disability studies, the specter of globalization. Or, perhaps more properly, specters, and perhaps they are more properly specters of counterglobalization (the proper is so elusive and specters so difficult to discern). Following Jacques Derrida, we might invoke Marcellus's charge when confronted with the ghost of Hamlet's father ("Thou art a scholar; speak to it, Horatio"), but we should simultaneously remember Derrida's forewarning: "There has never been a scholar who really, and as scholar, deals with ghosts. A traditional scholar does not believe in ghosts—nor in all that could be called the virtual space of spectrality" (*Specters of Marx* 11).

There are a few reasons why we don't like to think about disability studies as being haunted. First, we are, currently, busily, rapidly being incorporated: "to incorporate: to give material form to." As I suggest in chapter 5, we have programs, institutes, university press lines, and high-profile national conferences. Who has the time these days, let alone the inclination, to consider how the house we are building—right now, right here, in the present—is haunted? Second, honestly, we like to think about disability studies *doing* the haunting: "I'm the nightmare booga you flirt with in dreams/ Cause I emphatically demonstrate: It ain't what it seems" (Wade 409). Indeed, some of our most cherished theses demonstrate how invested we are in haunting. Consider, for instance, Douglas Baynton's assertion that "disability is everywhere in history, once you begin looking for it, but conspicuously absent in the histories we write" (qtd. in Longmore and Umansky, "Introduction" 2) or, even more directly, Lennard J. Davis's insistence that the "specter may be crippled, deaf, blind, spasming or chronically ill—but it is clearly no longer willing to be relegated to the fringes of culture and academic study" (*Bending over Backwards* 34). Absences that are somehow preternaturally present, spaces of academic work and study that are not what they seem, academics startled by us or refusing outright to acknowledge our existence—we like, in short, to *do* the haunting. Perhaps this is evident most directly in the truism I discuss and complicate at the end of chapter 5—the oft-repeated invocation of what we might call the spectral disability yet to come: "If we live long enough, disability is the one identity we will all inhabit."

I do think crip theory should continue to conjure up the disability to come, though—as I hope to suggest—we might do more to keep the discussion about what we mean by that, the disability to come, open. But, to call back Derrida calling back Hamlet calling up a disability image, the time is out of joint—our time, crip time, these spectacular and terrible times—and, in the interest of another future altogether, we should not at this point avoid considering the ways in which disability studies itself is haunted.

In a December 2003 report in *LA Weekly*, Marc Cooper tells the story of Tijuana, Mexico's "Wall of the Dead." Earlier in 2003, activists from Tijuana—from what Gloria Anzaldúa calls "el otro lado"—nailed brightly painted coffins to a wall along the road leading to the airport. "Each coffin," Cooper explains, "is inscribed with a year, running from the mid-'90s to the present, and a death toll: the number of Mexicans who have died while attempting to cross the border. In 1995, the toll was 61. In 2000, the number of dead had risen to 499." When Cooper wrote his piece at the end of 2003, he explained that, by October, the death toll was already almost four hundred ("On the Border of Hypocrisy").

The idea that everyone will be disabled if they live long enough has been, at its best, an incredibly generative disability studies insight. When Michael Bérubé titles an essay "If I Should Live So Long," for instance, he accesses the hope and generativity the insight affords. Rather than being a timeless truth, however, it is a rhetorical point, and as such, what's important is how it functions: in one way in one context, quite differently in another. In this brief epilogue, I speculate about how the rhetorical point—everyone will be disabled if they live long enough—functions around global bodies, and perhaps, to begin, around the coffins Cooper describes, around this particular body count. The numbers are high enough—61, 87, 149, 499, they read—for us to know that some of those crossing were already disabled (even if they were passing as though they were not). The majority of those making the trip, however, well, didn't

live long enough. Which should haunt us, all of us still living, but particularly those of us living and working in the United States.

If disability studies or the disability rights movement has gone global,
if—like LGBT studies before it—the field is increasingly concerned with
global bodies or desires, then it behooves us to think through what that
concern means. In what follows, then, I first introduce and explore the
question: What do we talk about when we talk about global bodies? After
considering five possibilities, I turn once again to some of the questions
of identity and identification that have haunted this book, inflecting those
questions—this time—through the unlikely disability studies query, "why
shop at Wal-Mart?" I conclude this epilogue, and *Crip Theory*, with the
briefest reinvocation of specters and the disability to come.

When we talk about "global bodies," we might intend, first, for that
phrase to merely *supplement* the foundational work, largely focused on
the United States and Europe, that has already been done in disability
studies. That work, to again take the MLA's *Disability Studies: Enabling
the Humanities* volume as representative, is "about integration in the
widest sense." As it has put forward disability "as a subject of critical inquiry and a category of critical analysis," disability studies has largely focused on excavating the complex workings of stigma in Euro-American
cultures; on critiquing literary, filmic, and visual representations; and on
tracing the formation of disability minority identities that might speak
back to exclusionary able-bodied discourses and institutions (Snyder et
al., "Introduction" 3). If global bodies—bodies from elsewhere—supplement this project, it would presumably be with an eye toward extension
or completion of it. But of course, and dangerously, the supplement supplements, it adds only to replace, and there is no guarantee that even the
most foundational disability studies theses will function in the same way
when we talk about global bodies (Derrida, *Of Grammatology* 145). Perhaps, for instance, just as gay identity initially seemed quite local and located when historians turned their attention elsewhere, so, too, might disability identity.

Second, when we talk about global bodies, we might mean not new
subjects in the field but the field as a whole, moving out to cover a much
larger terrain—at times disability studies, like (true confessions) queer
studies before it, does purport to be about everything. And it's not as if
there isn't some truth to that. This meaning of global bodies, however,
also comes with its dangers. When a field covers a larger terrain and purports to be about everything (and again, some variants of queer studies

are in my mind here), there is always the danger that trumping, transcending, and even colonizing will displace the more urgent work—especially urgent in these times—of coalition. I would argue that this is what happens to a certain extent in Lennard Davis's *Bending over Backwards: Disability, Dismodernism, and Other Difficult Positions*. According to Davis, since African American, queer, and feminist thought inadvertently reinforced a reactionary identity politics even as they attempted to dismantle it, disability studies might provide a way out—as an emergent discourse it is, apparently, less caught up in the tendency to rigidify that other movements exhibit. Instead of embracing an identity position, or a crypto-identity position, disability studies could be at the vanguard of a new postidentity world. "Rather than ignore the unstable nature of disability," Davis writes, "rather than try to fix it, we should amplify that quality to distinguish it from other identity groups that have . . . reached the limits of their own projects" (26). Davis calls his version of postidentity, post-postmodern politics, "dismodernism" and offers it, missionary-like, as the good news for other "identity groups." Here, then, we are not talking about supplementing disability studies with a discussion of global bodies but, rather, about disability studies as a global (or globalizing) body. Dismodernism saves all of us from the perceived failures of other progressive movements and extends to queers, people of color, and feminists, in particular, a new and better way.

Despite my fundamental sympathy with a postidentity politics, I would insist that the conversations about identity trouble in feminism, queer theory, critical race theory, and other allied fields have been much more complex and contested than Davis allows. Indeed, the reason I have a fundamental sympathy with a postidentity politics is because of the work that has been done in those fields. Like many missionaries before him, Davis did not really bother to research thoroughly, in advance, the belief systems or cultural conversations already in place among those who would be rescued. As I hope *Crip Theory* has consistently suggested, we need a postidentity politics of sorts, but a postidentity politics that allows us to work together, one that acknowledges the complex and contradictory histories of our various movements, drawing on and learning from those histories rather than transcending them. We can't afford to position any body of thought, not even disability studies, as global in the sense of offering *the* subject position, *the* key.[1]

Third, and equally problematically, global bodies might signify a certain cosmopolitanism. Global bodies, in this sense, are bodies that inhabit and move between global cities. Global cities, as Saskia Sassen and others have demonstrated, "are centers for the servicing and financing of international trade, investment, and headquarter operations" (xxiii). For those living in, working in, and moving between such sites, national boundaries have become less and less important; my own university, for instance, is well known for preparing large numbers of international finance and international relations students to function in this new global space, and many of them do indeed move between Washington, New York, London, Tokyo, Bombay, and other locations with ease. As do many academics in the humanities and social sciences; as Richard Rorty writes: "This frightening economic cosmopolitanism . . . has, as a byproduct, an agreeable cultural cosmopolitanism. Platoons of vital young entrepreneurs fill the front cabins of transoceanic jets, while the back cabins are weighted down with paunchy professors like myself, zipping off to interdisciplinary conferences held in pleasant places" (qtd. in Bérubé, "American Studies without Exceptions" 110).

Fourth, and related to those vital young entrepreneurs, global bodies might not refer to people at all. Twentieth-century modernity established "global bodies" such as the League of Nations and the United Nations; the age of Empire has privileged more diffuse "global bodies" such as the World Bank, the International Monetary Fund, and—of course—multinational corporations. And perhaps we shouldn't be so surprised at this dominant understanding of global bodies in an era where public spaces and public cultures around the world have been circumscribed. Since the postmodern, neoliberal consensus holds that free trade should be protected above all other freedoms and that agents or players in the market should be given as much latitude and autonomy as possible, global entities like Microsoft and McDonalds have, after all, effectively functioned as persons, their ongoing embodiment more vouchsafed than any of us with bodies of mere flesh and blood.

Finally, and seemingly as against the previous two meanings, global bodies might refer to another kind of mobile and productive force—to those, for example, whom Grace Chang has called "disposable domestics." These are the figures populating the informal economy undergirding the formal economy of any global city, or of any city that purports to be global. National and international financial crises, brought on or exacerbated by "free trade" agreements, by ongoing legacies of colonialism such as massive debt, and by the structural adjustment programs of the World Bank and IMF, have created a largely female, migrant workforce.

In the United States and Canada, in particular, immigrant women of color have been transformed into what Chang calls a "super-exploitable, low-wage workforce to staff the nation's nursing homes, ever-increasing sweatshops, and middle-class households" (xii).

Disability identity as such never appears in Chang's book *Disposable Domestics*, but the story she tells of the ways in which these immigrant women of color are incorporated into contemporary service economies is a disability story nonetheless. Anti-immigrant discourses and policies have worked to keep this workforce contingent, temporary, disposable, and far away from public services, including health care and education. Many of the individuals and groups Chang writes about are themselves elderly, sick, or disabled, even though they might never identify as such, and even though—or perhaps precisely because—illness, disability, and age are often cause for termination where they are employed. For example, when sixty-five-year old Natie Llever was fired by Casa San Miguel in Concord, California, where she had been working as a certified nursing assistant, she was told, "You can no longer do this job because of your age. You are a sickly woman, and we want a young and strong worker for this job" (Chang 93). Youth, strength, and ability, however, are commodities that are both desirable and, in Chang's words, "disposable" in regard to this workforce—long hours and hard labor ensure that a system that wants "young and strong workers" is always haunted by disability, and the need for surplus profit ensures that a system that generates disability must immediately conjure it away when it appears. I'm not arguing that disability in Chang's story should be understood once again through a rubric of loss, lack, or pity; a vibrant disability identity politics has successfully challenged those able-bodied notions. I am arguing that if disability studies turns its attention to global bodies, then—in coalition with feminist, queer, postcolonial and other movements—we need to develop new vocabularies, disability vocabularies, for analyzing postmodern subject positions like the one Chang writes about.

In the interest of new vocabularies and practices, I turn again to Wal-Mart, where—on October 23, 2003—250 janitors at sixty different stores were arrested by the INS and deported. But before putting names and faces to those global bodies (this group of detainees came from Russia, Poland, Lithuania, and other eastern European locations) I want to first invoke some perhaps more familiar Wal-Mart images. A human relations management style at Wal-Mart has worked to link the company's name—in the consciousness of consumers—with friendliness or neighborliness, diversity, education, and access. The advertising campaigns that have attempted to forward this image have often included images of disability. In the words of U.S. Equal Employment Opportunity Commission Chair Cari M. Dominguez: "Everyone is familiar with Wal-Mart's compelling national television advertisements featuring people with disabilities as valued employees" (U.S. Equal Employment Opportunity Commission).

Dominguez called forth these compelling advertisements in 2001, in response to the case of Jeremy Fass and William Darnell, whom Wal-Mart refused to hire because they are deaf. A Tucson court sided with Fass and Darnell, and as part of the settlement, Wal-Mart agreed to air ads telling the story of the two would-be employees, thereby, in the words of Katherine Kruse, one of the attorneys involved in the case, "educat[ing] the public about discrimination against people with disabilities, and in particular the barriers faced by hearing impaired applicants and employees" (U.S. Equal Employment Opportunity Commission).

Emphasizing people with disabilities as valued employees, Dominguez deflects attention away from the rather embarrassing ad featuring Fass and Darnell (it was scheduled to air at least once a day for only two weeks in Phoenix and Tucson) and onto the national ads we all, as Dominguez insists, already know well. And there are, of course, several. Taking Dominguez's lead and temporarily spectralizing Fass and Darnell, the advertisement I would like to call forth, with pleasure, features a Wal-Mart "associate" using a motorized wheelchair. In the advertisement, the associate establishes an intimate, conversational tone with viewers: he takes us up and down the aisles at the store where there are always low prices—always—and as he does so, he lets us know just how great it is to work for Wal-Mart.

As far as I know, none of those arrested on October 23, 2003, as of yet use wheelchairs, though some of the eastern European cities from which they come are without question particularly difficult to negotiate with a wheelchair. Nonetheless, despite my uncertainty as to their status as wheelchair users or not, turning to the group of detainees, I want to introduce at least one more Wal-Mart story into the mix here, and ultimately I'll call it a disability story. Although we never met, and although the INS has effectively declared that he is not part of my imagined community, Pavel worked at a Wal-Mart store just down the road from me, in Lynchburg, Virginia. In February 2003, Pavel happened across a website for United States cleaning jobs paying four times what he was earning as a restaurant manager in the Czech Republic. He flew from Prague to New York on a tourist visa and took a bus to Lynchburg, where a subcontractor delivered him to a giant Wal-Mart. . . . Pavel immediately began on the midnight shift and . . . soon learned that he would never receive a night off. He said he worked every night for the next eight months. (Greenhouse 2).

Pavel was one of those arrested in October 2003. Before he was deported, he told a reporter that "he received $380 in cash for his 56-hour work-weeks. That came to $6.79 an hour, and he did not receive time-and-a-half for overtime" (Greenhouse 2). With Pavel and others, the subcontractors in fact violated most U.S. labor laws—overtime, Worker's Compensation, Social Security. Wal-Mart officials denied that the company itself had anything to do with these violations, and as far as I know, and as of this writing, there are still no plans to air ads educating the public about discrimination against undocumented workers.

All of this leaves us, here at the end of *Crip Theory*, with a range of dissonant images. The man in the motorized wheelchair very well might have a highly developed sense, even an activist sense, of disability identity; clearly, on some level, Fass and Darnell do, since they turn to the Americans with Disabilities Act for protection. Whether Pavel's identity is disabled or able-bodied, or whether such a notion of "identity" surrounding embodiment even resonates for him, it's clear that it would have been better for him, like those memorialized on the wall in Tijuana, like all of those passing through San Diego or Lynchburg or Washington, D.C., without identification papers, never to have been identified.

And, again, Wal-Mart in fact claims that these workers *cannot* be identified, not with Wal-Mart, at least, not with any of us here in the United States; they were supply workers, never officially members of the Wal-Mart team. What does it mean, though, to think of these workers as supplemental, especially—and this is particularly uncomfortable—supplemental to the man in the motorized wheelchair, or to Fass and Darnell? From Paul K. Longmore in 1985 ("Positive images in commercials . . . reflect the growing socio-political perception of disabled people as a minority group and the increasing impact of the disability civil rights movement"; "Screening Stereotypes" 37) to Rosemarie Garland-Thomson in 2001 ("In the aggregate, contemporary advertising casts disabled people as simply one of many variations that compose the market to which they appeal"; "Seeing the Disabled" 368), we've tended to at least see disability ads as benign and more often as a mark of progress. Yet post–October 23, 2003, isn't it incumbent on us to see these images as haunted? And I do mean these images—I don't want to put forward a reading, in other words, that simply sees Wal-Mart as haunted: doing some basically good, liberal things *at the very least* in diverse national television ads despite the specters in the closet, or sweeping out the closet. In the aggregate, embodied identities that appear in contemporary advertising—and we could easily spin it out here, to encompass the gay couple shopping at IKEA or the many colors of Benetton—simultaneously compose (in a few senses, materializing *and* reassuring) a viewing self and make unthinkable other embodiments, other identifications. I might sympathize with Pavel, but if I recognize and take on the identities that Wal-Mart recognizes and takes on, he cannot be me; I won't, I can't, see him as disabled or gay, or anything else that can be booked in the multicultural present, in my present (this despite the fact that he's literally been booked and sent back to Prague).

Yet what might result from comprehending global bodies, Pavel and others, in relation to disability? Deciding, *against* the preferred reading of the more familiar Wal-Mart advertisements, to recognize or re-cognize disposable domestics, broadly conceived, as disabled (despite the simple point from Chang that the work they came to do and the conditions under which they do it are disabling) runs the risk of merely metaphorizing, or perhaps of spectralizing, disability. Taking that risk, however, invoking a disability that is not yet here—not yet here in space, or in time—strikes me as nonetheless true to a certain disability studies logic. After all, whether it's the adage of everyone will be disabled if they live long enough, or the urgent call for a postidentity politics, or Harriet McBryde Johnson's report on the "disability gulag"—that terrible future space that an able-bodied culture has constructed, where she, or you, or I might end up—it's clear that we're inescapably haunted by the disability to come. And the disability to come, the one we invoke, has often been frightening, as is suggested not only by the able-bodied recoil disability activists and disability studies scholars have consistently, and rightly, criticized, but also by Johnson's quite reasonable desire not to be lost forever in nursing homes or other institutions.

There are other ways of summoning the future, however. Despite the fact that these frightening futures make it difficult to do so, what might it mean to welcome the disability to come, to desire it? What might it mean to shape worlds capable of welcoming the disability to come? In such terrible times, is it even possible to ask the question that way?

Deferring a straightforward answer, I hope that crip theory nonetheless works to welcome the disability to come. The idea intentionally deploys two Derridean notions—first, welcoming, an always-impossible act but one that cannot wait, an act that entails acknowledging the other that haunts the self; and, second, the democracy to come. At the end of *Politics of Friendship*, Derrida writes: "For democracy remains to come . . . belonging to the time of the promise, it will always remain, in each of its future times, to come: even when there is democracy, it never exists, it is never present, it remains the theme of a non-presentable concept" (306). The disability to come, likewise, perhaps, will and should always belong to the time of the promise—the promise to Pavel and McBryde Johnson, to global bodies, to specters of disability in the borderlands or elsewhere. It's a crip promise that we will always comprehend disability otherwise and that we will, collectively, somehow access other worlds and futures.

Notes

NOTES TO THE INTRODUCTION

1. Eve Kosofsky Sedgwick writes: "To the degree that heterosexuality does not function as a sexuality . . . there are stubborn barriers to making it accountable, to making it so much as visible, in the framework of projects of historicizing and hence denaturalizing sexuality. The making historically visible of heterosexuality is difficult because, under its institutional pseudonyms such as Inheritance, Marriage, Dynasty, Family, Domesticity, and Population, heterosexuality has been permitted to masquerade so fully as History itself—when it has not presented itself as the totality of Romance" (*Tendencies* 10–11). David M. Halperin, similarly, argues: "By constituting homosexuality as an object of knowledge, heterosexuality also constitutes itself as a privileged stance of subjectivity—as the very condition of knowledge—and thereby avoids becoming an object of knowledge itself, the target of a possible critique. . . . (Heterosexuality, not homosexuality, then, is truly 'the love that dare not speak its name')" (47–48).

2. On the policing and containment of homosexuality, especially during the McCarthy era, see John D'Emilio, "The Homosexual Menace: The Politics of Sexuality in Cold War America."

3. My title for this introduction is itself of course indebted to feminist critiques of heteronormativity, specifically Adrienne Rich's 1980 article "Compulsory Heterosexuality and Lesbian Existence." In 1976, the Brussels Tribunal on Crimes against Women identified "compulsory heterosexuality" as one such crime (Rich 196). Earlier, in her important article "The Traffic in Women: Notes on the 'Political Economy' of Sex," Gayle S. Rubin examined the ways in which "obligatory heterosexuality" and "compulsory heterosexuality" function in what she theorized as a larger "sex/gender system" (179, 198; qtd. in Katz, *Invention* 132). For work attentive to how constructions of race and sexuality are interwoven, see Roderick A. Ferguson, *Aberrations in Black: Toward a Queer of Color Critique*; Mattie Udora Richardson, "No More Secrets, No More Lies: African American History and Compulsory Heterosexuality"; Siobhan Somerville, *Queering the Color Line: Race and the Invention of Homosexuality*

in American Culture; and Mason Stokes, *The Color of Sex: Whiteness, Hetero-sexuality, and the Fictions of White Supremacy.*

4. On the discursive production of the natural order of things, see Michel Foucault, *The Order of Things: An Archaeology of the Human Sciences.* Eli Clare's *Exile and Pride: Disability, Queerness, and Liberation* (1999) was a landmark text for the development of queer/disability studies, as were a number of edited volumes, including Raymond Luczak's *Eyes of Desire: A Deaf Gay and Lesbian Reader* (1993); Shelley Tremain's *Pushing the Limits: Disabled Dykes Produce Culture* (1996); Victoria A. Brownworth and Susan Raffo's *Restricted Access: Lesbians on Disability* (1999); Robert McRuer and Abby L. Wilkerson's *Desiring Disability: Queer Theory Meets Disability Studies* (2003); and Bob Guter and John R. Killacky's *Queer Crips: Disabled Gay Men and Their Stories* (2004).

5. As with many texts in the voluminous tradition here invoked, in *Crip Theory* I attempt to put forward a cultural materialist perspective that combines poststructuralist techniques of close reading and literary analysis, or inquiries into how language works to shape and reshape a range of contested meanings, with a materialist commitment to locating (but not fixing) the production of those meanings—and the contradictory texts, identities, and cultures that convey them—within economic structures, processes, and relations. A cultural material-ist perspective understands these economic processes as both constraining and enabling culture and social change without being fully or finally determinate. Such an understanding of culture and political economy is still described well by Stuart Hall's classic essay, "The Problem of Ideology: Marxism without Guaran-tees." A range of other important work in cultural studies (including work in queer, feminist, critical race, and disability theory) is engaged and cited through-out *Crip Theory*; an extremely partial list of some foundational cultural studies texts that have influenced this book includes Bérubé, *Public Access*; Denning; du Gay et al.; Grossberg et al.; Hall et al.; Haraway; Hebdige; Hoggart; Morley and Chen; Nelson and Gaonkar; Ross; Williams, *Keywords*; and Williams, *Marxism and Literature.* The term "crip" itself emerged in disability movements as an ap-propriation and revaluation of the derogatory term "cripple," and its positive va-lences are, at this point, multiple. I discuss the uses of "crip" directly in chapter 1.

6. In lesbian, gay, bisexual, and transgendered (LGBT) studies, Alexandra Chasin's *Selling Out: The Lesbian and Gay Movement Goes to Market* is one of the most important books to emerge in the last several years that acknowledges and engages critically these shifting relations of visibility. D'Emilio's *The World Turned: Essays on Gay History, Politics, and Culture* marks through its very title the fact that significant changes have taken place over the past decade; if throughout the twentieth century, the homosexual menace was more visible than an LGBT movement understood as part of the mainstream of U.S. politics, that is no longer necessarily the case.

7. The title of my introduction notwithstanding, I am ultimately less interested, here and in chapter 1 in a specific critique of Rich's essay and more interested in locating compulsory able-bodiedness in the larger history of compulsory heterosexuality and in laying the foundation for a queer understanding of critical disability and crip theory. For an important disability studies essay that effectively, and much more directly, attends to Rich's work (as well as, at least in part, an earlier essay of mine also titled "Compulsory Able-Bodiedness and Queer/Disabled Existence"), see Alison Kafer's "Compulsory Bodies: Reflections on Heterosexuality and Able-bodiedness." The special issue of the *Journal of Women's History* in which Kafer's essay appears, titled "Women's History in the New Millennium: Adrienne Rich's 'Compulsory Heterosexuality and Lesbian Existence'—A Retrospective" (Rupp 9–89), provides a respectful yet critically engaged analysis of Rich that is particularly attentive to how the essay functioned historically.

8. I engage Rosemarie Garland-Thomson's theory of the normate more extensively in chapter 5.

9. Disability studies is not the only field Norah Vincent has attacked in the mainstream media; see her article "The Future of Queer: Wedded to Orthodoxy," which mocks academic queer theory. As I hope *Crip Theory* will consistently demonstrate, neither being disabled nor LGBT in and of itself guarantees the critical consciousness generated in the disability rights or LGBT movements, or in queer or crip theory: Vincent herself is a lesbian journalist, but her writing clearly supports both able-bodied and heterosexual norms. Instead of a stigmaphilic response to queer/disabled existence, finding "a commonality with those who suffer from stigma, and in this alternative realm [learning] to value the very things the rest of the world despises" (Warner, *Trouble with Normal* 43), Vincent reproduces the dominant culture's stigmaphobic response. See Michael Warner's discussion of Erving Goffman's concepts of stigmaphobe and stigmaphile (41–45). Since this introduction is ultimately concerned with the emergence of more flexible able-bodied/heterosexual subjects, however, I want to emphasize that Vincent's positions are not only extreme but increasingly outmoded, although I think that such positions are currently more common in relation to ability/disability than to heterosexuality/homosexuality. Kafer's "Compulsory Bodies" is particularly good at thinking through the uneven historical shifts in the systems of compulsory heterosexuality and compulsory able-bodiedness. "Able-bodiedness," she writes, "has been cast as separate from politics, as a universal ideal and a normal way of life, in much the same way as heterosexuality in the 1970s and early 1980s (and, in some contexts, still today)" (79). Kafer implies, nonetheless, that the two systems are always intertwined, have shared developmental paths, and will hopefully share a future demise: "[the systems are] pervasive, buil into the foundations of our culture, but . . . not monolithic" (81).

10. I discuss the rise of industrial capitalism and the attendant emergence of able-bodied ideologies (with particular attention to able-bodied domesticity) in chapter 2.

11. My interest in this section is in drawing out the ways in which compulsory heterosexuality depends on compulsory able-bodiedness (and vice versa); my rewriting of Judith Butler with and on the terms of disability studies should thus be read (in this introduction and in chapter 1) not merely as a celebratory application of her work but as a critique of some of its elisions. Given the canonical status of Butler's theories, the terms of embodiment I highlight here do not and cannot obscure the sex/gender terms that remain in play behind them. Moreover, my intention is, in fact, to keep those terms in play, drawing out—with my brackets—terms that actually were obscured by a theory of heterosexuality not attentive to its dependency on able-bodiedness. For an excellent overview and analysis of the use of Butler in disability studies, see Ellen Samuels's "Critical Divides: Judith Butler's Body Theory and the Question of Disability."

12. For a discussion of what he calls dominant, residual, and emergent discourses, see Raymond Williams, *Marxism and Literature* 121–127. A discourse is "residual" not because it is a weak or uncommon: "The residual, by definition, has been effectively formed in the past, but it is still active in the cultural process, not only and often not at all as an element of the past, but as an effective element of the present" (122). Williams's terms enable us to think through the ways in which different forms of compulsory heterosexuality and compulsory able-bodiedness coexist and influence each other.

13. By 1990 and 1991, in fact, a journal such as *Radical America* could publish two special issues on lesbian and gay cultures under the title "Becoming a Spectacle: Lesbian and Gay Politics and Culture in the Nineties." On the disability rights movement, see Joseph P. Shapiro, *No Pity: People with Disabilities Forging a New Civil Rights Movement*; and Doris Zames Fleischer and Frieda Zames, *The Disability Rights Movement: From Charity to Confrontation*.

14. Ronald Bayer overviews the gay activism that led the American Psychiatric Association to remove homosexuality from its list of mental disorders in 1974 in *Homosexuality and American Psychiatry: The Politics of Diagnosis*.

15. See my own overview of how gay and lesbian theorists and activists have critiqued homosexual coming-out stories, particularly for their scripted, and thus predictable, forms (McRuer, *Queer Renaissance* 32–39). One of the best essays in this vein is Biddy Martin's "Lesbian Identity and Autobiographical Difference[s]." Building on the work of Carrie Sandahl, I discuss what might be understood as the very different process of coming out crip in chapter 1.

16. For discussion of the Koch incident, see Jonathan Ned Katz, "Invention of Heterosexuality" 24–25, and Douglas Crimp, "Right On, Girlfriend!" 306. For an analysis of public response to Magic Johnson's revelation, see David Román, *Acts of Intervention: Performance, Gay Culture, and AIDS* 160–164.

Because Johnson's 1991 announcement of his HIV status came at a moment when the media was insistently putting forward the message "AIDS is not just a gay disease," he was explicitly and repeatedly linked to the identity "heterosexual"; inescapably, he became one of the decade's most openly heterosexual figures. Jan Zita Grover discusses how the phrase "heterosexual community" gained currency during the AIDS crisis in "AIDS: Keywords" 24–25.

17. For a variety of perspectives from within and around queer theory on the Clinton-Lewinsky affair, see Warner, *Trouble with Normal* 17–24; Jeffrey Falla, "Disorderly Consumption and Capitalism: The Privilege of Sex Addiction"; and Lauren Berlant and Lisa Duggan, *Our Monica, Ourselves: The Clinton Affair and the National Interest.*

18. By definition, of course, a discourse of "timelessness" makes it possible for historical shifts like the ones I'm excavating to pass unnoticed, which is one reason that theories such as Butler's (which demonstrate that identity is contingent on temporality) function so effectively as a counterpoint to hegemonic conceptions of gender and sexuality. Although Butler's theories have been widely cited, however, it has perhaps been less remarked how centrally and critically they themselves participate in a particular moment (of openness and even spectacle) in the history of heterosexuality.

19. Emily Martin's discursive study of the varied uses of "flexibility" allows us to differentiate between the flexibility of corporate strategies and the (potentially) more critical flexibility associated with, say, some versions of feminist theory. This is not to say that feminism or any other critical discourse is immune (to use Martin's language) to the problems associated with flexibility in our time; it is simply to underscore that liberal, radical, or progressive resignifications or reappropriations of the term are not essentially impossible (it would not be a keyword of the present moment if that were the case; in Williams's sense, something emerges as a keyword only if struggles over its meaning, however sedimented, can be traced).

20. For other analyses of neoliberalism and flexibility that are variously attentive to cultural representation or to the appropriation of discourses (including discourses of flexibility itself) generated in the new social movements, see Lisa Duggan, *The Twilight of Equality: Neoliberalism, Cultural Politics, and the Attack on Democracy*; Thomas Frank, *One Market under God: Extreme Capitalism, Market Populism, and the End of Economic Democracy*; Michael Hardt and Antonio Negri, *Empire* (esp. 272–276); Naomi Klein, *No Logo*; and Aihwa Ong, *Flexible Citizenship: The Cultural Logics of Transnationality*. Duggan's study provides the most nuanced account of the intersectionality of political economy and the identity politics put forward by new social movements; she is sharply critical of Frank and Klein for reducing "both the historical range and the social bases for identity politics" in their rush to point out how various identities have been seemingly—or, more important, solely—co-opted by neoliberalism (74–75).

21. Heteronormative, able-bodied epiphanies are probably most common in mainstream films and television movies about AIDS, even—or perhaps especially—when those films are marketed as "new" and "daring," like the 1997 Christopher Reeve–directed HBO film, *In the Gloaming*, in which the disabled, queer character dies (yet again) at the end, but not before effecting a healing of the heteronormative family. I focus in this introduction on a non-AIDS-related film about disability and homosexuality because I think that the epiphanic processes I theorize here have a much wider currency and can be found in many cultural texts that attempt to represent queerness and/or disability. For an extended discussion of both *In the Gloaming* and the Nuveen Investment Corporation advertisement in which Reeve—through computer simulation—is shown walking, see McRuer, "Critical Investments: AIDS, Christopher Reeve, and Queer/Disability Studies."

22. The idea of staring back comes from Kenny Fries, *Staring Back: The Disability Experience from the Inside Out*. Because ideologies of treatment and "cure" are arguably still the central—and even in some instances the exclusive—organizing principles for people with obsessive-compulsive disorder or some other mental or behavioral disabilities, it is currently easier for blind people, Deaf people, people who use wheelchairs, and people with visible bodily differences to embrace the minoritized identity put forward by the disability rights movement. This is not to say that a reverse discourse or minority consciousness around OCD is impossible (it seems to me that a reverse discourse is virtually always possible), but that there has been fairly little space for, or collective discussion of, such a consciousness, and thus it is at this point more difficult to imagine. Although Emily Colas, in *Just Checking: Scenes from the Life of an Obsessive-Compulsive*, is not at all in conversation with the disability rights movement and only partially comprehends a minority identity, her work nonetheless points toward other possibilities, if only because Colas herself, and not the psychiatric establishment, tells the story. I take up OCD in somewhat different ways in the conclusion to chapter 3.

23. In this entire section, I am indebted to Martin Norden's overview in *The Cinema of Isolation: A History of Physical Disability in the Movies*. For other important early analyses of how disability functions in film, see Paul K. Longmore's "Screening Stereotypes: Images of Disabled People," and E. Keith Byrd and Randolph B. Pipes's "Feature Films and Disability." Byrd and Pipes, in particular, see a relationship between cultural representations of mental and physical disability.

24. In fact, in *Just Checking* Colas's worries often produce concern for other people; when she hits a chipmunk while driving home from her children's school, she repeatedly returns to confirm that she has not hit a small child (108–109). Even medical information on obsessive-compulsive disorder, which would be more complicit than personal narrative in objectifying the person who suffers

from the disorder, emphasizes that obsessive-compulsive behavior generally does not result in harm or insult to others. See American Psychiatric Association, *Diagnostic and Statistical Manual of Mental Disorders*, 4th ed. 417–423.

25. Marta Russell's "New Freedom Initiative: Survival of the Fittest 'Equality'" is the best disability analysis of the New Freedom Initiative. For information on Scott Evertz, the gay Republican appointed by Bush, see "Bush Appoints Gay Man to Head AIDS Office" and "A Quiet Thumbs Up."

26. On the history of the AIDS Coalition to Unleash Power (ACT UP), see Douglas Crimp and Adam Rolston's *AIDS DemoGraphics*. Audre Lorde recounts her experiences with breast cancer and imagines a movement of one-breasted women in *The Cancer Journals*. For accounts of the Rolling Quads and the Independent Living Movement and the Deaf President Now action, see Shapiro 41–58 and 74–85. Deaf activists have insisted for some time that deafness should not be understood as a disability and that Deaf people, instead, should be understood as having a distinct language and culture. As the disability rights movement has matured, however, some Deaf activists and scholars in Deaf studies have rethought this position and have claimed disability (that is, disability revalued by a disability rights movement and disability studies) in an attempt to affirm a coalition with other people with disabilities. It is precisely such a reclaiming of disability that I want to stress here with my emphasis on severe disability.

NOTES TO CHAPTER I

1. "Understood and imaged," in Teresa de Lauretis's formulation, certainly provides an opening for engagement with art and activism, but that engagement is not realized. My hope is that the theoretical context in which crip theory is developing is more concerned with explicitly articulating what Wahneema Lubiano calls "bridge discourses" (qtd. in Duggan, Introduction to *Sex Wars* 248, n.1). For Duggan, bridge discourses are "political languages and strategies that can open dialogue across discursive gaps [such as, for instance, the gap or perceived gap between the theorizing that artists, activists, and academics perform], generate critical challenges from one location to another, and produce negotiated interventions and actions" (Introduction to *Sex Wars* 2). It is possible to read de Lauretis's note as specifically critical only of the emergent activism of what she calls "the Queer Nation Group" (Introduction to "Queer Theory" xvii), a group that formed and generated direct actions in multiple locations over the course of the early 1990s. However, I see de Lauretis's insistence that there is "no relation" between queer theory and even the Queer Nation group, narrowly defined, to be emblematic of a larger academic distancing from activist and artistic theorizing. Despite the limited identity politics put forward by Queer Nation, it seems to me that their actions were also nonetheless "queer" and "theory," and they emerged

from the same historical moment that generated the *differences* volume. For an important attempt to think through the cultural work performed by Queer Nation, see Lauren Berlant and Elizabeth Freeman's "Queer Nationality."

2. Since its emergence, queer theory's origins have proliferated. Robyn Wiegman credits de Lauretis with coining the term (17); William B. Turner—and many others—trace the beginnings of queer theory to Michel Foucault and *The History of Sexuality, Volume 1: An Introduction*. Annamarie Jagose rightly extends the "queer" work of Foucault backward, considering its connection to other "constructionist" work done by LGBT historians and sociologists in the 1960s and 1970s, largely outside the academy. The play with identity, systemic critiques, and coalitions that emerged (and often fractured) in early 1980s feminist activism around sexual freedom and late 1980s AIDS activism (particularly the activism associated with ACT UP) were also, in many ways, "queer" or "queer theory" (on the feminist "sex wars," see Duggan and Hunter; on the history of ACT UP, see Crimp and Rolston). José Esteban Muñoz credits, as an originary text, the 1981 anthology *This Bridge Called My Back: Writings by Radical Women of Color* (Muñoz 21–22; cf. McRuer, *Queer Renaissance* 232, n.40); I discuss Muñoz's citation of this text more thoroughly later in this chapter. Many academic courses reviewing queer theory employ, or even begin with, Gayle S. Rubin's groundbreaking "Thinking Sex: Notes for a Radical Theory of the Politics of Sexuality," Judith Butler's *Gender Trouble: Feminism and the Subversion of Identity*, or Eve Kosofsky Sedgwick's *Epistemology of the Closet*. I find an understanding of the origins of queer theory as proliferating (especially as such a model inescapably and desirably conjures up notions of a monstrous birth) preferable to a straight reproductive model that would establish a proper or legitimate lineage, and I hope that a similar understanding of crip theory is already in circulation. Although, as far as I know, this project is the first to use the concept in its title, the authorship of crip theory is various, multiple, diffuse, contradictory, and contested.

3. It would be impossible to provide a comprehensive listing of all the locations where crip practices and identifications have materialized. For a range of deployments of the term and its variants, see Clare; Ferris; Finkelstein, "Only Thing"; Guter and Killacky; Hershey; Hockenberry; Mairs; McRuer and Wilkerson; Milam; Mitchell and Snyder, *Self-Preservation*; Mitchell and Snyder, "Talking about *Talking Back*"; Mitchell and Snyder, *Vital Signs*; Russell *Beyond Ramps*; Sandahl, "Queering the Crip or Cripping the Queer?"; Sandahl et al.; Widom. Performance venues seem particularly well-suited to the capacious understanding of the term "crip" I introduce, via Carrie Sandahl, in the next paragraph; the Austin-based Actual Lives Theatre Troupe, the Tallahassee-based Mickee Faust Club, and the San Francisco/Oakland-based Wry Crips Disabled Women's Theatre Project are just a few of the groups to explore (and expand) the meaning of crip through performance. The direct actions noted in this para-

graph have often been associated with ADAPT, a militant disability rights group whose name initially stood for American Disabled for Accessible Public Transport and later for American Disabled for Attendant Programs Today (Shapiro 127–139, 251; Fleischer and Zames 104–105). On sledgehammers and the emergence of curb cuts, see Shapiro 126. On the Independent Living Movement, see Shapiro 49–58; Fleischer and Zames 33–48.

4. Although Sandahl invokes here the idea of *being*, coming out crip, and the queer/crip performances of Robert DeFelice, Terry Galloway, Julia Trahan, and Greg Walloch, which she discusses, simultaneously put in motion a playful deferral of definitive and substantive notions of being. As I hope the snapshot approach in this chapter demonstrates, committed deferral (in the interest of imaginative identification, performative possibility, and ongoing struggle) is one of the contingent foundations on which crip theory is built. In a discussion of the title sketch and other pieces included in the 2001 compilation directed by Eli Kabillio, *F**K the Disabled*, Walloch himself informed me that he writes much of his own material by attending closely to the unusual and unexpected things that people say and then considering "suppose this were true."

5. The curb cut has often served as one of the premier examples of universal design: if cuts were "intended" for those who use wheelchairs, they have been used, perhaps unexpectedly, by many other people and for many different reasons.

6. Dissent, as it is employed here, does not simply entail disagreement or critique but making public and political (and thus open to contestation) conditions or relations that are widely accepted as natural. Dissent makes clear that those conditions or relations have been naturalized and that a hegemonic formation has (only temporarily) emerged through consent that can be actively and collectively refused (Duggan, Introduction 5; McRuer and Wilkerson 10). This understanding of dissent animates *Crip Theory* as a whole; I most directly discuss the Gramscian theory of hegemony on which it is based in chapter 5.

7. For an important exception to this queer tendency to elide the contributions of feminists of color, see Linda Garber's textured consideration of the relationship between lesbian feminism and queer theory, *Identity Poetics: Race, Class, and the Lesbian-Feminist Roots of Queer Theory*.

8. Roderick A. Ferguson, in turn, positions his own queer project, *Aberrations in Black: Toward a Queer of Color Critique*, in a line of descent from both Muñoz and women of color feminism (4–5). Ferguson defines queer of color analysis as a process that "interrogates social formations as the intersections of race, gender, sexuality, and class, with particular interest in how those formations correspond with and diverge from nationalist ideals and practices. Queer of color analysis is a heterogeneous enterprise made up of women of color feminism, materialist analysis, poststructuralist theory, and queer critique" (149, n.1). Ferguson may not immediately locate disability in this description of his

project, but I quote his useful and committed formulation of queer of color analysis, and position it in relation to the work of figures like Muñoz and Gloria Anzaldúa, in order to stress that such intersectional analyses likewise must be central to the project of crip theory (especially as crip theory attempts to think beyond the nation or nationalism). Ferguson, in fact, names disability directly in later chapters, and it has a particularly important role in his brilliant reading of Ralph Ellison's *Invisible Man* (*Aberrations in Black* 54–81).

9. See for instance, Anzaldúa's essay "To(o) Queer the Writer—Loca, escritora y chicana," which writes what Muñoz calls "disidentification" into the very title: while "to queer" might be read as an imperative, "too queer" must simultaneously be read as a caution. Chela Sandoval calls such disidentificatory practices "differential movement":

> the methodology of the oppressed and its technologies of resistance are constantly reorganized to self-consciously reappropriate and reapportion ideology, and in doing so, they serve to make the languages of emancipation more subtle, more rich, multiple, supple, and flexible, with "all possible degrees of dignity" at their disposal. This reappropriation of ideology insists on the ability of consciousness to meta-ideologize, to move in, through, and outside of dominant ideology through the technology of differential movement. (112)

The flexible bodies I discussed in my introduction to this volume are not really flexible in Sandoval's sense, precisely because they are essentially stripped of "all possible degrees of dignity." In other words, hegemonic flexibility is resisted, or even transformed, through Sandoval's differential coupling of flexibility and the dignity she associates with women-of-color feminism. It seems to me that crip communities know a great deal about such dignity and about the technology of differential movement Sandoval describes (even if they might, in the spirit of critical coalition she calls for, insist that what Sandoval calls an "ability to meta-ideologize" is not contingent on able-bodiedness).

10. Although it does not use the term, I count S. Naomi Finkelstein's poem "Upon the Passing of Gloria Anzaldúa—May 2004" as one such fledgling effort to affirm Anzaldúa's connection to crip community. Not only has the queer diabetes community to whom Finkelstein directly offers her poem interrogated the critical possibilities afforded by crip (or sicko, or fabulous) identification; Finkelstein herself (a Seattle-based writer and activist) has done a great deal to move forward progressive, coalitional, and sex radical crip theory and praxis. See, for example, her essay "The Only Thing You Have to Do Is Live."

11. On the border between the living and the dead in modernity, see Roach; Holland. Despite what may still strike some readers as an unlikely identification of Anzaldúa with disability or crip theory, it seems to me that even in the list I have quoted there are already provocative openings to precisely such an identification: What does Anzaldúa mean by the squint-eyed? Who has, historically,

been associated with the "half-dead," even as they have contested such an association? Although again disability is not directly named, Anzaldúa's final footnote in the first section of *Borderlands/La Frontera: The New Mestiza* opens the door to an even more complicated discussion of these questions: "Out of the twenty-two border counties in the four border states, Hidalgo County . . . is the most poverty-stricken county in the nation as well as the largest home base (along with Imperial in California) for migrant workers. It was here that I was born and raised. I am amazed that both it and I have survived" (98, n.10). According to the most recent U.S. Census Bureau information, seventeen years later (2004, and the year of Anzaldúa's death), the number of people living with any disability (26.92 percent) or with a severe disability (14.51 percent) in Hidalgo County was slightly higher than it was for the rest of the nation (24.11 and 12.21 percent, respectively). The poverty rate, however, remained significantly higher than elsewhere: 41.9 percent, as compared to 18.1 percent for the rest of the country, with Hildago residents holding a median income of only $17,619, compared with $31,553 for the rest of the country. The population the Census Bureau counted as "Percent Hispanic origin or non-White" was 85.85 percent in Hidalgo County; the Bureau estimated this category to be 24.36 percent of the U.S. more generally. All of these numbers, however, quite likely do not even begin to describe disability in the borderlands or the world Anzaldúa left behind; the figure she describes as *la mojada, la mujer indocumentada* (*Borderlands/La Frontera* 12), in particular, can (by definition) have only a spectral presence at best in official U.S. documents, from county-level employment and disability figures put out by the Census Bureau to claims made (and documented) in the name of the Americans with Disabilities Act (ADA). "With/out documents" undoubtedly has several layers of meaning when considering disability in a place like Hildago County (as it does when I briefly consider disability in Washington, D.C., in the conclusion to this chapter).

  12. Coalition is both an effect of and condition of possibility for Cheryl Marie Wade's work, as it is for Anzaldúa's. Wade's poem first appeared in print in the lesbian feminist journal *Sinister Wisdom* and was later anthologized in *The Disability Studies Reader*. Print versions of the poem include the dedication "to all my disabled sisters, to the activists in the streets and on the stages, to the millions of Sharon Kowalskis without a Karen Thompson, to all my sisters and brothers in the pits, closets, and institutions of enlightened societies everywhere" ("Poems" 408). I provide a reading of Karen Thompson and Julie Andrzejewski's memoir *Why Can't Sharon Kowalski Come Home?*, and the Thompson-Kowalski story more generally, in chapter 2.

  13. Not Dead Yet is an activist group that has specifically protested advocates of assisted suicide such as Jack Kevorkian; Not Dead Yet contends that supporters of assisted suicide depend on the unquestioned belief that disabled lives are not worth living. They also argue that a cultural focus on assisted suicide diverts

attention away from pain remediation and other important issues, such as the injustices perpetuated by corporate health care systems. *Diseased Pariah News* was an Oakland-based zine published sporadically throughout the 1990s; its editors, claiming "diseased pariah" status, resisted the normalization, sentimentalization, and banalization of the AIDS crisis. For a thorough consideration of a range of terms like *gimp* and *freak*, see Clare 67–101; for an exploration and celebration of "mad pride," see Curtis et al. In regard to "crip" itself, I could note at this point, following Jacques Derrida, that—in a book titled *Crip Theory*—"the irreplaceable character of this signifier, which everything seemed to grant it, was laid out like a trap" (*Dissemination* 220). As the constant proliferation of crip terms should suggest, however, "what counts here is not the lexical richness, the semantic infiniteness of a word or concept, its depth or breadth, the sedimentation that has produced inside it two contradictory layers of signification (continuity and discontinuity, inside and outside, identity and difference, etc.). What counts here is the formal or syntactical *praxis* that composes and decomposes it" (*Dissemination* 220). For more on "de-composing bodies," see chapter 4.

14. It seems to me that Butler wrote this passage at a historical moment when the critiques of "queer" she notes were most pronounced; thus this particular passage, while open-ended, favors an interpretation of "critically queer" largely *critical of* (deployments of) queerness, even if queerness that is *critically urgent* is still legible in what she writes. Since then, in ways that were perhaps still unexpected in 1993, "queer" has been mobilized anew by some of the groups Butler cites (and perhaps most obviously in opposition to an increasingly normalized movement much more likely to pass under the sign "gay," or at best "LGBT"): not only in academic studies such as Muñoz's and Ferguson's, but also in activist groups such as Queers for Racial and Economic Justice and the multiracial coalition that has launched Gay Shame actions in San Francisco and elsewhere (see Gay Shame San Francisco, which is "committed to a queer extravaganza that brings direct action to astounding levels of theatricality"; cf. Sycamore). On the use of "queer" within feminist disability studies, Alison Kafer writes: "When referring to the work of more recent gender theorists, I use the word 'queer.' I find it to be a more accurate and inclusive term for the range of concerns, gender identities, and orientations [in feminist disability studies and activism]. Moreover, I believe 'queer' allows for a relationship between sexuality and disability in ways that 'lesbian' does not" (86, n. 3).

15. I am relying on a range of sources for my account of the World Social Forum, including Fisher and Ponniah; Klein, *Fences and Windows* 193–207; Mertes; Notes from Nowhere. For discussions on the disability protest in Mumbai, I am indebted to email conversations with Anne Finger and Jean Stewart, who witnessed the event; for some of the quite limited reporting on it, see Hewitt; S. Kumar; Mulama.

16. In his analysis of an earlier era of progressive political and cultural ac-

tivism, Michael Denning notes an important feminist critique of the mid-twentieth-century "Cultural Front":

> The feminist critique of Popular Front culture goes beyond the sexual politics of the movement, arguing that the symbolic systems and aesthetic ideologies of the Popular Front were inscribed with what might be called a "gender unconscious." . . . the symbolic systems of the Popular Front drew on a traditional iconography and rhetoric of manhood and womanhood that was at odds with the utopian and emancipatory hopes of the movement. (136–137)

Although he does not discount this critique, Denning goes on to complicate it. My own concern in this section, however, is that the symbolic and theoretical systems of counterglobalization are inscribed with a disability unconscious, a now-traditional iconography and rhetoric of ability/disability often at odds with the emancipatory hopes of the Movement of Movements. I suggest later in this chapter that the disability unconscious is pronounced in the work of many cultural geographers.

17. For more on these issues in relation to what I call "the disability to come," see the epilogue to this book. It should be clear that in *Crip Theory* I favor the latter project, even though neoliberalism has clearly already emerged in this book as a primary target. It is doubtful, however, that various global events or spaces, including Mumbai 2004, would be accessible for some crip activists without the educational, employment, and health opportunities that emerged under the aegis of the welfare state. There may be many disabled people in or from the United States, for instance, who participated in a range of turn-of-the-century counterglobalization efforts (including the World Social Forums) who could do so because they came of age in a post–Education for All Handicapped Children Act world (this act was later renamed the Individuals with Disabilities Education Act [IDEA]). I am not arguing, contra Hardt and Negri, for a nostalgic return to earlier and partial solutions. I am simply suggesting in this section, in solidarity with the Mumbai protestors, that the Left's desire for new social bodies often neglects consideration of the histories and futures of actual disabled bodies.

18. I am sympathetic enough to Hardt and Negri's analysis to suggest that "crip multitude" should be something of a redundancy, but that will only really be the case as the crip literacies articulated in Mumbai and elsewhere are disseminated. It is worth pointing out that the Society for Disability Studies (SDS) has of late actively moved toward creating non-national spaces that are still broadly accessible; under the leadership of its most recent presidents (Anne Finger and Jim Ferris) and (U.S. and Canadian) board of directors, SDS networked with disability activists and scholars in Central America to consider holding the organization's meeting in San Jose, Costa Rica, in 2007. SDS 2007 is founded on the dual commitment to the theoretical accessibility implicit in the idea that another

world is possible and to the literal and local accessibility that will make it possible for people with disabilities from across North America to begin realizing that idea.

19. Marco Hewitt, in a brief meditation on his experiences at WSF 2004, notes that both India's independence movement and its first trade union emerged in Mumbai, in 1885 and 1890, respectively; these and other historical factors made the city a good choice for the first World Social Forum to be held outside Brazil. The "pits" Abidi invokes, however, extend beyond the site of the conference; the city's "suitably radical history" does not change the fact that Mumbai is currently "over-crowded and polluted, and does not have the advantage of a progressive local government like Porto Alegre" (Hewitt). The projects of the PT in Porto Alegre included road repair and other work on the actual physical space of the city. Hewitt writes that "Mumbai is home to nearly 20 million people, half of whom either live in slums or on the streets. The sheer degree and conspicuousness of urban poverty in Mumbai shocked many international participants of the forum." Although a study of the actual physical space of Mumbai as it connects to disability remains to be written, the Partners for Urban Knowledge, Action and Research (PUKAR), Mumbai, headed by Arjun Appadurai, is involved in important cultural studies projects and initiatives on gender and space, the public sphere, the range of "cultures of writing that exist in the city of Mumbai, across linguistic, disciplinary and social divides," and "the location of Mumbai in the global economic shift from manufacturing to services." For more critical (and creative) work on Mumbai and its history, see Dwivedi and Mehrotra; Mehta.

20. I am particularly grateful to Jean Stewart for sharing with me both her photographs and the paper she read for this panel. "Disability, Capitalism, and War" is a good example of the global disability solidarity and multifaceted crip literacy I invoke in this section; Stewart critiques the slashing of state-sponsored social service programs while simultaneously imagining and putting into motion a global disability consciousness. I am also grateful to Jean Parker for sending me her tapes from the "Disability in a Global Perspective" panel.

21. My thanks to Sharon L. Snyder for allowing me to quote our personal correspondence. Harlan Hahn is one of the scholars and activists interviewed in *Vital Signs*.

22. For critical analyses of *Paris Is Burning*, see Browning 159–172; Butler, *Bodies That Matter* 121–140; hooks 145–156.

23. It is perhaps telling that Derrida locates mimesis generally within what he calls a "clinical paradigm" (*Dissemination* 191–192), given the film's failure to repeat or imitate "vital signs" faithfully, its noncompliance with clinical procedures or protocols.

24. I am particularly grateful to Sammie Moshenberg and Dan Moshenberg (pictured in the text) for information on the AIDS crisis in South Africa; my dis-

cussion of Zackie Achmat, TAC, and the December 9, 2003, agreement relies on the following material: TAC: Treatment Action Campaign; Boseley; "Competition Commission"; Musbach; Rivière; Rosenberg; Smetherman; Steinglass; J. Wright. Mandela himself has been generally supportive of TAC's work; the group was the initial recipient, in 2003, of the Nelson Mandela Award for Health and Human Rights. However, although Mandela has appeared in some venues wearing one of TAC's HIV POSITIVE t-shirts, there was initially some controversy over the TAC t-shirt that included his photograph in an HIV POSITIVE t-shirt (see "Mandela Does Not Endorse").

25. Edward King's discussion of the "Safer Sex—Keep It Up!" campaign underscores the fragility of such queer projects of solidarity. The contingent universalization of HIV/AIDS that this project attempted to posit for gay men was during this period matched (or trumped) by a "de-gaying" of AIDS that put forward a de-politicized, humanistic universalization. "We're all living with AIDS," in this latter context, essentially functioned as a straight dilution of queer projects of solidarity. Cindy Patton, in *Fatal Advice: How Safe-Sex Education Went Wrong*, too, while endorsing emancipatory models, implies that they were never dominant and that their promise has never been fully realized. In some ways, TAC's contingent universalization of HIV/AIDS, even as it may be indebted to these earlier queer efforts, does much more to sustain an emancipatory model. I talk more about the contingent universalization of queerness and disability in chapter 4. The oxymoron attempts to name a theory that has always been linked to praxis; if and when contingent universalization is not linked to praxis, it rigidifies into the humanistic universalization that is a legacy of the Enlightenment and that has been critiqued by countless feminist and queer theorists.

26. As of this writing, TAC continues to monitor Boehringer Ingelheim's and GlaxoSmithKline's compliance with the December 2003 agreement. Implementation of key licensing agreements has been slow (see "Mobilise to Build").

27. On HIV-negative identity for gay men, see Walt Odets, *In the Shadow of an Epidemic: Being HIV-Negative in the Age of AIDS*. Odets's study makes clear that self-conscious HIV-negative identities have been shaped in intimate proximity to the HIV/AIDS crisis—or, even more directly, in intimate proximity to HIV. For Odets, HIV-negative identity does not simply mean being free from HIV and in some ways means the opposite, despite the distancing and disavowal that intimacy generates, alongside and attending desire. The vast majority of people who are free from HIV would not recognize themselves in Odets's book or in the complex psychological and cultural conditions that are part of HIV-negative identity.

28. I use "Mika" and "Glen" when referring to Foster and Winkler as they are represented in and by *The Littlest Groom*; I use their surnames otherwise. For cultural studies work on reality television, see Andrejevic; Dovey; Friedman; Murray and Ouellette; Tincknell and Raghuram.

29. My criticism of Judith Halberstam is minor; "Pimp My Bride" is an otherwise astute article, written for the mainstream press, on the politics of representation (of race, gender, and sexuality) on reality television. Although even in her most recent work, "disability" still does not appear in the index (or directly in the body of the text), there are countless points where Halberstam's work, with its careful attention to identity and embodiment, nevertheless potentially intersects with the work of disability studies: see, for example, Halberstam, *Female Masculinity*; Halberstam, *In a Queer Time and Place*; Volcano and Halberstam, *The Drag King Book*. For more media coverage on *The Littlest Groom*, see Rosenthal; Starr; Susman.

30. The circuit of culture in which *The Littlest Groom* (and the reality television industry more generally) is located, of course, extends far beyond Malibu and the Los Angeles region (encompassing the locations where parts for television equipment are manufactured, the regions from which the gardeners and maids who tend and clean Malibu properties hail, and so forth). My point in this section is not to suggest that attention to the site of production allows for a finally comprehensive account of the meanings of *The Littlest Groom* or any other text (that is, a definitive answer or solution as to what a text or image means) but, rather, to propose that crip theory should always proliferate questions, including the questions "Where was this text produced?" and "What other—competing, alternative, crip, or queer—disability meanings and experiences are discernible in and around this space?"

31. The optimism I am emphasizing here should be understood through Antonio Gramsci's famous insistence on pessimism of the intellect and optimism of the will.

32. Crip theory may be allied with cyborg theory, as my borrowing of Donna J. Haraway's language suggests, but it is relatively autonomous from it as well, mostly because cyborg theory has rarely engaged disability as anything more than metaphor. Crip theory—in and with its optimistic ambivalence—might additionally be situated in opposition to Lennard J. Davis's theory of "dismodernism," in which he positions disability studies as a sort of transcendent solution to the problems besetting other fields concerned with—or seemingly hung up on—identity (*Bending over Backwards* 9–32). Haraway's feminist analysis of the cyborg is one of literally thousands of examples countering Davis's claim that feminism, queer theory, African American studies, and other critical projects are caught in "the dead end of identity politics" and in need of a new solution or key that might serve as "*the* postmodern subject position" (29, 14; emphasis mine). I discuss dismodernism again briefly in the epilogue to this book. Rather than identifying the ways in which any of the fields scholars and activists work in might provide a, or the, critical or theoretical key, crip theory might well approach the question backward: How does the work we do generate not just solu-

tions but problems? What issues are never identified in our fields and movements as they are currently constituted? Why?

33. Mitchell and Snyder's theory of "narrative prosthesis" suggests that disability functions "throughout history as a crutch upon which literary narratives lean for their representational power, disruptive potentiality, and analytical insight" (49). Although I would qualify the transhistorical applicability Mitchell and Snyder give to their theory, I do find it extremely useful for understanding a range of modern and postmodern, literary and nonliterary, narrative strategies.

34. For introductions to cultural geography particularly focusing on Los Angeles, see Scott and Soja; Soja; Villa and Sánchez. Mike Davis has been loosely associated with the Los Angeles "school" of cultural geography, particularly since his groundbreaking *City of Quartz: Excavating the Future in Los Angeles.* Edward W. Soja's original consideration of Los Angeles is worth quoting at length:

> [Los Angeles's] spatiality challenges orthodox analysis and interpretation, for it too seems limitless and constantly in motion, never still enough to encompass, too filled with "other spaces" to be informatively described. Looking at Los Angeles from the inside, introspectively, one tends to see only fragments and immediacies, fixed sites of myopic understanding impulsively generated to represent the whole. To the more far-sighted outsider, the visible aggregate of the whole of Los Angeles churns so confusingly that it induces little more than illusionary stereotypes or self-serving caricatures—if its reality is ever seen at all. (222)

Although the analysis of Los Angeles here seems absolutely contingent on images (both literal images and mental images, including the mental images Soja himself evokes in this passage), for Soja these images clutter and confound; the ways in which they are "conflicting" seems only and inevitably unsettling. Moreover, "other spaces," at least as they are constructed here, similarly confound, a term suggesting not only confusion or perplexity but also—in more obscure or archaic senses—failure, ruin, and damnation. Images and other spaces, in other words, both give rise to and (ultimately) obscure the spatial meanings and the political economy of Los Angeles. As Rosalyn Deutsche points out, beneath this anxiety about images and other spaces, one can discern Soja's (unacknowledged) belief that, if only these images could be cleared up or away, if the churning could be stilled, the economic base *might* be understood more fully. Deutsche argues that this unacknowledged desire introduces into cultural geography a masculinism that discounts or short-circuits postmodern feminist work on the image and its inextricable connection to political economy (195–202). My argument that cultural geography exhibits an ableism that has the potential to short-circuit disability studies work is in accord with Deutsche's feminist critique. However, I would grant my argument a crip specificity, given the ways in which disability so often serves as primary evidence of the excesses of capitalism (and I am not arguing that disability should be an aside to a consideration of the excesses of capitalism but, rather, that disability work on the image and the disability rights movement make available other ways of comprehending disability that should also be taken into account). Davis is certainly less totalizing and more attentive to "other spaces" than Soja and many other cultural geographers, but disability is still not generally an acknowledged part of te mix he analyzes.

35. Even if an error in any of these stories is directly traceable and could thus theoretically be fixed—if, for instance, it could be demonstrated that Tom Hayden misread Davis and "Continuous Revolution in Progress" became "Continuing Revolution in Progress"—it still contributes to the mythologizing of the Crips (as the story that quite openly depends upon "error"—Crib becoming Crip—demonstrates). Although in chapter 5 I am focused on disability mythologies in Roland Barthes's sense of the term, by calling any of these stories "myths" in this chapter, I do not intend to discount them. Mythologizing here, additionally, does not necessarily mean idolizing or making legendary, although clearly such a concretization of meaning is a danger in any discussion of the Crips and Bloods and one of the reasons Los Angeles youth join the gangs. I'm less interested, in this section, in clearing away mythology and unveiling the "true" story of the Crips (or even the "true" disability aspects of that story) than I am in considering how these various mythologies, emerging as images in this particular location, work and how they might be woven into the larger project of crip theory. I'm also interested, here and throughout *Crip Theory*, in opening up meanings and possibilities, calling back other ways of being, and calling forth alternative crip futures.

36. Remaining attentive to what will have also been, of course, allows us to recognize an alternative crippin' in the 1992 peace treaty that is still nonetheless not the answer or key. As Susan Anderson points out, the "Crips/Bloods document reveals a faith, amounting to an apotheosis, in the virtues of capitalism, the responsiveness of government, and the goodwill of the community" (360). Los Angeles's failure to deliver illustrates some of the ways in which that faith was misplaced (and displaced).

37. I am aware that some disability activists or scholars—clearly, Marta Russell not among them—will avoid the term "crip" when talking about Los Angeles, because of the presence of Crip gang members. I respect that choice, even if I want to question it somewhat: if the decision to forego the use of crip comes from an assumption (recognized or unrecognized) that L.A. Crip reality has little to do with disability as we know it or think we know it, then the decision contradicts crip theory, as I'm delineating it in this chapter—permanently partial, contradictory, and oriented toward future affinities. The point is not to insist on a particular nomenclature (again, crip is only a term and not the only term) but to probe why and when we disclaim connections to other fields and movements

in lieu of (perhaps safer) analyses of more recognizable (disabled) objects or texts like *The Littlest Groom*.

38. The Kerik scandal was widely covered in December 2004; see, for instance, Jim VandeHei and Mike Allen, "White House Puts Blame on Kerik."

NOTES TO CHAPTER 2

1. For a consideration of queer ceremonies and "forms of belonging" (including weddings) that reflect desires in excess of the desire for state-sanctioned marriage, see Elizabeth Freeman's *The Wedding Complex: Forms of Belonging in Modern American Culture*. See also my own brief essay, McRuer, "'Marry' Me?"

2. For a consideration of queerness, disability, and homelessness, see my discussion of Susana Aikin and Carlos Aparicio's documentary *The Transformation* in chapter 3.

3. For critiques of lesbian and gay consumerism and the construction, especially in the 1990s, of lesbian and gay target markets, see Alexandra Chasin's *Selling Out: The Lesbian and Gay Movement Goes to Market* and Rosemary Hennessy's *Profit and Pleasure: Sexual Identities in Late Capitalism*. On the "trouble with normal" generally and the problems with the movement toward gay marriage in particular, see Michael Warner's *The Trouble with Normal: Sex, Politics, and the Ethics of Queer Life*. Warner's chapter "Beyond Gay Marriage" remains the most eloquent and important critique of the gay marriage movement (81–147). For a more recent and less critical overview of the movement, see George Chauncey's *Why Marriage? The History Shaping Today's Debate over Gay Equality*. I consider popular televisual images of queerness more directly in chapter 5; I discuss the Human Rights Campaign's notorious Millennium March in chapter 4.

4. For post-Habermasian work on the public sphere, see Oskar Negt and Alexandar Kluge's *Public Sphere and Experience: Toward an Analysis of the Bourgeois and Proletarian Public Sphere*; Miriam Hansen's foreword to *Public Sphere and Experience* (ix–xli); and Nancy Fraser's *Justice Interruptus: Critical Reflections on the "Postsocialist" Condition*, especially chapter 3, "Rethinking the Public Sphere: A Contribution to the Critique of Actually Existing Democracy" (69–98). For queer work on the public sphere, see Warner's *Publics and Counterpublics*; Eric O. Clarke's *Virtuous Vice: Homoeroticism and the Public Sphere*; and José Esteban Muñoz's *Disidentifications: Queers of Color and the Performance of Politics*, especially chapter 6, "Pedro Zamora's *Real World* of Counterpublicity" (143–160).

5. For a critical discussion of paradigmatic images of poster children, see chapter 5, especially the section subtitled "The Return of the Transgressive: Burning Candles for Bob Flanagan."

228 | Notes to Chapter 2

6. Lisa Duggan's essay "Holy Matrimony!" was published as a cover story seven years after Gabriel Rotello's "Creating a New Gay Culture: Balancing Fidelity and Freedom," suggesting that—during the 2004 election when the liberal consensus was most pronounced—the *Nation* had moved to the left on this issue. Duggan's article critiques gay marriage and links it to other neoliberal projects of privatization such as "welfare reform." As of this writing, Duggan's article remains the most prominent queer critique of gay marriage to be published in a mainstream media venue. See also Greg Wharton and Ian Philips's anthology *I Do, I Don't: Queers on Marriage*, which reprints "Holy Matrimony!"

7. For a consideration of Michel Foucault's relevance to disability studies, see Shelley Lynn Tremain's *Foucault and the Government of Disability*.

8. See Cindy Patton's *Fatal Advice: How Safe-Sex Education Went Wrong*. In her "AIDS: Keywords," Jan Zita Grover discusses the second AIDS forum, held in Denver in 1983, where people living with AIDS explicitly rejected the dominant languages of blame and fear that were circulating around them (26–27).

9. On AIDS care networks, see Philip M. Kayal's *Bearing Witness: Gay Men's Health Crisis and the Politics of AIDS*. Risa Denenberg overviews some of the feminist health care traditions that influenced early AIDS activism in "A History of the Lesbian Health Movement."

10. On the identity of the "invalid woman," see Diane Price Herndl's important study *Invalid Women: Figuring Feminine Illness in American Fiction and Culture, 1840–1940*.

11. For a discussion of "race suicide," see Priscilla Wald's "Cultures and Carriers: 'Typhoid Mary' and the Science of Social Control" 201–206.

12. Information on Bertha Flaten, the Faribault State School, and similar institutions was included as part of the Smithsonian National Museum of American History's exhibition, "The Disability Rights Movement."

13. See, for instance, Susan Wendell's *The Rejected Body: Feminist Philosophical Reflections on Disability* 19–22.

14. As I work through the text of *Why Can't Sharon Kowalski Come Home?* in this section, I will use "Karen" and "Sharon" to refer to the women as they are represented in the text, and "Thompson" and "Kowalski" at other times (to refer to Thompson as author, or to the women outside the text).

15. My emphasis on becoming crip in this brief conclusion is partly intended to direct attention away from any heroic reading of Thompson the individual. Above and beyond any individual, the text itself— and, more important, the movements that generated it—put forward a crip expansiveness, an imaginative sense of what public cultures of queerness and disability might look like.

16. The gay marriage movement has not forwarded a single proposal that would validate and protect the Thompson-Kowalski-Bresser union, Thompson's occasional work for the Human Rights Campaign notwithstanding. Historically, various forms of the disability movement, feminism, and gay liberation—forms

that remain vital today—could value, and even make contingently representative, such a union. The HRC, in an era of "family values" can invoke, generically and vaguely, the importance of valuing LGBT family forms, but they are not about to encourage legislation to protect a threesome.

NOTES TO CHAPTER 3

1. Through my invocation of thirty years of collective action, I intend to call back, specifically, activist efforts that directly marked "black" as beautiful, proud, and powerful: Black Pride, Black Power, Black Arts. The collective action responsible for these resignifications of "black," of course, depended on other, prior, forms of individual and communal self-definition. Robert F. Reid-Pharr, in his essay "The Shock of Gary Fisher" (in *Black Gay Man*), traces this tradition of resignification all the way back to Frederick Douglass. I am following Reid-Pharr by arguing that Fisher diverges from more recognizable, or hegemonic, forms of black identification (and specifically the black gay identification Belton associates with Marlon Riggs and others) (Reid-Pharr 142–144). I engage "The Shock of Gary Fisher" more later in this chapter, linking it to issues of disability, rehabilitation, and degradation.

2. "When AIDS Ends" was the title used on the cover of the *New York Times Magazine* on November 10, 1996; on the inside, Andrew Sullivan's title was "When Plagues End: Notes on the Twilight of an Epidemic." David Román discusses the 1996 *New York Times Magazine* and *Time* covers briefly in his perceptive article "Not-about-AIDS" (1). For an excellent consideration of Sullivan's piece in relation to (white, black, and Latino) gay male identification, HIV/AIDS, homelessness, and public space (all of which are similarly concerns in the present chapter), see Phillip Brian Harper's "Gay Male Identities, Personal Privacy, and Relations of Public Exchange: Notes on Directions for Queer Critique." Harper's queer theory of "discursive admissiveness" (which he counterposes to "discursive sacrifice") has affinity with the crip theory of noncompliance this chapter advances (23).

3. "Is This a Great Time or What?" was the question put forward by a famous MCI commercial from around 1996. My use of the slogan in relation to *Wired* follows Thomas Frank, who, in *One Market under God: Extreme Capitalism, Market Populism, and the End of Economic Democracy*, uses it more generally as a catch-phrase for compulsory, neoliberal structures of feeling in the 1990s (51–87, 172, 187–188). Frank demonstrates that, by the 1990s, neoliberalism had begun to appropriate rhetorical styles (and liberatory content) from the liberal and radical social movements of the previous decades; the appropriation of rhetoric associated with liberation movements made it appear as though a global, unfettered market was the only site where real democracy could function. Intellectuals or policymakers who dared to question the functioning of the

market were "elites" and "cynics" (45–46, 260–263). Frank argues that market populism essentially allowed only one proper stance toward the market: aligning yourself with those who believed in "freedom" and "choice" meant striking a pose of childlike awe before the workings of the new economy (230–234). The *Time* magazine cover featuring Ho redeploys these rhetorical strategies, encouraging not only wonder and awe in the presence of Ho's amazing vision but also a heady sense that people living with HIV/AIDS will now have new "choices." The cover effectively disallows interrogation of the ways in which global capitalism (and specifically the multinational pharmaceutical companies most invested in the traffic in protease inhibitors) reins in or constrains justice for people with HIV/AIDS, short-circuiting their capacity to exercise choice in relation to the collective future. Activists in Vancouver were well aware of how market populism was functioning around the story of protease inhibitors; Eric Sawyer of ACT UP New York, in a speech critiquing "AIDS Profiteers," stated bluntly: "I am afraid that you all will miss the real message from this conference. I speak especially to the media, who have started the spin that 'the cure is here, let's dance.'" For a report on the positions and direct actions put forward by ACT UP and other activist groups in Vancouver, see "ACT UP @ Vancouver"; the report includes Sawyer's speech. For an important overview of HIV/AIDS treatment activism and activists' development of sophisticated political, economic, and scientific vocabularies, see Treichler 278–314.

4. On gay men of color and HIV/AIDS, see C. Cohen; Diaz; Harper, "Gay Male Identities"; Manalansan; Vernon.

5. For Stuart Hall et al., "policing the crisis" does not entail simply facing and managing an already-existing "crisis," but calling it up, enforcing it, and displacing the larger political, economic, and cultural anxieties and issues that attend it. In Hall et al.'s sense, then, 1996—with its demands for wonder, awe, and celebration—would be part of a larger effort to police the crisis, even as (or precisely because) activist invocations and analyses of "the AIDS crisis" and the structures that sustain it were disciplined. I intend "Around 1996"—like Cindy Patton's "Around 1989," in *Fatal Advice: How Safe-Sex Education Went Wrong* (3)—to mark a particularly-charged moment in the history of policing the AIDS crisis.

6. I am indebted in this chapter not only to Jacques Derrida's analysis of poison, cure, and the *pharmakon* in "Plato's Pharmacy" (*Dissemination* 61–171), but also to his later work on hospitality (see, in particular, *Of Hospitality: Anne Dufourmantelle Invites Jacques Derrida to Respond*) and on mourning: "Is the most distressing, or even the most deadly infidelity that of a *possible mourning* which would interiorize within us the image, idol, or ideal of the other who is dead and lives only in us? Or is it that of the impossible mourning, which, leaving the other his alterity, respecting thus his infinite remove, either refuses to take or is incapable of taking the other within oneself, as in the tomb or the vault of

some narcissism?" (*Memoires for Paul de Man* 6). By placing this chapter at the crip "limits" of rehabilitation, I am of course not calling for the elimination or destruction of rehabilitative therapies or for some sort of pure noncompliance, as though that were possible; I am, rather, trying to think how the limit is always at work in and on rehab, enabling or making rehab as we understand it possible (cf. Derrida, *Positions* 6, 12).

7. In *A History of Disability*, Henri-Jacques Stiker makes it quite clear that both those who are institutionalized and those who are reintegrated into society are caught up in the larger rehabilitative system:

There are those who bear the label [disabled] but who have been identified as nonintegrable. These are individuals whose affliction has been called too serious. All kinds of special institutions have been created for them: MAS [Mobility Assistance Services], group homes, sheltered workshops, nursing homes. Thus the general label of disabled is further subdivided into severe cases, mild cases, etc. The integration of some of these facilitates the recognition of others as unadaptable. (152–153)

8. On the return of African American troops who had been segregated while fighting in World War I and the linkage between this return and new forms of distinct and militant identity (that is, forms of identity that would seem to be opposed to the identity desired and generated by rehabilitation), see Lewis 3–24.

9. One of Roderick A. Ferguson's primary targets in *Aberrations in Black* is canonical sociology; his critique of the ways in which this field essentially "diagnosed" the problems of the African American family makes clear that sociology was another arena "saturated by the discourse of physical rehabilitation." Ferguson's chapter on *Invisible Man*, moreover, particularly suggests that some African Americans of necessity were "rehabilitated" and achieved (or were perceived to achieve) the assumed prior, normal state Stiker analyzes; it was this group that was, in turn, most readily integrated into a range of modern institutions as a result of the civil rights movement. This normalization process, however, further marginalized "other African American subjects because of class difference and disability, as well as gender/sexual nonconformity" (66).

10. People with HIV/AIDS were almost excluded from the Americans with Disabilities Act on both legislative and judicial levels: on the legislative side, some conservative lawmakers were specifically wary of including HIV/AIDS, and some groups explicitly lobbied for its exclusion; on the judicial side, the first Supreme Court case testing the limits of the ADA was a case, *Bragdon v. Abbott*, involving asymptomatic HIV/AIDS. In *Bragdon v. Abbott*, Justices interpreted the ADA as indeed applicable to asymptomatic people with HIV/AIDS.

11. Initially associated with mainline Protestantism but in the late twentieth century virtually canonical within Fundamentalist Christian circles, *In His Steps, or What Would Jesus Do?* even spawned WWJD? merchandise such as lapel pins and coffee mugs. I say that the text was virtually canonical in this context be-

cause, although it is at times taught in Fundamentalist Christian educational venues, it is known largely through its subtitle and through the merchandise associated with that subtitle. Most Christian consumers of the merchandise, although they undoubtedly expect to be blessed for their conformity, are likely unaware that Sheldon's novel literally represents a town made more productive through individuals' constant monitoring of how their movements match up with Jesus's idealized movements. The longstanding engagement between rehabilitation and Fundamentalist Christianity is not guaranteed; put differently, it is a hegemonic formation. Fundamentalist Christianity and rehab, in other words, don't have to go together—*modern* (even "undeniably moderne") rehab could at times be read in opposition to an *antimodern* (and -anticorporate) Fundamentalist Christianity (think here of certain sects, for instance, refusing blood transfusions). Just as Fundamentalism's anticorporatism strikes me as increasingly residual in the United States (especially in the wake of the 2004 elections), however, so, too, does its potential to critique dominant discourses of rehabilitation. WWJD? consumers and ministries like Terry's have been more than content to repeat rehabilitative truths without question (even if those truths are articulated to more properly religious discourses of salvation).

12. Given Harry Braverman's concern with industrial capitalism, I am taking a bit of literary license with his theses; I recognize, in other words, that the economies into which Ricardo and others in Aikin and Aparicio's *The Transformation* are incorporated are different from, more flexible than, the economies Braverman discusses (industrial capitalism more directly gave rise to the conflicts in the Iron Range of Minnesota that I considered in chapter 2). In some ways, Ricardo's job is an example of what Evan Watkins calls "the new literacy" that "privileges . . . a flexible and lifelong willingness to engage in creative responses in continually new and shifting conditions" ("World Bank Literacy" 18). However, despite the fact that Ricardo's story-telling will ostensibly require more creativity than what is demanded from the workers (from the first two-thirds of the twentieth century) in Braverman's study, Ricardo's work is still degraded, according to Braverman's terms. Neoliberalism still locates the most crucial forms of conception elsewhere, largely apart from the majority of laborers negotiating the new literacy (on the most basic level, for instance, workers like Ricardo played no role in conceiving the new literacy they are now required to execute).

13. I am grateful to the graduate students in my fall 2000 course "Conceptualizing Genders" for a particularly engaging discussion of Gigi's function in *The Transformation*.

14. I do not intend to fetishize academic queer theory here; like crip theory, as I suggested in chapter 1, queer theory and praxis emerge as much or more from nonacademic spaces. My point here is more concerned with how (and through what paradoxes) queer speech or writing becomes authoritative. Even the high antiassimilationism of a book like Matt Bernstein Sycamore's *Revolting Behav-*

ior: Queer Strategies for Resisting Assimilation challenges authoritative strategies largely through spaces (including, say, Amazon.com or Barnes and Noble Bookstores) where that challenge is in some sense proper (and the book itself, of course, becomes property through commodity exchange). This is not to say that the revolting ideas in *Revolting Behavior* (or even the book itself) are not in circulation outside of authoritative spaces; as I hope this chapter demonstrates, authoritative spaces, on the contrary, are policed so heavily because of the revolting ideas, behaviors, and bodies in circulation outside their borders.

15. My invocation of "we know what that means" is of course not to suggest that "nigger" does not have multiple valences—on the most obvious level, the term historically has incredibly different valences for white and black speakers, and in majority white or majority black speaking contexts (for a discussion of the term's multiple valences, see Randall Kennedy's *Nigger: The Strange Career of a Troublesome Word*). Fisher's deployment of the term is ambivalent in all senses—regardless of who "we" are, we think "we know what that means," and Fisher is disturbing because he exceeds what we think we know. To call back Derrida, I might say in this note, before returning to the body of my text, that "to a considerable degree, we have already said all we *meant to say.* Our lexicon at any rate is not far from being exhausted. With the exception of this or that supplement, our questions will have nothing more to name but the texture of the text, reading and writing, mastery and play, the paradoxes of supplementarity, and the graphic relations between the living and the dead. . . . Since we have already said everything, the reader must bear with us if we continue on awhile" (*Dissemination* 65).

16. It is perhaps premature, less than a decade after its publication, to make pronouncements on the amount of critical attention to Fisher. Nonetheless, despite the fact that the publication context for *Gary in Your Pocket*—connected so directly to Sedgwick's work as both teacher and queer theorist, located in the prestigious Series Q from Duke University Press, introduced by Belton, and blurbed by Marilyn Hacker and Randall Kenan—could hardly be more conducive for critical attention, Reid-Pharr's essay remains the only significant consideration of it. On this theme, Reid-Pharr writes, "I have been struck by how difficult the text seems to have been for those people—white, black, and otherwise—who have encountered it. Indeed responses have ranged from righteous indignation toward the text and its editor . . . to a rather maddening inarticulateness" (149).

17. On the inception of disability movements in Berkeley, see Shapiro 41–73. For an oral history of the AIDS Epidemic in San Francisco, see Benjamin Shepard, *White Nights and Ascending Shadows: A History of the San Francisco AIDS Epidemic.*

18. According to Sedgwick, Fisher began graduate work at Berkeley in 1984: "Continuing to live in San Francisco and commute across the bay, he did well in

graduate school, was admitted to the Ph.D. program after three semesters, became a gifted teacher of composition and of American and African-American literature, and developed strong friendships with a few other graduate students" (274). A few of the journal entries included in *Gary in Your Pocket* represent Fisher working through complex issues of race, desire, and power in American literature, most notably an entry dated January 31, 1987, attempting to answer the question "Where's a black reader's desire?" in Herman Melville's "Benito Cereno" (201). Fisher writes in this entry of the pleasure in what he calls "the S and M game" in "Benito Cereno" and links that game to the complicated (and deadly serious) play of domination and submission in other texts, including William Faulkner's *Light in August* and Richard Wright's *Native Son* (*Gary in Your Pocket* 201–203).

19. I'm calling the Alvin Ailey American Dance Theater a space of disability because of how thoroughly it has remained associated with Ailey's legacy and, indeed, with HIV/AIDS. Fisher himself associates it with both as he writes about leaving the Alta Bates Summit Medical Center to attend a performance. Fisher's timeline in this journal entry, incidentally, is slightly off—he writes (in 1993) that Ailey had died eight years earlier; it had only been four. Alvin Ailey died in 1989 at the age of fifty-eight. The Alvin Ailey American Dance Theater continues to thrive today.

20. Although my reading of Marlon Riggs's *Tongues Untied* is indebted to Ferguson, I am diverging from him through my emphasis on the ways in which liberal ideologies captivate the film's nationalist conclusion. The overdetermined linearity of the film's conclusion ("we're black black black black gay gay gay gay!" men marching in a pride parade shout) is at odds with some of the film's more aberrant moments, including a beautiful scene focused on a lone black drag queen wandering (or perhaps working) the streets. A reading of this scene opens Ferguson's *Aberrations in Black* (1–2). I find *Tongues Untied* to be one of the richest and most teachable texts of the LGBT 1990s, and I have used it in the classroom innumerable times since its release. However, the first time I taught *Tongues Untied* next to Fisher (or—true confessions—next to Fisher mediated through Reid-Pharr's essay on him), my students were tellingly tongue-tied. The first effect of the juxtaposition, in other words, was a difficult and extended silence in the classroom—which was then followed by one of the best class discussions I have ever experienced. My thanks to the members of my Queer Cultural Studies class from fall 2002, in particular Nathan Weiner and Miriam Greenberg.

21. I am drawing attention here to the ways in which men of color participate in SM subcultures partly because Fisher seems to me to have consistently noticed their participation; on this point, then, I read *Gary in Your Pocket* slightly differently than Reid-Pharr, who suggests that men of color are "hailed" only "infrequently" in Fisher's text (*Black Gay Man* 143). It is not only the journal entries,

moreover, but the stories included in the first half of *Gary in Your Pocket* that suggest that Fisher's San Francisco years were marked by careful observation of both white people and people of color and by constant theorizing about how little about race, gender, sexuality, and embodiment is apparent on the surface of quotidian relations and conversations.

NOTES TO CHAPTER 4

1. Kenneth Burke develops the following thesis throughout the final section of his 1950 *A Rhetoric of Motives*: "Order, the Secret, and the Kill. To study the nature of rhetoric, the relation between rhetoric and dialectic, and the application of both to human relations in general, is to circulate about these three motives" (265). Despite Burke's emphasis on relations among the various elements, order remains the privileged term, and is in fact the title of the section (181–333).

2. A significant body of work in composition theory, focused in various and contestatory ways on "process," has taken up some of the questions I introduce here; I locate myself in relation to that work in a later section of this chapter. Although I have revised them slightly, I draw the preceding paragraphs from my introduction to the second edition of "Composing a Writing Program: An Alternative Handbook for the Program in Rhetoric and Composition at the George Washington University." The second edition of this document, which was printed in August 1999, was collectively authored by twenty members of George Washington University's Expository Writing Program and was edited by Angela Hewett and myself. "Composing a Writing Program" included, among many other topics, discussion of the wide range of composition theories that were in circulation at the university. At the time, faculty in the program intended to revise this document continually, although there was debate about whether it should take a temporarily final form annually or whether it should appear online, allowing for the more obvious deferment of any "final" form. A great deal of agitation, however, attended the second edition: although the final copying bill was relatively small, there was concern that the university, via the English department, had paid for the document, which included a section openly discussing efforts on the part of graduate students and part-time faculty around the country to unionize (in actuality, the document was collectively paid for by members of the Writing Program; see following note 4). In my conclusion to this chapter, I return to localized agitation and consider some of the ways in which GWU has designed initiatives that in effect work to contain what I call in this chapter "decomposition."

3. This chapter directly builds on the critique of neoliberalism, flexible bodies, and compulsory able-bodiedness that I put forward in chapter 1. One could certainly argue that the truth of the corporate university is far from universally

acknowledged because, as the work of Paulo Freire has repeatedly suggested, knowledge requires praxis to be genuine: "The oppressed must confront reality critically, simultaneously objectifying and acting upon that reality. A mere perception of reality not followed by this critical intervention will not lead to a transformation of objective reality—precisely because it is not a true perception" (*Pedagogy of the Oppressed* 34). For a thorough discussion of the corporate university, see Cary Nelson and Stephen Watt's *Academic Keywords: A Devil's Dictionary for Higher Education* (84–98). According to Nelson and Watt, corporate universities include "universities that adopt profit-oriented corporate values," "universities that adopt corporate-style management and accounting techniques," and "universities that instill corporate culture in their students and staff" (89–90). A March 21, 2003, *Chronicle of Higher Education* article succinctly details the ways in which composition programs are particularly invested in (or, conversely, are serving as investments for) the corporate university; in a paragraph nodding directly toward GWU, the writer of the piece suggests that "scholarship in the humanities has always kept its distance from the business school. But in some recent work in composition studies, ideas about discourse mingle with concepts from the corporate world" (McLemee A16). For recent work in and around composition studies that addresses the issues I take up in this introduction, see the articles included in Marc Bousquet et al., *Tenured Bosses and Disposable Teachers: Writing Instruction in the Managed University*, and in Tony Scott et al., *Composition as Management Science*, which was published as a special issue of *Workplace: A Journal for Academic Labor*. See also Connors; Horner; Johnson et al.; Schell and Stock; Slaughter; and Watkins, *Work Time*.

4. For an important volume of essays linking disability theory to rhetoric and composition, see James C. Wilson and Cynthia Lewiecki-Wilson's *Embodied Rhetorics: Disability in Language and Culture*. In turn, this chapter links queer/disability theory and (or in) rhetoric and composition to critiques of the corporate university (or, more broadly, links work on political economy in composition to work on identity politics in composition). Given the increasing prominence of Writing in the Disciplines (WID) initiatives around the country, there are many ways in which the writing classrooms I am locating as "ours" are not simply those dedicated to first-year writing. At the very least, I intend for the concerns about writing, discipline, and embodiment in higher education that I am putting forward to be relevant beyond that particular, introductory space and for progressive faculty members in various locations to be concerned about what is happening in first-year writing classrooms. Moreover, my use of "inaugurate" to describe the de-composing queer/disability theory I describe in this chapter purposefully implies that something should (always and continuously) follow. The practices that might follow upon a theory of de-composition include—but are not limited to—direct participation in labor movements and

unionizing drives. My open advocacy of such drives here, including the ongoing drive to organize adjunct faculty at GWU, has in fact been partially paid for by GWU; I'm grateful to the university for leave time in 2004 to complete this book project, as well as for office supplies, a copying budget, and a computer. "Paid for," of course, mystifies the fact that my labor and the labor of others has generated surplus value for the university; I hope that the theories I explore in this chapter, and *Crip Theory* in general, consistently emphasize that value might be realized in other ways.

5. Just as my exploration of rehabilitative noncompliance in chapter 4 was influenced by the work of Jacques Derrida, my advocacy for a certain loss of composure in sites committed to composition has affinities with what he, reflecting on the nature of justice, describes as a necessary "experience of the impossible" ("Force of Law" 947). De-composition is an experience of the impossible, and as such cannot simply be implemented (or—even more—administered) by a writing program, except perhaps—to continue drawing out the Derridean implications of my argument—the democratic writing program to come. Justice, for Derrida, "is yet, to come" ("Force of Law" 969), though it is also, "however unpresentable it may be. . . . that which must not wait" ("Force of Law" 967). The present chapter is also indebted, as I hope my coda suggests, to Derrida's *Specters of Marx: The State of the Debt, the Work of Mourning, and the New International.* For work in composition theory attentive to deconstruction, see Covino; Jarratt; and Neel.

6. My point is perhaps best exemplified by certain forms of expressivism that explicitly move from (handwritten) freewriting to a printed text. Neither freewriting nor the linkage between the composed self and an orderly written text, however, is confined solely to expressivist classrooms.

7. The "indiscipline" Foucault theorizes near the end of *Discipline and Punish*, whereby the "useful delinquency" required and produced by the prison system refuses pathologization and insolently speaks back to bourgeois discourses of law and order (280, 290–292), also floats free of its initial location in and around the legal system and has affinities with what I am calling "de-composition."

8. Rosalyn Deutsche's work on art, public space, and democracy, with its analysis of a range of political and artistic movements intent on challenging those who "presume that the task of democracy is to settle, rather than sustain, conflict" has strongly influenced my thinking about these issues (270).

9. I am referring here first to Matthew Shepard, the gay University of Wyoming student who was murdered by Russell Henderson and Aaron McKinney in 1998. Henderson and McKinney beat Shepard, tied him to a deer fence, and left him for dead; the murder gained unprecedented nationwide media coverage. My second reference is to the deaths, from 1993 to the present, of more than one hundred residents of the District of Columbia who were living in group

homes for the mentally disabled that were overseen by the mismanaged and negligent Mental Retardation and Developmental Disabilities Administration (a division of the Department of Human Services). The deaths were due to unsafe, unsanitary, and abusive conditions.

10. Rosemarie Garland-Thomson argues, in her foundational *Extraordinary Bodies: Figuring Physical Disability in American Culture and Literature*, that "disability studies should become a universalizing discourse in the way that Sedgwick imagines gay studies and feminism to be" (22). The project of contingent universalization is one attempt both to take Garland-Thomson's call seriously and to hold in generative tension Sedgwick's "minoritizing" and "universalizing" understandings of sexuality and identity (*Epistemology of the Closet* 1). For another politicized example of contingent universalization that specifically distinguishes the process from more recognizable forms of humanistic universalization, see my discussion of South Africa's Treatment Action Campaign (TAC) in chapter 2. In the introduction to "Desiring Disability: Queer Theory Meets Disability Studies," McRuer and Abby L. Wilkerson further develop the notion of queerness and disability as desirable.

11. In Roland Barthes's terms, the virtually orgasmic and identity-disintegrating "text of bliss" is impossible to sustain in the context of a culture that privileges the text of pleasure: "the text that contents, fills, grants euphoria; the text that comes from culture and does not break with it, is linked to a *comfortable* practice of reading" (*Pleasure of the Text* 14).

12. Given the commitment to cultural studies pedagogy and content in the composition classroom that I detail in the next section, there are ways in which I am aligned with what has been called the "postprocess" movement in composition theory rather than with expressivist attempts to "discover" the processes individual writers' employ or some attempts, by cognitivists and others, to delineate the components of "the" writing process. For overviews of debates about process in composition, see the collection edited by Lad Tobin and Thomas Newkirk, *Taking Stock: The Writing Process Movement in the 90s*, as well as Tobin's useful essay, "Process Pedagogy," which provides a snapshot of the emergence of the postprocess movement (13–16). For more on postprocess theory, see Truman Kent, *Post-Process Theory: Betond the Writing Process Paradigm*.

13. Since programs for the Composition and Cultural Studies Conference for Student Writers are available online, at http://www.gwu.edu/%7Eenglish/ccsc/, and since these programs include links to actual presentations and email addresses for the authors, some students report being contacted years later for information on their topics. In 2002, one student was contacted by Hollywood producers who were putting together a website for the film *The Hours*. At its height, the conference involved GWU students, faculty, and staff, as well as stu-

dents and faculty from American and Georgetown Universities and some leaders from local Washington, D.C., activist groups such as Homes Not Jails and Neighbors Consejo. The involvement of American and Georgetown Universities was largely due to the fact that some part-time GWU composition instructors were also teaching sections of composition at those universities. Angela Hewett and I discuss the emergence of the Composition and Cultural Studies Conference in "Composing Student Activists."

14. Syllabi for my courses on AIDS and the media and disability studies are available online at the "Disability Studies in the Humanities" website: http://www.georgetown.edu/crossroads/interests/ds-hum/.

15. Although, as Lennard J. Davis points out, "reading/writing has been unproblematically thought of as a process that involves hearing and vocalizing" (*Enforcing Normalcy* 101), the process is more properly understood through what Davis calls "deafness as a critical modality" (100), since, in fact, reading and writing do *not* involve hearing and vocalizing (no one reading these words is actually hearing me speak them). The listserv that I discuss in this paragraph similarly highlights the ways in which deafness as a critical modality organizes many of our communicative processes.

16. Although Wilkerson and Michael Bérubé are both known as disability studies scholars, Ralph Cintron had not at the time considered his work in that context. The chapter from *Angels' Town* which I had students read, however, "A Boy and His Wall" (98–129), is concerned among other things with the ways in which some members of the Latino/a community Cintron studied were tracked—as "learning disabled"—through the education system. Cintron's critique of this tracking and attention to the social construction of learning disability resonate with a great deal of scholarship in disability studies. I am grateful to Cintron, Bérubé, and Wilkerson for their virtual participation in my class.

17. Some neoconservative gay critics would undoubtedly say, as Andrew Sullivan and Bruce Bawer have indeed been saying in numerous articles and public appearances for some time, that such a critique is out of touch with the times and that the gay movement has developed beyond such radicalism. I would counter that the success of the "A16" protests against the World Bank and the International Monetary Fund (IMF)—protests that brought together thousands of participants from around the country and that were held a week before the Millennium March on Washington (MMOW)—suggest that in actuality the normalizing MMOW (held one week after the anti–World Bank/IMF protests) was out of touch with the times. The A16 protests, endorsed by the National Lesbian and Gay Task Force, various ACT UP chapters, and many other groups, were much queerer (in the critical sense) than the MMOW. For an overview of the A16 protests, along with other "dispatches from the front lines of the globalization debate," see Naomi Klein's *Fences and Windows*.

18. For coverage of the controversies, see Joshua Gamson, "Whose Millennium March?" and Karla Solheim, "Militant Marketing March." See also Chasin 214–219.

19. Information on GWU's new University Writing Program, marking it as "a cornerstone in GW's Strategic Plan for Academic Excellence" is available online at http://www2.gwu.edu/~uwp/. For the *AAC&U News* article, see "George Washington University Rewrites Its Writing Program." In my interpretation, the reasons the very language of "cultural studies" has been proscribed include both the historical association of cultural studies pedagogy with politically engaged and left-leaning scholarship and the administrative need to generate knowledge about the new program, for audiences such as readers of *AAC&U News*, that clearly marks it as different from, and indeed unconnected to, the old.

20. Abby L. Wilkerson was hired in 2002 with a joint appointment in the University Writing Program and the department of English. The courses I am noting here are from the spring 2004 semester: Gustavo Guerra's "Sexuality, Identity, and Other Contemporary Anxieties: Latin American Thought and Culture" and Christy Zink's "A Congress of Freaks: Cultural Oddities, Strange Folks, and Proud Outsiders." Although we both remain committed to composing bodies and de-composition, Moshenberg and I, among the few tenured members of the old Writing Program, were folded back into the English department or relocated to other programs. I teach critical theory and special topics in cultural studies in English, and Moshenberg is currently the director of the Women's Studies Program.

NOTES TO CHAPTER 5

1. Although I had written about HIV/AIDS and culture, my own direct involvement in disability studies (where I would now most immediately locate my scholarly and political commitments) literally commenced with such an invitation from Garland-Thomson, who encouraged me to write my first piece on the intersections of queer theory and disability studies. The essay, "Compulsory Able-Bodiedness and Queer/Disabled Existence," appeared in the MLA volume I discuss in this chapter (and now appears, revised and expanded, as the introduction to this book).

2. The Society for Disability Studies (SDS) has been holding an annual convention for almost two decades, and—as I note in chapter 1—a few other significant conferences focused directly on disability studies in the humanities were held in the mid-1990s, including "Discourses of Disability in the Humanities" (University of Puerto Rico, Mayaguez), "This/Ability: An Interdisciplinary Conference on Disability and the Arts" (University of Michigan, Ann Arbor), and "Gender and Disability Studies" (Rutgers University). A six-week summer institute on disability studies, funded by the National Endowment for the Humani-

ties (NEH), was held at San Francisco State in summer 2000. As of this writing, the MLA's Emory conference was both the most prestigious and high-profile single event for the discipline of disability studies, given that the conference was extremely well funded and that presentations were by invitation. *PMLA* has a circulation of more than 30,000 members and subscribers—a number that far exceeds the circulation numbers for other journals that had previously published special issues or clusters on disability studies.

3. I am obviously echoing (or stealing) Amazon.com's famous phrase here. The books listed are essentially *Queer Eye for the Straight Guy* spin-offs, as *Esquire's Guide* (written in 1999 but repackaged and re-released following the success of *Queer Eye*) is coauthored by dining expert Ted Allen and *Off the Cuff* by fashion expert Carson Kressley. For other critical work on *Queer Eye*, see Baldwin; Keller. In 2005, *GLQ: A Journal of Lesbian and Gay Studies* published a special cluster of short, critical pieces on *Queer Eye*, edited by Chris Straayer and Tom Waugh ("Queer TV Style" 95–117). Although none of the essays directly addresses issues of disability, Anna McCarthy's selection, "Crab People from the Center of the Earth," has the most affinity with my own analysis, since it links *Queer Eye* to what Laurie Ouellette calls "the neoliberal project of reality TV" (McCarthy 98).

4. Although *Boy Meets Boy* also naturalizes sexual identity (given that the twist for the show depends on some of the men being "really" straight), the rapprochement between gay and straight men is ultimately less successful, in that the show constructs a built-in hostility between (straight) deceiving and (gay) deceived figures. As I underscore in this section, the idea of a distinct gay, minority identity was historically challenging or even threatening (the Marxist founders of the Mattachine Society in the early 1950s wanted to emphasize, with their minority thesis, that homosexuals had been *constituted* as a minority by an oppressive heterosexual culture and that such a minority could speak back, and act, in its own interests), but the early twenty-first-century "queer" identity in *Queer Eye*, also a minoritized identity, is largely nonthreatening and contained precisely through an implicit appeal to distinction. *Queer Eye* is thus (brilliantly, in the breadth of the containments it is able to effect) distinct from both threatening identitarian and anti-identitarian queer traditions.

5. The achievement of such carnivalesque spaces, however, can be quite difficult (though the difficulty should not make such spaces any less desirable). If, for Mikhail Bakhtin, the carnivalesque involves a "temporary suspension of all hierarchic distinctions and barriers among men . . . and of the prohibitions of usual life" (15), I am in part attempting here to theorize the ways in which suspension of one hierarchic distinction consolidates another.

6. Franklin D. Roosevelt himself, in fact, is arguably part of this cultural advance: the struggle to represent the 32nd president as (realistically) disabled in the FDR memorial in Washington, D.C. culminated, on January 10, 2001, with

the unveiling of the first public statue of any world leader seated in the wheel-chair he or she used. For more on the FDR memorial, see following note 16.

7. On "critically disabled" or "severely disabled" perspectives, see the conclusion to the introduction to *Crip Theory*. Later in this chapter, I discuss the ways in which Bob Flanagan works with, around, and on the classic twentieth-century poster child image.

8. The actions listed here are not by definition (or essentially) radical; their status as "transgressive," in my mind, suggests less that they mark a *definitive* better way and more that they invoke a range of alternative, expansive futures. Judith Heumann herself in fact participated in the HEW takeover; her later emergence as a representative figure in neoliberal state and international financial institutions attests both to the difficulty of sustaining the transgressive mode and to the overdetermination of the realistic mode. In April 1977, activists occupied the offices of the Health, Education, and Welfare Department in San Francisco, essentially shutting down government operations there. They were protesting the failure to implement Section 504 of the Rehabilitation Act of 1973, which prohibited federal agencies, or any institution that received federal funding, from discriminating against people with disabilities (Shapiro 64–70). The protests at the Stonewall Inn bar in New York City, in which patrons fought back during what had been a routine police raid, are often understood to mark the beginning of the contemporary gay liberation movement. Sex Panic! was a group that mobilized a range of actions and "teach-ins" during the mid-1990s to oppose the ways in which neoconservative gay writers were advocating the couple form as most desirable for LGBT people and as most likely to stem the spread of HIV. The Battle for Seattle in November 1999 refers to protests mobilized by a wide coalition of groups—environmentalists, union members, Lesbian Avengers, Students against Sweatshops—in opposition to the World Trade Organization (WTO), which was holding its meetings in Seattle at the time.

9. The queerness of Barthes's project has been noted most famously by D. A. Miller in *Bringing out Roland Barthes*; this chapter, with its tentative effort to position Barthes as a crip theorist, might be taken as an extension of that work. (Although our projects are somewhat different, Tobin Siebers also articulates Barthes to disability theory in "Words Stare Like a Glass Eye: From Literary to Visual to Disability Studies and Back Again.") It is, perhaps, notable that one of Barthes's early publications, "On Gide and His Journal," appeared in *Existences*, which—as Susan Sontag, who edited *A Barthes Reader*, notes—was the magazine for the Sanatorium des Etudiantes de France, where Barthes was interred for tuberculosis both in 1942 and from 1943 to 1945. "On Gide and His Journal," published when Barthes was literally enclosed in a sanatorium, opens, "Reluctant to enclose Gide in a system I knew would never content me, I was vainly trying to find some connection among these notes" (3). Given that Barthes

both read avidly and spent a great deal of time simply observing others around him during his years in the sanatorium, a case could be made that his incisive theoretical project is at least in part a disabled project. Put differently, *Mythologies* could be comprehended as crip theory *avant la lettre*.

10. I have generally followed the usage in Andrea Juno and V. Vale's *Bob Flanagan, Supermasochist*—"CF" for cystic fibrosis and "SM" for sadomasochism—in this chapter, although a range of other usages are also possible (including cf and C-F; sm, s/m, and S/m). The term "bdsm" incorporates both SM and "bondage and domination." Children's alphabet blocks with the capital letters C, F, S, and M were also included in "Visiting Hours," so my CF and SM usage in this chapter follows that performance piece (Juno and Vale 66). Placing this section of my chapter alongside my discussion of Gary Fisher in chapter 3 will imply, no doubt, that, at the very least, complicated bottoms are interesting, if not downright sexy. While chapter 3 was concerned with the limits of rehabilitation, however, my focus on Flanagan here is more concerned with thinking the limits of (disability) media and representation.

11. Both Richard Kim's formulation (cited in Duggan "Down There") and my adaptation of it here are indebted to Walter Benjamin's "Theses on the Philosophy of History": "To articulate the past historically does not mean to recognize it 'the way it really was.' It means to seize hold of a memory as it flashes up at a moment of danger. Historical materialism wishes to retain that image of the past which unexpectedly appears to man singled out by history at a moment of danger" (255).

12. Given how foundational this tradition of disability studies theorizing has been, this volume, *Crip Theory*, is itself partly built on it. To call back Barthes, however, we might acknowledge that this tradition—which often puts forward a new metaphor, disability as minority identity, to exorcise more problematic metaphors—is "moderately symbolic," while the possibilities Flanagan's images put into play are "radically symbolic" ("From Work to Text" 158). The good intentions of the realist tradition generally require eliding the metaphoricity of "disability as minority identity."

13. Flanagan's performances, moreover (such as those documented in Kirby Dick's *Sick: The Life and Death of Bob Flanagan, Supermasochist*), invariably incorporate camp humor; in this sense, they are even more directly linked to the filmic practices Matthew Tinkcomm discusses in *Working Like a Homosexual: Camp, Capital, Cinema*. Flanagan often stresses that public performances of SM are framed by a principle of consent (see, for instance, Juno and Vale 89).

14. On the discovery and invention of new erotic and sexual possibilities, see Bob Guter and John R. Killacky's anthology *Queer Crips: Disabled Gay Men and Their Stories*. The stories in *Queer Crips* are nonheteronormative in the broadest sense; it is in fact quite striking how much the convergence of disability

244 | Notes to Chapter 5

and homosexuality in *Queer Crips* appears to authorize erotic inventiveness and play (conversely, the anthology implies that compulsory heterosexuality and compulsory able-bodiedness constrict such inventiveness).

15. Flanagan's poem appears to target explicitly what Michel Foucault called "scientia sexualis," the Western, confession-oriented, practice of extracting the preexisting truth from sex. In contrast, "Why" and Flanagan's performances more generally (especially performances conducted in subcultural space) put forward what Foucault calls "ars erotica," where "truth" is generated in and through the erotic experience itself (*History of Sexuality* 57–59).

16. In "Gramsci's Relevance for the Study of Race and Ethnicity," Stuart Hall writes that the term "hegemony" marks "a very particular, historically specific, and temporary 'moment' in the life of a society. . . . Such periods of 'settlement' are unlikely to persist forever. There is nothing automatic about them. They have to be actively constructed and positively maintained." The maintenance of hegemonic formations has a "multi-arena character": "Mastery is not simply imposed or dominative in character. Effectively, it results from winning a substantial degree of popular consent" (424). The disabled realism of the FDR memorial is a good example of the hegemony I am discussing here at work: both disabled and nondisabled people consented to the realistic representation of FDR as disabled, including both political conservatives and members of the Roosevelt family who had formerly resisted such a representation. It is not particularly controversial at this point to acknowledge FDR's disability. At the same time, however, the New Deal that FDR helped to secure has been, over the past three decades, dismantled. Increasingly, FDR has been positioned less as an architect of the New Deal and more as a (disabled) great man in history—one who has tellingly been linked, more and more, to Ronald Reagan, who essentially undid Roosevelt's legacy. Newt Gingrich, following Reagan's death in 2004, even called Reagan the "heir to FDR" and labeled the two men "the two most effective presidents of the 20th century" ("The Heir to FDR"). I would certainly not suggest that the realistic representation of FDR seated in a wheelchair is a bad thing (again, who could suggest such a thing!). There is, nonetheless, a danger that the representation will facilitate a neoliberal forgetting of other aspects of midtwentieth-century political economy. One way for teachers to address this dilemma might be to suggest, transgressively, that another struggle over Washington, D.C., space (contemporaneous with the struggle to represent FDR as disabled) was a disability struggle. I am thinking of the fight to keep the U.S. Congress from renaming National Airport "Ronald Reagan National Airport" (this was uncontroversial at the federal level but highly controversial at the local level; even after the airport was renamed, residents of northern Virginia lobbied hard to keep Reagan's name off of highway and Metro signs). Considering with students how disabled and nondisabled figures on the Right and Left might have been positioned in the two struggles (one successful and one unsuccessful), and

why, would at least help interrupt the disarticulation of political economy and identity politics that helps the realistic mode function efficiently.

17. To link two different aspects of Garland-Thomson's project to the distinctions D'Emilio puts forward, we might say that her emphasis on "ordinary bodies" is more reform-oriented, while her earlier emphasis on "extraordinary bodies" is in many ways more liberationist-oriented, calling the system's bluff.

NOTES TO THE EPILOGUE

1. Some of the material in the preceding two paragraphs, as well as the material below on Grace Chang's *Disposable Domestics: Immigrant Women Workers in the Global Economy*, is drawn from my essay "We Were Never Identified: Feminism, Queer Theory, and a Disabled World" and is used here by permission.

Works Cited

"ACT UP @ Vancouver." Report on the 11th International Conference on AIDS, Vancouver, Canada, July 7–12, 1996. Available at http://www.actupny.org/reports/reportvancouver.html. Accessed 23 January 2005.

Aikin, Susana, and Carlos Aparicio, dir. *The Transformation.* Frameline Distribution, 2005. Premiered PBS *P.O.V.* series, 9 July 1996.

Allen, Ted, Kyan Douglas, Thom Filicia, Carson Kressley, and Jai Rodriguez. *Queer Eye for the Straight Guy: The Fab 5's Guide to Looking Better, Cooking Better, Dressing Better, Behaving Better, and Living Better.* New York: Clarkson Potter, 2004.

Alonso, Alejandro A. "Territoriality among African-American Street Gangs in Los Angeles." Master's thesis, Department of Geography, University of Southern California, May 1999.

Alta Bates Summit Medical Center. "About Us." Berkeley, California. Available at http://www.altabates.com/about/. Accessed 6 February 2005.

American Psychiatric Association. "Obsessive-Compulsive Disorder." *Diagnostic and Statistical Manual of Mental Disorders*, 4th ed., 417–423. Washington, D.C.: APA, 1994.

Anderson, Susan. "A City Called Heaven: Black Enchantment and Despair in Los Angeles." In *The City: Los Angeles and Urban Theory at the End of the Twentieth Century*, ed. Allen J. Scott and Edward W. Soja, 336–364. Berkeley: University of California Press, 1996.

Andrejevic, Mark. "The Kindler, Gentler Gaze of Big Brother: Reality TV in the Era of Digital Capitalism." *New Media and Society* 4.2 (June 2002): 251–270.

Anzaldúa, Gloria. *Borderlands/La Frontera: The New Mestiza.* San Francisco: Aunt Lute, 1987.

———. "La Prieta." In *This Bridge Called My Back: Writings by Radical Women of Color*, ed. Cherríe Moraga and Gloria Anzaldúa, 198–209. New York: Kitchen Table, 1981.

———. "To(o) Queer the Writer—Loca, escritora y chicana." In *InVersions: Writings by Dykes, Queers, and Lesbians*, ed. Betsy Warland, 249–263. Vancouver: Press Gang, 1991.

Bakhtin, Mikhail. *Rabelais and His World*. Trans. Helene Iswolsky. Blooming-ton: Indiana University Press, 1984.

Baldwin, Gayle R. "What a Difference a Gay Makes: Queering the Magic Negro." Journal of Religion and Popular Culture 5 (Fall 2003). Available at http://www.usask.ca/relst/jrpc/. Accessed 26 January 2005.

Balfanz-Vertiz, Kristin, Richard Meldrum, and Joel Irizarry. "Reintegrating the VASCI Population." Power Point Presentation. Chicago: Schwab Rehabilita-tion Hospital, 12 October 2003.

Barthes, Roland. "From Work to Text." Trans. Stephen Heath. In *Image/Music/Text*, ed. Stephen Heath, 155–164. New York: Hill and Wang, 1977. Originally published 1971.

———. *Mythologies*. Trans. Anette Lavers. New York: Hill and Wang, 1972. Originally published 1957.

———. "On Gide and His Journal." Trans. Richard Howard. In *A Barthes Reader*, ed. Susan Sontag, 3–17. New York: Hill and Wang, 1983. Originally published 1942.

———. *The Pleasure of the Text*. Trans. Richard Miller. New York: Hill and Wang, 1975.

Bayer, Ronald. *Homosexuality and American Psychiatry: The Politics of Diag-nosis*. Princeton, N.J.: Princeton University Press, 1987.

"Becoming a Spectacle: Lesbian and Gay Politics and Culture in the Nineties." *Radical America* 24.4, 25.1 (1990–1991).

Bello, Walden. "The Global South." In *A Movement of Movements: Is Another World Really Possible?* ed. Tom Mertes, 49–69. London: Verso, 2004.

Belton, Don. Introduction to *Gary in Your Pocket: Stories and Notebooks of Gary Fisher*, ed. Eve Kosofsky Sedgwick, vii–xii. Durham, N.C.: Duke Uni-versity Press, 1996.

Benjamin, Walter. "Theses on the Philosophy of History." Trans. Harry Zohn. In *Illuminations: Essays and Reflections*, ed. Hannah Arendt, 253–264. New York: Harcourt, 1968. Originally published 1950.

Berlant, Lauren, and Lisa Duggan, eds. *Our Monica, Ourselves: The Clinton Affair and the National Interest*. New York: New York University Press, 2001.

Berlant, Lauren, and Elizabeth Freeman. "Queer Nationality." In *Fear of a Queer Planet: Queer Politics and Social Theory*, ed. Michael Warner, 193–229. Minneapolis: University of Minnesota Press, 1993.

Bérubé, Michael. "Afterword: If I Should Live So Long." In *Disability Studies: Enabling the Humanities*, ed. Sharon L. Snyder, Brenda Jo Brueggemann, and Rosemarie Garland-Thomson, 337–343. New York: Modern Language Asso-ciation, 2002.

———. "American Studies without Exceptions." *PMLA: Publications of the Modern Language Association of America* 118.1 (January 2003): 103–113.

———. *Life As We Know It: A Father, a Family, and an Exceptional Child*. New York: Vintage, 1996.

———. *Public Access: Literary Theory and American Cultural Politics*. London: Verso, 1994.

Borradori, Giovanna. *Philosophy in a Time of Terror: Dialogues with Jürgen Habermas and Jacques Derrida*. Chicago: University of Chicago Press, 2003.

Boseley, Sarah. "Pharmaceutical Companies Charging Unfair Prices for Essential Aids Medicines, Says South African Commission: Ruling Opens the Door for Cut-Price HIV Drugs." *Guardian* (17 October 2003): 17.

Bousquet, Marc, Tony Scott, and Leo Parascondola, eds. *Tenured Bosses and Disposable Teachers: Writing Instruction in the Managed University*. Carbondale: Southern Illinois University Press, 2003.

Braverman, Harry. *Labor and Monopoly Capital: The Degradation of Work in the Twentieth Century*. 25th anniv. ed. New York: Monthly Review, 1998. Originally published 1974.

Brooks, James L., dir. *As Good As It Gets*. Perf. Jack Nicholson, Helen Hunt, and Greg Kinnear. TriStar, 1997.

Browning, Barbara. *Infectious Rhythm: Metaphors of Contagion and the Spread of African Culture*. New York: Routledge, 1998.

Brownworth, Victoria A., and Susan Raffo, eds. *Restricted Access: Lesbians on Disability*. Seattle: Seal, 1999.

Burke, Kenneth. *A Rhetoric of Motives*. Berkeley: University of California Press, 1969. Originally published 1950.

"Bush Appoints Gay Man to Head AIDS Office." *CNN News* (9 April 2001). Available at http://www.cnn.com/2001/ALLPOLITICS/04/09/bush.aids.02. Accessed 2 November 2004.

Butler, Judith. *Bodies That Matter: On the Discursive Limits of "Sex."* New York: Routledge, 1993.

———. "Critically Queer." *GLQ: A Journal of Lesbian and Gay Studies* 1.1 (1993): 17–32.

———. *Gender Trouble: Feminism and the Subversion of Identity*. New York: Routledge, 1990.

———. "Imitation and Gender Insubordination." In *Inside/Out: Lesbian Theories, Gay Theories*, ed. Diana Fuss, 13–31. New York: Routledge, 1991.

Byrd, E. Keith, and Randolph B. Pipes. "Feature Films and Disability." *Journal of Rehabilitation* 74 (1981): 51–53, 80.

Champagne, John. *The Ethics of Marginality: A New Approach to Gay Studies*. Minneapolis: University of Minnesota Press, 1995.

Chang, Grace. *Disposable Domestics: Immigrant Women Workers in the Global Economy*. Cambridge, Mass.: South End, 2000.

Charles, Casey. *The Sharon Kowalski Case: Lesbian and Gay Rights on Trial*. Lawrence: University Press of Kansas, 2003.

Chasin, Alexandra. *Selling Out: The Lesbian and Gay Movement Goes to Market*. New York: St. Martin's, 2000.

Chauncey, George. *Why Marriage? The History Shaping Today's Debate over Gay Equality*. New York: Basic, 2004.

Cintron, Ralph. *Angels' Town: Chero Ways, Gang Life, and Rhetorics of the Everyday*. Boston: Beacon, 1997.

Clare, Eli. *Exile and Pride: Disability, Queerness, and Liberation*. Cambridge, Mass.: South End, 1999.

Clarke, Eric O. *Virtuous Vice: Homoeroticism and the Public Sphere*. Durham, N.C.: Duke University Press, 2000.

Cohen, Cathy J. *The Boundaries of Blackness: AIDS and the Breakdown of Black Politics*. Chicago: University of Chicago Press, 1999.

Cohen, Jeffrey J. *Medieval Identity Machines*. Minneapolis: University of Minnesota Press, 2003.

Colas, Emily. *Just Checking: Scenes from the Life of an Obsessive-Compulsive*. New York: Pocket, 1998.

Combahee River Collective. "The Combahee River Collective Statement." In *Home Girls: A Black Feminist Anthology*, ed. Barbara Smith, 272–282. New York: Kitchen Table–Women of Color Press.

"Competition Commission Settlement Agreements Secure Access to Affordable Life-Saving Antiretroviral Medicines." *TAC Newsletter* (10 December 2003). Available at http://www.tac.org.za/newsletter/news_2003.htm. Accessed 25 October 2004.

"Composition and Cultural Studies Conference for Student Writers." Proceedings of a conference held at George Washington University. Available at http://www.gwu.edu/%7Eenglish/ccsc/. Accessed 11 February 2005.

Compton, Michelle. "Ruminations." Entry in *Dragonflypond*, 4 January 1998. Available at http://www.dragonflypond.com/rumination/bob.html. Accessed 17 September 2004.

Connors, Robert J. "Composition History and Disciplinarity." In *History, Reflection, and Narrative: The Professionalization of Composition 1963–1983*, ed. Mary Rosner, Beth Boehm, and Debra Journet, 3–22. Stamford, Conn.: Ablex, 2000.

Cooper, Marc. "On the Border of Hypocrisy: The Unintended Consequences of Getting Tough on Illegal Immigration." *LA Weekly* (5 December 2003). Available at http://www.laweekly.com/ink/04/02/features-cooper.php. Accessed 2 March 2005.

Covino, William A. "Rhetoric Is Back: Derrida, Feyerabend, Geertz, and the Lessons of History." In *Rhetoric: Concepts, Definitions, Boundaries*, ed. William A. Covino and David A. Jolliffe, 311–318. Boston: Allyn and Bacon, 1995.

Crimp, Douglas. "Right On, Girlfriend!" In *Fear of a Queer Planet: Queer Poli-*

tics and Social Theory, ed. Michael Warner, 300–320. Minneapolis: University of Minnesota Press, 1993.

Crimp, Douglas, with Adam Rolston. *AIDS DemoGraphics*. Seattle: Bay, 1990.

Curtis, Ted, Robert Dellar, Esther Leslie, and Ben Watson. *Mad Pride: A Celebration of Mad Culture*. London: Chipmunkapublishing, 2000.

Dahir, Mubarak. "Profile in Courage." Interview with Governor Howard Dean. *Advocate* (23 May 2000): 60–61.

Davis, Lennard J. *Bending over Backwards: Disability, Dismodernism, and Other Difficult Positions*. New York: New York University Press, 2002.

———. *Enforcing Normalcy: Disability, Deafness, and the Body*. New York: Verso, 1995.

Davis, Mike. *City of Quartz: Excavating the Future in Los Angeles*. New York: Vintage, 1990.

———. *Ecology of Fear: Los Angeles and the Imagination of Disaster*. New York: Vintage, 1998.

———. "Uprising and Repression in L.A.: An Interview with Mike Davis by the *CovertAction Information Bulletin*." In *Reading Rodney King/Reading Urban Uprising*, ed. Robert Gooding-Williams, 142–154. New York: Routledge, 1993.

de Lauretis, Teresa. "Film and the Visible." In *How Do I Look? Queer Film and Video*, ed. Bad Object-Choices, 223–276. Seattle: Bay, 1991.

———, ed. Introduction to "Queer Theory: Lesbian and Gay Sexualities." *differences: A Journal of Feminist Cultural Studies* 3.2 (Summer 1991): iii–xviii.

D'Emilio, John. "Capitalism and Gay Identity." In *Powers of Desire: The Politics of Sexuality*, ed. Ann Snitow, Christine Stansell, and Sharon Thompson, 100–116. New York: Monthly Review Press, 1983.

———. "The Homosexual Menace: The Politics of Sexuality in Cold War America." In *Passion and Power: Sexuality in History*, ed. Kathy Peiss and Christina Simmons, with Robert A. Padgug, 226–240. Philadelphia: Temple University Press, 1989.

———. *Making Trouble: Essays on Gay History, Politics, and the University*. New York: Routledge, 1992.

———. *Sexual Politics, Sexual Communities: The Making of a Homosexual Minority in the United States, 1940–1970*. Chicago: University of Chicago Press, 1983.

———. *The World Turned: Essays on Gay History, Politics, and Culture*. Durham, N.C.: Duke University Press, 2000.

Denenberg, Risa. "A History of the Lesbian Health Movement." In *Caring for Ourselves: The Lesbian Health Book*, ed. Jocelyn White and Marissa C. Martinez, 3–22. Seattle: Seal, 1997.

Denning, Michael. *The Cultural Front: The Laboring of American Culture in the Twentieth Century*. London: Verso, 1997.

Derrida, Jacques. *Dissemination.* Trans. Barbara Johnson. Chicago: University of Chicago Press, 1981.

———. "Force of Law: The 'Mystical Foundation of Authority.'" Trans. Mary Quaintance. *Cardoza Law Review* 11.5–6 (1990): 921–1045.

———. *Memoires for Paul de Man.* Rev. ed. New York: Columbia University Press, 1989.

———. *Of Grammatology.* Trans. Gayatri Chakravorty Spivak. Baltimore: Johns Hopkins University Press, 1974.

———. *Of Hospitality: Anne Dufourmantelle Invites Jacques Derrida to Respond.* Trans. Rachel Bowlby. Stanford, Calif.: Stanford University Press, 2000.

———. *Politics of Friendship.* Trans. George Collins. London: Verso, 1997.

———. *Positions.* Trans. Alan Bass. Chicago: University of Chicago Press, 1981.

———. *The Post Card: From Socrates to Freud and Beyond.* Trans. Alan Bass. Chicago: University of Chicago Press, 1987.

———. *Specters of Marx: The State of the Debt, the Work of Mourning, and the New International.* Trans. Peggy Kamuf. New York: Routledge, 1994.

Deutsche, Rosalyn. *Evictions: Art and Spatial Politics.* Cambridge: MIT Press, 1996.

Devlieger, Patrick, and Miriam Hertz, dir. *The Disabling Bullet.* University of Illinois at Chicago, Department of Disability and Human Development, 1999.

Diaz, Rafael M. *Latino Gay Men and HIV: Culture, Sexuality, and Risk Behavior.* New York: Routledge, 1997.

Dick, Kirby, dir. *Sick: The Life and Death of Bob Flanagan, Supermasochist.* Lions Gate Films, 1997.

"Disability in the Mainstream: Bank Appoints Prominent New Disability Adviser." DevNews Media Center (3 June 2002). Available at http://web.worldbank.org. Accessed 17 September 2004.

"Disability Studies in the Humanities." Available at http://www.georgetown.edu/crossroads/interests/ds-hum/. Accessed 11 February 2005.

Dovey, Jon. "Reality TV." In *The Television Genre Book*, ed. Glen Creeber, Toby Miller, and John Tulloch, 134–135, 137. London: British Film Institute, 2001.

du Gay, Paul, Stuart Hall, Linda Janes, Hugh MacKay, and Keith Negus. *Doing Cultural Studies: The Story of the Sony Walkman.* London: Sage, 1997.

Duggan, Lisa. "Down There: The Queer South and the Future of History Writing." *GLQ: A Journal of Lesbian and Gay Studies* 8.3 (2002): 379–387.

———. "Holy Matrimony!" *Nation* (15 March 2004): 14–19.

———. Introduction to *Sex Wars: Sexual Dissent and Political Culture*, by Lisa Duggan and Nan D. Hunter, 1–14. New York: Routledge, 1995.

————. *The Twilight of Equality: Neoliberalism, Cultural Politics, and the Attack on Democracy*. Boston: Beacon, 2003.

Duggan, Lisa, and Nan D. Hunter. *Sex Wars: Sexual Dissent and Political Culture*. New York: Routledge, 1995.

Dwivedi, Sharada, and Rahul Mehrotra. *Bombay: The Cities Within*. Bombay: Eminence Designs, 2001.

Edelman, Lee. *Homographesis: Essays in Gay Literary and Cultural Theory*. New York: Routledge, 1994.

Egan, Robert, dir. *Weights*. Perf. Lynn Manning at Urban Stages, New York City. January 9–February 1, 2004.

Ehrenreich, Barbara, and Deirdre English. *For Her Own Good: 150 Years of the Experts' Advice to Women*. New York: Anchor, 1978.

Erni, John Nguyet. *Unstable Frontiers: Technomedicine and the Cultural Politics of "Curing" AIDS*. Minneapolis: University of Minnesota Press, 1994.

Ewald, Laura. "New Program Addresses Student Writing Skills." *GW Magazine: A Magazine for Alumni and Friends* (Fall 2004): 3.

Falla, Jeffrey. "Disorderly Consumption and Capitalism: The Privilege of Sex Addiction." *College Literature* 28.1 (Winter 2001): 49–55.

Ferguson, Roderick A. *Aberrations in Black: Toward a Queer of Color Critique*. Minneapolis: University of Minnesota Press, 2004.

Ferris, Jim. *The Hospital Poems*. Charlotte, N.C.: Main Street Rag, 2004.

Finkelstein, S. Naomi. "The Only Thing You Have to Do Is Live." *GLQ: A Journal of Lesbian and Gay Studies* 9.1–2 (2003): 307–319.

————. "Upon the Passing of Gloria Anzaldúa—May 2004." Entry at *Queering Diabetes*. Available at http://www.queeringdiabetes.org/substance/upon_the_passing_of_gloria_anzal.htm. Accessed 9 October 2004.

Fisher, Gary. *Gary in Your Pocket: Stories and Notebooks of Gary Fisher*. Ed. Eve Kosofsky Sedgwick. Durham, N.C.: Duke University Press, 1996.

Fisher, William F., and Thomas Ponniah, eds. *Another World Is Possible: Popular Alternatives to Globalization at the World Social Forum*. London: Zed, 2003.

Flanagan, Bob. *The Pain Journal*. Los Angeles: Semiotext(e), 2000.

————. "Why." In *Bob Flanagan: Supermasochist*, ed. Andrea Juno and V. Vale. RE/Search People Series, Vol. 1., 64–65. San Francisco: RE/Search, 1993.

Fleischer, Doris Zames, and Frieda Zames. *The Disability Rights Movement: From Charity to Confrontation*. Philadelphia: Temple University Press, 2001.

Foley, Barbara. "Looking Backward, 2002–1969: Campus Activism in the Era of Globalization." In *World Bank Literature*, ed. Amitava Kumar, 26–39. Minneapolis: University of Minnesota Press, 2003.

Foucault, Michel. *Discipline and Punish: The Birth of the Prison*. Trans. Alan Sheridan. New York: Vintage, 1977.

——. *The History of Sexuality.* Vol. 1: *An Introduction.* Trans. Robert Hurley. New York: Vintage, 1978.

——. *The Order of Things: An Archaeology of the Human Sciences.* New York: Vintage, 1970.

"FOX Thinks Small for New Reality Series." *Zap2it TV News* (27 January 2004). Available at http://tv.zap2it.com/tveditorial/tve_main/1,1002,271%7C85975%7C1%7C,00.html. Accessed 26 October 2004.

Frank, Thomas. *The Conquest of Cool: Business Culture, Counterculture, and the Rise of Hip Consumerism.* Chicago: University of Chicago Press, 1998.

——. *One Market under God: Extreme Capitalism, Market Populism, and the End of Economic Democracy.* New York: Anchor, 2001.

Fraser, Nancy. *Justice Interruptus: Critical Reflections on the "Postsocialist" Condition.* New York: Routledge, 1997.

Freeman, Elizabeth. *The Wedding Complex: Forms of Belonging in Modern American Culture.* Durham, N.C.: Duke University Press, 2002.

Freire, Paulo. *Pedagogy of Freedom: Ethics, Democracy, and Civic Courage.* Lanham: Rowman and Littlefield, 1998.

——. *Pedagogy of the Oppressed.* Rev. 20th anniv. ed. New York: Continuum, 1993. Originally published 1970.

Freud, Sigmund. "Three Contributions to the Theory of Sex." In *The Basic Writings of Sigmund Freud,* ed. and trans. A. A. Brill, 551–629. New York: Modern Library, 1938. Originally published 1915.

Friedman, James, ed. *Reality Squared: Televisual Discourse on the Real.* New Brunswick, N.J.: Rutgers University Press, 2002.

Fries, Kenny, ed. *Staring Back: The Disability Experience from the Inside Out.* New York: Plume, 1997.

Gamson, Joshua. "Whose Millennium March?" *Nation* (17 April 2000): 10.

Garber, Linda. *Identity Poetics: Race, Class, and the Lesbian-Feminist Roots of Queer Theory.* New York: Columbia University Press, 2001.

Garland-Thomson, Rosemarie. *Extraordinary Bodies: Figuring Physical Disability in American Culture and Literature.* New York: Columbia University Press, 1997.

——. "The Politics of Staring: Visual Rhetorics of Disability in Popular Photography." In *Disability Studies: Enabling the Humanities,* ed. Sharon L. Snyder, Brenda Jo Brueggemann, and Rosemarie Garland-Thomson, 56–75. New York: Modern Language Association, 2002.

——. "Seeing the Disabled: Visual Rhetorics of Disability in Popular Photography." In *The New Disability History: American Perspectives,* ed. Paul K. Longmore and Lauri Umansky, 335–374. New York: New York University Press, 2001.

Gates, Henry Louis, Jr. *The Signifying Monkey: A Theory of African-American Literary Criticism.* New York: Oxford University Press, 1988.

Gay Shame San Francisco. Available at http://www.gayshamesf.org/home.htm. Accessed 12 October 2004.

George Washington University. University Writing Program Home Page. Available at http://www2.gwu.edu/~uwp/. Accessed 15 February 2005.

"George Washington University Rewrites Its Writing Program." *AAC&U News* (December 2003). Available at http://www.aacu.org/aacu_news/December03/feature.cfm. Accessed 22 December 2003.

Gill, Carol J. "Questioning Continuum." In *The Ragged Edge: The Disability Experience from the Pages of the First Fifteen Years of "The Disability Rag,"* ed. B. Shaw, 42–49. Louisville, Ky.: Advocado.

Gingrich, Newt. "The Heir to FDR." American Enterprise Institute for Public Policy Research (8 June 2004). Available at http://www.aei.org/publications/pubID.20665,filter.all/pub_detail.asp. Accessed 23 June 2005.

Glitz, Michael. "Queer Eye Confidential." *Advocate* (2 September 2003): 40–44.

Greenhouse, Stephen. "Illegally in the U.S., and Never a Day off at Wal-Mart." *New York Times* (5 November 2003): 2.

Grossberg, Lawrence, Cary Nelson, and Paula Treichler, eds. *Cultural Studies.* New York: Routledge, 1992.

Grover, Jan Zita. "AIDS: Keywords." In *AIDS: Cultural Analysis, Cultural Activism,* ed. Douglas Crimp, 17–30. Cambridge: MIT Press, 1987.

Guter, Bob, and John R. Killacky, eds. *Queer Crips: Disabled Gay Men and Their Stories.* New York: Harrington Park, 2004.

Halberstam, Judith. *Female Masculinity.* Durham, N.C.: Duke University Press, 1998.

———. *In a Queer Time and Place: Transgender Bodies, Subcultural Lives.* New York: New York University Press, 2005.

———. "Pimp My Bride: Reality TV Gives Marriage an Extreme Makeover." *Nation* (5 July 2004): 44–46.

Hall, Stuart. "Gramsci's Relevance for the Study of Race and Ethnicity." In *Stuart Hall: Critical Dialogues in Cultural Studies,* ed. David Morley and Kuan-Hsing Chen, 411–440. London: Routledge, 1996.

———. "The Problem of Ideology: Marxism without Guarantees." In *Stuart Hall: Critical Dialogues in Cultural Studies,* ed. David Morley and Kuan-Hsing Chen, 25–70. London: Routledge, 1996.

———. "What Is This 'Black' in Black Popular Culture?" In *Stuart Hall: Critical Dialogues in Cultural Studies,* ed. David Morley and Kuan-Hsing Chen, 465–475. London: Routledge, 1996.

Hall, Stuart, Chas Critcher, Tony Jefferson, Jon N. Clarke, and Brian Roberts. *Policing the Crisis: Mugging, the State, and Law and Order.* London: Macmillan, 1979.

Halperin, David M. *Saint Foucault: Towards a Gay Hagiography.* New York: Oxford University Press, 1995.

Hansen, Miriam. Foreword to *Public Sphere and Experience: Toward an Analysis of the Bourgeois and Proletarian Public Sphere,* by Oskar Negt and Alexander Kluge. Trans. Peter Labanyi, Jamie Owen Daniel, and Assenka Oksiloff. Minneapolis: University of Minnesota Press, 1993. ix–xli.

Haraway, Donna J. *Simians, Cyborgs, and Women: The Reinvention of Nature.* New York: Routledge, 1991.

Hardt, Michael. "Today's Bandung?" In *A Movement of Movements: Is Another World Really Possible?* ed. Tom Mertes, 230–236. London: Verso, 2004.

Hardt, Michael, and Antonio Negri. *Empire.* Cambridge: Harvard University Press, 2000.

———. *Multitude.* New York: Penguin, 2004.

Harper, Phillip Brian. "Gay Male Identities, Personal Privacy, and Relations of Public Exchange: Notes on Directions for Queer Critique." *Social Text* 52–53 (Fall/Winter 1997): 5–29.

Harvey, David. *The Condition of Postmodernity: An Enquiry into the Origins of Cultural Change.* Cambridge, U.K.: Blackwell, 1990.

———. *Spaces of Hope.* Berkeley: University of California Press, 2000.

Hayden, Tom. *Street Wars: Gangs and the Future of Violence.* New York: New, 2004.

Hebdige, Dick. *Subculture: The Meaning of Style.* London: Routledge, 1979.

Hennessy, Rosemary. *Profit and Pleasure: Sexual Identities in Late Capitalism.* New York: Routledge, 2000.

———. "¡Ya Basta! We Are Rising Up! World Bank Culture and Collective Opposition in the North." In *World Bank Literature,* ed. Amitava Kumar, 40–55. Minneapolis: University of Minnesota Press, 2003.

Herndl, Diane Price. *Invalid Women: Figuring Feminine Illness in American Fiction and Culture, 1840–1940.* Chapel Hill: University of North Carolina Press, 1993.

Hershey, Laura. "Crip Commentary: Laura Hershey's Whenever Web Column." Available at http://www.cripcommentary.com. Accessed 6 October 2004.

Hewett, Angela, and Robert McRuer, eds. "Composing a Writing Program: An Alternative Handbook for the Program in Rhetoric and Composition at the George Washington University." 2nd ed. Unpublished manuscript, 1999.

———. "Composing Student Activists, Relocating Student Writing." In *Public Works: Student Writing as Public Text,* ed. Emily J. Isaacs and Phoebe Jackson, 97–106. Portsmouth, N.H.: Heinemann, 2001.

Hewitt, Marco. "Reflections after Mumbai 2004: Reflections on the Global Justice Movement after the Mumbai World Social Forum." Project SafeCom Inc. Available at http://members.westnet.com.au/jackhsmit/mumbai2004.htm. Accessed 12 October 2004.

Hockenberry, John. *Moving Violations: War Zones, Wheelchairs, and Declarations of Independence.* New York: Hyperion, 1995.

Hoggart, Richard. *The Uses of Literacy.* New Brunswick, N.J.: Transaction, 1998. Originally published 1957.

Holland, Sharon. *Raising the Dead: Readings of Death and (Black) Subjectivity.* Durham, N.C.: Duke University Press, 2000.

hooks, bell. *Black Looks: Race and Representation.* Cambridge, Mass.: South End, 1992.

Horner, Bruce. *Terms of Work for Composition: A Materialist Critique.* Albany: SUNY Press, 2000.

Hunter, Nan D. "Sexual Dissent and the Family: The Sharon Kowalski Case." In *Sex Wars: Sexual Dissent and Political Culture,* by Lisa Duggan and Nan D. Hunter, 101–106. New York: Routledge, 1995.

Jagose, Annamarie. *Queer Theory: An Introduction.* New York: New York University Press, 1996.

Jarratt, Susan C. *Rereading the Sophists: Classical Rhetoric Refigured.* Carbondale: Southern Illinois University Press, 1991.

Johnson, Benjamin, Patrick Kavanagh, and Kevin Mattson, eds. *Steal This University: The Rise of the Corporate University and the Academic Labor Movement.* New York: Routledge, 2003.

Johnson, Harriet McBryde. "The Disability Gulag." *New York Times* (23 November 2003): 59.

Juno, Andrea, and V. Vale, eds. *Bob Flanagan: Supermasochist.* RE/Search People Series, Vol. 1. San Francisco: RE/Search, 1993.

Kabillio, Eli, dir. *F**K the Disabled.* Perf. Greg Walloch. Mad Dog, 2001.

Kafer, Alison. "Compulsory Bodies: Reflections on Heterosexuality and Ablebodiedness." *Journal of Women's History* 15.3 (Autumn 2003):77–89.

Kalb, Rosalind C. *Multiple Sclerosis: A Guide for Families.* New York: Demos Vermande, 1998.

Katz, Jonathan Ned. "The Invention of Heterosexuality." *Socialist Review* 20.1 (1990): 7–34.

———. *The Invention of Heterosexuality.* New York: Dutton, 1995.

Kauffman, Linda S. *Bad Girls and Sick Boys: Fantasies in Contemporary Art and Culture.* Berkeley: University of California Press, 1998.

Kayal, Philip M. *Bearing Witness: Gay Men's Health Crisis and the Politics of AIDS.* Boulder, Colo.: Westview, 1993.

Keller, James. "'Does He Think We Are Not Watching?': Straight Guys and the *Queer Eye Panopticon.*" *Studies in Popular Culture* 26.3 (April 2004): 49–60.

Kennedy, Randall. *Nigger: The Strange Career of a Troublesome Word.* New York: Pantheon, 2002.

Kent, Thomas, ed. *Post-Process Theory: Beyond the Writing Process Paradigm.* Carbondale: Southern Illinois University Press, 1999.

King, Edward. *Safety in Numbers: Safer Sex and Gay Men.* New York: Routledge, 1993.

Kittay, Eva Feder. *Love's Labor: Essays on Women, Equality, and Dependency.* New York: Routledge, 1999.

Klein, Naomi. *Fences and Windows: Dispatches from the Front Lines of the Globalization Debate.* New York: Picador, 2002.

————. *No Logo.* New York: Picador, 2000.

Kressley, Carson. *Off the Cuff: The Essential Style Guide for Men—and the Women Who Love Them.* New York: Dutton, 2004.

Kumar, Amitava, ed. *World Bank Literature.* Minneapolis: University of Minnesota Press, 2003.

Kumar, Salil. "Will the World Social Forum Listen?" Report at Rediff.com India (17 January 2004). Available at http://www.rediff.com/news/2004/jan/17wsf .htm. Accessed 12 October 2004.

Kushner, Tony. "Foreword: Notes toward a Theater of the Fabulous." In *Staging Lives: An Anthology of Contemporary Gay Theater*, ed. John M. Clum, vii–ix. Boulder, Colo.: Westview, 1996.

Leland, John, and Mark Miller. "Can Gays 'Convert'?" *Newsweek* (17 August 1998): 47–50.

Lewis, David Levering. *When Harlem Was in Vogue.* New York: Oxford University Press, 1981.

Linton, Simi. *Claiming Disability: Knowledge and Identity.* New York: New York University Press, 1998.

Livingston, Jennie, dir. *Paris Is Burning.* Off While Productions, 1990.

Longmore, Paul K. "Conspicuous Contribution and American Cultural Dilemmas: Telethon Rituals of Cleansing and Renewal." In *The Body and Physical Difference: Discourses of Disability*, ed. David T. Mitchell and Sharon L. Snyder, 134–158. Ann Arbor: University of Michigan Press, 1997.

————. "Screening Stereotypes: Images of Disabled People." *Social Policy* 16 (Summer 1985): 31–37.

Longmore, Paul K., and Lauri Umansky. "Introduction: Disability History: From the Margins to the Mainstream." In *The New Disability History: American Perspectives*, ed. Paul K. Longmore and Lauri Umansky, 1–29. New York: New York University Press, 2001.

Lorde, Audre. *The Cancer Journals.* 2nd ed. San Francisco: Aunt Lute, 1980.

————. *Sister Outsider: Essays and Speeches.* Freedom, Calif.: Crossing Press, 1984.

Luczak, Raymond, ed. *Eyes of Desire: A Deaf Gay and Lesbian Reader.* Boston: Alyson, 1993.

Mairs, Nancy. *Plaintext.* Tucson: University of Arizona Press, 1986.

Make-a-Wish Foundation. "About Us." Available at http://www.wish.org/home/ aboutus.htm. Accessed 6 February 2005.

Manalansan, Martin F., IV. *Global Divas: Filipino Gay Men in the Diaspora.* Durham, N.C.: Duke University Press, 2003.

"Mandela Does Not Endorse TAC March on Parliament." ANC Daily News Briefing (12 February 2003). Available at http://www.anc.org.za/anc/newsbrief/2003/news0213.txt. Accessed 25 October 2004.

Marble, John. "Ex-Gay Pride: Interview with John Paulk." *Advocate* (5 June 2001): 27–31.

Martin, Biddy. "Lesbian Identity and Autobiographical Difference[s]." In *Life/Lines: Theorizing Women's Autobiography*, ed. Bella Brodzki and Celeste Schenk, 77–103. Ithaca, N.Y.: Cornell University Press, 1988.

Martin, Del, and Phyllis Lyon. *Lesbian/Woman*. Rev. ed. New York: Bantam, 1983. Originally published 1972.

Martin, Emily. *Flexible Bodies: The Role of Immunity in American Culture from the Days of Polio to the Age of AIDS*. Boston: Beacon, 1994.

Marx, Karl. *Capital*. Vol. 1. Trans. Samuel Moore and Edward Aveling. In *The Marx-Engels Reader*, ed. Robert C. Tucker, 294–438. 2nd ed. New York: Norton, 1978. Originally published 1867.

———. "Economic and Philosophic Manuscripts of 1844." Trans. Martin Milligan. In *The Marx-Engels Reader*, ed. Robert C. Tucker, 66–125. 2nd ed. New York: Norton, 1978. Originally published 1844.

Marx, Karl, and Friedrich Engels. "Manifesto of the Communist Party." In *The Marx-Engels Reader*, ed. Robert C. Tucker, 469–500. 2nd ed. New York: Norton, 1978. Originally published 1848.

McCarthy, Anna. "Crab People from the Center of the Earth." *GLQ: A Journal of Lesbian and Gay Studies* 11.1 (2005): 97–101..

McLemee, Scott. "Deconstructing Composition." *Chronicle of Higher Education* (21 March 2003): A16.

McRuer, Robert. "As Good As It Gets: Queer Theory and Critical Disability." *GLQ: A Journal of Lesbian and Gay Studies* 9.1–2 (2003): 79–105.

———. "Composing Bodies; or, De-Composition: Queer Theory, Disability Studies, and Alternative Corporealities." *JAC: A Quarterly Journal for the Interdisciplinary Study of Rhetoric, Culture, Literacy, and Politics* 24.1 (2004): 47–78.

———. "Compulsory Able-Bodiedness and Queer/Disabled Existence." In *Disability Studies: Enabling the Humanities*, ed. Sharon L. Snyder, Brenda Jo Brueggemann, and Rosemarie Garland-Thomson, 88–99. New York: Modern Language Association, 2002.

———. "Crip Eye for the Normate Guy: Queer Theory and the Disciplining of Disability Studies." *PMLA: Publications of the Modern Language Association of America* 120.2 (2005): 586–592.

———. "Critical Investments: AIDS, Christopher Reeve, and Queer/Disability Studies." In *Thinking the Limits of the Body*, ed. Jeffrey Jerome Cohen and Gail Weiss, 145–163. Albany: SUNY Press, 2003.

————. "'Marry' Me?" Report for Alternatives to Marriage Project. Available at http://www.unmarried.org/marryme.html. Accessed 13 March 2005.

————. *The Queer Renaissance: Contemporary American Literature and the Reinvention of Lesbian and Gay Identities.* New York: New York University Press, 1997.

————. "We Were Never Identified: Feminism, Queer Theory, and a Disabled World." *Radical History Review* 94 (Winter 2006): 148–154.

McRuer, Robert, and Abby L. Wilkerson, eds. "Desiring Disability: Queer Theory Meets Disability Studies." Special issue of *GLQ: A Journal of Lesbian and Gay Studies* 9.1–2 (2003).

Mehta, Suketu. *Maximum City: Bombay Lost and Found.* New York: Knopf, 2005.

Mertes, Tom, ed. *A Movement of Movements: Is Another World Really Possible?* London: Verso, 2004.

Milam, Lorenzo Wilson. *The Cripple Liberation Front Marching Band Blues.* San Diego: MHO and MHO Works, 1984.

Miller, D.A. *Bringing out Roland Barthes.* Berkeley: University of California Press, 1992.

Mitchell, David T., and Sharon L. Snyder, eds. *The Body and Physical Difference: Discourses of Disability.* Ann Arbor: University of Michigan Press, 1997.

————. "The Eugenic Atlantic: Race, Disability, and the Making of an International Eugenics Science, 1800–1945." *Disability and Society* 18.7 (2003): 843–864.

————. *Narrative Prosthesis: Disability and the Dependencies of Discourse.* Ann Arbor: University of Michigan Press, 2000.

————, dir. *Self-Preservation: The Art of Riva Lehrer.* Brace Yourselves Productions, 2004.

————. "Talking about *Talking Back*: Afterthoughts on the Making of the Disability Documentary *Vital Signs: Crip Culture Talks Back*." In *Points of Contact: Disability, Art, and Culture.*, ed. Susan Crutchfield and Marcy Epstein, 197–217. Ann Arbor: University of Michigan Press, 2000.

————, dir. *Vital Signs: Crip Culture Talks Back.* Brace Yourselves Productions, 1996.

"Mobilise to Build a Better Public Health Service: Resolutions of TAC National Executive Committee Meeting—14 to 15 May 2004." *TAC Newsletter* (20 May 2004). Available at http://www.tac.org.za/newsletter/2004/ns20_05_2004.htm. Accessed 25 October 2004.

Moraga, Cherríe, and Gloria Anzaldúa, eds. *This Bridge Called My Back: Writings by Radical Women of Color.* New York: Kitchen Table, 1981.

Morley, David, and Kuan-Hsing Chen, eds. *Stuart Hall: Critical Dialogues in Cultural Studies.* London: Routledge, 1996.

Mulama, Joyce. "WSF Marginalising the Marginalized?" *Terraviva Online*: The Independent Newspaper of the World Social Forum IV (16–21 January 2004). Available at http://www.ipsnews.net/focus/tv_mumbai/viewstory .asp?idn=261. Accessed 10 March 2004.

Muñoz, José Esteban. *Disidentifications: Queers of Color and the Performance of Politics*. Minneapolis: University of Minnesota Press, 1999.

Murray, Susan, and Laurie Ouellette, eds. *Reality TV: Remaking Television Culture*. New York: New York University Press, 2004.

Musbach, Tom. "2003 Gay.com Person of the Year: Zackie Achmat." *Gay.com News*. Available at http://www.gay.com/news/roundups/package.html?ser num=770. Accessed 25 October 2004.

Neel, Jasper. *Plato, Derrida, and Writing*. Carbondale: Southern Illinois University Press, 1988.

Negt, Oskar, and Alexander Kluge. *Public Sphere and Experience: Toward an Analysis of the Bourgeois and Proletarian Public Sphere*. Trans. Peter Labanyi, Jamie Owen Daniel, and Assenka Oksiloff. Minneapolis: University of Minnesota Press, 1993.

Nelson, Cary, and Dilip Parameshwar Gaonkar, eds. *Disciplinarity and Dissent in Cultural Studies*. New York: Routledge, 1996.

Nelson, Cary, and Stephen Watt. *Academic Keywords: A Devil's Dictionary for Higher Education*. New York: Routledge, 1999.

Norden, Martin F. *The Cinema of Isolation: A History of Physical Disability in the Movies*. New Brunswick, N.J.: Rutgers University Press, 1994.

Notes from Nowhere. *We Are Everywhere: The Irresistible Rise of Global Anti-capitalism*. London: Verso, 2003.

Odets, Walt. *In the Shadow of an Epidemic: Being HIV-Negative in the Age of AIDS*. Durham, N.C.: Duke University Press, 1995.

Omelianuk, Scott, and Ted Allen. *Esquire's Things a Man Should Know about Style*. New York: Riverhead, 1999.

Ong, Aihwa. *Flexible Citizenship: The Cultural Logics of Transnationality*. Durham, N.C.: Duke University Press, 1999.

Parker, Richard. *Beneath the Equator: Cultures of Desire, Male Homosexuality, and Emerging Gay Communities in Brazil*. New York: Routledge, 1999.

Partners for Urban Knowledge, Action and Research, Mumbai (PUKAR). Available at http://www.pukar.org.in/pukar/. Accessed 25 June 2005.

Patton, Cindy. *Fatal Advice: How Safe-Sex Education Went Wrong*. Durham, N.C.: Duke University Press, 1996.

———. *Inventing AIDS*. New York: Routledge, 1990.

Paulk, John. *Not Afraid to Change: The Remarkable Story of How One Man Overcame Homosexuality*. Mukilteo, Wash.: WinePress, 2000.

"A Quiet Thumbs Up." *Advocate* (22 May 2001): 17.

Reeve, Christopher, dir. *In the Gloaming*. Perf. Glenn Close, Robert Sean Leonard, and David Straithairn. HBO, 1997.

Reid-Pharr, Robert F. *Black Gay Man: Essays*. New York: New York University Press, 2001.

Rich, Adrienne. "Compulsory Heterosexuality and Lesbian Existence." In *Powers of Desire: The Politics of Sexuality*, ed. Ann Snitow, Christine Stansell, and Sharon Thompson, 177–205. New York: Monthly Review, 1983. Originally published 1980.

Richardson, Mattie Udora. "No More Secrets, No More Lies: African American History and Compulsory Heterosexuality." *Journal of Women's History* 15.3 (Autumn 2003): 63–76.

Riggs, Marlon, dir. *Tongues Untied*. Frameline Distribution, 1989.

Rivière, Philippe. "At Last, Generic Anti-AIDS Medicine for Sub-Saharan Africa." Trans. Gulliver Cragg. *Le Monde Diplomatique/English Edition* (12 December 2003). Available at http://mondediplo.com/2003/12/19aids. Accessed 25 October 2004.

Roach, Joseph. *Cities of the Dead: Circum-Atlantic Performance*. New York: Columbia University Press, 1996.

Román, David. *Acts of Intervention: Performance, Gay Culture, and AIDS*. Bloomington: Indiana University Press, 1998.

———. "Not-about-AIDS." *GLQ: A Journal of Lesbian and Gay Studies* 6.1 (2000): 1–28.

Rosenberg, Tina. "In South Africa, a Hero Measured by the Advance of a Deadly Disease." *New York Times* (13 January 2003): A20.

Rosenthal, Phil. "'Littlest Groom' Shows Fox's Bar Not Too High." *Chicago Sun-Times* (16 February 2004): 51.

Ross, Andrew. *No Respect: Intellectuals and Popular Culture*. New York: Routledge, 1989.

Rotello, Gabriel. "Creating a New Gay Culture: Balancing Fidelity and Freedom." *Nation* (21 April 1997): 11–15.

Rubin, Gayle S. "Thinking Sex: Notes for a Radical Theory of the Politics of Sexuality." In *The Lesbian and Gay Studies Reader*, ed. Henry Abelove, Michèle Aina Barale, and David M. Halperin, 3–44. New York: Routledge, 1993. Originally published 1984.

Rupp, Leila J., ed. "Women's History in the New Millennium: Adrienne Rich's 'Compulsory Heterosexuality and Lesbian Existence'—A Retrospective." *Journal of Women's History* 15.3 (Autumn 2003): 9–89.

Russell, Marta. *Beyond Ramps: Disability at the End of the Social Contract*. Monroe: Common Courage, 1998.

———. "New Freedom Initiative: Survival of the Fittest 'Equality.'" *Znet Daily Commentaries* (23 February 2001). Available at http://www.zmag.org/sustainers/content/2001-02/23russell.htm. Accessed 2 November 2004.

Russo, Vito. *The Celluloid Closet: Homosexuality in the Movies.* 2nd ed. New York: Harper and Row, 1987.

Samuels, Ellen. "Critical Divides: Judith Butler's Body Theory and the Question of Disability Studies." *NWSA [National Women's Studies Association] Journal* 14.3 (Fall 2002): 58–76.

Sandahl, Carrie. "Black Man, Blind Man: Disability Identity Politics and Performance." *Theatre Journal* 56 (2004): 579–602.

———. "Queering the Crip or Cripping the Queer? Intersections of Queer and Crip Identities in Solo Autobiographical Performance." *GLQ: A Journal of Lesbian and Gay Studies* 9.1–2 (2003): 25–56.

Sandahl, Carrie, Terry Galloway, Joan Lipkin, and Julia Trahan. "All-Girl Action: Crip Queer Women in Performance." Roundtable Discussion. First International Queer Disability Conference. San Francisco State University. 2 June 2002. Online transcript available at http://www.disabilityhistory.org/dwa/queer/panel_allgirl.html. Accessed 6 October 2004.

Sandoval, Chela. *Methodology of the Oppressed.* Minneapolis: University of Minnesota Press, 2000.

Sassen, Saskia. *Globalization and Its Discontents: Essays on the New Mobility of People and Money.* New York: New, 1998.

Schell, Eileen E., and Patricia Lambert Stock, eds. *Moving a Mountain: Transforming the Role of Contingent Faculty in Composition Studies and Higher Education.* Urbana, Ill.: National Council of Teachers of English, 2001.

Schneider, Marj. "Home among the Trees: A Visit with Karen Thompson, Sharon Kowalski, and Patty Bresser." In *Restricted Access: Lesbians on Disability*, ed. Victoria A. Brownworth and Susan Raffo, 6–17. Seattle: Seal, 1999.

Schulman, Sarah. *Stagestruck: Theater, AIDS, and the Marketing of Gay America.* Durham, N.C.: Duke University Press, 1998.

Scott, Allen J., and Edward W. Soja, eds. *The City: Los Angeles and Urban Theory at the End of the Twentieth Century.* Berkeley: University of California Press, 1996.

Scott, Tony, Leo Parascondola, and Tony Baker, eds. *Composition as Management Science.* Spec. issue of *Workplace: A Journal for Academic Labor* 4.1 (2003). Available at http://128.164.127.31/redirect?http://www.louisville.edu/journal/workplace/issue7/issue7frontpage.html. Accessed 15 December 2003.

Sedgwick, Eve Kosofsky. *Epistemology of the Closet.* Berkeley: University of California Press, 1990.

———, ed. *Gary in Your Pocket: Stories and Notebooks of Gary Fisher.* Durham, N.C.: Duke University Press, 1996.

———. "Inside Henry James: Toward a Lexicon for *The Art of the Novel*." In *Negotiating Lesbian and Gay Subjects*, ed. Monica Dorenkamp and Richard Henke, 131–146. New York: Routledge, 1995.

————. *Tendencies*. Durham, N.C.: Duke University Press, 1993.

Serlin, David. *Replaceable You: Engineering the Body in Postwar America.* Chicago: University of Chicago Press, 2004.

Shapiro, Joseph P. *No Pity: People with Disabilities Forging a New Civil Rights Movement.* New York: Times Books, 1993.

Sheldon, Charles M. *In His Steps, or What Would Jesus Do?* New York: Revell, 1993. Originally published 1897.

Shepard, Benjamin. *White Nights and Ascending Shadows: A History of the San Francisco AIDS Epidemic.* London: Cassell, 1997.

Siebers, Tobin. "Words Stare Like a Glass Eye: From Literary to Visual to Disability Studies and Back Again." *PMLA: Publications of the Modern Language Association of America* 119.5 (October 2004): 1315–1324.

Slaughter, Sheila. *Academic Capitalism: Politics, Policies, and the Entrepreneurial University.* Baltimore: Johns Hopkins University Press, 1999.

Smetherman, Jo-Anne. "TAC: We'll Take AIDS Corpses to Parliament." *Cape Times* (9 May 2003): 1.

Smith, Anna Deavere. *Twilight: Los Angeles, 1992.* New York: Anchor, 1994.

Smithsonian National Museum of American History. "The Disability Rights Movement." Exhibit, July 2000–July 2001. Available at http://americanhistory.si.edu/disabilityrights/index.html. Accessed 22 February 2005.

Snyder, Sharon L. "Geographies of Uneven Development: How Does One Make Disability Integral to Higher Education?" *PMLA: Publications of the Modern Language Association of America* 120.2 (March 2005): 533–541.

Snyder, Sharon L., Brenda Jo Brueggemann, and Rosemarie Garland-Thomson, eds. *Disability Studies: Enabling the Humanities.* New York: Modern Language Association, 2002.

————. "Introduction: Integrating Disability into Teaching and Scholarship." In *Disability Studies: Enabling the Humanities*, ed. Sharon L. Snyder, Brenda Jo Brueggemann, and Rosemarie Garland-Thomson, 1–12. New York: Modern Language Association, 2002.

Soja, Edward W. *Postmodern Geographies: The Reassertion of Space in Critical Social Theory.* London: Verso, 1989.

Solheim, Karla. "Militant Marketing March." *Mother Jones* (25 April 2000). Available at http://www.motherjones.com/commentary/columns/2000/04/mmow.html. Accessed 15 December 2003.

Somerville, Siobhan. *Queering the Color Line: Race and the Invention of Homosexuality in American Culture.* Durham, N.C.: Duke University Press, 2000.

Song, David, Gideon P. Naude, Debra Ann Gilmore, and Fred Bongard. "Gang Warfare: The Medical Repercussions." *Journal of Trauma: Injury, Infection, and Critical Care* 40.5 (1996): 810–815.

Stacey, Judith. *Brave New Families: Stories of Domestic Upheaval in Late Twentieth Century America.* New York: Basic, 1990.

Starr, Michael. "Reality TV's First 'Mini' Series." *New York Post* (28 January 2004): 79.

Steinglass, Matt. "Killing Him Softly: Zackie Achmat Is Dying in the Name of South Africa's AIDS Victims. Why Doesn't He Want to Make a Big Deal out of It?" *Boston Globe* (8 December 2002): D1.

Stewart, Jean. "Disability, Capitalism, and War." Paper Presented at panel on Disability in a Global Perspective: Nothing about Us without Us. World Social Forum, Mumbai, 18 January 2004.

Stiker, Henri-Jacques. *A History of Disability*. Rev. ed. Trans. William Sayers. Ann Arbor: University of Michigan Press, 1999. Originally published 1982; revised 1997.

Stokes, Mason. *The Color of Sex: Whiteness, Heterosexuality, and the Fictions of White Supremacy*. Durham, N.C.: Duke University Press, 2001.

Straayer, Chris, and Tom Waugh, eds. "Queer TV Style." *GLQ: A Journal of Lesbian and Gay Studies* 11.1 (2005): 95–117.

Sullivan, Andrew. "When Plagues End: Notes on the Twilight of an Epidemic." *New York Times Magazine* (10 November 1996): 52–62.

Susman, Carolyn. "'Little People' Say of Reality Show: What's the Big Deal?" *Palm Beach Post* (21 February 2004): 1D.

Sycamore, Matt Bernstein, aka Mattilda, ed. *Revolting Behavior: Queer Strategies for Resisting Assimilation*. San Francisco: Soft Skull, 2004.

TAC: Treatment Action Campaign. "About TAC." Available at http://www.tac .org.za/. Accessed 25 October 2004.

Thompson, Karen, and Julie Andrzejewski. *Why Can't Sharon Kowalski Come Home?* San Francisco: Aunt Lute, 1988.

Thornton, Tamar Plakins. *Handwriting in America: A Cultural History*. New Haven, Conn.: Yale University Press, 1996.

Tincknell, Estella, and Parvati Raghuram. "Big Brother: Reconfiguring the 'Active' Audience of Cultural Studies?" *European Journal of Cultural Studies* 5.2 (May 2002): 199–215.

Tinkcomm, Matthew. *Working Like a Homosexual: Camp, Capital, Cinema*. Durham, N.C.: Duke University Press, 2002.

Tobin, Lad. "Process Pedagogy." In *A Guide to Composition Pedagogies*, ed. Gary Tate, Amy Rupiper, and Kurt Schick, 1–18. New York: Oxford University Press, 2001.

Tobin, Lad, and Thomas Newkirk, eds. *Taking Stock: The Writing Process Movement in the 90s*. Portsmouth, N.H.: Boynton and Cook, 1994.

Tongson, Karen. "White Men Are Hysterical." *GLQ: A Journal of Lesbian and Gay Studies* 10.4 (2004): 631–633.

Treichler, Paula A. *How to Have Theory in an Epidemic: Cultural Chronicles of AIDS*. Durham, N.C.: Duke University Press, 1999.

Tremain, Shelley Lynn, ed. *Foucault and the Government of Disability*. Ann Arbor: University of Michigan Press, 2005.

———. *Pushing the Limits: Disabled Dykes Produce Culture*. Toronto: Women's Press, 1996.

Trent, James W., Jr. *Inventing the Feeble Mind: A History of Mental Retardation in the United States*. Berkeley: University of California Press, 1994.

Turner, Tina. "What's Love Got to Do with It." *Simply the Best*. Capital Records, 1991.

Turner, William B. *A Genealogy of Queer Theory*. Philadelphia: Temple University Press, 2000.

United States Census Bureau. "Census Disability Data: Texas. Selected Population Characteristics for States and Counties Including Model-Based Estimates of the Prevalence of Specific Disabilities among Persons 16 and Over" (Table 3). Available at http://www.census.gov/hhes/www/disable/census/disapick.html. Accessed 10 October 2004.

United States Equal Employment Opportunity Commission. "Wal-Mart Agrees to Air TV Ad and Pay $427,000 after Court Finds Retailer in Contempt of Court." Available at http://www.eeoc.gov/press/9–20–01.html. Accessed 20 December 2003.

VandeHei, Jim, and Mike Allen. "White House Puts Blame on Kerik." *Washington Post* (12 December 2004): A01.

Vernon, Irene S. *Killing Us Softly: Native Americans and HIV/AIDS*. Lincoln: University of Nebraska Press, 2001.

Villa, Raúl Homero, and George J. Sánchez, eds. "Los Angeles and the Future of Urban Cultures." *American Quarterly* 56.3 (September 2004).

Vincent, Norah. "Enabling Disabled Scholarship." *Salon* (18 August 1999). Available at http://www.salon.com/books/it/1999/08/18/disability. Accessed 7 October 2004.

———. "The Future of Queer: Wedded to Orthodoxy." *Village Voice* (22 February 2000): 16.

Volcano, Del LaGrace, and Judith "Jack" Halberstam. *The Drag King Book*. London: Serpent's Tail, 1999.

Wade, Cheryl Marie. "Poems." In *The Disability Studies Reader*, ed. Lennard J. Davis, 408–409. New York: Routledge, 1997.

Wade, Cheryl Marie, and Jerry Smith, dir. *Disability Culture Rap*. Advocating Change Together, 2000.

Wald, Priscilla. "Cultures and Carriers: 'Typhoid Mary' and the Science of Social Control." *Social Text* 52–53 (Fall/Winter 1997): 181–214.

Warner, Michael, ed. *Fear of a Queer Planet: Queer Politics and Social Theory*. Minneapolis: University of Minnesota Press, 1993.

———. "Normal and Normaller: Beyond Gay Marriage." *GLQ: A Journal of Lesbian and Gay Studies* 5.2 (1999): 119–171.

———. *Publics and Counterpublics*. New York: Zone, 2002.

———. *The Trouble with Normal: Sex, Politics, and the Ethics of Queer Life.* New York: Free Press, 1999.

Watkins, Evan. *Work Time: English Departments and the Circulation of Cultural Value*. Palo Alto, Calif.: Stanford University Press, 1989.

———. "World Bank Literacy and the Culture of Jobs." In *World Bank Literature*, ed. Amitava Kumar, 12–25. Minneapolis: University of Minnesota Press, 2003.

Wendell, Susan. *The Rejected Body: Feminist Philosophical Reflections on Disability*. New York: Routledge, 1996.

Wharton, Greg, and Ian Philips, eds. *I Do, I Don't: Queers on Marriage*. San Francisco: Suspect Thoughts, 2004.

Widom, Rebecca. "I'm a Sicko." Entry in *Queering Diabetes*. Available at http://www.queeringdiabetes.org/sicko_journal/020611_sicko.htm. Accessed 6 October 2004.

Wiegman, Robyn. "Introduction: Mapping the Lesbian Postmodern." In *The Lesbian Postmodern*, ed. Laura Doan, 1–20. New York: Columbia University Press, 1994.

Williams, Raymond. *Keywords: A Vocabulary of Culture and Society*. Rev. ed. New York: Oxford University Press, 1983.

———. *Marxism and Literature*. Oxford: Oxford University Press, 1977.

Wilson, James C., and Cynthia Lewiecki-Wilson, eds. *Embodied Rhetorics: Disability in Language and Culture*. Carbondale: Southern Illinois University Press, 2001.

Wright, Joe. "Commentary: South African AIDS Activist Group Treatment Action Campaign Is Using Bold T-Shirts to Send Message." Report on *All Things Considered*, National Public Radio. Broadcast 20 November 2003.

Wright, Talmadge. *Out of Place: Homeless Mobilizations, Subcities, and Contested Landscapes*. Albany: SUNY Press, 1997.

Index

269

Cystic fibrosis, 5, 181–182, 186,
187–191, 243n10
Cystic Fibrosis Foundation, 188–189

Dahir, Mubarak, 79
Darnell, William, 205, 206
Davis, Lennard J., 7, 199–200, 202,
224n32, 239n15
Davis, Mike, 60–62, 64–65, 66,
67–68, 168, 225–226n34, 226n35
Deaf culture, 31, 90, 160, 215n26
Deafness, 8–9, 205, 239n15
Deaf President Now action, 31, 90,
215n26
Dean, Howard, 79
DeFelice, Robert, 50, 217n4
Defense of Marriage Act (DOMA), 81
Degeneres, Ellen, 164, 190
Degradation: racial, 4, 105, 132–133,
140–143; and rehabilitation,
108–110, 110–111, 122–124, 131,
143–145
Delany, Samuel R., 198
de Lauretis, Teresa, 33, 50, 96,
215n1, 216n2
D'Emilio, John, 163, 194, 209n2,
210n6, 245n17; "Capitalism and
Gay Identity," 4, 81, 86–88
Democratic party, 28–29, 79
Denenberg, Risa, 228n9
Denning, Michael, 210n5,
220–221n16
Denny, Simone, 173
Derrida, Jacques, 5–6, 127, 128, 199,
200, 201, 208, 220n13, 222n23,
230–231n6, 233n15, 237n5
Deutsche, Rosalyn, 225n34, 237n8
Devlieger, Patrick, 55
Diabetes, 38, 161, 218n10
Diaz, Rafael M., 230n4
DiCaprio, Leonardo, 15
Dick, Kirby, 182, 243n13

Dion, Celine, 15
Disability: and compulsory able-bodiedness, 2, 7–8, 35–37, 156–157,
197–198, 240n1; as critical disability, 3, 30–32, 158, 179, 197,
242n7; and cultural geography,
64–65, 69–70, 72, 225–226n34;
cultural model of, 151; and democracy, 5–6, 42–48, 102, 195, 208;
and humor, 176–177; and identity
politics, 3, 35, 51–52, 60, 71,
89–90, 112, 141, 195–196,
197–198, 202, 243n12,
244–245n16; medical model of,
151, 172, 177; and metaphor, 51,
65, 177, 183–184, 207, 224n32,
243n12; and photography, 171,
177–180, 191–193, 194–196; and
post-identity politics, 71, 141, 145,
202; and queerness, 2, 11, 24–28,
29, 49, 80–81, 101–102, 149,
150–151, 176–177, 210n4, 240n1,
243–244n13; universalizing, 149,
157, 223n25, 238n10
Disability Culture Rap (Cheryl Marie
Wade and Jerry Smith), 39–40
Disability rights movement, 2, 7, 31,
89–90, 141, 151, 157, 163,
178–179, 194, 212n13,
228–229n16
Disability studies, 7, 50–53, 69–70,
89–90, 211n9, 224–225n32,
243n12; and composition, 149,
151, 159, 161, 169, 170, 239n14;
disciplining of, 171–173, 197–198,
240–241n2
"Disability Studies and the University" (Emory University), 173
The Disabling Bullet (Patrick Devlieger and Miriam Hertz), 65, 69
"Discourses of Disability in the
Humanities" (University of

Foucault, Michel, 1, 20–21, 22, 84,
91, 92, 93, 153, 210n4, 216n2,
228n7, 237n7, 244n15
Frank, Thomas, 108, 169, 213n20,
229–230n3
Fraser, Nancy, 227n4
Freaks Are Family, 164–165
Freak show, 58–59, 60, 93, 169,
192–193
Freeman, Elizabeth, 216n1, 227n1
Free Sharon Kowalski groups, 100
Freire, Paulo, 170, 236n3
Freud, Sigmund, 1
Friedman, James, 223n28
Fries, Kenny, 50, 214n22
Futurity, 41, 67, 144–145, 155, 170,
226n35, 226–227n37, 237n5,
242n8; and Bob Flanagan,
182–183, 188, 189, 191, 193–194;
and the disability to come, 5–6,
200–201, 207–208, 221n17

Galloway, Terry, 217n4
Gamson, Joshua, 240n18
Gangs. *See* Crips (Los Angeles)
Gaonkar, Dilip Parameshwar,
210n5
Garber, Linda, 217n7
Garland-Thomson, Rosemarie, 7,
197, 211n8, 238n10, 240n1,
245n17; "Seeing the Disabled: Vi-
sual Rhetorics of Disability in Pop-
ular Culture," 5, 171–173,
177–180, 181, 183, 185, 191–193,
194–195, 206
Gates, Daryl, 68
Gates, Henry Louis, Jr., 137
Gay liberation, 2, 12, 83, 163,
212n13, 228–229n16, 242n8
Gay Shame San Francisco, 198,
220n14
Geffen, Nathan, 56

Gender, 9–10, 90–91, 150–151,
220–221n16; and sexuality, 209n3.
See also Transgender lives
"Gender and Disability Studies" (Rut-
gers University), 240n2
Ghai, Anita, 48
Gill, Carol, 51, 157
Gingrich, Newt, 244n16
GlaxoSmithKline (GSK), 56, 223n26
Globalization, 3, 42–48, 71–72, 90,
144, 194–197, 199, 201–208,
221n16, 221n17, 239n17
Goffman, Erving, 82, 211n9
Gooding, Jr., Cuba, 29
Goodrich, Henrietta, 90
Gramsci, Antonio, 192, 217n6,
224n31, 244n16
Greenhouse, Stephen, 206
Grossberg, Lawrence, 210n5
Group homes, 237–238n9
Grover, Jan Zita, 213n16, 228n8
Guerra, Gustavo, 240n20
Guter, Bob, 210n4, 216n3,
243–244n14

Habermas, Jürgen, 81, 227n4
Hacker, Marilyn, 233n16
Hahn, Harlan, 52, 222n21
Halberstam, Judith, 59, 224n29
Hall, Stuart, 149–150, 169–170,
210n5, 230n5, 244n16
Halperin, David, 31, 150, 193,
209n1
Hamlet, 199, 200
Hansen, Miriam, 227n4
Haraway, Donna, 63, 159, 210n5,
224n32
Hardt, Michael, 46–47, 148, 166,
196, 213n20, 221n17, 221n18
Harper, Phillip Brian, 198, 229n2,
230n4
Harvey, David, 12, 17, 145

Ong, Aihwa, 213n20
Ouellette, Laurie, 223n28, 241n3

Paris Is Burning (Jennie Livingston), 50, 222n22
Parker, Jean, 48, 222n20
Partners for Urban Knowledge, Action and Research (PUKAR), 222n19
Patton, Cindy, 55, 85, 223n25, 228n8, 230n5
Paulk, Anne, 13
Paulk, John, 13–14
Philip, Ian, 228n6
Photography, 171, 177–180, 182, 191–193, 194–196
Pipes, Randolph B., 214n23
Police brutality, 63, 67–68, 70
Ponniah, Thomas, 220n15
Poster children, 82, 179, 187–191, 194, 227n5, 242n7
Postmodernity, 2, 17–19, 34–35, 153, 159, 202, 203, 204
Poujade, Pierre-Marie, 180
Protease inhibitors, 56, 107–108, 144, 230n3
Public Broadcasting System (PBS), 104, 124
Public cultures, 3, 4, 30–31, 35, 71–72, 81, 86–90, 101–102, 198, 203, 227n4, 228n15

Queer: activism, 33, 38, 191, 215–216n1; as concept, 31, 37–42, 150, 220n14, 241n4; as critical queerness, 3, 30–32, 40–41, 158, 183, 198, 220n14
Queer Eye for the Straight Guy (Bravo TV), 5, 173–177, 178, 191, 194, 197, 241n3, 241n4
Queer Nation, 215–216n1
Queers for Racial and Economic Justice, 220n14

Queer theory, 33–34, 174–175, 176, 198, 201–202, 211n9, 215–216n1, 216n2, 217n7, 232n14; and composition, 149–150, 150–152, 155, 170

Race: in disability studies, 69–70; and domesticity, 91; and sexuality, 104–107, 140–143, 209–210n3, 220n14
Radical Faeries, 164
Raffo, Susan, 210n4
Raghuram, Parvati, 223n28
Reagan, Ronald, 244–245n16
Reeve, Christopher, 214n21
Rehabilitation, 4, 103–104, 108–116, 230–231n6, 231n7, 231n8, 231n9, 232n11; and crip noncompliance, 4, 133–140, 229n2, 237n5; and identity politics, 112, 141, 143–145
Reid-Pharr, Robert F., 132, 133, 140–141, 143–144, 229n1, 233n16, 234n20, 234n21
Religion, 4, 13, 94, 97–98, 231–232n11; in *The Transformation*, 104, 116–117, 118, 119–121, 122, 124, 126, 127, 129, 130
Republican party, 28–29
Revolutionary nationalism, 106, 141–143, 234n20
Rhetoric. *See* Composition theory
Rich, Adrienne: "Compulsory Heterosexuality and Lesbian Existence," 6, 209n3, 211n7
Richardson, Mattie Udora, 209n3
Riggs, Marlon, 105–106, 133, 142, 229n1, 234n20
Rivière, Philippe, 56, 223n24
Roach, Joseph, 218n11
Rolling Quads, 31, 89, 215n26
Rolston, Adam, 215n26, 216n2
Román, David, 212n16, 229n2

Romney, Mitt, 77
Ronald Reagan National Airport,
 244–245n16
Roosevelt, Franklin Delano, 178,
 241–242n6, 244n16. *See also* FDR
 Memorial
Roosevelt, Theodore, 91
Rorty, Richard, 203
Rose, Sheree, 181–182, 184, 186,
 189, 190, 194, 198
Rosenberg, Tina, 223n24
Rosenthal, Phil, 224n29
Ross, Andrew, 210n5
Rotello, Gabriel, 82–83, 85, 228n6
Roy, Arundhati, 48
Rubin, Gayle S., 209n3, 216n2
Russell, Marta, 62–63, 72, 215n25,
 226n37
Russo, Vito, 28

Sadomasochism, 5, 104–105, 133,
 138, 140, 142–143, 181–182,
 183–191, 192, 193, 234n18,
 234n21, 243n10, 243n13
The Salt Mines (Susana Aiken and
 Carlos Aparicio), 104, 124, 125
Samuels, Ellen, 212n11
Sánchez, George J., 225n34
Sandahl, Carrie, 34, 36, 50, 51,
 52–53, 139, 212n15, 216n3,
 217n4
Sandoval, Chela, 218n9
San Francisco, 77–78, 86, 105,
 133–134, 142, 198, 233n17
Sassen, Saskia, 203
Sawyer, Eric, 230n3
Schell, Eileen E., 236n3
Schulman, Sarah, 164
Scientific management, 88–89,
 90–95
Scott, Allen J., 225n34
Scott, Tony, 236n3

Seattle. *See* Battle for Seattle
Sedgwick, Eve Kosofsky, 4, 104, 106,
 131, 133, 134–135, 137, 138, 140,
 150, 156, 209n1, 216n2, 233n16,
 233–234n18, 238n10
Serlin, David, 113–114, 115, 116
Sex Panic!, 180, 242n8
Shapiro, Joseph P., 212n13, 215n26,
 217n3, 233n17, 242n8
Sheldon, Charles, 121, 232n11
Shepard, Benjamin, 233n17
Shepard, Matthew, 237n9
*Sick: The Life and Death of Bob
 Flanagan, Supermasochist* (Kirby
 Dick), 182, 188, 189–191, 243n13
Siebers, Tobin, 242n9
Slaughter, Sheila, 236n3
Smetherman, Jo-Anne, 223n24
Smith, Anna Deavere, 63–64, 70
Smith, Jerry, 39
Smithsonian National Museum of
 American History, 90, 228n12
Snyder, Sharon L., 48–53, 65, 72,
 216n3, 222n21, 225n33
Society for Disability Studies (SDS),
 221–222n18
Soja, Edward W., 225–226n34
Solheim, Karla, 240n18
Somerville, Siobhan, 209–210n3
Song, David, 69
Sontag, Susan, 242n9
South Africa, 34, 53–57, 222–223n24
Stacey, Judith, 94
Starr, Michael, 224n29
Steinglass, Matt, 223n24
Stock, Patricia Lambert, 236n3
Stratton, Charles S., 59
Stewart, Jean, 48, 220n15, 222n20
Stigma, 35–36, 82, 85, 211n9
Stiker, Henri Jacques, 110–115, 116,
 121–122, 231n7
Stokes, Mason, 210n3

About the Author

Robert McRuer is an associate professor of English at the George Washington University, where he teaches critical theory, disability studies, and queer studies. He is the author of *The Queer Renaissance: Contemporary American Literature and the Reinvention of Lesbian and Gay Identities* and co-editor, with Abby L. Wilkerson, of "Desiring Disability: Queer Theory Meets Disability Studies," which appeared as a special issue of *GLQ: A Journal of Lesbian and Gay Studies*.